D1156641

Programming Languages:
Structures and Models

The PWS Series in Computer Science

· SECOND EDITION ·

Programming Languages: Structures and Models

Herbert L. Dershem
Michael J. Jipping

Department of Computer Science
Hope College

PWS Publishing Company

I(T)P   **An International Thomson Publishing Company**

Boston • Albany • Belmont • Bonn • Cincinnati • Detroit • London
Madrid • Melbourne • Mexico City • New York • Paris • Singapore • Tokyo
Toronto • Washington

WITHDRAWN
ITHACA COLLEGE LIBRARY

ACW 2027

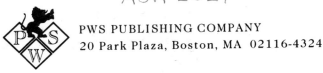

PWS PUBLISHING COMPANY
20 Park Plaza, Boston, MA 02116-4324

Copyright © 1995 by PWS Publishing Company, a division of International Thomson Publishing Inc.

All rights reserved. No part of this book may be reproduced, stored in a retrieval system, or transcribed, in any form or by any means — electronic, mechanical, photocopying, recording, or otherwise — without the prior written permission of PWS Publishing Company.

 International Thomson Publishing
The trademark ITP is used under license.

For more information, contact:

PWS Publishing Co.
20 Park Plaza
Boston, MA 02116

International Thomson Publishing Europe
Berkshire House I68–I73
High Holborn
London WC1V 7AA
England

International Thomson Publishing Asia
221 Henderson Road
#05–10 Henderson Building
Singapore 0315

International Thomson Publishing Japan
Hirakawacho Kyowa Building, 31
2-2-1 Hirakawacho
Chiyoda-ku, Tokyo 102
Japan

International Thomson Editores
Campos Eliseos 385, Piso 7
Col. Polanco
11560 Mexico D.F., Mexico

International Thomson Publishing GmbH
Königswinterer Strasse 418
53227 Bonn, Germany

Thomas Nelson Australia
102 Dodds Street
South Melbourne, 3205
Victoria, Australia

Nelson Canada
1120 Birchmount Road
Scarborough, Ontario
Canada M1K 5G4

Library of Congress Cataloging-in-Publication Data
Dershem, Herbert.
   Programming languages: structures and models / Herbert
   L. Dershem, Michael J. Jipping
     p. cm.
   Includes bibliographical references and index.
   ISBN 0-534-94740-9
   1. Programming languages (Electronic computers)
   I. Jipping, Michael J. II. Title.
QA76.7.D47   1995   94-24921
005.13 — dc20   CIP

This book is printed on recycled, acid-free paper.

QA
76.7
D 465
1995

Sponsoring Editor: Michael J. Sugarman
Developmental Editor: Mary Thomas
Production Editor: Abigail M. Heim
Marketing Manager: Nathan Wilbur
Manufacturing Coordinator: Lisa Flanagan
Editorial Assistant: Benjamin Steinberg

Interior/Cover Designer: Abigail M. Heim
Interior Illustrator: Pre-Press Company, Inc.
Cover Artist: Michael Tcherevkoff, © The IMAGEBank, Inc.
Typesetter: Pre-Press Company, Inc.
Cover Printer: John P. Pow Company, Inc.
Text Printer and Binder: Quebecor Printing/Martinsburg

Printed and bound in the United States of America.
95 96 97 98 99 — 9 8 7 6 5 4 3 2

Contents

CHAPTER **10**   **Scheme: A Functional-Oriented Language**   **261**

CHAPTER **11**   **ML: A Typed Functional Language**   **281**

CHAPTER **12**   **An Overview of the Logic-Oriented Model**   **299**

Preface

Programming Languages: Structures and Models, Second Edition — a first course for undergraduates in programming languages — presents the fundamental features and concepts common to all programming languages, while also giving students experience using a variety of actual languages and a basic understanding of supporting theoretical principles.

Organization

The text organizes languages into five fundamental computational models, or paradigms — imperative, functional, logic-oriented, object-oriented, and distributed parallel — chosen for their importance in the field of computer science or anticipated importance in the near future.

The imperative model is presented first and includes a description of those fundamental features of programming languages that are commonly found in imperative languages. Because many basic concepts common to all models are present in imperative languages, the presentation of the four nonimperative models that follows focuses on their unique features.

Use of Model Languages

Each of the five programming language paradigms is described through the use of a model language that exhibits the important aspects of that paradigm. For the imperative model, Ada serves as the model language because of the richness of its features, especially in data abstraction and concurrency. For those instructors who wish to use a language other than Ada as the empirical model, C and Modula-2 are described in Chapters 7 and 8, with the topics appearing there in the same order as in Chapters 3 through 6. Chapters 7 and 8 can therefore be covered in parallel with Chapters 3 through 6 if desired.

Backus' FP is used as the model functional language while hypothetical languages are constructed to represent the logic-oriented and object-oriented models. In all cases, the model languages form a standard against which other languages exhibiting properties of that model are compared. Several such languages are discussed under each model. For the distributed parallel model, two example languages representing very different approaches are discussed, rather than a model language.

Laboratory Exercises

Laboratory exercises are included at the end of most chapters to reinforce the concepts with actual programming practice. These lab exercises require the students to write programs and usually to exercise some language found in that chapter, determining how that feature is implemented.

Most of these exercises are language independent and can be assigned for any appropriate language that is available. Repeating a given exercise for several different languages has proven very instructive for students. Most of the laboratory exercises are also stated very generally to permit the instructor maximum latitude in adapting them to the local environment.

New to the Second Edition

Based on the suggestions of many users of the first edition and reviewers of this text, the following major modifications have been made:

- A section has been added on the semantic specification of languages.
- The treatment of the imperative model has been compressed from six to four chapters to permit an expanded treatment of the other models.
- The distributed parallel model has been added, with Ada and Occam used as example languages.
- Discussion of the functional model has been expanded from one to three chapters, adding ML as an example language.
- The object-oriented model presentation has been expanded from one to three chapters.
- Treatment of the logic-oriented model has been expanded from one to two chapters.
- Exercises and laboratory exercises have been added and exercises from the first edition have been revised and improved.

Audience

The prerequisite for this book is completion of the first two courses in a computer science curriculum, including experience in programming in one structured imperative language. Pascal is used in examples throughout the book with the assumption that the reader is familiar with that language. However, students whose first language was C++, Ada, or Modula-2 will have no trouble in understanding the Pascal examples.

The objective of this book is for the student to become an intelligent user of programming languages, able to choose an appropriate language for an application, make effective and efficient use of a language in software development, and quickly learn new languages. This book is not intended as a final preparation for programming language implementers, designers, or researchers, although it provides appropriate background preparation for more advanced courses in these areas.

Suggestions for Use

This text contains more material than can be comfortably covered in a single-term undergraduate course. Many different courses can be taught from this book:

1. **Imperative model only** — Chapters 1–8 are covered in detail and students do a significant amount of programming in several imperative languages that are new to them.

2. **Imperative model plus survey of other models** — This course covers Chapters 1–8, introducing students to only one new imperative language, perhaps Ada. Chapters 9, 12, 14, and 17 are then covered with little, if any, programming in the nonimperative models.

3. **Imperative model plus one or two other models** — Chapters 1–6 are covered, with students programming in no new imperative languages. Rather, the students use imperative languages that they already know. One or two of the other models are then covered in detail, introducing the students to one or more languages and having them program in those languages. The other nonimperative models are quickly surveyed without any student programming experience in those models.

4. **All models** — This course gives approximately equal time to all five models presented in this book or to some subset, at the instructor's discretion. Chapters 3–6 are treated briefly, relying heavily on the students' prior experience. Previously learned languages are used for programming exercises throughout. Selected chapters from 9–19 are covered in detail, giving students programming experience with one language representing each model.

An *Instructor's Manual*, available from the publisher, contains complete solutions to text exercises and a list of sources for language translators.

Acknowledgments

The following reviewers provided many helpful comments, which greatly improved the accuracy and coverage of this book for the second edition:

George W. Ball
Alfred University

John Crenshaw
Western Kentucky University

Andrew Gelsey
Rutgers University

Rachelle Heller
George Washington University

Mary Lou Hines
University of Missouri — Kansas City

Dalton R. Hunkins
Saint Bonaventure University

Richard G. Larson
University of Illinois — Chicago

Bruce Mabis
University of Southern Indiana

Bruce Maxim
University of Michigan — Dearborn

Andrew Oldroyd
Washington University

Gary Potts
Saint Joseph's College

Robert S. Roos
Smith College

John Sigle
Louisiana State University — Shreveport

John A. Wenzel
Albion College

I-Ling Yen
Michigan State University

The authors would again like to acknowledge the comments and suggestions of the reviewers who helped to shape the first edition: Anthony Aaby, *Bucknell University*; Boumediene Belkhouche, *Tulane University*; Bill Buckles, *Tulane University*; Frank A. Chimenti, *Liberty University*; Robert Crawford, *Western Kentucky University*; Al Cripps, *Middle Tennessee State University*; Thomas Gendreau, *University of Wisconsin*; David Oakland, *Drake University*; Prakash Panangaden, *Cornell University*; Richard Pattis, *University of Washington*; John Peterson, *University of Arizona*; John Remmers, *Eastern Michigan University*; Ken Slonneger, *University of Iowa*; Victor Terrana, *Indiana State University*; Barbara Tulley, *Elizabethtown College*.

The students in the Hope College CSCI 383 course and cadets in CS 359 at the United States Air Force Academy provided many helpful comments during the class testing of preliminary versions of this book. In addition, colleagues Dave Cook and Ricky Sward were very helpful in making suggestions for improvements.

We greatly appreciate the patience and support of our wives, Katie and Peg, throughout our work on this project.

Herbert L. Dershem
Michael J. Jipping

Introduction and Overview

1.1 What Is a Programming Language?

A language is a systematic set of rules for communicating ideas. With a natural language, such as English, this communication is between people, and the language is used in both spoken and written forms.

Programming languages differ from natural languages in several important ways. First, the primary communication is between a person and a computer, although programming languages are also useful for communication between people. The second major difference is in the content of the communications, which, in the case of programming languages, is known as a program. Programs are expressions of solutions to problems that are specific enough to give the receiver of the program sufficient information to carry out the solution. A third unique feature of communication via a programming language is the medium used. Because a computer is the intended receiver, this has traditionally meant that programs are represented symbolically as strings of characters, as opposed, for example, to audible sounds. Although modern programming environments have somewhat released programmers from this restriction, all languages that we discuss in this book have been designed for this mode of communication.

Our working definition for a programming language is

A programming language is a language that is intended to be used by a person to express a process by which a computer can solve a problem.

The four key components in this definition of a programming language are

1. *processor*—the machine that will carry out the process described by the program
2. *person*—the programmer who serves as the source of the process and who wishes to communicate it to the processor
3. *process*—the activity being described by the program
4. *problem*—the actual system or environment that the process is intended to model

Five models for programming languages are detailed in this text. Four of these models represent the point of view of one of the preceding four components.

The imperative model is based on the processor's perspective. This outlook is reflected in the sequential execution of commands and the use of a changeable data store, concepts that are based on the way computers execute programs at the machine language level. In the past, imperative was the predominant paradigm for languages, because such languages were easiest to translate into a form suitable for machine execution. Programs written in a language of this model consist of a sequence of modifications to the processor's storage.

The logic-oriented model is most closely related to the perspective of the person. It looks at the problem from the logical point of view. The program is a logical description of the problem expressed in a formal way, similar to the manner that a human brain would reason about the problem.

The functional model focuses on the process of solving the problem. The functional view results in programs that describe, in an abstract way, the operations that must be performed to solve the problem.

The object-oriented model reflects most closely the actual problem itself. A program in a language of this model consists of objects that send messages to each other. These objects in the program correspond directly to actual objects in the problem space, such as people, machines, departments, documents, and so on.

The fifth model of languages discussed in this book, the distributed/parallel model, incorporates the views of all four of the components to permit the description of multiple, simultaneous processes.

In this book, we will look at all five of these models, or paradigms, and the ways they are represented in programming languages. We will also find that all programming languages provide some combination of these viewpoints to allow for efficiency in the construction and execution of programs.

1.2 Why Study Programming Languages?

You will receive five major benefits from the study of the structure and models of programming languages.

1. *You will improve your problem-solving ability.* Experts tell us that facility and understanding of natural language affects our ability to think and form ideas. Similarly, a thorough understanding of programming languages can increase our ability to think about approaches to problems. This is especially true when we have the ability to think about a problem from a number of different perspectives using the various models of languages described in Section 1.1.

2. *You will be able to make better use of a programming language.* The study of programming language structures will give you a better understanding of the function and implementation of these structures. Then, when you are programming, you will be better able to use the language to its greatest potential and to do so in an efficient way. Understanding the power of a language will enable you better to utilize that power.

3. *You will be able to choose an appropriate language more intelligently.* In the 1960s and 1970s, programmers could seldom select the language they would use. All programmers working for a given organization were expected to program in the language that was the "standard" for that site. In many cases, only one computer was available, and only one language was implemented on that computer. Frequently, the local programmers knew how to program just in that one language as well, because that was all that was necessary.

   This situation changed dramatically in the 1980s and 1990s. In the first place, the improved technology of computers and language translators has made many languages available on present-day machines, even on the smallest personal computers. In addition, programmers who have completed courses such as the one for which this book is intended have experience with and an understanding of a variety of languages.

   Therefore, it is common practice today for the programmer to choose a language for a given project from among several possibilities. Whereas in the past this choice was determined by the language allowed, the one implemented on the computer system, or the knowledge of the programmer, today a programmer with an understanding of programming languages can choose the language that makes the problem solution easiest and most efficient.

4. *You will find it easier to learn new programming languages.* As we study the development of programming languages, we find that new languages and enhancements to present languages are continually being introduced. We also see that throughout this development, there are key concepts that remain constant as well as new facilities that are added.

   An important consequence of the study of programming languages is that it enables you to learn new languages and new capabilities of existing languages as they are developed. Through a thorough understanding of programming language models, you can quickly assess a new language in comparison with those models and determine the ways in which the new language adheres to a model and ways in which it differs.

5. *You will become a better language designer.*　　　This benefit is more important than it first appears. Few people ever have the desire or the opportunity to design their own programming language. Although you may be one of these people, most likely you are not. However, if we hold to our view that language is a means of communication between a person and a computer, then every computer system that is developed must have a language embedded within it to provide for human-machine interaction. A good understanding of programming language principles can greatly assist in this interface design.

In addition, many modern languages are extensible in a variety of ways. This means that the programmer can enhance the language through the addition of new data types and operators. With these languages, every program is actually a new language design in the sense that the programmer has the power to enhance the original language.

1.3　A Brief History of Programming Languages

It is helpful for understanding programming languages to have some appreciation of their history. Much has been written on this topic, including Sammet (1969) and Wexelblat (1981).

In the historical overview that follows, we have limited our consideration to those languages that are either used extensively today or that originated important concepts for today's languages. Thousands of languages have been implemented, and most of these have made important contributions to the field. We have necessarily limited our consideration to the 15 that we feel have had the greatest impact.

We have structured this history into three periods. The first is a period of about a decade, beginning in 1955, during which the first higher-level languages were being developed with a wide variety of philosophies and concepts. The second period—1965 to 1971—was a time of consolidation around the model of one language, ALGOL 60, with the development of a number of new languages derived from ALGOL 60 but extending it by adding important new features. In the final period, 1972 and after, the results of earlier research on languages were pulled together to introduce new models and approaches for programming languages.

1.3.1 ▪ The Early Languages

FORTRAN　　The distinction of being the first widely used higher-level programming language is held by FORTRAN. Prior to its implementation, many people were skeptical about the possibility of a language being compiled successfully and efficiently. FORTRAN quickly erased such skepticism and became a very popular language; it is still in use more than 35 years later.

Most early languages were named by acronyms. We indicate this in a language's name by writing it in uppercase letters. We also display the full name in parentheses after the first mention of the language's name. FORTRAN

(FORmula TRANslation) was designed in 1954 and implemented several years later by John Backus at IBM. It was specifically designed for a single machine, the IBM 704, and still bears the marks of some of the idiosyncrasies of that machine. It has evolved through the years into a language that incorporates many modern language facilities while still maintaining its original character.

FORTRAN was designed for solving scientific problems and therefore adopted an algebraic notation. Because it was a pioneer language, it made many contributions to language development. Included among these were (1) variables and assignment statements, (2) the concept of types, (3) modularity through the use of subprograms, (4) conditional and iterative control structures, and (5) formatted input/output.

COBOL Although much early programming was scientific in nature, in the 1950s many business applications were being programmed as well, and the requirements of such programming were not handled well by FORTRAN. There was an evident need for a common language suitable to these business applications. In 1959, through the initiative of the U.S. Department of Defense, a committee was formed to develop a language to meet these needs. This committee, called the CODASYL Committee, consisted of representatives from computer manufacturers and the Department of Defense. The resulting language, COBOL (COmmon Business Oriented Language), was first implemented in 1960 and soon became the standard for business data processing applications.

Beyond the difference in their intended applications, there were two major differences in the ways FORTRAN and COBOL were developed. FORTRAN was the effort of one organization, IBM, whereas COBOL resulted from the cooperative effort of many organizations. Furthermore, FORTRAN was designed to be run on a single machine; in fact, the architecture of that machine affected many of the design decisions. COBOL, on the other hand, was designed independently of any specific computer, with the intention that it be implemented on all computers.

Like FORTRAN, COBOL has evolved over the years as new standards have been developed. It has also continued to be used extensively over a 30-year period. Its strengths are in the manipulation of files and in handling fixed-decimal data.

One of the primary objectives of COBOL was that its code be English-like. For this reason, COBOL programs tend to be very wordy, and many programmers find this cumbersome. However, the English-like property of COBOL was an early attempt at designing a language to facilitate the readability of programs and thus was an important contribution to the development of later languages. The other major contribution of COBOL was the introduction of a heterogeneous data structure, the record, which became an important component of later languages.

ALGOL 60 The ALGOL (ALGorithmic Oriented Language) 60 language had a European origin and was designed by an international committee. The first version was called ALGOL 58, after the year of its introduction, but in 1960 the finished product, ALGOL 60, was published. Although it never enjoyed the commercial popularity of FORTRAN and COBOL, it is the most important language of this era in terms of its influence on later language development.

Like FORTRAN, ALGOL 60 was designed for use in scientific problem solving. Unlike FORTRAN, it was designed independently of an implementation. This was both a major asset and a major liability of the ALGOL 60 language. Its machine independence permitted the designers to be more creative, but it made implementation much more difficult.

One of the greatest impacts ALGOL 60 had was a result of its description, as found in Naur (1963). This report became the accepted definition of the language and was a model of clarity and completeness. A major contribution from this report was the introduction of BNF notation for defining the syntax of the language. This notation is described in Chapter 2 and is used throughout this book.

ALGOL 60 was used on only a limited basis, mostly by research computer scientists in the United States and Europeans. Its use in commercial applications was hindered by the absence of standard input/output facilities in its description and the lack of interest in the language by large computer vendors. ALGOL 60 did, however, become the standard for the publication of algorithms and had a profound effect on future language development.

Some of the major contributions of ALGOL 60 to later languages were (1) block structure: the ability to create blocks of statements for the scope of variables and the extent of influence of control statement; (2) structured control statements: `if-then-else` and the use of a general condition for iteration control; and (3) recursion: the ability of a procedure to call itself.

LISP   Like FORTRAN and COBOL, LISP (LISt Processing) is a language that was developed for a specific application and is still extensively used today. LISP was developed by John McCarthy in the Artificial Intelligence Group at M.I.T. in the late 1950s as a language to support artificial intelligence research. It was first implemented in 1960 on the IBM 704. It has remained the primary programming language for artificial intelligence through the years. Common LISP was defined in 1981 as an informal standard and has since become officially recognized.

LISP pioneered the idea of nonnumeric, or symbolic, computing. It also introduced as its basic data structure the concept of the linked list. The LISP language is functional in nature. This means that rather than specifying operations as a sequential set of statements, LISP specifies the invocation of a function, using composition of functions as the main device for specifying multiple actions. This model of computation is defined and explored in Chapter 9, and a description of the Scheme dialect of the LISP language is presented in Chapter 10.

LISP also used the same basic construct, the S-expression, to represent both data and program, thus allowing a program to be accessed as data and data to be executed as a program.

APL   Still another language designed in the late 1950s was APL (A Programming Language), which was the creation of Kenneth Iverson. Iverson did his initial work on the language at Harvard and later continued development at IBM. APL was enthusiastically received by a number of programmers. It consisted of many powerful operators and a simple, mathematical notation. The availability of this large number of operators required a large character set and made implementation of the language difficult. The mathematical nature of APL discouraged programmers who were not adept at mathematics. The definition of APL was specified in Iverson (1962).

The primary data structure of APL is the array, and the language features operators that apply to an entire array. Iterative processing is accomplished by placing the data in an array and applying a single operator to that entire array. The variables of APL are untyped, taking on the type of the objects assigned to them.

APL is especially useful for mathematical and array processing applications. Because of its powerful operators and compact notation, a great pastime among APL programmers is the construction of one-line programs. Such programs actually use APL in a purely functional manner that very closely matches the functional model.

BASIC   The BASIC (Beginners All-purpose Symbolic Instruction Code) language was developed at Dartmouth College by Thomas Kurtz and John Kemeny in the mid-1960s. Its objective was to be easy for undergraduate students to learn and to use the interactive programming environment that was also under development at Dartmouth at that time.

BASIC was quite popular in academic circles over the next decade, but its greatest popularity came with the arrival of the microcomputer in the mid-1970s. The marketers of microcomputers needed a language that would be useful to the consumer. The two major criteria were that the language be easy to learn and that it exploit the interactive environment provided by the microcomputer. Because BASIC was designed a decade earlier to meet these same two objectives, it was chosen as the language that was provided with all of the early microcomputers.

Although the microcomputer gave BASIC an important place in the history of programming languages, BASIC contributed little to the development of programming language technology. Perhaps its greatest contribution was that it was one of the first languages to provide an interactive programming environment, including the interpretive execution of programs, as a part of the language.

1.3.2 ▪ ALGOL-based Languages

The six languages described in the preceding section represent the first wave of language development. The next wave built on the ideas and concepts of that first wave. The most important languages to appear in the latter half of the 1960s were based on the key concepts of the ALGOL 60 language. Four of these ALGOL-based languages are described in the following paragraphs.

PL/I   The philosophy behind PL/I (Programming Language/I), developed at IBM in the mid-1960s, was the replacement of the multitude of languages that were in use for specific applications with one general-purpose language. The approach used was to incorporate features from each of the earlier languages into PL/I. For example, PL/I included the block structure, control structures, and recursion from ALGOL 60, subprograms and formatted input/output from FORTRAN, file manipulation and the record structure from COBOL, dynamic storage allocation and linked structures from LISP, and the array operations from APL.

PL/I, although highly promoted by IBM, never became as popular as its designers hoped. The major difficulty was a lack of cohesiveness in the language design, which contained many different features implemented in many different ways. The language was complex, difficult to learn, and difficult to implement. Two possible remedies for these problems were included in the language: The use of many defaults that could remain transparent to the user, and the intention that a programmer needed to learn only a subset of the language for a given application. These remedies proved to be inadequate, however.

Two features of PL/I that have significantly impacted later language development are interrupt-handling, the ability to execute specified procedures when an exceptional condition occurs, and multitasking, the specification of tasks that can be performed concurrently. These topics are explored in Chapters 5 and 17, respectively.

Simula 67   Ole-Johan Dahl and Kristen Nygaard developed Simula 67 at the Norwegian Computing Center in the early 1960s. The original work was based on ALGOL 60 and was intended to be a language for system description and simulation programming. The first version was called Simula 1. The designers soon discovered that this language had potential beyond simulation; to realize this potential they extended the original design to Simula 67.

The major contribution of Simula 67 is the concept of class. A class is an encapsulation of data and procedures, which can be instantiated in a number of objects. The class of Simula 67 is the forerunner of abstract data types as implemented in Ada and Modula-2 (see Chapter 6) and of classes from the object-oriented languages Smalltalk and C++ (see Chapters 15 and 16). The latter two languages also adopted from Simula 67 the hierarchy of classes with inheritance of components.

ALGOL 68   Although its name implies that it is an improved version of ALGOL 60, ALGOL 68 is actually a rather radical departure from its predecessor. It was designed to be a general-purpose language, as opposed to having the scientific orientation of ALGOL 60.

ALGOL 68 never gained acceptance even to the limited level attained by ALGOL 60. This was, in part, because the original description (van Wijngaarden et al. 1969) was difficult to understand, using notation and terminology that were foreign to many of its readers.

The major design philosophy of ALGOL 68 is also its major contribution, namely, orthogonality. A language that is orthogonal has a relatively small number of basic constructs and a set of rules for combining those constructs. It is then possible to combine these constructs using any of the rules with predictable results. This approach is in opposition to that of PL/I, which included a large number of independent constructs.

Pascal The most popular of this second wave of ALGOL-based languages is Pascal, developed by Niklaus Wirth in 1969 and named for the mathematician Blaise Pascal. Wirth's goal was to provide a language that is simple to learn, supportive of structured programming, and easily implemented. He intended it to be a language suitable for use in the teaching of programming. The defining document is provided by Jensen and Wirth (1985).

By the early 1980s, Pascal had become by far the most commonly used language for teaching programming at the college level. By the middle 1980s it also had become popular as a production language on microcomputers.

Pascal's flexible control structures, user-defined data types, and file, record, and set data structures have made it a model for many of the languages of the next stage of development.

1.3.3 ▪ Languages of the Eighties

Although each of the following five languages was actually designed in the 1970s, their major impact on computing occurred in the 1980s. The designers of these languages benefited greatly from experience with earlier languages, and all the languages include features that take advantage of modern hardware and software technology.

The first two languages use entirely different models of computing than the earlier languages, whereas the last three continue development in the ALGOL line, following what we call the imperative model.

Prolog Developed at the University of Marseilles in France in 1977, Prolog was designed for artificial intelligence applications and is based on formal logic. The logic-oriented model of programming served as a basis for Prolog, but Prolog falls short of the model's ideal of clauses that describe the problem and can be expressed in an order-independent way. This model and Prolog are described in Chapters 12 and 13.

Prolog has become a competitor with LISP for artificial intelligence research. It received higher visibility in the early 1980s when it was chosen as the language of the Japanese Fifth Generation Project.

Smalltalk Alan Kay developed Smalltalk at the Xerox Palo Alto Research Center in the early 1970s as a part of the Dynabook project.

The two distinguishing features of Smalltalk are its environment and the strict use of the object-oriented model. The Smalltalk language is embedded within a graphical environment, which includes pop-up menus, windows, and the use of a mouse device for input. This environment has served as the prototype for many modern programming environments, including those of the Apple Macintosh and Microsoft Windows.

Smalltalk is designed around the Simula 67 class concept and includes encapsulation, inheritance, and instantiation. All operations in Smalltalk consist of objects sending messages to other objects. Smalltalk and the object-oriented model are described in Chapters 14 and 15.

This highly extensible and interactive language will undoubtedly have a major impact on future language development.

C   The language C was developed at Bell Laboratories in the early 1970s as a language for implementing the UNIX operating system. C is a powerful language with facilities for accessing raw data stored in memory as well as accessing memory through data types and structures of the language. The standard for the C language is defined by Kernighan and Ritchie (1988).

The objective of C is to provide a language that has access to low-level data and generates efficient code. The language has an extensive set of operators. As a result, programs often are expressed with compact code at the expense of readability. A description of the C language is given in Chapter 7.

C has grown in popularity in conjunction with the acceptance of UNIX as an operating system. C is an excellent language for the construction of portable system programs. Many of C's early limitations have been removed in its enhancement, C++, which also includes object-oriented features and is described in Chapter 16.

Modula-2   Niklaus Wirth, designer of Pascal, developed Modula-2 in the late 1970s as an improvement to Pascal, especially for use in systems programming. Wirth developed the language as a part of the Lilith project, whose goal was the creation of an integrated hardware/software system. The result—as described in Wirth (1985)—is an excellent general-purpose language that has replaced Pascal as a teaching language in some universities. Modula-2 is described in Chapter 8.

Modula-2 offers the following improvements over Pascal:

1. Modules can be used to implement abstract data types.

2. All control structures have a termination keyword.

3. Coroutines provide for interleaved execution.

4. Procedure types can be declared.

The modules of Modula-2 make it an excellent language for use in large software-development projects.

Ada   In the early 1970s, the United States Department of Defense initiated a project to obtain a suitable programming language for the development of embedded systems. An embedded system is a computer system that operates as a part of a larger system. A large portion of the work done by the Department of Defense is on these embedded systems.

After evaluating existing languages against the criteria desired, the Department of Defense decided that no language existed that met the needs and a new language should be designed.

In 1977, a competition was initiated among four contractors to design a suitable language. In 1979 the winning design was chosen, and the resulting language was given the name Ada, after Ada Augusta Byron, the Countess of Lovelace and daughter of Lord Byron. She was a collaborator with Charles Babbage in his work on the analytical engine in the nineteenth century and is considered by some to have originated some of the key ideas that led to programming.

The standard for Ada is given by the Reference Manual (American National Standards Institute 1983). Every compiler that aspires to be called an Ada compiler must be validated by the Department of Defense. Subsets and supersets of the language are not permitted.

Ada is based primarily on Pascal, but it uses the class concept of Simula 67 in its abstract data-type facility called a package, adopts the exception-handling features of PL/I, and provides an extensive tasking facility for concurrent processing.

Ada has been chosen as the primary example of an imperative language in this book because of its wide range of facilities and the fact that its structure is representative of the class of imperative languages.

Preliminary Concepts

This chapter presents a number of concepts that are necessary for a complete understanding of the remainder of the text, including language specification, and a description of several languages that can be used to describe the syntax of other languages. These are called *metalanguages* and will prove useful throughout the book for expressing language syntax. Approaches that are used to describe formally the semantics of a programming language are briefly outlined. The structure of a programming language is frequently affected by the process used to translate programs from that language into an executable form: an overview of that translation process is presented.

A number of characteristics of a programming language that enhance its effectiveness are outlined, standards against which languages and their various features can be judged are described, and criteria useful for choosing the appropriate language for a given application are listed.

2.1 An Overview of Language Specification

The specification of a natural language, such as English, evolves over time through the usage of those who communicate in that language. But problems arise when the population that communicates in that language is widely separated geographically and culturally. In this case, dialects develop that inhibit the ability of some groups to communicate with others, even though they share the same language. For this reason, formal specification of natural languages are created in the form of dictionaries and guides to grammar and style, so there is common, formalized description of the language.

Usually, even people who speak different dialects of the same language are able to communicate without a common specification, because natural languages have a great deal of built-in redundancy and people are able to derive meaning from statements intelligently even if they do not understand everything. It is even more important, however, for programming languages to be formally specified, because they lack the redundancy of natural languages, and one of the parties that communicates (the computer) requires strict conformance of expressions to the rules of the language in order to understand their meaning. There are three classes of people who need formal programming language specifications:

1. *Language designers* — those who design a language need some means to express the language they create.

2. *Language implementors* — those who write compilers and interpreters for languages need to have a formal specification to describe unambiguously the language they are implementing. Compilers and interpreters are actually language specifications that describe a language to the computer.

3. *Language users* — those who program in a language must have specifications that formally describe legal structures and the meaning of those structures so that they can form correct programs in that language.

With programming languages, it is convenient to divide their formal specification into two parts: syntax and semantics. The reason for this division is that each of these two has its own set of tools used in expressing its part of the specification.

Syntax refers to the description of those sets of strings that represent valid structures in a language. In fact, a syntactic specification divides the set of all strings of characters into two mutually exclusive groups: those that are in the language and those that are not. Tools used to specify syntax formally must, therefore, consist of rules that can be applied to a string of characters in order to determine in which of the two groups it lies. This set of rules is the syntactic specification of a language. The tool that we introduce and use in the book for syntactic specification is EBNF, a language used to describe the syntax of other languages.

The **semantics** of a programming language associate a meaning with each syntactically valid construct. More specifically, the semantics of a language describe the actions that will occur when the program associated with any valid construct in that language is executed by a computer. On a functional level, the semantic specification gives a way of determining, for any valid program and any valid input to that program, what the resulting output of that program will be.

To understand the difference between syntactic and semantic specifications, let us suppose we have such specifications for some hypothetical language Z. The syntactic specification of the language will describe a process whereby any string of characters can be tested as to whether they form a valid program in Z. The semantic specification of Z will define a notation by which any string that passes the syntactic test can have its actions specified. As you can see from this illustration, the application of the syntactic specification precedes that of the semantic specification.

In the following two sections we examine some tools for constructing syntax and semantic specifications. You will see there that syntactic specification is a much more exact process than semantic specification. Whereas the tool introduced for syntactic specification is universally accepted because it can so thoroughly specify syntax, there is no tool that is similarly successful in semantic specification. Three approaches to semantic specification are presented in Section 2.3.

2.2   Syntax Specification

Recall from Section 2.1 that the description of a language is commonly broken into two parts: syntax and semantics. The syntax of a language is the set of rules that determine which constructs are correctly formed programs and which are not. The semantics of a language is the description of the way a syntactically correct program is interpreted, or carried out. For example, the syntax of Pascal tells us that

```
a := b;
```

forms a correct assignment statement, whereas the interpretation of the statement as "replace the value of a with the current value of b" is a result of Pascal's semantics.

In our discussions in this text, we will use a specific formal tool, known as *EBNF*, to describe language syntax. EBNF is defined in detail in Section 2.2.2. Language syntax specification is important for two reasons. First, it is useful in describing a language, and this is the way that we will use it throughout the text to describe both real and theoretical programming language constructs. But language specifications are also useful in the verification of the validity of programs, because they give us a set of rules against which an allegedly legal program can be tested. Such syntactic verification is typically carried out by language translation programs such as compilers.

2.2.1 ▪ Grammars

The syntax of a language is described by a **grammar**, which is a set of rules that defines all of the valid constructs that can be accepted in the language. The basic elements of a grammar are as follows:

1. *Set of terminal symbols* — These symbols are the atomic (nondivisible) symbols that can be combined to form valid constructs in the language. **Terminal symbols** most commonly are a set of characters, although some languages may consider certain character strings to be symbols as well.

2. *Set of nonterminal symbols* — These symbols are not included in the program text of the language itself but are symbols used to represent intermediate definitions within the language as defined by productions. These **nonterminal symbols** represent syntactic classes or categories.

3. *Set of productions* — A **production** is a definition of a nonterminal symbol. It is of the form

   x ::= y

   where *x* is a nonterminal symbol and *y* is a sequence of symbols, each of which can be either terminal or nonterminal.

4. *Goal symbol* — One of the set of nonterminal symbols is specified as the **goal symbol**. This is also sometimes called the distinguished symbol or the start symbol.

Two rules must be obeyed for these three components to form a grammar:

1. Every nonterminal symbol must appear to the left of the ::= of at least one production.

2. The goal symbol must not appear to the right of the ::= of any production.

To illustrate this concept of a grammar, let us construct a simple grammar for describing a calculator language. This grammar is given in Figure 2.1. Note that this grammar has 16 terminal symbols and 8 nonterminals. Also note that every nonterminal except for the goal symbol has multiple productions defining it. Although such multiple productions are not required, they are common and represent alternate definitions. You can also see that recursive productions are permitted, that is, productions where the nonterminal being defined is also found in its own definition on the right-hand side of the production.

FIGURE 2.1 **Grammar for Calculator Language**

```
Terminal Symbols: 0 1 2 3 4 5 6 7 8 9 + - * / = .

Nonterminal Symbols:    calculation
                        expression
                        value
                        number
                        unsigned
                        digit
                        sign
                        operator

Goal Symbol:    calculation
```

(continues)

```
Productions:
1.    calculation  ::=        expression =
2.    expression   ::=        value
3.    expression   ::=        value operator expression
4.    value        ::=        number
5.    value        ::=        sign number
6.    number       ::=        unsigned
7.    number       ::=        unsigned . unsigned
8.    unsigned     ::=        digit
9.    unsigned     ::=        digit unsigned
10.   digit        ::=        0
11.   digit        ::=        1
12.   digit        ::=        2
13.   digit        ::=        3
14.   digit        ::=        4
15.   digit        ::=        5
16.   digit        ::=        6
17.   digit        ::=        7
18.   digit        ::=        8
19.   digit        ::=        9
20.   sign         ::=        +
21.   sign         ::=        -
22.   operator     ::=        +
23.   operator     ::=        -
24.   operator     ::=        *
25.   operator     ::=        /
```

There are two ways that a grammar such as that found in Figure 2.1 can be used. The first is to generate valid programs in the language. If we begin with the goal symbol and at each step substitute some definition for a nonterminal, proceeding until all remaining symbols are terminal symbols, we have generated a valid program. Examine the generation sequence found in Figure 2.2. At each step, the leftmost nonterminal was replaced by a definition from one of the productions. Because multiple productions might apply to any nonterminal, there are multiple choices that can be made. The choice of a production to apply is arbitrary in these cases. The choice of the leftmost nonterminal for expansion was also arbitrary. An infinite number of valid calculations can be generated in this way.

The second way a grammar can be used is in the reduction of a valid program back to the goal symbol through the reverse application of productions. This verifies that a string of terminal symbols is indeed a program in the language defined by the grammar. This derivation is possible only if a prudent choice is made of the sequence of productions to be applied, as in Figure 2.3. For example, an initial choice of sign for + would have led to an early dead end in our reduction. Furthermore, if this process is attempted on a string that is not a valid program, the goal symbol can never be reached.

FIGURE **2.2**   **Generation of a Calculation Using the Grammar in Figure 2.1**

```
Current String                                Production Applied
calculation                                           1
expression =                                          3
value operator expression =                           4
number operator expression =                          6
unsigned operator expression =                        9
digit unsigned operator expression =                 12
2 unsigned operator expression =                      8
2 digit operator expression =                        15
25 operator expression =                             24
25* expression =                                      2
25* value =                                           4
25* number =                                          7
25* unsigned . unsigned =                             8
25* digit . unsigned =                               11
25*1. unsigned =                                      8
25*1. digit =                                        15
25*1.5=
```

FIGURE **2.3**   **Verification that** 6+3 / 12= **Is a Calculation**

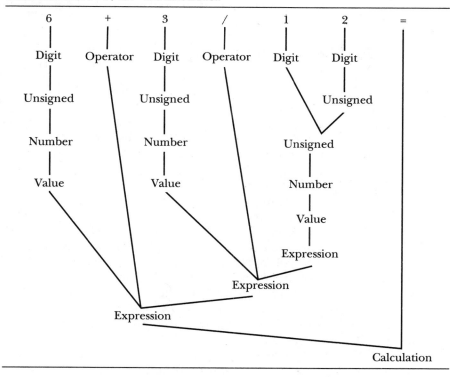

FIGURE 2.4   **Reduction of an Invalid String**

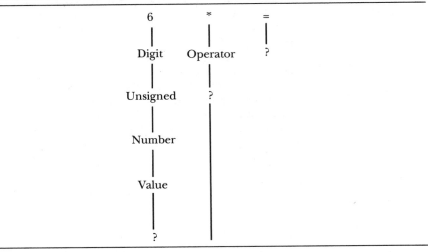

Figure 2.4 shows this through an example, where every step is uniquely determined and the final string matches none of the productions' right-hand sides.

2.2.2 ▪ BNF and EBNF

In this section we describe a language for expressing grammars. Because this is a language for describing languages, we call it a **metalanguage**. The metalanguage we describe is **BNF**, which stands for **Backus-Naur Form**. This language was created to express the syntax of ALGOL 60 and has become the standard metalanguage. We will use BNF along with three extensions to describe syntax throughout this text. The extended language is called **EBNF**, for **Extended BNF**.

The metalanguage described in the previous section is what we will define as BNF, with one notational addition. In BNF, nonterminals will have their names enclosed in angle brackets (< >) to allow a string of characters in a nonterminal name to be distinguished from the corresponding string of terminal characters. For example, the nonterminal symbol <id> can be distinguished from id, a string of two terminal symbols. See Figure 2.5 for a BNF definition of the calculator grammar.

We are now ready to add three features to BNF to transform it into our EBNF. These features do not add any capabilities to the language, but rather enhance the compactness of the expression. These features are in such common use that many people include them in the definition of BNF.

The first new feature, **alternation**, is the use of the or symbol to express alternative definitions for the same nonterminal within a single production. This symbol is a vertical bar. For example, the set of productions

FIGURE **2.5**   **Calculator Grammar in BNF**

```
<calculation>  ::=  <expression> =
<expression>   ::=  <value>
<expression>   ::=  <value> <operator> <expression>
<value>        ::=  <number>
<value>        ::=  <sign> <number>
<number>       ::=  <unsigned>
<number>       ::=  <unsigned> . <unsigned>
<unsigned>     ::=  <digit>
<unsigned>     ::=  <digit> <unsigned>
<digit>        ::=  0
<digit>        ::=  1
<digit>        ::=  2
<digit>        ::=  3
<digit>        ::=  4
<digit>        ::=  5
<digit>        ::=  6
<digit>        ::=  7
<digit>        ::=  8
<digit>        ::=  9
<sign>         ::=  +
<sign>         ::=  -
<operator>     ::=  +
<operator>     ::=  -
<operator>     ::=  *
<operator>     ::=  /
```

```
<odd> ::= 1
<odd> ::= 3
<odd> ::= 5
<odd> ::= 7
<odd> ::= 9
```

can be compressed using this notation to

```
<odd> ::= 1 | 3 | 5 | 7 | 9
```

We also add **optionality** by use of brackets ([]) to specify an optional item and **repetition** by use of the braces ({}) to specify a repeated item. The brackets indicate zero or one occurrence of the enclosed specification, whereas the braces indicate zero or more repetitions of the enclosed specification.

For example, the production

```
<goal> ::= [a] b {c}
```

specifies the following strings as valid goals:

```
b
ab
```

```
bc
abc
bcc
abcc
bccc
abccc
.
.
.
.
```

This notation indicates that zero or one a is followed by one b and zero or more c's.

Although these brackets and braces are simply defined, their interpretation can be quite complicated when they are nested and/or include the or metasymbol. Consider, for example, the production

```
<goal> ::= [{a} b] {d | e}
```

Although this expresses a production compactly, we see that some clarity has been lost in the process, because the definition is rather complex.

One final extension that we will find helpful is the use of parentheses to group parts of the specification for priority in evaluation. Parentheses are necessary primarily to eliminate ambiguity in the application of alternation and concatenation. For example, parentheses can specify whether the production

```
<x> ::= a b | c
```

means

```
<x> ::= (a b) | c  or  <x> ::= a (b | c)
```

The first of these interpretations would recognize the string c, whereas the second would not. The second would recognize ac, but the first would not.

When used with care, these extensions can improve not only the compactness, but also the clarity of grammar definitions. Figure 2.6 shows how these extensions can be used in defining our calculator grammar. As you can see, this new notation frequently eliminates the need for recursion and alternatives.

One purpose of EBNF is to enhance the clarity of expression for grammars. There is one difficulty that arises in its use when a symbol used in EBNF (a metasymbol) is also a terminal symbol in a grammar. For example, if | were a terminal symbol in the grammar being defined, then the production

FIGURE 2.6   **Calculator Grammar in EBNF**

```
<calculation>  ::= <expression> =
<expression>   ::= <value> [<operator> <expression>]
<value>        ::= [<sign>] <unsigned> [. <unsigned>]
<unsigned>     ::= <digit> {<digit>}
<digit>        ::= 0 | 1 | 2 | 3 | 4 | 5 | 6 | 7 | 8 | 9
<sign>         ::= + | -
<operator>     ::= + | - | * | /
```

```
<x> ::= a | b
```

could be interpreted in either of two ways. First, the nonterminal x might have two alternative definitions, a or b, if | is interpreted as a metasymbol. If, however, | is interpreted as a terminal symbol of the grammar, a single definition consisting of three terminal symbols is specified.

We avoid this confusion by using the following convention: When a metasymbol is also a terminal symbol of the grammar being defined, the symbol will be underlined when it is to represent the terminal symbol and will represent the metasymbol otherwise. Using this convention, the preceding production would represent two alternative single-symbol definitions of x. If we wished to express the three-symbol definition, it would be written

```
<x> ::= a | b
```

2.2.3 ▪ Syntax Diagrams

A somewhat different approach to expressing grammars was used by Wirth in his definition of Pascal. This tool is called a **syntax diagram**. It expresses productions as two-dimensional directed graphs whose nodes are symbols. The possible paths through the graph represent the possible sequences of symbols that define the nonterminal of the production.

Terminal symbols are represented by ovals and nonterminals, by rectangular nodes. Syntax diagrams have the advantage of using two dimensions to enhance understandability. Their disadvantage is the difficulty in generating the diagrams using a linear input device, such as a keyboard. Figure 2.7 shows the syntax diagram for our calculator grammar.

2.2.4 ▪ Problems with Specifications

The grammars that can be described by BNF and, equivalently, by EBNF are known as *context-free grammars*. This terminology indicates that the valid definitions of a nonterminal symbol are independent of the context in which the symbol is found. Most programming languages cannot be completely specified by a context-free grammar because they contain some rules that are *context sensitive*, meaning that their nonterminal definition depends on context. For example, the common requirement that a variable must be declared before it is used cannot be expressed in a context-free grammar, because the validity of a variable depends upon whether its declaration is in the context of its use or not. Although formal tools do exist to express context-sensitive grammars, these are much more complex than the context-free tools we have already seen. These context-sensitive tools are, therefore, not commonly used in language specification. The common approach is to specify formally the context-free portion of a language's syntax using BNF or a similar tool, and informally specify the context-sensitive portion in English text.

Another problem in formal specification is that of ambiguity. Ambiguity occurs when there is more than one possible derivation tree associated with a

FIGURE 2.7   **Syntax Diagram for Calculator Grammar**

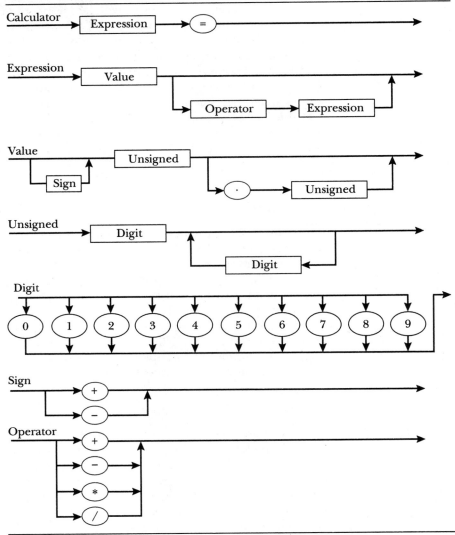

given valid string in a language. To illustrate this, consider the grammar in Figure 2.6 as modified by replacing the production for <expression> by

```
<expression> ::= <value> |
               (<expression> <operator> <expression>)
```

The resulting grammar is an **ambiguous grammar**, as Figure 2.8 demonstrates. Here, two different valid derivation trees are given for the string

```
4 + 2 * 3 =
```

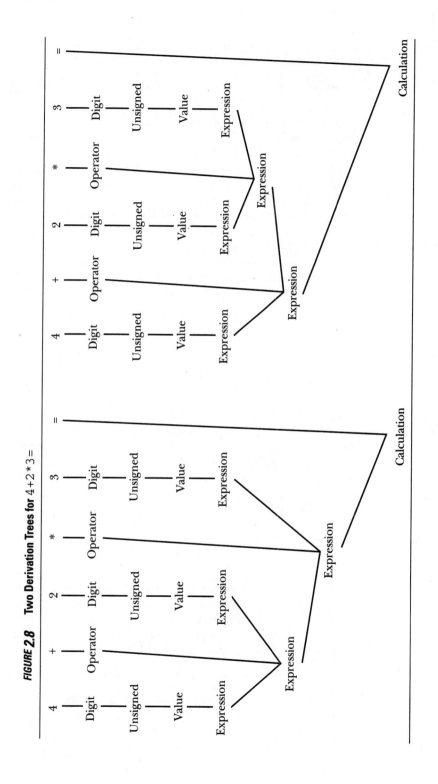

FIGURE 2.8 Two Derivation Trees for $4+2*3=$

If the grammar is being used only to determine whether the string is valid or not, this ambiguity causes no problem, because either derivation is sufficient for this purpose. Often, however, a grammar is used to interpret the meaning of the string as well. Notice that in this case, the two possible derivations have different meanings in the sense that they imply that the two operators are applied in the opposite order when the statement is executed. The application of the first tree then represents a calculation whose result is 18, whereas the second tree represents a calculation whose result is 10.

It is useful to eliminate ambiguity by modifying the grammar whenever possible. There are no general techniques for doing this. Rather, each situation must be carefully analyzed to find and eliminate the ambiguities. Some languages have no possible representation through an unambiguous grammar, so attempts to find such representations are fruitless. Such languages are called **ambiguous languages**.

The grammar of Figure 2.6 results in the derivation of a tree equivalent to the second tree of Figure 2.8. In general, this grammar specifies the application of operators from right to left. This order is reversed from the left-to-right application that we commonly expect. Careful examination shows that we could generate a left-to-right operator application if the production for `expression` is replaced by

```
<expression> ::= [<expression> <operator>] <value>
```

The difference between this production and the one given in Figure 2.6 is the placement of the recursive symbol with respect to the operator. When the recursive symbol is to the left of the operator, the operator will be applied left to right, and when it is to the right, the operator will be applied right to left.

We frequently wish to override the left-to-right application of operators in arithmetic expressions in order to give certain operators precedence over others. For example, it is common for multiplication and division to be given precedence over addition and subtraction. In this way the expression

```
6 + 3 * 4
```

is evaluated by applying the multiplication first, even though it lies to the right of the addition.

Grammars can be constructed that implement precedence by inserting additional nonterminal symbols for each level of precedence. The lower the level of precedence for an operator, the nearer to the goal symbol it is applied. In order to implement the precedence rule stated earlier, we include the following productions in our calculator grammar:

```
<expression>  ::= [<expression> <addoperator>] <term>
<term>        ::= [<term> <multoperator>] <value>
<addoperator> ::= + | -
<multoperator>::= * | /
```

Notice that by using left recursion in each case, we have also specified left-to-right order among operators of the same precedence. It would, of course, be possible to reverse the order for some precedence levels to become right-to-left by making the corresponding productions right recursive.

2.3 Semantics Specification

Although the syntax of a language can be nicely described in a formal manner by the use of tools such as BNF, the semantics are a different matter. Even though tools are available, which we briefly describe in this section, these tools are too complex to describe the semantics of a practical language in an easily interpreted way. Therefore, semantics are usually described in English, a tool that is understandable enough but unfortunately lacks the formalism we desire.

In spite of its complexity, formal semantic specification is desirable, because it allows the actions of programs to be described in an unambiguous, machine-independent way, just as formal syntactic specifications describe legal program syntax. In addition, formal semantics provide a standard and a reference for the testing or verification of language translation systems.

In this section we briefly describe three approaches to formal semantics specification, each of which corresponds to one of the language models presented in this book. The first approach, **operational semantics**, is based on the imperative model of languages, describing the semantics of a language by mapping programs in that language into equivalent programs implemented on an **abstract machine**. **Denotational semantics** use the functional model of languages to map programs in a language into equivalent functions. The final approach, **axiomatic semantics**, is based on the logic model of programming languages. It describes the action of a program by determining logical assertions that hold before and after its execution.

Each of the three approaches is illustrated by application to a variation of the calculator grammar used in the previous section. That variation is given in Figure 2.9.

FIGURE **2.9**   **Calculator Grammar for Semantic Specification**

```
<calculation>      ::=    <expression> =
<expression>       ::=    <value> | <value> <operator>
                          <expression>
<value>            ::=    [<sign>]<integer-part> | [<sign>]|
                          <integer-part>.<digit>
<integer-part>     ::=    <digit> | <integer-part> <digit>
<decimal-part>     ::=    <digit> | <digit> <decimal-part>
<digit>            ::=    0 | 1 | 2 | 3 | 4 | 5 | 6 | 7 | 8 | 9
<sign>             ::=    + | -
<operator>         ::=    + | - | * | /
```

2.3.1   ▪   Operational Semantics

The operational approach to semantic specification defines the meaning of any statement in a language by providing a means of translating that statement into an equivalent statement in another language. In order for this technique to be useful, the new language must be one whose semantics are unambiguous and completely understood by the user.

As an example, if we already understand the Pascal programming language, an operational semantic specification for Ada might consist of a program that translates any Ada program into an equivalent Pascal program. But this reduces the problem to a semantic specification of Pascal, which, since Pascal is approximately the same level of complexity as Ada, is nearly as difficult to accomplish.

Therefore, the most useful operational semantic specification would automate a translation from the source language to a lower-level language — that is, one whose semantics can be defined more simply. The lowest-level language in this sense is machine language, because its semantics are completely and unambiguously defined by the architecture of the machine. An operational semantic specifier that generates machine language is also known as a *compiler*, and for those who are fluent in machine language, a compiler fulfills the role of a semantic specification. However, the machine language of a real computer may be more detailed than we wish for the purpose of semantic specification. Therefore, operational semantic specifications are usually based on translation to the language of an abstract machine that contains only the essential parts of a machine language. The implementation of a compiler for the source language can then be reduced to producing a translator from the abstract machine language to the target machine language.

The most famous abstract machine used for this purpose was the **Vienna Definition Language** developed by Wegner (1972) for the semantic description of PL/I. This abstract machine definition was important from a theoretical point of view, but it did not come into popular use because the semantic descriptions were very complex.

To illustrate the operational approach to semantic specification, we use a simple stack machine as our abstract machine. Its machine language contains six instructions:

`push value`	Push the given value on the stack.
`pop`	Pop the top value from the stack.
`add`	Add the top two values, replacing them with their sum.
`sub`	Subtract the top two values, replacing them with their difference.
`mult`	Multiply the top two values, replacing them with their product.
`div`	Divide the top two values, replacing them with their quotient.

The semantic description of the calculator language now consists of the stack machine code that is to be generated for each syntax rule in the grammar. For example, the syntax rule

```
<integer-part> ::= <integer-part> <digit>
```

would be replaced by the following stack machine code:

```
[the code generated by the right-hand-side <integer-part>]
push 10
mult
[the code generated by <digit>, which leaves that result on
 top of the stack]
add
```

This code requires some explanation. The code is a recursive definition of the code for <integer-part> in that the code for another <integer-part> is included within it. The second and third steps multiply that value by 10, whereas the fourth and fifth steps add the value of <digit>.

Let's assume that the code generated by the right-hand side, <integer-part>, results in a value of 28 being placed on top of the stack and the code generated by <digit> results in 7 being placed on top. Then the preceding code would be equivalent to the following, with the stack shown to the right.

```
[push 28]          28
push 10            10 28
mult               280
[push 7]           7   280
add                287
```

A complete definition of the semantics of the calculator language is found in Figure 2.10. Here the code generated by a syntactic structure is represented by that structure's name.

FIGURE **2.10**   **Operational Semantics for Calculator Language**

```
<calculation>    ::=    <expression> =              <expression>
                                                    pop

<expression>     ::=    <value>                     <value>
                        |
                        <value> <operator> <expression>   <expression>
                                                          <value>
                                                          <operator>

<value>          ::=    [<sign>]<integer-part>      <integer-part>
                                                    [<sign>]
                        |
                        [<sign>]|<integer-part>.<digit>   <integer-part>
                                                          <decimal-part>
                                                          add
                                                          [<sign>]
```

(continues)

```
<integer-part>  ::=   <digit>                                 <digit>
                      |
                      <integer-part> <digit>                  <integer-part>
                                                              push 10
                                                              mult
                                                              <digit>
                                                              add

<decimal-part>  ::=   <digit>                                 push 10
                                                              <digit>
                                                              div

                      |
                      <digit> <decimal-part>                  push 10
                                                              <decimal-part>
                                                              div
                                                              push 10
                                                              <digit>
                                                              div
                                                              add

<digit>         ::=   0                                       push 0
                      |
                      1                                       push 1
                      |
                      ...                                     ...
                      |
                      9                                       push 9

<sign>          ::=   +                                       nop
                      |
                      -                                       push -1
                                                              mult

<operator>      ::=   +                                       add
                      |
                      -                                       sub
                      |
                      *                                       mult
                      |
                      /                                       div
```

We now examine the abstract machine program generated by the calculation

```
1.5*-40=
```

Figure 2.11 shows the stack machine code generated by our model, along with the accompanying syntax structures. This diagram is the parse tree for the calculation and illustrates the process by which the stack machine program is generated as you examine it from right to left. For example, the goal `calculation` is semantically represented by

```
expression
pop
```

where `expression` is then further parsed into

```
expression
value
```

and `pop` is a statement in our stack machine language.

The items in parentheses in Figure 2.11 represent the portion of the source string represented by each syntactic component. The left column is the stack machine code generated that is equivalent to the original expression.

2.3.2 ▪ Denotational Semantics

The operational approach maps each syntax production into a sequence of abstract machine language statements, but the denotational approach maps each production into a function. For each nonterminal symbol on the right-hand side of a production, the generated function includes a call on the function defined for that nonterminal. The theory behind this approach was originally developed by Scott and Strachey (1971).

The final function generated for the goal symbol accepts as its parameter a program written in the language that is being described and has as its result the output that the given program should generate. Specifically, if the final function for the calculator grammar was given by F_c, the application of this function to a syntactically valid string would give the correct result of the calculation — for example,

```
Fc('2+3=') = '5'
```

Let us first examine how a function can be derived from a production. We choose the production

```
<integer-part> ::= <integer-part> <digit>
```

from our calculator grammar. We specify the function `IP` defined by this production to be

```
IP(<integer-part><digit>) = 10*IP(<integer-part>) + D(<digit>)
```

where `D` is the function associated with `<digit>`. Note that this is a recursive definition of function `IP`, but a nonrecursive alternative definition is associated with the production

```
<integer-part> ::= <digit>
```

namely,

```
IP(<digit>) = D(<digit>)
```

FIGURE 2.11   Stack Machine Program for 1.5*-40

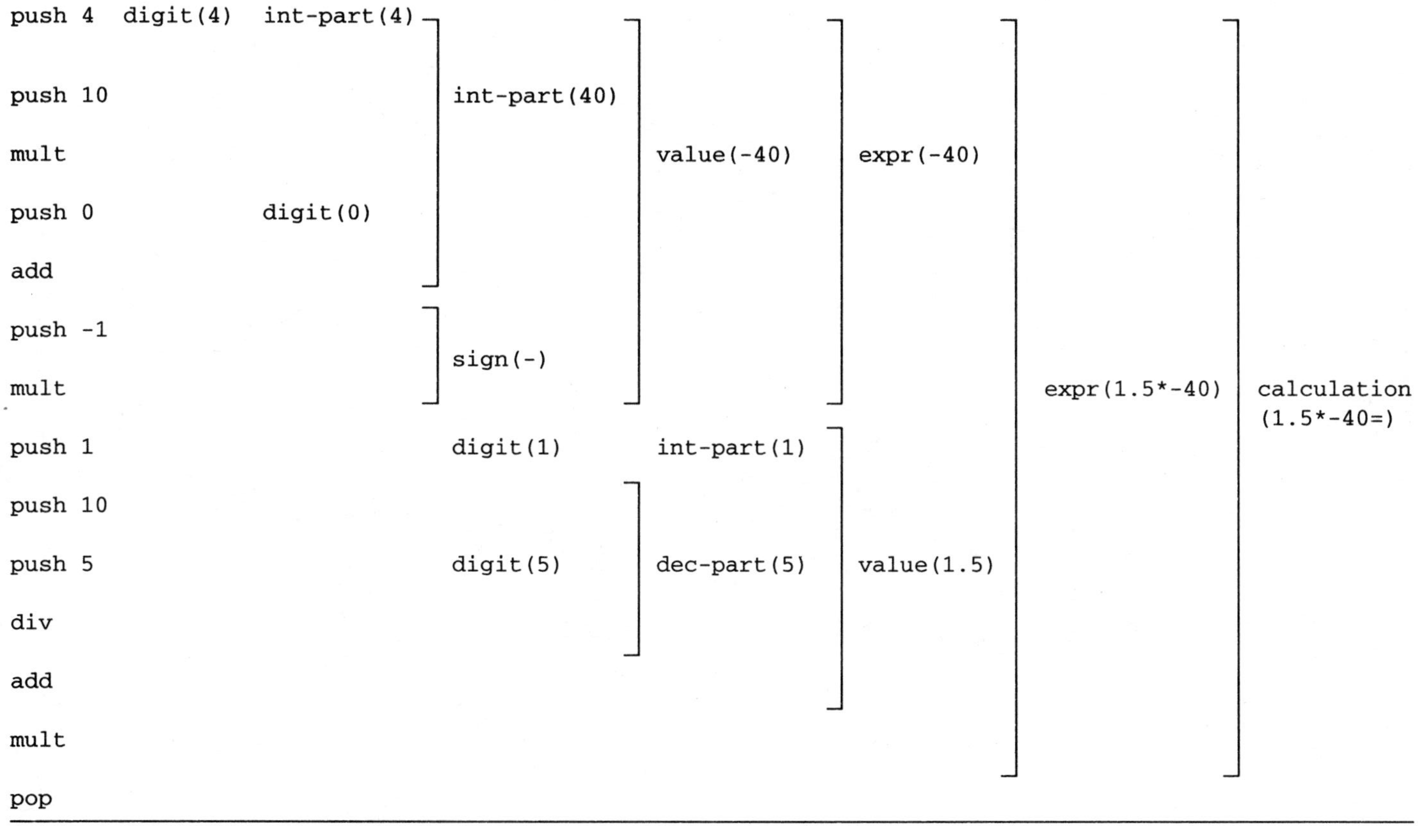

```
push 4     digit(4)    int-part(4)

push 10
                       int-part(40)    value(-40)

mult

push 0     digit(0)

add

push -1

mult                   sign(-)

push 1     digit(1)    int-part(1)

push 10

push 5     digit(5)    dec-part(5)     value(1.5)

div

add

mult

pop
```

value(-40) ─ expr(-40) ─ expr(1.5*-40) ─ calculation (1.5*-40=)

Therefore, if we expand the definition of `'245'`, we see that

```
IP('245') = 10 * IP('24') + D('5')
          = 10 * (10 * IP('2') + D('4')) + D('5')
          = 10 * (10 * D('2') + D('4')) + D('5')
```

where the first two lines apply the recursive definition of `IP` and the last line applies the nonrecursive one.

A complete denotational description of our calculator grammar is given in Figure 2.12. The function definitions found there are self-explanatory. Figure 2.13 contains the evaluation of the function `C` for the string `'1.5*-40='`. Each line of this evaluation is the application of one or more functions from the specification of Figure 2.12.

Note that this semantic description is simplified by two properties of our language. First, the language admits no input, so all our functions are constant functions. Suppose, for example, that a construct reads an integer and outputs its double. Its function could then be defined as

```
D(<double>) = [f(x) = 2*x]
```

FIGURE 2.12 **Denotational Semantic Description of Calculator Language**

`C(<expression> =)`	`=`	`E(<expression>)`
`E(<value>)`	`=`	`V(<value>)`
`E(<value>+<expression>)`	`=`	`V(<value>) +`
		`E(<expression>)`
`E(<value>-<expression>)`	`=`	`V(<value>) -`
		`E(<expression>)`
`E(<value>*<expression>)`	`=`	`V(<value>) *`
		`E(<expression>)`
`E(<value>/<expression>)`	`=`	`V(<value>) /`
		`E(<expression>)`
`V(+ <value>)`	`=`	`V(<value>)`
`V(- <value>)`	`=`	`- V(<value>)`
`V(<integer-part>)`	`=`	`IP(<integer-part>)`
`V(<integer-part>.<decimal-part>)`	`=`	`IP(<integer-part>)+`
		`DP(<decimal-part>)`
`IP(<digit>)`	`=`	`D(<digit>)`
`IP(<integer-part><digit>)`	`=`	`10*IP(<integer-part>)+`
		`D(<digit>)`
`DP(<digit>)`	`=`	`0.1*D(<digit>)`
`DP(<digit><decimal-part>)`	`=`	`0.1*(DP(<decimal-part>)+`
		`D(<digit>))`
`D('0')`	`=`	`0`
`D('1')`	`=`	`1`
`...`		`...`
`D('9')`	`=`	`9`

FIGURE 2.13   **Derivation of Denotational Function for** `1.5*-40`

```
C('1.5*-40=') =
E('1.5*-40') =
V('1.5')*E('-40') =
(IP('1')+DP('5'))*E('-40') =
(D('1')+0.1*D('5'))*E('-40') =
(1 + 0.1*5)*E('-40') =
1.5*V('-40') =
1.5*(-V('40')) =
1.5*(-IP('40')) =
1.5*(-(10*IP('4')+D('0'))) =
1.5*(-(10*D('4')+D('0'))) =
1.5*(-(10*4+0)) =
1.5*(-40) =
-60
```

The second simplifying property of our language is that no construct produces side effects that change the computing environment. In cases where side effects can be produced, the computing environment, such as the data store, must be included as input and output to the specified function, allowing the syntactic structure to modify the environment as well.

2.3.3 ▪ Axiomatic Semantics

The axiomatic method of specifying semantics is based on the logic model of computing. It makes use of logical **assertions**, which are statements that are either true or false. For each syntactic definition, the axiomatic method specifies the assertions that are assumed to be true before the execution of the syntactic unit, known as the **precondition**, and the assertion that then must be true after the unit's execution, called the **postcondition**. The first major work on this approach was done by Hoare (1969).

Like the logic model, the axiomatic approach to semantic specification is nonprocedural in nature. Rather than specifying the actions that a syntactic unit performs, as the operational and denotational approaches do, this approach describes the effect of the action in the form of the postcondition.

Although the axiomatic approach requires extensive background in predicate calculus and its use in the semantic description of programming languages can be quite difficult to understand, it is easy to apply this approach to the semantic definition of our calculator language. In order to do this, we introduce some helpful notation. First, we express the assertion that a syntactic structure S evaluates to a given value v by the notation

```
<S> → v
```

We then express precondition and postcondition pairs by placing the precondition on top of the postcondition and dividing them by a line.

As an example, consider the axiomatic semantic description of the syntax rule

```
<integer-part> ::= <integer-part> <digit>
```

We would write this in our notation as follows:

$$\frac{\text{<integer-part>}_r \rightarrow v_1 \text{ and <digit> } \rightarrow v_2}{\text{<integer-part>}_1 \rightarrow 10*v_1 + v_2}$$

This notation indicates that if the precondition is that the two constituent syntactic units evaluate to v_1 and v_2, the postcondition is that the defined unit evaluates to $10*v_1+v_2$. Note the use of the subscripts r and 1 to differentiate between the occurrences of <integer-part> on the left and right sides of the production.

A complete axiomatic definition of our calculator language is given in Figure 2.14. Productions with no precondition are represented by leaving the expression above the line blank. See definitions of <digit> and <sign> in Figure 2.14.

FIGURE 2.14 **Axiomatic Semantic Description of Calculator Language**

`<calculation> ::= <expression>`	$\dfrac{\text{<expression>} \rightarrow v}{\text{output } v}$
`<expression> ::= <value>`	$\dfrac{\text{<value>} \rightarrow v}{\text{<expression>} \rightarrow v}$
<code> |</code>	
`<value><operator><expression>`	$\dfrac{\text{<expr>}_r \rightarrow v_1 \text{ and <value> } \rightarrow v_2}{\text{<expr>}_1 \rightarrow \text{apply(<operator>,} v_1, v_2)}$
`<value> ::= [<sign>]<int-part>`	$\dfrac{\text{<int-part> } \rightarrow v_1 \text{ [and <sign } \rightarrow v_2\text{>]}}{\text{<value> } \rightarrow v_1[*v_2]}$
<code> |</code>	
`[<sign>]<int-part><dec-part>`	$\dfrac{\text{<int-part>} \rightarrow v_1 \text{ and <dec-part>} \rightarrow v_2 \text{ [and <sign>} \rightarrow v_3]}{\text{<value>} \rightarrow [v_3*](v_1+v_2)}$
`<int-part> ::= <digit>`	$\dfrac{\text{<digit> } \rightarrow v}{\text{<int-part> } \rightarrow v}$
<code> |</code>	
`<int-part> <digit>`	$\dfrac{\text{<int-part>}_r \rightarrow v_1 \text{ and <digit>} \rightarrow v_2}{\text{<int-part>}_1 \rightarrow 10*v_1+v_2}$
`<dec-part> ::= <digit>`	$\dfrac{\text{<digit> } \rightarrow v}{\text{<dec-part> } \rightarrow v/10}$
<code> |</code>	
`<digit><dec-part>`	$\dfrac{\text{<digit>} \rightarrow v_1 \text{ and <dec-part>}_r \rightarrow v_2}{\text{<dec-part>}_1 \rightarrow v_1 + (v_2/10)}$

```
<digit> ::= 0
                                                        ————————
          |                                             <digit> → 0
          1
                                                        ————————
         ...                                            <digit> → 1
          |
          9
                                                        ————————
<sign> ::= +                                            <digit> → 9

          |                                             ————————
          -                                             <sign> → 1

                                                        ————————
                                                        <sign> → -1
```

Let us examine the second definition of <value> in Figure 2.14. It states that when <value> is represented by

[<sign>] <int-part> <dec-part>

the semantics rule is stated in English as follows:

> If <int-part> is the value v_1 and <dec-part> is the value v_2 and <sign>, if present, is v_3, then <value> has the value v1 + v2 if <sign> is not present or v_3 * (v_1 + v_2) if <sign> is present.

2.4 Language Translation

The purpose of any language is communication between two parties, a sender and a receiver. With natural language, the communication is between two people, who alternate between the sending and receiving roles. With programming languages, the communication is between a programmer and a language-translation program. Communication in a programming language is sent by the programmer and received by the translation program. There is also communication in the opposite direction in the form of diagnostic messages and other information about the translation; however, this communication is not in the programming language itself but is usually in English, some cryptic codes, or a combination of the two.

The purpose of a language-translation program is to accept a set of instructions written in a programming language and to cause the activities specified by these instructions to be carried out by the receiving computer. Therefore, a language-translation program accepts as input a program in a programming language and makes it possible for the activities specified by this program to be carried out, either by translating the program into an equivalent program in a language that is already executable or by directly carrying out the activities specified by the translation program.

In order to understand a language and judge its effectiveness, we must have some understanding of the capabilities and needs of both the sender and the receiver. This text is concerned primarily with languages from the point of view of the sender. Other books examine languages from the point of view of the receiver. These latter books are useful in courses on compiler analysis and design.

In this section we briefly describe the properties of translation programs. Our intent is that as we study programming languages from the perspective of the programmer, you might gain some understanding of the perspective of the translation program located at the receiving end of this communication.

2.4.1 ▪ Compilers and Interpreters

There are two fundamental approaches to language translation: compilation and interpretation. In order to help explain the difference between these two approaches, we will examine an analogy.

Suppose that you have a German gardener who speaks no English, and you speak no German. Every day you prepare a list in English of instructions to the gardener for his tasks that day. You present this list to him upon his arrival in the morning. The gardener must then use a German-English dictionary that you provide to translate your instructions so that he can perform the requested tasks.

We will consider two approaches that the gardener might take to this translation task. The first is the interpretive approach. Here he translates the first instruction and then performs the task described by that instruction. Next he translates the second instruction and performs that task. He continues in this manner until all tasks are completed or until his workday is over.

With the second approach — the compilation approach — the gardener first translates all the instructions on the list from English to German, recording all the translated instructions. He then takes this translated list of German instructions and begins performing the requested tasks.

As we examine these two approaches, we note some advantages of each. Interpretation has the advantage that if for some reason the gardener does not complete all the jobs specified, he has not wasted time translating descriptions of tasks that he will not do. Also, if one of the instructions is not executable, the gardener is able to point out the troublesome instruction to you on your English list, because he knows where he is translating at the moment. This may not be possible under compilation.

Compilation is advantageous if there is a need to repeat the same activity several times, because the translated version is saved and can be referred to again later. For example, if the instructions included

1. Mow the front lawn.
2. Prune shrubs in front lawn.
3. Rake front lawn.
4. Repeat steps 1–3 for the back lawn.

the interpretive gardener would have to retranslate instructions 1 to 3 when he reached instruction 4, because we assume that he does not save the translated version either on paper or in his head. The compiling gardener would not need to retranslate, because he would have saved the complete set of translated instructions. Another case of repetition of a translated instruction would occur if the instructions for this Monday read, "Repeat the jobs you did last Monday." We assume the compiling gardener, in anticipation of such a circumstance, saves each day's translated instructions, and this Monday needs only to retrieve the list from last Monday rather than translate at all. The interpreting gardener would not have recorded the translated instructions and would need to repeat the translation process.

The application of this analogy to programming language translation is straightforward. We will refer to translation programs using these two techniques as *interpreters* and *compilers*. An **interpreter** translates one statement of a program at a time and then calls a routine to complete the execution of that statement. A **compiler** produces from the given input program another program that is equivalent to the original but in a language that is executable. This resulting program may be in a language that is directly executable, such as machine language, or indirectly executable, such as another language for which a translator already exists.

The relative advantages of interpreters and compilers are similar to those of the gardener's two processes. An interpreter has the advantage of not translating statements that are never executed and of being able to relate back to the corresponding instruction in the programming language from every point of the execution. The compiler, on the other hand, only needs to translate each statement once, no matter how many times the statement is executed. This is applicable in both the case of iteration and that of repeated executions of the same program.

The advantages of a compiler generally outweigh those of an interpreter in practice, and this form of translation is by far the one most frequently used. For this reason, and because compilation is a more complex process, we focus on the activities of a compiler in the remainder of this section.

2.4.2 ▪ Overview of the Compilation Process

The purpose of a compiler is to translate a program written in a source language into an equivalent program expressed in a language that is executable directly by the machine. These two programs are called the *source program* and the *object program*. The language of the object program is called the *target language*. Figure 2.15 shows an overview of the compilation process where the object program is directly executable. The time during which the compiler is executing is known as **compile time**. The time during which the object program is executing is called **run time**.

The compilation can be broken down into several phases. These phases are conceptual and specify activities that all compilers perform, although frequently the activities of several phases may be combined and performed simultaneously. These phases and their corresponding inputs and outputs are illustrated in Figure 2.16.

FIGURE **2.15** **Compilation Process Overview**

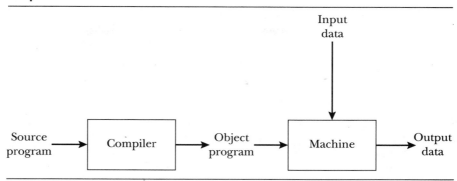

Under this model, the program takes on three intermediate forms, the **to-ken string**, the **parse tree**, and the **abstract program**. These are each discussed in later sections describing the steps that produce them.

An additional important data structure in the compilation process is the symbol table. The **symbol table** contains an entry for every user-defined symbol or identifier included in the source program. This table is used to communicate between phases. It associates each identifier's name with its attributes, or properties. The attributes included vary from compiler to compiler and from phase to phase in a single compiler. They may include indications of type, location, and status. Symbol table entries are created during lexical analysis, but the table is modified and referenced by both semantic analysis and code generation.

2.4.3 ▪ Lexical Analysis

The purpose of the *lexical analyzer* (also known as the *scanner*) is to transform the source program in the form of a character string into a string of tokens. A *token* is a symbol that expresses the nature of a language element, as abstracted from the string of characters that represents it. Some characters may translate directly into tokens — for example, operators and punctuation marks. Other tokens may be formed from strings of characters, such as reserved words, statement labels, variables, and constants. The lexical analyzer must determine the appropriate token for a string of characters from the characters themselves and their context.

Some tokens, such as identifiers, may have names associated with them. In this case, there will be a reference to an entry in the symbol table attached to the token that represents that identifier. The first time a given identifier is encountered in the source program, it is entered into the symbol table. Subsequent occurrences will result in references to that symbol table entry being included in the token.

Some characters in the source program will result in no token entries. In particular, this will include characters whose purpose it is to serve as separators between token elements in the source program.

FIGURE **2.16**   **Phases of Compilation**

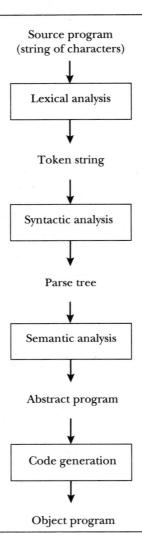

Source program
(string of characters)

Lexical analysis

Token string

Syntactic analysis

Parse tree

Semantic analysis

Abstract program

Code generation

Object program

The output from **lexical analysis** is, therefore, a string of pairs, where one element of the pair identifies the class of the token and the other element points to the entry in the symbol table where attributes of this particular token will be found. Some tokens, such as those for operators and reserved words, will contain an empty pointer, because no further attributes are required.

For example, the Pascal statement

```
x := substr(x,1,4) + '...';
```

could, after lexical analysis, be represented by the following sequence of pairs:

```
(identifier, ptr1)
(colon, nil)
(equal, nil)
(identifier, ptr2)
(leftparen, nil)
(identifier, ptr1)
(comma, nil)
(integer, ptr3)
(comma, nil)
(integer, ptr4)
(rightparen, nil)
(plus, nil)
(string, ptr5)
(semicolon, nil)
```

All identifiers and constants contain pointers to corresponding symbol table entries. The two references to the identifier x both point to the same entry in the symbol table, `ptr1`. In practice, abbreviated codes are used to identify token types instead of the more descriptive names used here.

2.4.4 ▪ Syntactic Analysis

Syntactic analysis is the process of applying a grammar to form the derivation tree for a program from the sequence of tokens generated by the lexical analysis process. This process is called *parsing*. There are two strategies that can be applied for this purpose: top-down and bottom-up.

Top-down parsing starts with the goal symbol and replaces that symbol with one of its alternative definitions that has the potential to match the string of tokens, resulting in nonterminals within the definitions being matched to substrings of the original token string. These nonterminals are, in turn, replaced by one of their definitions, and so on, until no unmatched nonterminals remain. This top-down process corresponds to the generation of a valid string, as shown in Figure 2.2, only in this case, the generation is directed toward a specific string of terminal symbols and the steps are retained to form the derivation tree.

Frequently, a sequence of definition substitutions leads to a dead end in the generation process, at which point the top-down parser must resort to *backtracking*. Backtracking refers to the process of backing up to the most recent substitution where there are untested alternative definitions and attempting to use one of those alternatives in the generation process.

Bottom-up parsing starts with a string of tokens and attempts to match its substrings to the right-hand sides of productions and substituting the defined nonterminal, continuing until the entire string is replaced by the goal symbol. This process proceeds as in Figure 2.3, with the derivation tree resulting.

2.4.5 ▪ Semantic Analysis

Semantic analysis uses the parse tree generated during syntactic analysis to generate a program in some abstract programming language, a form of operational semantic specification. This abstract language is typically a machine language for some simple, hypothetical machine designed to be compatible with the data types and operations of the source language. This abstract language is intended to be an intermediate step between the source and target languages of the compiler.

One of the primary purposes of this abstract language is to enhance portability of the language. By *portability* we mean the ability to translate the programming language easily into multiple target languages. With a suitable choice for the abstract language, compilers sharing the same source language but having different target languages could share the same code for the first three phases of the compilation process. Once a compiler is written for a given source language, writing one for the same source language but a different target language would require only developing a new code-generation phase for mapping the abstract language into the object language.

Intermediate languages usually resemble a high-level assembly language. The semantic analyzer calls a translation procedure that is identified with the syntactic class of the statement as determined by the syntax analysis. Each syntactic class has a corresponding translation procedure that analyzes the constituent parts of the parse tree and constructs the equivalent intermediate language form of the statement.

Another job of the semantic analyzer is the detection of context-sensitive errors such as mismatched types and undeclared variables. It also completes symbol table entries.

2.4.6 ▪ Code Generation

Code generation consists of replacing abstract language statements by parameterized object code templates. Therefore, the two steps in the code-generation process are matching a statement or sequence of statements in the abstract language to some pattern and, from that pattern, extracting a number of elements that will serve as parametric values. Next, the object code template that matches that pattern is obtained and the parameter values are substituted. This filled-in template is then passed on as a part of the generated object program.

Let us consider a simple example to illustrate this use of templates. Suppose our intermediate language uses a three-address instruction set, and one such instruction is represented by the template

```
ADD a,b,c
```

This instruction specifies that the operand located in a is to be added to the operand located in b and the result is to be stored in the location specified by operand c. Such a template may be translated by the code generator into a sequence of instructions in a two-address target language given by

```
MOVE loc(a),R1
ADD  loc(b),R1
MOVE R1,loc(c)
```

where R1 represents register 1 and loc is a function that returns the address of its identifier operand as it is found in the symbol table.

2.4.7 ▪ Optimization

Compiler **optimization** refers to the process of transforming a program into an equivalent program that will result in a more efficient execution. This modification might be performed on the source program, on the object program, or on any of the intermediate forms the program takes during the compilation process. The goal is to produce a program that will execute faster while still matching the functionality of the original source program. The word *optimization* is actually too strong, because it implies that the best of all possible equivalent programs will be produced. In practice, we can only hope to improve the run-time efficiency, not to optimize it.

Two forms of optimization that we will discuss are object-independent optimization and object-dependent optimization. *Object-independent optimization* can be performed on the source program prior to the compilation process, or on any of the intermediate forms up to the abstract program. It involves the identification of unnecessarily long or redundant run-time activities. Simple examples are computation at compile time of expressions whose values are known, repetition of identical computations, and operators that can be replaced by equivalent but faster operators.

Object-dependent optimization can be performed only on the object program and uses properties of the target language itself to reduce execution time. One such transformation is the use of registers to retain values that are reused later, thus avoiding recalculation. Another common technique is replacing operations by those having faster target instructions. Examples of this situation include the replacement of multiplication by a power of 2 with a shift instruction or using an increment instruction in place of adding 1. Such optimization might also be used to take advantage of parallel processing capabilities of the target language to perform independent computations.

2.5 Language Design Characteristics

The primary goal of a programming language is to assist the programmer in the software-development process. This includes assistance in the design, implementation, testing, verification, and maintenance of the software.

There are a number of characteristics of a language that contribute to this goal. These characteristics are all present within any language in varying degrees, and there is often a trade-off among two or more of them. In this section, we will discuss five of these characteristics. Although this list is by no means complete, it includes those that the authors believe to be the most significant for programming language effectiveness.

2.5.1 ▪ Simplicity

A programming language should strive for simplicity in both semantics and syntax. Semantic simplicity implies that the language contains a minimal number of concepts and structures. These concepts should be natural, quickly learned, and easily understood with little danger of misinterpretation.

Syntactic simplicity requires that the syntax represent each concept in one and only one way and that this representation be as easily understood as possible. This does not necessarily imply that the syntax be as concise as possible, because conciseness is often counterproductive to readability. It does exclude multiple representations of the same semantic concept and syntactic representations that are easily confused.

2.5.2 ▪ Abstraction

An **abstraction** is a representation of an object that includes only the relevant attributes of the original object, ignoring those attributes that are irrelevant to the purpose at hand. For example, a box score for a baseball game contains a summary of the performance of each player and is an abstraction of the game itself, including only those details relevant to those interested in its contents. A further abstraction of the game would be just the score.

A programming language's ability to express and use abstractions is important at both the data and procedural level. With data, the programmer is able to work more effectively by using simpler abstractions that do not include many irrelevant details of data objects. With procedures, abstractions facilitate good design practices and modularity.

The level to which a language implements the hiding of irrelevant details in the creation and use of abstractions is important to its ability to support effective design, implementation, and modification of programs.

2.5.3 ▪ Expressiveness

Expressiveness refers to the ease with which an object can be represented. In relation to programming languages, this means the language should permit the natural representation of both data objects and procedures. Appropriate data structures and control structures are corresponding examples of this.

Expressiveness may conflict with simplicity, because more expressiveness will frequently result in greater complexity in the language. Also, expressiveness is related to the problem domain. For example, language features that are expressive for artificial intelligence are probably not expressive for engineering applications. In order to resolve this conflict between expressiveness and simplicity, the current trend is for languages to restrict their problem domain to provide both characteristics.

2.5.4 ▪ Orthogonality

Simplicity requires a language to incorporate as few concepts as possible. Expressiveness requires that the concepts closely match the objects that they represent while abstraction eliminates irrelevant details. **Orthogonality** refers to the interaction between concepts — namely, the degree to which different concepts can be combined with each other in a consistent manner.

Violations of orthogonality occur when two concepts cannot interact with each other or when they interact in a manner inconsistent with their other interactions. For example, if a language does not allow a string to be passed as a parameter, the two concepts "string" and "parameter" may not interact, and hence there is a lack of orthogonality. If a language uses the operator : = for integer assignment and <- for string assignment, then the concept "assignment" interacts inconsistently with the concepts of "integer" and "string."

Orthogonality reduces the number of exceptions to the rules of a language and makes the language easier to learn and remember. It is easier to remember that := means assignment for all types than to remember a handful of exceptions to this rule.

Orthogonality can lead to difficulties, however, in situations where certain combinations of concepts are difficult to implement. This is particularly true when the combination is unlikely to occur or is completely impossible.

2.5.5 ▪ Portability

The ability to maintain programs is affected by all of the first four characteristics in the sense that they all encourage ease of program understanding and modification. One major maintenance problem that these characteristics do not address is the movement of a program from one computer to another. The **portability** of a language is much greater when a machine-independent standard exists for that language. For some languages the standard is an official standard constructed and approved by a standards organization such as the American National Standards Institute (ANSI). For others, the standard may be a de facto standard that has informally developed through the use of the language. Some languages for which formal standards are defined are FORTRAN, COBOL, Ada, Common LISP, C, and Pascal.

2.6 Choice of Language

As a result of the large number of programming languages in existence, a programmer with a given application must make a choice of the language to use. In this section, we describe seven criteria that are important considerations when making this decision.

2.6.1 ▪ Implementation

The implementation of the language refers to the language translator that is used. There are two important considerations related to the implementation: its availability and its efficiency.

The availability of a language obviously impacts the decision as to whether to use it or not for a given application. For example, a language that is not available on many small computers is, therefore, not a feasible choice if programs must be written on such machines. Even when a translator exists, its cost may make it impossible to use.

The efficiency of an implementation refers to the speed of execution of the object programs created by the translator. FORTRAN is frequently chosen for an application because FORTRAN compilers often contain many optimization features and therefore produce very efficient object code. Efficiency is a factor when the application has specific speed requirements.

2.6.2 ▪ Programmer Knowledge

Although it would be nice to assume that all programmers (and especially those who have read this book) are equally adept at programming in every language, this is certainly not the case. Primarily as a result of the programmer's education and experience, he or she typically favors one or two languages and is most effective when using those languages. Although learning a new, more appropriate language for a given application would certainly be a broadening experience, it is one that an employer is seldom eager to support financially.

An even more frequent factor is the knowledge of other programmers within the organization. Those other programmers may be responsible for validating, testing, modifying, or maintaining the program, so the cost of using an unfamiliar language would include training costs for many people.

This factor in the choice of a language is a major reason why FORTRAN and COBOL continue to be very popular in spite of the availability of many more effective languages.

2.6.3 ▪ Portability

If the ability to run an application on a variety of computers is important, then portability is a significant criterion in language choice. Languages that adhere to standards, such as FORTRAN, COBOL, and Ada, are much safer choices in this situation than are languages whose implementations are machine dependent and result in more time and expense when porting to a new system.

2.6.4 ▪ Syntax

Some applications are better accommodated by the syntax of one language than others. For example, the syntax of FORTRAN was designed to meet the requirements of expressing mathematical programs, whereas the English-like syntax of COBOL makes it a good choice when it is desirable to make the program understandable to nonprogrammers. More modern languages such as Pascal and Ada have syntax that makes the expression of control structures easier.

2.6.5 ▪ Semantics

The semantics of a language can be a significant factor in its choice for a given application. If an application requires or is facilitated by a certain language feature, then a language might be chosen that provides that capability. For example, if concurrent processing is required for a given application, a language with concurrent features, such as Ada, might be chosen. Often processing of an application is greatly simplified by the use of recursion, making languages that support recursion strong candidates.

2.6.6 ▪ Programming Environment

The presence of a rich programming environment to support software development can be a factor in the choice of a language. If the language resides in an environment that provides a context-sensitive editor, a symbolic debugger, a source code control system, windowing, or any of a number of other software-development tools, the effort required to produce the software can be greatly reduced. Although some of these features are available in language-independent environments, such as operating systems, often they are specific to a single language implementation. The availability of libraries of programs that interface with programs in a given language might also be an important factor.

2.6.7 ▪ Model of Computation

A final consideration in the selection of a programming language is the model of computation on which the language is based. Section 1.1 discusses the models emphasized in this text, and certain applications adapt most easily to one model over the others. For example, if the application requires a significant amount of heuristic searching, a language adhering to the logic-oriented model would be appropriate. Simulations are usually most easily implemented using the object-oriented model.

2.6.8 ▪ An Example

Consider the following real-life situation.

> A researcher requires a program that will generate all possible combinations of a collection of objects, apply a metric to each combination, and report the results of the application. The application of the metric involves comparing each object to each of the other objects in every combination. Thus, this task is iterative at several levels and could be coded to exploit recursion. The first question the researcher must answer is, which language should be used?

We consider the seven criteria just discussed. The researcher is really only concerned with the resulting measurements; thus, the speed of the implementation is not an issue. This is to be a locally written program with a specific purpose and a short lifetime; so that programmer knowledge and portability concerns can be ignored. The researcher likes to program but not in cryptic languages, so syntax is an issue. A language whose semantics provides easy iteration and/or natural recursion would allow for a simpler and better understood program. Also, a model of computation that allows a simple, abstract representation of the objects and the metric is desired here.

In this situation, the researcher chooses the language Prolog as the programming language for the project. Prolog implements the logical model of computation (see Chapter 12) and provides a simple and natural mechanism for recursively generating the combinations necessary. The objects can be represented at a very abstract level, and the metric can be simplified because of the simpler object representation. The Prolog program is quite short (40 lines of semimodular code) and easy to understand. Because Prolog is typically interpreted and the interpreter on the researcher's computer is not very fast, the program will take a long time to compute the necessary results. The researcher will begin data collection on a Friday and, returning on Monday, will find it takes more than 2 days to complete data collection.

Now, we reconsider the seven criteria under different circumstances. The researcher wants to work this metric application into a collection of programs that will be used by other people. Now performance is an issue; that is, 52 hours is not an acceptable time to wait for a program to collect metric data. But, the researcher discovers that the speed of the Prolog interpreter at the work site cannot be improved and another interpreter cannot be obtained. In addition, the researcher wants to share the code with others and wants someone else (a research assistant) to support the code. Thus, a different language must be chosen that compiles to much faster code, that is portable, and that is known by many other programmers.

The new language chosen for the project is C. The big advantage to C is that it compiles to very fast code and it is very portable. It also provides natural support for both complex iteration and recursion. The new program is much longer than the Prolog version (because the objects cannot be abstractly represented), but it is also much faster. The program is now 200 lines long, but it runs in less than 2 hours.

C H A P T E R **2**   **Terms**

syntax	goal symbol
semantics	metalanguage
grammar	Backus-Naur Form (BNF)
terminal symbols	Extended BNF (EBNF)
nonterminal symbols	alternation
production	optionality

repetition

syntax diagrams

ambiguous grammar

ambiguous language

operational semantics

abstract machine

denotational semantics

axiomatic semantics

Vienna Definition Language

assertion

precondition

postcondition

interpreter

compiler

compile time

run time

token string

parse tree

abstract program

symbol table

lexical analysis

syntactic analysis

semantic analysis

code generation

optimization

abstraction

orthogonality

portability

C H A P T E R 2 Discussion Questions

1. What are the advantages and disadvantages of using EBNF as opposed to BNF?

2. What are the advantages and disadvantages of using syntax diagrams as opposed to EBNF or BNF?

3. What are some context-sensitive rules found in most programming languages?

4. Under what circumstances is an interpreter preferable to a compiler? What circumstances make a compiler preferable?

5. Compare the three methods for semantic description of languages in terms of understandability and usefulness.

6. List other important language design characteristics in addition to the five given in Section 2.5.

7. Discuss the seven criteria that should be kept in mind in the choice of a programming language.

C H A P T E R 2 Exercises

1. Determine whether each of the following is a valid calculation in the calculator language of Figure 2.5. If so, show its derivation tree. If not, tell why not.

   a. `4+2=`
   b. `6=`
   c. `21-14/7=`
   d. `6-(2+5)=`
   e. `+4+2=`
   f. `6+-3=`
   g. `4.0-6.1=`
   h. `4.-6.1=`

2. Given the EBNF production

    ```
    <goal> ::= [{ab}c]{d}e
    ```

    determine which of the following form valid goal nonterminals.

    a. abcde
    b. ce
    c. abe
    d. ababce
    e. ccee
    f. dddde
    g. cddd
    h. aabbce
    i. e
    j. cccccce

3. Translate the following grammars expressed in EBNF into BNF. *Note:* You may need to add nonterminals.

    a.
    ```
    <goal> ::= [<a>]{xy}<b>
    <a>    ::= z{z}
    <b>    ::= x[y]z
    ```

    b.
    ```
    <goal>       ::= <expression>
    <expression> ::= <term> {+ <expression>}
    <term>       ::= <factor> {* <term>}
    <factor>     ::= a | b | c | (<expression>)
    ```

4. Translate each of the following grammars expressed in BNF into a more succinct EBNF form.

    a.
    ```
    <goal> ::= <a>
    <goal> ::= x <b> <a>
    <a>    ::= y
    <a>    ::= x <a>
    <b>    ::= <a>
    <b>    ::= <a> <b>
    <b>    ::= y <b>
    ```

    b.
    ```
    <goal> ::= <a>
    <a>    ::= <b>
    <a>    ::= x <a>
    <b>    ::= <c>
    <b>    ::= y <c>
    <c>    ::= z
    <c>    ::= z <c>
    ```

5. Construct syntax diagrams for the grammars described in Exercises 3 and 4.

6. Consider the following ambiguous grammar:

```
<goal> ::= <expression>
<expression> ::= <item>
                      | <expression> + <expression>
                      | <expression> * <expression>
```

Rewrite this as an unambiguous grammar in which

a. + and * have equal precedence and both are performed left to right.

b. * has precedence over + and both are performed right to left.

c. + has precedence over *, + is performed left to right, and * is performed right to left.

7. Indicate how the following Pascal code fragment could be optimized by a compiler. Do this by rewriting the fragment in optimized form.

```
u := 10;
x := 3 * y - 7;
while x > 0 do
  begin
    if 3 * y > z then
      z := z + 1
    else
      x := x + u;
  end;
```

8. A certain magazine distributor stores each subscription it distributes in a database and assigns each subscription a code number. That code number looks like

```
JIP081#03018701890189019001900190019178
```

Here the first three letters of the code are the first three letters of the subscriber's last name. The next three characters are the first three numbers in the street address. This field is omitted if there is no street address (for example, the address is a post office box). The next character is always a number sign (#). The next two characters indicate the number of subscription terms, which can be an integer from 1 to 99. The following four characters indicate the starting date of the first subscription term in the format mmyy. A pair of start/end dates is given for each subscription term. The last two characters in the code form a two-digit ID code for the magazine.

In the preceding sample code, the fields are interpreted as follows:

JIP	First three letters of subscriber's last name
081	First three digits of street address
#	Number sign
03	Number of subscription terms
0187	Start date of term 1
0189	End date of term 1
0189	Start date of term 2
0190	End date of term 2
0190	Start date of term 3
0790	End date of term 3
78	Magazine ID code

Give a specification for a language that recognizes all forms of subscription code numbers using BNF and syntax diagrams (not EBNF). Be sure your language accepts exactly what is specified earlier — nothing more or less. You may have to invent a few names for nonterminal symbols. You may assume that `<letter>` and `<digit>` are nonterminal symbols and are predefined for your use.

9. Consider your specification for Exercise 8. For each of the following strings, give a derivation and a parse tree.

    a. `JIP081#03018701890589069000591129278`
    b. `SMI#010719128733`

10. The following EBNF specification is ambiguous:

    ```
    <stmt> ::= if <expr> then <stmt>
             | if <expr> then <stmt> else <stmt>
             | <others>
    ```

    Assume that `<expr>` and `<others>` are defined elsewhere and that they describe a Boolean expression and other statements, respectively.

    a. Show that the specification is ambiguous.
    b. Give a different specification that describes the identical language, but that is unambiguous. Do not give further definitions to `<expr>` and `<others>`.

11. Consider this language specification:

    ```
    <E> ::= <E> * <E>
    <E> ::= [<E>] ^ <E>
    <E> ::= c
    ```

    The set of terminal symbols is {c, *, ^} and `<E>` is the only nonterminal symbol. The start symbol is obviously `<E>`.

    a. Give a derivation and parse tree for the string

    ```
    c * c ^ c * ^ c
    ```

    b. The preceding specification is ambiguous. Give a proof of its ambiguity.

12. Give a BNF specification for the language that consists of an even number of a's followed by an odd number of b's.

13. Write the semantic description of the following programs in the stack machine language, using the semantic description in Figure 2.10:

    a. `-17+2.41/5=`
    b. `1.2/3+2=`

14. Derive the denotational function for each for the following calculations for the extended calculator language of Figure 2.9.

    a. `-17+2.41/5=`
    b. `1.2/3+2=`

15. Suppose the following production is added to the calculator grammar as a monadic square operator:

    ```
    <sqr-op> ::= @
    ```

    a. How would this change the operational semantics specification in Figure 2.10?

    b. How would this change the denotational semantics specification in Figure 2.12?

    c. How would this change the axiomatic semantics specification in Figure 2.14?

C H A P T E R **2** **Laboratory Exercises**

1. Write an interpreter for the calculator language described in this chapter.

2. Write a program that translates a grammar written in EBNF into a BNF grammar.

3. Write a program that accepts as input an expression in calculator language and generates the parse tree for that expression.

4. Write a simulator for the stack machine described in this chapter. Then implement the calculator language on that simulated machine.

· C H A P T E R · 3

An Overview of the Imperative Model

3.1 ▪ Data Types and Bindings
3.2 ▪ Execution Units and Scope of Binding
3.3 ▪ Control Structures

The imperative model of programming languages was created to mimic, as closely as possible, the actions of computers at the machine language level. At that level, computers operate with two major units — the central processing unit (CPU), where computations are performed, and the memory, where data are stored.

The typical unit of execution in machine language, which may or may not be a single instruction, consists of the following four steps:

1. Obtain the addresses of locations for a result and one or more operands.

2. Obtain the operand data from the operand location(s).

3. Compute result data from the operand data.

4. Store the result data in the result location.

For example, a simple assignment statement such as

```
A := B + C;
```

is executed as follows:

1. Obtain the addresses of A, B, and C.

2. Obtain the data from the addresses of B and C.

3. Compute the result of B + C.

4. Store the result in the location of A.

Imperative programming languages have abstracted away the use of addresses in favor of names but otherwise have retained these four steps as a standard program unit. This unit of execution has become the fundamental execution unit of imperative languages and is called the *assignment statement*. The BNF form for such a statement is given by

```
<name> <assignment operator> <expression>
```

where the first component, name, represents the result location, the second component is an operator that signifies assignment (:= in Pascal and Ada, for example) and the third component is an expression that specifies the names of the operands and the computation to be performed.

Fundamental to the performance of this assignment is the establishment and use of a number of *bindings*. In step 1 of the preceding execution model, a binding between names and locations must be used to obtain the locations of the operands and result. In step 2, a binding between location and value must be referenced to establish operand values. And, finally, in step 4 a new binding between the result location and its computed value must be established. A view of programming languages from the perspective of bindings is presented in Section 3.1.

In step 3 of our model unit of execution, the computations depend on the interpretation of the data and of the operations that are defined. Programming languages relate data and operations through the mechanism known as *type*. In Section 3.1 we also discuss the role of type in the binding and computation process and review the properties of several fundamental types.

A further consideration related to the binding of names and locations is the ability to establish and change these bindings within the program. The part of the program in which a name-location binding is preserved is called the *scope of the binding*. In Section 3.2 we examine ways in which scope of binding can be defined within a language.

Another feature of the imperative model is the sequential execution of program steps. When this sequential execution needs to be modified, programming language features called *control structures* are used. A review of common control structures is found in Section 3.3.

3.1   Data Types and Bindings

3.1.1 ▪ Bindings

The abstraction that we will use to express the assignment statement activity in imperative languages is the data object. A **data object** consists of a four-tuple (L, N, V, T), where L is the location, N is the name, V is the value, and T is the type of the object. We call the determination of one of these components a **binding**. The implication here is that some of these bindings can be changed at certain times for a given data object.

Figure 3.1 shows a visualization of a data object and its bindings. The four bindings are all represented as lines from the data object to the corresponding objects to which it is bound. The **storage space**, from which **location bindings** are selected, is the set of virtual storage locations available within the computer system on which the program will be executed. This space is completely invisible to the programmer, who needs to know only that the binding takes place and when and does not need to know the specific location to which the data object is bound.

The time at which a binding takes place is often an important consideration. There are three times when bindings can occur:

1. **compile time** — when the program is being translated into machine language

2. **load time** — when the machine language program generated by the compiler is being assigned to particular locations within the storage space of the computer

3. **run time** — when the program is being executed

For convenience, the **location binding** commonly occurs at load time. We will see later that bindings to locations can occur during run time as well.

3.1.2 ▪ Identifiers

The **identifier space** of a language is the collection of all possible names that can be given to data objects. In addition, program units are also bound to names selected from the same identifier space.

In this text we use boxes to highlight language components, which include the description of the component for the Ada language. This also provides a template for expressing these components for new languages that you might encounter. The laboratory exercises frequently ask you to do this activity.

The accompanying box defines the identifier space as the set of all character strings of length 1 or longer beginning with a letter, containing only letters, digits, or underscores, and ending with a letter or digit. We will use EBNF notation to express language components, where possible, to avoid ambiguity.

```
Identifier Space
Language: Ada
Definition:

   <identifier> ::= <letter> {[underline]<letter_or_digit>}

Usage: The domain of names available for data objects and program units is
expressed in this way. Uppercase and lowercase are not distinguishable.
```

The **name binding** for a data object typically occurs at compile time at the point where a declaration is encountered by the compiler.

Note that name binding becomes a more complex issue when we are dealing with aggregate data objects such as arrays and records. Such aggregate

FIGURE **3.1** **Data Object and Bindings**

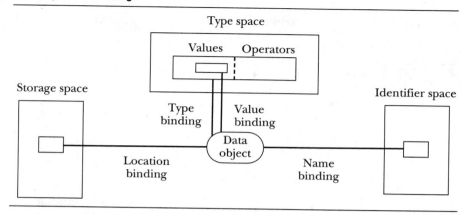

data objects, although bound to a single name, are bound to multiple locations. In addition, although the individual components are data objects themselves, with type, value, and location bindings, they do not have a binding to a simple name in the identifier space. Rather, each component is identified by a compound binding of some form.

For example, if ITEM is a record variable with one of its components being ID, then the simple name ITEM is bound to several locations corresponding to the collection of component data objects of the aggregate object ITEM. Moreover, the compound name ITEM.ID is bound to a single data object. We will ignore such complications in our present discussion by limiting our attention to simple, or scalar, data objects with simple name bindings.

3.1.3 ▪ Types

The **type space** of a language is the set of all possible types that can be bound to a simple data object. Each type is, itself, a space of possible values to which a data object of that type can be bound and a set of operations that apply to objects of that type. Therefore, the type and value bindings are two phases of the same binding, with the type binding restricting the possible values to which an object can be bound and defining the set of operations that can be applied to the data object. We can, therefore, think of a type as a set of values and a set of operations. A data object is usually bound to its type at compile time through a **type declaration** in a programming language.

```
Data Object Declaration
    Language: Ada
    Definition:
      <data object declaration> ::=
         <identifier list> : constant <type> := <expression>
       | <identifier list> : <type> [:= <expression>]
```

> Usage: One or more data objects are created at compile time. The objects result from binding each identifier in the identifier list to the type indicated. If := <expression> is present, a binding of the data object to the value indicated by the expression occurs at compile time. If constant is present, that value binding must be included and will remain in effect for the life of the data object.

To illustrate the effect of a declaration, consider the following sample declarations:

```
A : integer;
B : integer := 1;
C : constant integer := 1;
```

The effects of these three declarations on bindings at compile time are indicated in Figure 3.2. Double lines indicate bindings that will hold for the life of the data object. Single lines indicate bindings that may be modified at run time.

3.1.4 ▪ **Operators, Functions, and Expressions**

Another important consideration is the syntax a language uses to specify the operations performed when computing. In general, **operators** are of two types, monadic and dyadic. **Monadic operators** have one operand whereas **dyadic operators** have two. The standard format for monadic operators is **prefix** form, with the operator preceding the operand:

```
<Monadic Operation> ::= <operator> <operand>
```

Dyadic operations are commonly expressed in **infix** form, with the operator between the two operands:

```
<Infix Dyadic Operation> ::= <operand> <operator> <operand>
```

Functions are another form of operation, but they can have an unlimited number of operands. The form of function calls in an imperative language is typically the prefix form, using parentheses. This is expressed by

```
<Function call> ::= <function identifier>[ (<operand>
                    {,<operand>})]
```

This format specifies that functions with no operands are called by their identifier alone, although some languages require an empty set of parentheses for such a call.

A further consideration in the evaluation of **expressions** is the order in which operations are performed. For example, the expression

```
6 + 2 * 3
```

could be evaluated as 24 if the addition is performed first. Or it could be evaluated as 12 if the multiplication is performed first. The most common rules

FIGURE **3.2** **Sample Declarations**

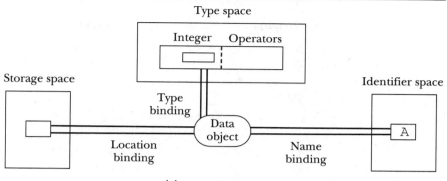

(a) A : integer;

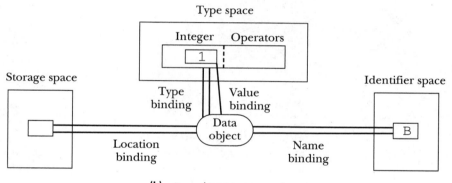

(b) B : integer := 1;

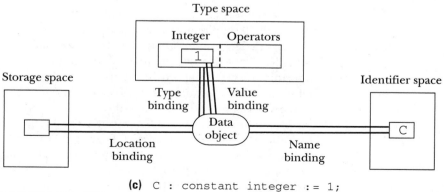

(c) C : constant integer := 1;

for determining order of evaluation in an imperative language with, for example, operations +, −, *, /, and ** is as follows:

1. Operations inside parentheses are performed first.

2. Next, operations are performed in the following order:

```
first:   **
second:  * and /
third:   + and -
```

3. Operations at the same level in step 2 are performed from left to right. (Some languages perform ** right to left.)

These rules, which are summarized in the accompanying box, can be represented in EBNF, as previously described in Chapter 2.

```
Expression Evaluation
Language: Ada
 Operators: <operand> <operator> <operand>

          Order determined by:
              1. parentheses
              2. precedence
              3. left-to-right if equal precedence

 Functions: <identifier> [(<operand> {, <operand>})]
```

Although this **precedence** convention is common among imperative languages, it should be noted that some languages use other strategies for expression evaluation, such as prefix notation for dyadic operations, no precedence levels, or right-to-left evaluation among operators of equal precedence.

3.1.5 ▪ Type Binding and Type Checking

Although types are bound to data objects at compile time in most languages, it is possible for this binding to occur at run time as well. The languages APL and Smalltalk implement such dynamic binding.

Whereas declarations are used to bind data objects to types at compile time, dynamically typed languages need no declarations. The type of a data object is determined by the type of its value. Therefore, whenever a data object is bound to a different value, it takes on the type of that newly bound value.

Type checking is the process of determining the type of a specified data object. Such checking by the computer can be of great assistance in the detection and prevention of errors. Type checking can occur at compile time, at run time, or not at all. A language is said to be **strongly typed** if all type checking that is feasible to do at compile time is done then and all other type checking is done at run time. Pascal is nearly strongly typed, but it is not quite because of two exceptions: subrange types and variant records.

Consider, for example, the following Pascal program:

```
type soft = record
              case test:boolean of
                 true : (first:1..20);
                 false : (second:char);
              end;

var x,y:soft;
    c:char;

begin
 ...
 c := x.second;
 y.first := 2 * x.first;
 ...
end.
```

Pascal violates strong typing in this program for two reasons. First, when x.second is used, Pascal is unable to check at compile time that the second variant part of x is in effect. Second, at the assignment statement to y.first, there will be a type violation if x.first is greater than 10, and it is not possible to determine this at compile time. In both of these cases a run time check could be made, but Pascal does not provide it. Ada does provide for run-time checking of both of these situations and is, therefore, strongly typed.

There are two possible alternatives for those situations where types cannot be checked at compile time. First, the types might not be checked at all, which is what typically happens in the preceding cases for Pascal. This situation places the burden of type checking on the programmer and can lead to serious undetected errors. The second possibility is that the type can be checked at run time. Such dynamic type checking can be expensive in terms of execution time, because a check must be performed every time a data object is referenced. It is also expensive in its use of memory, because a type indicator must be stored as a part of every data value.

Dynamically typed languages bind types to data objects at run time and permit those bindings to be changed. **Statically typed languages** bind types to data objects at compile time and hence can check types at either compile time or run time.

3.1.6 ▪ **Type Conversion**

Another major issue in dealing with types is the way in which a data object of one type is converted to another type if the two types are mixed in the evaluation of an expression. Operators usually require both operands to be of the same type. This situation includes the assignment operator whose left operand is the result data object and whose right operand is an expression that represents a value to be bound to the result data object.

The two common strategies for converting an operand to a consistent type are *implicit* and *explicit conversion*. **Implicit type conversion** is often called **type coercion**. Such coercions may occur automatically when certain type mixtures occur. For example, real and integer operand mixtures might result in the integer operand being converted to a real of equivalent value, if possible. This result is, indeed, often possible because many integers have an equivalent real representation. The only exception to this case is when the integer is the left operand of an assignment. In this case, the real is truncated to an integer before assignment occurs, because an opposite coercion would require changing the type binding of the target data object, a change which is not normally permitted. Languages that permit implicit coercions provide a list of all pairs of types for which implied coercion is permitted. Nonpermissible pairs are flagged as errors.

The second option, **explicit type conversion**, makes the implicit mixing of types illegal. Instead, explicit functions are required to specify the conversion from one type to another. These functions can be given unique names for each conversion, such as INTEGER_TO_REAL, or, as in Ada, can permit conversion by a function name that matches the name of the target type and that accepts operands of any allowable type. For example, in Ada, the function FLOAT converts from any allowable type to float type. Such conversions are normally allowed between derived types and their parent types or between various numeric types.

Pascal permits some explicit and some implicit type conversions. For example, integer-to-real conversions are implicit, although explicit functions round and trunc must be used to convert from real to integer.

A question arises as to what actually constitutes different types and when there is a need for type conversion. Consider the following declarations in Ada:

```
type T1 is INTEGER range 0..10;
type T2 is INTEGER range 0..10;
A:T1;
B,C:T1;
D:T2;
```

The question is, Which of the variables A, B, C, D are considered to be of the same type? Another way of stating this is to ask, Which of the following assignments are legal?

```
A:=B;
A:=D;
B:=C;
```

Three possible definitions of **type equivalence** are given here in order of increasing restrictiveness:

1. **Domain equivalence** — Two data objects are of equivalent type if they have the same domain of possible values associated with their types. This situation is also known as *structural equivalence*. Under domain equivalence, A, B, C, D are all of equivalent type and can be operands that share the same operator without any type conversion.

2. **Name equivalence** — Two data objects are of equivalent type if they are typed by the same name. Under name equivalence, A, B, C are all of equivalent type, but D is not, because it was bound to a type T2 — which differs from the name T1 of the type of the other three variables. This is the type equivalence implemented in Ada.

3. **Declaration equivalence** — Two data objects are of equivalent type if they are bound to their type in the same declaration. Under declaration equivalence, only B and C are of equivalent type, because they are bound to a type in the same declaration.

The previous discussion ignores the issue of **anonymous types** — that is, those types associated directly with variables through declaration without being given a name. For example, in Ada we might declare

```
E,F : array (1..10) of INTEGER;
G   : array (1..10) of INTEGER;
```

The interpretations of these declarations using domain and declaration equivalent are obvious. However, the interpretation of name equivalence for anonymous types needs more careful definition. The rule used by Ada is that no two objects of anonymous type are name equivalent. This means that E, F, and G are all considered to be of different types under name equivalence.

3.1.7 ▪ Subtypes and Derived Types

A difficulty arises when the domain of one type is a subset of the domain of another. The operations between the two types might have a logical definition without type conversion, even though type conversion will be required under any of the definitions of type equivalence.

For example, consider the following situation in a hypothetical language:

```
A:INTEGER;
B: 0..100;
```

The assignment statement

```
A:=B;
```

although obviously meaningful, will be illegal in a language that requires explicit type conversion. One way of dealing with this situation is through the definition of subtypes. A **subtype** of a given parent type includes the same operators as the parent type, although its domain of values may be a subset of the parent type's domain. Operations, including assignment, are normally permitted between an operand of the subtype and an operand of the parent type. For example, the preceding assignment could be legalized by the following Ada declarations:

```
subtype T is INTEGER range 0..100;
A:INTEGER;
B:T;
```

This Ada construct enforces operational equivalence of data objects bound to the subtype with data objects bound to the parent type.

Another problem that can arise with subtypes is illustrated by the preceding declarations followed by the assignment

```
B:=A;
```

This assignment is possibly illegal, because A is bound to the parent type and may have a value outside the domain of the subtype T. For example, if A is bound to 101, the assignment is not legal. A language might handle this in three possible ways:

1. Check that the value of A is in the subtype domain at run time and flag the assignment as an error if not. This is the policy that Ada follows.

2. Flag such an assignment as an error at compile time even though it might execute correctly. This would avoid extra run-time checks.

3. Ignore the issue altogether by not checking subtypes.

An opposite situation to that addressed by subtypes occurs in languages that employ domain equivalence. Occasionally a programmer wishes to define two types with identical domains but make them operationally incompatible. For example, suppose we have

```
TYPE TIME is new FLOAT;
TYPE LENGTH is new FLOAT;
DURATION : TIME;
DISTANCE : LENGTH;
```

Although DURATION and DISTANCE share the same domain, it would not make sense to add two objects of these types. The reason for using different types TIME and LENGTH is to enforce this incompatibility. A language with domain equivalence should, therefore, permit an override of its basic mechanism to permit the declaration of separate, incompatible types with the same domain. One type will have the same properties as the other type but will not be equivalent in the sense of permitting a mixture of the two types without type conversion. This is called a **derived type** and is implemented in Ada, as shown in the preceding declarations of TIME and LENGTH. A derived type may also define a subtype that is not operationally equivalent to its containing type.

The type issues just discussed, as they are addressed in Ada, are summarized in the following box.

```
Type Issues
Language: Ada
  Type Conversion: Explicit, using the name of the
          target type as the conversion function
  Type Equivalence: Name

  Subtypes:
   <subtype declaration> ::=
      SUBTYPE <identifier> is <subtype definition>
```

```
Derived Types: <derived type declaration> ::=
    TYPE <identifier> is new <subtype definition>


Type Declaration:
    TYPE <identifier> is <type definition>
```

3.1.8 ▪ Scalar Data Types

Scalar data types are those data types that can be bound to **atomic data objects** in a language. An object is considered atomic if it cannot be broken down into component objects. Two classifications of such types are built-in and user-defined. **Built-in types** are included within the language definition and can be bound directly through the declaration of the data object. A **user-defined type** must be defined through a declaration of the type prior to its binding in a data object declaration.

In the following sections we examine the most common built-in scalar types by listing a number of their properties. The properties that we discuss include the following:

1. *Parameters* — Some types have parameters that determine, for example, the precision of a real or the subrange of an integer.

2. *Declaration format* — The format used in the declaration that binds the type to a data object will include the manner in which parameters are specified.

3. *Domain* — The set of values of a type is the domain of that type. This includes the syntax used to represent constants of that type within the language and their interpretation.

4. *Operations* — Operations defined on the type include operators and functions that are part of the definition of the language.

5. *Attributes* — Attributes differ from operators in that they are operations on a type whose results are properties of the type. In contrast, operators are operations on data objects whose results are other data objects.

6. *Conversion* — This category includes the permissible conversions between this type and other types and the syntax for performing them.

7. *Predefined constants* — These constants are named constants that are included in the language and need not be declared.

8. *Implementation* — Considerations in implementing a type include the representation of the type and the algorithms used in performing the operations.

3.1.9 ▪ Integer Type

Some languages have only a single integer numeric type called INTEGER, which has as its domain the set of integers that can be represented by the machine on which the language is implemented. The disadvantage of **integer type** is that the domain of the type is implementation dependent. Modern imperative languages permit the specification of subtypes of the type INTEGER that limit the domain of the type to a subrange of the machine's integer domain.

The definition of a subrange of integers is so common that it is often included even in languages that contain no general subrange capability. The specification of the subrange type is usually accomplished by supplying parametric values for the lower and upper end of the subrange. For example, in Pascal, an allowable subrange declaration is

```
type POSITIVE = 1..MAXINT;
```

The underlying type, INTEGER, for the subrange is implied by the type of constants that make up the range parameters. This is the convention of Pascal, though other languages require the specification of the parent type INTEGER. Ada permits either approach.

The use of such subranges can allow better type checking. Two options are available for type checking on subrange types. The first is to ignore type checking altogether, because such checking must be performed at run time when value bindings are made, and run-time checking is time consuming. The second option is to perform a run-time check every time a new value binding is performed. Many languages give the programmer the option of putting subrange checks into effect or not at the time of compilation.

A description of the properties of integers in Ada is given in the accompanying box.

```
Integer Type
Language: Ada
     Parameters: Range - specifies the lower and upper bound of integers
             included

     Declaration Format:

<integer definition> ::=
     INTEGER [RANGE <range specifier>] |
     RANGE <range specifier>

<range specifier>::= <integer constant> .. <integer constant>
     Domain: Integer values in the range specified by the declaration or
             by the implementation if no range is specified.
     Literals:
       <integer literal>::= [+] <integer> | - <integer>
             <integer> ::= digit {digit}
     Operations:
     Dyadic               Dyadic               Monadic
     Integer result       Boolean result       Integer Result
     + addition           > greater than       + identity
     - subtraction        < less than          - negation
```

```
* multiplication      >= gtr or equal    abs absolute
/ division            <= lss or equal        value
** exponentiation     = equal to
mod modulus           /= not equal to
rem remainder


Attributes: FIRST - the smallest value in type
            LAST - the largest value in type
Conversion: Function for conversion is type name.
            Type of operand may be any numeric type.
            Conversion from real value will round to the nearest
integer
Predefined Constants: in package SYSTEM
            MAX_INT - largest integer possible in
        default INTEGER type
            MIN_INT - smallest integer possible in
        default integer type
```

3.1.10 ▪ Real Type

Two possible parameters of **real type** are the number of significant digits and the scaling factor designating the number of digits to the right of the decimal point. For example, real numbers with 10 significant digits and a scale factor of 2 digits would be able to represent all numbers from

```
-99999999.99  to  99999999.99
```

spaced apart by steps of 0.01. The representation with these two parameters is called **fixed point**, and when fixed point is available in a language, it is usually provided in base 10 to permit exact decimal representations of quantities such as dollars and cents.

A more common real representation is **floating point**. This system includes the scale as a part of the value rather than as a parameter of the type. In this case, a pair of values is provided to represent a real value: the **mantissa**, whose precision is a parameter of the type, and the **exponent**, whose domain is another parameter of the type. Floating-point representation is usually stored with radix 2, taking advantage of the built-in floating-point commands of the machine on which the language is implemented.

Many languages give the programmer no control over the values of the parameters of reals, usually tying them to the particular implementation. Programs in these languages that use reals are therefore implementation dependent in the precision of their calculations.

Ada provides both fixed and floating point as well as a facility for specifying parameters of both. With fixed-point types, the parameters are the range of allowable values and the distance between consecutive reals within the defined type (see box on p. 66).

Real Type
Language: Ada

	Fixed Point	Floating Point

Parameters:

Fixed Point	Floating Point
Distance between consecutive values	Precision as number of decimal digits in mantissa
Range of allowable fixed-pt values	Range of allowable floating-point values

Declaration format:

Fixed Point	Floating Point
<fixed pt defn> ::= DELTA <distance> RANGE <range>	<floating pt defn> ::= DIGITS <precision> [RANGE <range>]

<range> ::= <real literal>..<real literal>

Domain:

Fixed Point	Floating Point
if d=distance and [lo,hi]=range then domain={lo,lo+d,...lo+Nd} where N is the largest integer such that lo+Nd<=hi	if p=precision and [lo,hi]=range then domain={p digit reals between lo and hi}

Attributes:

Fixed Point	Floating Point
DELTA - distance between values	DIGITS - number of decimal digits
MANTISSA - number of binary digits	MANTISSA - number of binary digits
	EPSILON - difference between 1.0 and next higher number
SMALL - smallest positive number	SMALL - smallest positive number
LARGE - largest positive number	LARGE - largest positive number
	EMAX - largest binary exponent

Literals:

<real literal>::=<integer literal> [.<integer>] [E <integer literal>]

Operations:

dyadic result same type   dyadic result Boolean   monadic result same type
+ - * / **   > < >= <= = /=   + - abs

Conversion: Function for conversion is type name. Type of operand may be any numeric type.

Predefined constants: In package SYSTEM
MAX_DIGITS - largest number of significant decimal digits allowed in floating pt types
MAX_MANTISSA - largest number of binary digits allowed in fixed-point type
FINE_DELTA - smallest delta allowed if range is -1.0..1.0

3.1.11 ▪ Boolean Type

The simplest type is **Boolean type**, whose domain consists of two values, one representing true and one representing false. The operators on this type are the logical operators, including the dyadic operators AND and OR and the monadic operator NOT.

In some situations, it is convenient to use the short-circuit form of these Boolean operators. To understand the role of **short-circuit operators**, consider the following Ada Boolean expression:

```
(I /= 0) AND (K/I > 6)
```

When the first condition is false, the second condition cannot be evaluated, because a division by zero would result. However, careful observation reveals that when the first condition is false, the second condition need not be evaluated, because the entire expression is guaranteed to be false anyway. A short-circuit AND operator is evaluated in the following way:

```
A AND B ≡ if A then B else FALSE
```

This avoids evaluation of B in the case where A is false. Similarly, a short-circuit OR can be defined by

```
A OR B ≡ if A then TRUE else B
```

This case avoids evaluation of B if A is true, because A true makes the expression true no matter what the value of B might be, even if it is not computable.

One way of making these short-circuit operators available is for the compiler automatically to generate code that evaluates AND and OR in this way. A better approach is to provide two new operators to carry out the short-circuit Boolean evaluations. Ada does this by providing the operators AND THEN and OR ELSE. This permits the programmer to specify explicitly the way Boolean operators are to be performed.

```
Boolean Type
Language: Ada
Declaration Format: <Boolean definition>::=BOOLEAN;
Domain: {FALSE,TRUE}
Literals: FALSE,TRUE
Operators:
dyadic result monadic result
   boolean         boolean
   AND             NOT
   OR
   XOR
  AND THEN
  OR ELSE
```

3.1.12 ▪ Pointer Type

Thus far data objects of every type we have discussed have a name, a value, and a location bound to them. The pointer data type complicates matters somewhat. The value of a pointer data object is itself the location of another data object. The definition of a pointer variable is illustrated in Figure 3.3.

Here, we see that two data objects are involved: the data object of pointer type (data object 1) and the data object to which it points (data object 2). In the case of **pointer types**, the data object is bound to a name and location, the same as with other types. The value bound to a pointer data object, however, is an element of the storage space. The value space for a pointer data object is, therefore, the storage space as shown in Figure 3.3. As with other types, the type and name bindings occur at compile time; the location binding, at load time; and the value binding, at run time.

The target data object (data object 2) differs quite a bit from those we have seen previously. First, we note that it has no name binding. It is not referenced by its name but rather through the data object that points to it. Secondly, the location and type bindings of this object must occur at run time, because the data object itself does not exist until run time, when the pointer data object is assigned a value. The binding of the pointer data object to a

FIGURE 3.3   **Pointer Type Bindings**

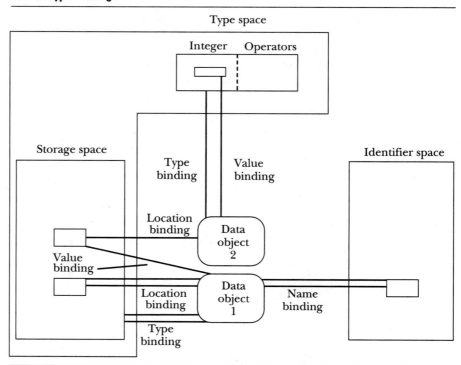

value implies the existence of the target data object and the binding of this target object to its location.

Pointer data objects are useful for constructing linked data structures for which storage is allocated dynamically at run time. This is especially useful for representing structured data whose size is not known beforehand, because it permits the structure to grow as the program is executed.

In most languages, the declaration of a data object of pointer type will specify as a parameter the type of the object to which it points. This is not true for all languages, however, as a parameterless declaration is possible if the type of the target data object is specified or implied at run time when the pointer data object is bound to a value (which is a location). This is known as *dynamic type binding for pointers.*

Pascal and Ada both require the specification of a type at compile time when declaring pointer variables. For example, the declaration of a variable to be of pointer type in Pascal takes the form

```
var P : ^TARGET_TYPE;
```

This indicates that the variable P will be a pointer to data objects of type TARGET_TYPE. The same declaration in Ada is written

```
P : access TARGET-TYPE;
```

The binding of a pointer variable to a value is done in two ways: *creation* and *assignment.* Creation of a new target data object and binding its location as value to the pointer data object is accomplished by a special procedure NEW in Pascal. For example,

```
NEW(P);
```

creates a new target object and binds P's value to the location of the new object. In Ada, the same effect is accomplished by assignment, as in

```
P := new TARGET-TYPE;
```

Ada also permits value initialization of the target object in the creation statement, whereas Pascal leaves that target object with an unbound value. For example, in Ada the access variable Q declared by

```
Q : access INTEGER;
```

could be initialized to point to an integer with value zero by the statement

```
Q := new INTEGER'(0);
```

Assignment of pointer objects occurs in the usual way, with the data object named on the left side of the assignment operator bound to the value resulting from evaluation of the right side.

A facility for deallocating a pointer data object is also a standard feature of pointer types. This results in the location being returned to the collection of available space for reassignment later in the program execution. In Pascal this is done by the procedure DISPOSE, and in Ada it is done by the procedure

FREE, which — although not part of standard Ada — has its Ada definition given in Section 13.2 of the Ada *Reference Manual.* Care must be taken in deallocation of the target object, because such deallocation may leave some pointer objects with value bindings to deallocated locations — that is, locations no longer bound to a target data object. Such pointers are said to be **dangling references**. A target data object that is no longer bound as a value to any pointer data object but that has not been deallocated is known as **garbage**. Because a target object is not bound to a name, it is impossible to access such garbage elements.

Dereferencing a pointer object is the process of obtaining the value of the target data object through a reference to the name of the pointer data objects. For example, in Pascal a pointer variable P is dereferenced by writing P^, meaning the data object bound to the location that is bound as a value to P. Dereferencing in Ada is done by writing P.ALL. Therefore, if P and Q are two pointer variables with the same target type,

```
P := Q;
```

assigns P the same value as is bound to Q, meaning they point to the same location. On the other hand,

```
P.ALL := Q.ALL;
```

binds the target object of P to the same value as is bound to the target object of Q. This difference is illustrated by Figure 3.4.

A final feature of pointer variables is the existence of a constant of pointer type that points to no location. In Pascal, this pointer constant is named NIL, whereas in Ada it is named NULL.

Pointer type for Ada is described in the box that follows.

```
Pointer Type
Language: Ada
Declaration Format:
  <pointer Definition> ::= ACCESS <target type>

Domain: set of locations of target type data objects

Operations: Dyadic-Result Boolean
            = /=
Allocation: NEW <target type> ['(<initial value>)]

Dereferencing:
    <pointer identifier> . ALL

    If target type is record, then
        <pointer identifier>.<component identifier>

Deallocation: FREE (<pointer identifier>)

Predefined constant: NULL
```

FIGURE **3.4**   **Pointer Assignments**

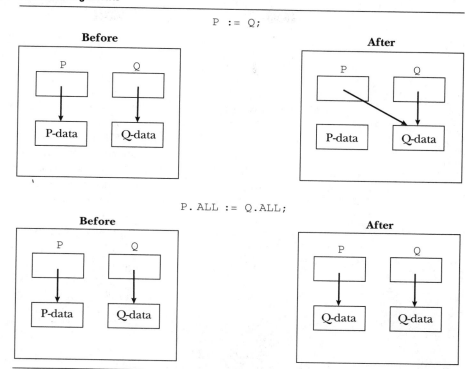

3.1.13 ▪ User-defined Types

In one sense, any type that a user declares in a type statement is a *user-defined type*. This could include all the types previously discussed. Many discussions of programming languages take the definition of user-defined types to include, in particular, subrange types. Because we considered subranges as parameters to built-in types, we do not include them in our discussion here.

The other common user-defined type is **enumerated type**. This type permits the user to define a type by listing the domain of the type. Languages typically permit the values of an enumerated type to be selected from the space of identifiers.

Enumerated types generally have their operations restricted to assignment and comparison, where the ordering for comparison is defined by the order that the elements of the domain are listed in the declaration.

A difficulty can arise with enumerated types when the same identifier is declared as a value for more than one such type. Some languages, such as Pascal, prohibit this. Other languages, such as Ada, permit it, interpreting the type of such a literal value identifier either from the context or by qualifying the literal by the type name. For example, the following declarations might be given within Ada:

```
type FRUIT is (APPLE,ORANGE,PEAR);
type COLOR is (RED,ORANGE,YELLOW,GREEN,BLUE,PURPLE);
F: FRUIT;
C: COLOR;
```

The statement

```
F := ORANGE;
```

would need no further qualification, because the context of the statement is sufficient to determine the type of ORANGE. If the context is not adequate for such determination, Ada permits the use of the form FRUIT′ORANGE.

Another issue is the ability to input or output enumerated types. Some languages forbid this, whereas others provide an automatic conversion between strings and enumerated types to make their input and output possible.

The following box specifies enumerated type in Ada.

```
Enumerated Type
Language: Ada
Declaration Format:
    <enumerated type definition> ::=
        (<enumeration literal> {,<enumeration literal>} )

    <enumeration literal>::=<identifier> | '<character>'

Domain: The set of values listed in the declaration
Attributes:
    FIRST - the first element listed in the type definition
    LAST - the last element listed in the type definition

Operations: dyadic - result Boolean
            > < >= <= = /=

Conversion: Only conversions between an enumerated type
            and its subranges are permitted.
```

3.2 Execution Units and Scope of Binding

In this section we examine the role of units of execution. These units are divisions of the executable program that are grouped together for a specific purpose. The largest unit is the program itself, which is the fundamental executable unit. Programs are frequently divided into smaller units called *blocks*, and the smallest, indivisible unit of a program is called a *statement*.

Execution units can be grouped together for a number of reasons, but the reason most closely related to the topic of this section is grouping to identify the scope of bindings.

3.2.1 ▪ **Statements**

The fundamental unit of execution in an imperative programming language is the **statement**. The statement accomplishes a single activity, making it roughly the counterpart of a sentence in a natural language. It is also considered to be the smallest translatable unit.

Some statements may contain other statements embedded within their structure. Conditional and iterative statements are examples of this, where the embedded statements constitute the domain of control. We call such statements **nested statements**.

In some languages, all statements have the same format. In essence, these languages have only one type of statement. Most imperative languages, however, have different formats for each of several types of statements, permitting more flexibility in expressing different activities. Ada, for example, has 11 different types of simple statements and 6 types of nested statements. Each of these 17 statement types has its own syntax.

Statements are also the units of execution that can be separately labeled for reference from other statements for activities such as branching. **Labels** permit the binding of a name to a statement. The time at which this binding occurs can be either compile time or run time. Compile-time binding, which is the standard practice of Pascal and Ada, permits reference to the labels within the body of the program unit. This works in the same way as the binding of names to data objects and enables reference from elsewhere in the program unit. The alternative is binding at run time. This permits, for example, the reading of a label identifier into a label variable and then referencing the label variable. This binding is identical to the binding of data objects and their values. APL and SNOBOL allow this type of label binding.

A programming language may require that each statement have a label (BASIC), or labels may be optional (Pascal). Labels may be selected from the space of integers (BASIC, FORTRAN, Pascal) or from the space of identifiers (Ada). Labels may be explicitly declared in order to specify their name binding (Pascal) or implicitly declared when attached to their statements (Ada). The syntax for including a label in a statement may identify the label by position or by punctuation. For example, FORTRAN reserves character positions 1 through 5 for the label of each statement, locating the label positionally. Pascal, on the other hand, separates the label from the remainder of the statement by a colon.

Another major issue with statement syntax is the method used to delimit statements. Perhaps the simplest is to delimit statements by lines in the program text, with each line containing one and only one statement. This has proved to be too restrictive, however, and requires special consideration for nested statements. A more common approach is the use of a punctuation mark to delimit statements. Pascal and Ada both use the semicolon, although there is a subtle difference in the meaning of this punctuation in these two languages. Ada uses the semicolon as a statement terminator, meaning the end of every statement is defined by the appearance of this punctuation mark. Pascal, on the other hand, uses the semicolon as a statement separator, which tends to be more confusing. This means that statements that are not immediately followed by another statement do not require a semicolon — for example, as in

```
   ...                  ...
  x:=x+1     or        x:=0
end                   else
   ...                  ...
```

This leads to a great deal of confusion among novice Pascal programmers concerning the appropriate use of semicolons.

The following box provides a summary of these points with respect to Ada.

```
Statements
Language: Ada
Simple statements: null, assignment, procedure call,
   exit, return, goto, entry call, delay, abort, raise,
   code

Nested statements: if, case, loop, block, accept, select

Label format:
   {<< <label identifier> >>} <statement>;

Label binding: compile time
Label declaration: implicit
Statement terminator:    ;
```

3.2.2 ▪ Blocks

The second level execution unit is the **block**, a collection of statements grouped together for a specific purpose. There are several reasons for forming blocks of statements:

1. *Scope of control structure* — In a conditional structure, it is necessary to form blocks of statements to indicate which statements are executed when a condition is true and which are executed when it is false. It is also necessary to block together statements that form the body of an iteration structure. Ways of expressing these blocks are discussed when control structures are introduced.

2. *Scope of procedural abstraction* — A set of statements is frequently blocked together to form a module that carries out a specific process. Such blocks are commonly in the form of procedures or functions and are useful for implementing top-down design of programs. These blocks have the added advantage of providing reusability of the module. Such blocks are discussed further in Chapter 5.

3. *Compilation units* — Statements are also blocked together to form compilation units. These blocks are compiled separately and then merged for exe-

cution. The capability of forming such blocks can be a useful tool in the program development process.

4. *Scope of bindings* — This type of block is the one of interest in this section. It is the block of statements over which specific bindings hold. Such a scope of binding often occurs in conjunction with blocks that serve other purposes as well, such as procedural abstraction and compilation units. In the following sections we focus on blocks that have the single purpose of defining the scope of bindings.

3.2.3 ▪ Scope of Name Binding

Blocks that define a scope of name binding usually contain two parts:

1. a declaration section, which defines the bindings that hold inside the block
2. an executable section, which contains the statements of the block over which the binding is to hold

Syntactically, this requires a marker for the beginning of the declaration section, a marker separating the declaration section and the statements, and a marker indicating the end of the block. We will develop a small pseudolanguage for expressing examples in this section. This pseudolanguage will use BLOCK to begin the block, BEGIN to separate declarations from statements, and END to end a block. The general structure of a block in our pseudolanguage is, therefore,

```
...
BLOCK A;
   DECLARE I;
BEGIN A
   ...              {I from A}
END A;
...
```

The declare statement in this example is used to bind the name I to a data object on entrance to block A. Our pseudolanguage will not bind type or value, because those elements are irrelevant for the present discussion. The three dots immediately following BEGIN indicate the statements of block A, and the comment to the right lists the bindings that hold in those statements. In this case, reference to I is to the binding made in block A. We use this notation for all of our examples in this section.

Within any block, there are two kinds of bindings: **Local bindings** are specified by the declarations of the block and **nonlocal bindings** are specified by declarations outside of the current block. Although some languages require a separate declaration of bindings that are inherited from the containing block, it is customary for a block to implicitly inherit bindings from the environment that directly contains it. This is particularly useful when we consider the possibility of nested blocks — for example,

```
PROGRAM P;
  DECLARE X;
BEGIN P
  ...                {X from P}
  BLOCK A;
    DECLARE Y;
  BEGIN A
  ...                {X from P, Y from A}
    BLOCK B;
      DECLARE Z;
    BEGIN B
    ...              {X from P, Y from A, Z from B}
    END B;
    ...              {X from P, Y from A}
  END A;
  ...                {X from P}
  BLOCK C;
    DECLARE Z;
  BEGIN C
  ...                {X from P, Z from C}
  END C;
  ...                {X from P}
END P;
```

In this example, we see that each block inherits the bindings of its containing block (including the main program, considered as the outermost block) and adds the bindings of its own declarations. These constitute nonlocal and local bindings, respectively.

The preceding scoping policy is known as **lexical scoping**, or **static scoping**. It can be summarized as follows:

1. If a name has a declaration within a block, that name is bound to the object specified in the declaration.

2. If a name has no declaration within a block, the name is bound to the same object to which it was bound in the block containing the present block in the program text. If the block has no containing block or the name is not bound in the containing block, then the name is unbound in the present block.

A situation known as **hole-in-scope** arises when a block redeclares a name already bound in the containing environment. In this case, the local declaration overrides the nonlocal binding, making the nonlocally bound data object inaccessible in the present block.

Consider the following example:

```
PROGRAM P;
  DECLARE X,Y;
BEGIN P
  ...                {X from P, Y from P}
```

```
     BLOCK A;
        DECLARE X,Z;
     BEGIN A
        ...                    {X from A, Y from P, Z from A}
     END A;
        ...                    {X from P, Y from P}
   END P;
```

The hole-in-scope refers to the fact that even though the x bound in program P exists during the execution of block A, it is not accessible in block A because the name x is bound by the local declaration there.

Some languages — Ada, for example — avoid the hole-in-scope problem by providing a way to specify a nonlocally bound object even when there is an object bound locally to the same name. In the preceding example, although identifier x used within block A would specify the locally bound object, the Ada notation P.X could be used to specify the object bound to x by declaration in block (program) P. This feature makes a data object available in the entire block in which it is declared, including subblocks that rebind its name, thus eliminating hole-in-scope.

An alternative to lexical scoping is called **dynamic scoping**. In this case, names are bound to objects at run time. We defer discussion of this strategy to Chapter 5.

3.2.4 ▪ Scope of Location Binding

Up to this point, we have considered only the scope of the name binding within a programming language. The assumption we have made is that the data object is bound to its location at load time and remains bound throughout the entire execution of the program. A side effect of this assumption is that upon reentry to a block, the block's locally bound variables can be assumed to have retained their values from the block's preceding execution. If a new location binding is made upon each entry to the block, no such assumption can be made.

Consider the following example in our pseudolanguage:

```
PROGRAM P;
   DECLARE I;
BEGIN P
   FOR I:= 1 TO 10 DO
      BLOCK A;
         DECLARE J;
      BEGIN A
         IF I=1 THEN
            J:=1;                {I from P, J from A}
         ELSE
            J:=J*I;
         END IF
      END A;
   END P;
```

In this program block A is executed 10 times. In order for the calculation to make sense the last 9 times, we must assume that the variable J, which is local to block A, retains its value from one execution of A to the next. The disadvantage of such a permanent location binding is that the storage for all blocks in a program must be reserved for the entire time the program is in execution.

The alternative is to bind the location as well as the name to the data object at run time upon entrance to a block, releasing that binding when the block is exited. This is called **dynamic storage allocation**, and the **extent** of such a binding is the period of time at run time when this location binding holds.

Let us reconsider the example program illustrating hole-in-scope.

```
PROGRAM P;
  DECLARE X,Y;
BEGIN P
  ...                {X from P, Y from P}
  BLOCK A;
    DECLARE X,Z;
  BEGIN A
    ...              {X from A, Y from P, Z from A}
  END A;
  ...                {X from P, Y from P}
END P;
```

Assuming dynamic storage allocation inside block A, the name X is bound to the location of the local variable. But upon completion of block A, the name X should revert back to its previous location binding from P. In practice, there can be many levels of nesting, each declaring a binding to the same name. Each binding must be recalled in reverse order as the blocks are exited.

The implementation of this nesting is accomplished through the use of **activation records**. Activation records are records that contain the information about an execution unit that is necessary in order to resume its execution after it has been suspended. We will need only a simple activation record to implement location binding in blocks. This simple record will be augmented later to provide additional capabilities.

For the purposes of location binding in blocks, the activation record must contain locations only for all locally bound data objects plus a pointer to the activation record of the block's containing block. As each block is entered, its activation record is placed on top of a stack. Similarly, the activation record is removed from the top of the stack when the block is exited.

Consider, for example, the following program. The progression of activation record stacks is shown in Figure 3.5.

```
PROGRAM P;
  DECLARE I,J;
BEGIN P
  BLOCK A;
    DECLARE I,K;
  BEGIN A
    BLOCK B;
```

```
          DECLARE I,L:INTEGER;
      BEGIN B;
        ...                {I from B, L from B, K from A, J from P}
      END B;
      ...                  {I from A, K from A, J from P}
    END A;
    BLOCK C;
      DECLARE I,N;
    BEGIN C
      ...                  {I from C, N from C, J from P}
    END C;
    ...                    {I from P, J from P}
  END P;
```

FIGURE **3.5**   **Contents of Activation Record Stack**

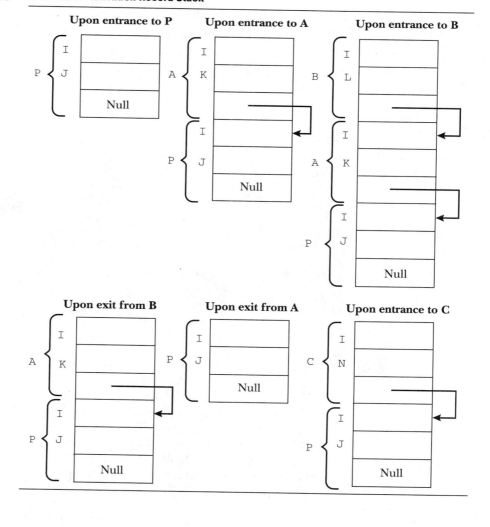

The use of the stack to locate data objects by name then proceeds as follows:

1. Look in the top activation record in the stack for an object bound to the given name.

2. If the object is not found, look in the activation record pointed to by the pointer to the containing block for the top activation record, continuing the search through the list of activation records until the appropriate data object is found.

This search can be shortened, because the structure of the stack and of each activation record is known at compile time. Therefore, the compiler could represent the location of a variable by a pair of integers (i,j), where i is the number of records up the list and j is the displacement of the desired location from the start of the activation record.

For example, in the preceding program, block B would represent each data object's location by the following pairs:

```
I  (0,0)    {0 records up the list, 0th element from start}
J  (2,1)    {2 records up the list, 1st element from start}
K  (1,1)    {1 record up the list, 1st element from start}
```

Finally, we conclude this section with a summary box of the block capabilities found in Ada.

```
Blocks
Language: Ada
Syntax:     [<block name identifier> :]
               [DECLARE
                   <declarations>]
               BEGIN
                   <statements>
               END [<block name identifier>];


Reference to data object whose binding is hidden:
       <block identifier> . <name identifier>
```

3.3　Control Structures

A programming language must do more than specify the actions that a computer should take. It must also specify the order in which those actions must occur. Because of the sequential nature of machine language execution, virtually all imperative languages follow the same pattern by adopting the sequential execution of statements. This means that after a statement has completed execution, the default for the choice of the next statement to be executed is the next physical statement in the program.

One of the obvious benefits of a programming language is its ability to modify the order of statement execution by presenting alternatives to the sequential mode. Facilities of a language that permit this are called **control structures**.

3.3.1 ▪ Conditional Structures

Conditional control structures determine the next block of statements to be executed based on the result of a test or a sequence of tests. Such structures are usually implemented through an **if statement**. We examine four forms of such statements.

Simple Conditional The simplest form of conditional control structure performs a single test, whose result it uses to determine whether or not to execute a specified block of statements. The two parts of the structure, therefore, are the Boolean expression that defines the condition and the block of statements that will be performed if the expression evaluates to true.

The typical form of the simple conditional is

```
if <boolean expression> then <block of statements>
```

The most frequent variation from language to language is the method of blocking the statements. Pascal and ALGOL 60, for example, consider the block of statements to be a single statement that can be made into a compound statement by enclosing multiple statements between begin and end. Ada and Modula 2, however, have specific keywords for ending the block of statements, Ada terminating with end if and Modula 2, with end. Neither of these languages needs a beginning-of-block marker, because then functions in this capacity.

Two-Alternative Conditional Every modern imperative programming language permits the extension of the simple conditional if statement to a two-alternative structure. This direct extension takes the form

```
if <Boolean expression> then
   <block of statements>
else
   <block of statements>
```

It is the addition of the else that makes apparent one disadvantage of the Pascal method of blocking statements in conditionals. It leads to the well-known **dangling else** problem in the case of nested conditionals. To illustrate this, consider the following Pascal fragment:

```
if x>0 then
  if x<10 then
  x:=x+1
else
  x:=x-1;
```

The else in this statement could be attached to either the first or the second if, depending on the way the language interprets this structure. Pascal, of course, has a rule for defining the semantics of this fragment: The else will always be matched with the nearest preceding if that is thus far unmatched with an else. In the case of our example, Pascal would match the else as our indenting suggests.

The use of required block markers, as in Ada and Modula-2, avoids this confusing syntax completely, because the termination of each conditional block is explicitly denoted. For example, the two ways of interpreting the preceding Pascal fragment could be written in Ada as

```
if x>0 then          if x>0 then
   if x<10 then          if x<10 then
      x:=x+1;               x:=x+1;
   else                  end if;
      x:=x-1;           else
   end if;                 x:=x-1;
end if;               end if;
```

Multialternative Conditional   Two forms of the multialternative conditional structure are found in modern imperative languages. The first and more general one permits any sequence of Boolean expressions to be tested, with the first true expression specifying the block of statements chosen for execution. The second form evaluates an expression and chooses the block of statements to be executed that corresponds to the value obtained.

Recent languages, such as Ada, permit the direct expression of the general multialternative structure through the use of separators for each condition. The general form in Ada is

```
if <condition-1> then
   <statement-block-1>
elsif <condition-2> then
   <statement-block-2>
...
elsif <condition-n> then
   <statement-block-n>
[else <statement-block-(n+1)>]
end if;
```

The conditions are tested in order until one is evaluated as true. Then the corresponding statement block is executed. If none of the conditions is true, the statement block following the else, if present, is executed. If no else clause is present and all conditions are false, none of the statement blocks is executed, and control passes to the statement following this entire construct. As soon as one condition is found to be true and its statement block has been executed, execution of the structure is completed, and no further conditions will be tested. Such a structure can be simulated in Pascal and other languages that lack the generalized structure of Ada by use of a nested if-then-else structure.

The **case structure** is more restrictive in that it is a special case of the `if-elsif-else` structure. In other words, any control structure created by a `case` statement can be duplicated directly by an `if-then-else` sequence without adding any complexity to the program.

The general form of a `case` structure, using Pascal syntax, is

```
case <expression> of
    <value 1> : <statement-block-1>
    <value 2> : <statement-block-2>
    ...
    <value n> : <statement-block-n>
end;
```

where the expression is first evaluated and the statement block whose corresponding value equals the evaluated result of the expression is then executed. Several key issues are pertinent to the implementation of the `case` structure in a language.

1. *What types are allowable for the expression?* It is usually necessary to restrict the types allowed in the expression of the `case` structure. In Ada and Pascal, for example, the expression is restricted to discrete types, namely, integers, characters, and enumerated types. In particular, this restriction rules out the use of strings or reals.

2. *How are multiple values that result in the same action represented?* Frequently, more than one value of the expression will prescribe the same action. It is helpful if the syntax of the language permits multiple alternatives expressed for the value without duplication of the action specification. Some languages permit ranges and/or lists to be included in the value field.

3. *What happens if the value of the expression is not specified among the `case` alternatives?* Three actions are possible if the value of the expression is not specified. First, the `case` construct may do nothing, acting like a null statement. Second, the action may be undefined. Finally, such an unspecified value might result in an error condition. Ada chooses this last approach. An exhaustive list that avoids this situation is more easily obtained when the language has a specifier that covers all alternatives not specified before. In Ada, this is the `others` alternative.

We conclude this section with a complete description of the conditional structures of Ada.

```
Conditional Structures
Language: Ada

if-statement ::= if <condition> then
                     <sequence-of-statements>
                 {elsif <condition> then
                     <sequence-of-statements>}
```

```
                    [else
                        <sequence-of-statements>]
                    end if;

case-statement ::= case <expression> is
                      <case-statement-alternative>
                      {<case-statement-alternative>}
                    [when others => <sequence-of-statements>]
                    end case;
case-statement-alternative ::=
                    when <choice> {|<choice>} =>
                              <sequence-of-statements>
choice ::= <discrete-constant> | <discrete-range>

Allowable types for case expression: integer, character, enumeration
All possible values of the expression's type must be included among the
choices.
All choices must be mutually exclusive.
```

Nondeterministic Conditional　　An important extension to the multialternative conditional has been suggested by Dijkstra (1975). The general form proposed is

```
if <condition-1> → <statement-sequence-1>
 when <condition-2> → <statement-sequence-2>
 ...
 when <condition-n> → <statement-sequence-n>
fi
```

This construct differs in several ways from the `if-elsif-else` construct. The preceding form evaluates all conditions, whereas the `if-elsif-else` evaluates only until a true condition occurs. Furthermore, in the case where more than one of the conditions is true, the alternative whose statement sequence is executed is chosen **nondeterministically**. In this situation, there is no rule for choosing among several possibilities, and any one of them could be chosen. If none of the conditions is true, the statement is considered to be in error. The conditions are often called **guards**, and the entire construct is called a **guarded command**.

Although Ada does not implement this construct in the generality of Dijkstra's definition, it does have a specialized version of it that is used to implement concurrency control. We study this in Chapter 18.

3.3.2　▪　Iterative Structures

One of the most powerful features of an imperative language is its ability to specify the repetition of a block of statements. Structures for doing this are called **iteration** structures. These structures are extremely important and raise many interesting issues. For convenience, we refer to the block of statements to be repeated as the body of the iteration.

Nonterminating Iteration The simplest form of iterative structure is a **nonterminating iteration**, which specifies the indefinite repetition of its body. Often, beginning programmers are cautioned to avoid such iterations because they will never terminate and hence will execute forever. In practice, however, there are frequently blocks of statements that execute in just this way. A communications program, for example, may have the following nonterminating structure:

```
do forever
  check for character sent
  if character is sent then process character
end do
```

Ada has a direct form that expresses a nonterminating iteration. In Ada, one writes

```
loop
  <sequence-of-statements>
end loop;
```

Pretest Iteration One fundamental capability of iterations is the ability to terminate based on the result of a test. Two factors can vary in the specification of this test: its placement and its logical direction. The placement of the test can either be before, after, or in the middle of the body of the iteration. We call these three choices pretest, posttest, and in-test iterations. The logical direction of an iteration specifies whether the test is a **termination test**, where a true condition indicates the iteration should halt, or a **continuation test**, where a false condition completes the iteration.

In Pascal, for example, the `while` statement indicates a **pretest iteration** with a continuation test. The Pascal `repeat-until` construct results in a posttest iteration with a termination test.

Once again, an important issue is the syntax for delimiting the statement block that serves as the body of the iteration. As with the `if` statement, Pascal assumes that the body is one statement, which can be expanded into a compound statement using `begin` and `end`. The technique of specifying a block of statements by special delimiters is used by Ada, whose syntax for the pretest iteration is

```
while <condition> loop
  <sequence-of-statements>
end loop;
```

The word `loop` signifies the beginning of the body, and `end loop` marks the end.

Posttest Iteration Whereas a pretest iteration provides a test before entry to the body of the iteration, a **posttest iteration** places the test after the body. Generally, pretest iteration is preferred over the posttest form because posttesting permits one execution of the loop body before the test is first performed. In Pascal, a posttest structure is available, the `repeat-until` construct. The `repeat-until` presents an inconsistency in Pascal in its method of delimiting the iteration body. This structure is the only control structure for which Pascal abandons the compound statement convention in favor of the use of keyword delimiters. In this case, the words `repeat` and `until` are used to delimit the iteration body.

The equivalence of the pretest and posttest iteration constructs is obvious. The inclusion of both constructs in a language is for the convenience of the programmer, who may choose the one most natural for any given iterative structure. Ada provides no posttest iteration construct but can simulate it by placing the in-test conditional at the end of the iteration body.

In-test Iteration   Occasionally, it is desirable to perform the test for terminating an iteration neither before nor after the execution of the body but, rather, somewhere in the middle. This case is called an **in-test iteration** and is a situation where it is often argued that the use of a `goto` statement is justified.

A much more restrictive construct than the `goto` can be used for this purpose, however — one whose only purpose is to exit from an iteration in the middle of its body. This situation has the advantage of permitting a flexible exit from a loop while not allowing indiscriminate branching within the program. This approach also avoids the need to use statement labels.

We examine the capabilities of such an in-test construct by discussing its Ada implementation, the `exit` statement. The format of this statement is

```
exit [when <condition>]
```

The condition, in this case, is a termination condition.

The general form of the in-test iteration in Ada is, therefore,

```
loop
  <top-body>
  exit when <condition>;
  <bottom-body>
end loop;
```

where the top and bottom bodies are those statements executed, respectively, before and after the test is performed.

A further extension of this construct is available to permit the termination of more than one nested iteration at the same time — for example,

```
loop
  <body-A>
  loop
    <body-B>
    exit when <condition>;
    <body-C>
  end loop;
  <body-D>
end loop;
```

In this situation, the `exit` statement is contained in both the outer and inner iterations. The definition of the Ada `exit` is that it exits from only the immediate containing iteration.

A facility is also provided in Ada, however, to permit the exit from several layers of iterations at the same time. This action is done by labeling the iterations and specifying the outermost iteration to be exited by naming its label in the `exit` statement. The preceding example could exit from the outer iteration in the following way:

```
OUTER: loop
        <body-A>
        loop
          <body-B>
          exit OUTER when <condition>;
          <body-C>
        end loop;
        <body-D>
      end loop OUTER;
```

Note that the label is attached to the `loop` statement with a colon separator and, in addition, must be appended to the `end loop` statement. This form of label is used for reference by `exit` statements only and may be attached only to `loop` statements. A separate syntax is used for general statement labels, and this syntax is described later.

The `exit` statement of Ada gives the programmer power beyond the simple in-test iteration. It provides the capability of multiple-exit iterations, because there is no limit to the number of exits that can occur within an iteration. This practice is discouraged, however, because it is counter to the goal of writing understandable programs.

The `exit` statement also permits the programmer to simulate the action of posttest iterations, a feature not directly included in Ada. An Ada posttest iteration can be written

```
loop
  <body>
  exit when <condition>;
end loop;
```

Another construct often confused with the `exit` is one that terminates the present pass of an iteration and begins the next pass, rather than terminating the entire iteration. Ada does not include such a statement, but the language C provides a `continue` statement for this purpose.

Fixed-Count Iteration The oldest of the iteration structures is the **fixed-count iteration**, which traces its roots back to the `do loop` of FORTRAN. This iteration is terminated after executing a specified number of times rather than when a specified condition occurs.

Fixed-count iterations are controlled by a variable known as the **iteration control variable (ICV)**. The general form of such an iteration is

```
for <ICV> := <initial> to <final> step <increment> do <body>
```

Here, ICV is a variable and `initial`, `final`, and `increment` are expressions of the same type as ICV. Based on this general form, we will address a number of important variations among languages in forming the fixed-count iteration.

1. *What types are permitted for the ICV?* In some languages only integers are permitted; in others, only numerics, including integers and reals, are allowed. Pascal and Ada both permit integer, character, and enumerated types, the same as those permitted in the control of a `case` structure. These types are permitted because they possess a built-in stepping function. In other words, each element has a natural successor. Real types do not possess this property and require explicit values for the increment if they are allowed.

2. *What is the scope of the ICV?* Most imperative languages require that the ICV be a variable that is bound in the execution unit containing the iteration. Ada, however, takes a different approach. The scope of an ICV in Ada is the body of the iteration for which it is declared. This means that its appearance in the iteration statement is equivalent to its declaration and binds it locally to a location. Upon completion of the iteration, the ICV is no longer bound to that location.

3. *Can the ICV be modified within the iteration body?* The modification of the ICV within the iteration body is dangerous in that it disrupts the sequence of values specified at the beginning of the iteration. For this reason, some languages, such as Ada, disallow modification of the ICV through either assignment or use as a modifiable argument to a procedure. Other languages place no restrictions on changing the ICV.

4. *What is the value of the ICV after termination of the iteration?* There are four different responses that languages give to this question. If the scope of the ICV is the iteration, as in Ada, the answer is obviously that the ICV no longer is bound to a location and hence has no value binding either. If the ICV maintains its location binding after termination of the iteration, it could be bound either to the value it had during the last iteration, to one increment beyond its value during the last iteration, or to an unspecified value. This last option means that, unlike with Ada, the ICV will have some value, but no guarantees are made as to what that value might be.

5. *When are the final and increment expressions evaluated?* This becomes an important issue when variables in these two expressions are modified inside the iteration. For example, the following Pascal program fragment would raise this issue:

```
for i:= 1 to n do
  n:=n+1;
```

If the final value n is reevaluated each time the iteration body is executed, this iteration will run forever for n initially positive. It turns out that for

Pascal, as with most imperative languages, both the final and the increment expressions are evaluated once, prior to the initial entry into the iteration. The changing of n in the preceding iteration body would, therefore, have no effect on the number of times the body is executed, and for positive n the preceding fragment is equivalent to the simple statement

```
n := 2*n;
```

6. *Is an increment other than successor permitted?* Although an increment expression was specified in the general form, some languages do not allow such a specification. Pascal and Ada, for example, permit only an increment of 1 for a numeric ICV. Nonnumeric ICVs are required to be of types where each element has a defined successor, making the implied effect of an increment setting the ICV to the successor element within the type.

7. *How is iteration backward through a range specified?* In languages that permit increment specification, a negative increment is usually used to indicate this type of iteration. Pascal, which has no explicit increment, replaces the keyword to with downto, as in

```
for i := 6 downto 1 do ...
```

Ada expresses the initial and final expressions together as a range in which initial must always be less than or equal to final. For the ICV to proceed backward through this range, the keywords in reverse must be appended — for example,

```
for I in reverse 1..6 loop ...
```

8. *Is transfer into the iteration permitted?* Because the parameters for a fixed-count iteration are evaluated and fixed when it is initially entered, branching to the interior of such an iteration without executing these initial evaluations can be very dangerous. Therefore, some languages, such as Ada, disallow such transfers. Pascal and many others allow these transfers to occur, although the results will be highly unpredictable.

9. *How is the iteration body delimited?* As with other iterations, the two approaches are (1) to allow the body to be a compound statement, or (2) to use keywords to delimit the block of statements forming the body. Pascal, as usual, follows the compound statement philosophy. Ada utilizes the keywords loop and end loop to delimit, as before.

The general form of the iteration statement in Ada includes all of the types of iteration that can be specified, including nonterminating, pretest, in-test, and fixed-count iterations.

```
Iteration
Language: Ada

  loop-statement::=
    [<loop-name>:]
    [while <condition> | for <identifier> in [reverse] <range>]        loop
```

```
        <sequence-of-statements>
    end loop [<loop-name>];

Pretest: continuation test is used with while option.

Posttest: no facility is provided for posttest.

In-test: statement of the form
        exit [<loop-name>] [when <condition>]
    exits from the named iteration or from the innermost
    iteration if no loop-name is present

Fixed count: for option implements fixed count iteration
  Types for ICV: integer, character, enumerated
  Scope of ICV: iteration body only
  ICV modification permitted inside iteration?: No
  Value of ICV after iteration: Not applicable
  When is range evaluated: Once, upon initial entry
  Permissible increments: +1 and -1
  Backward iteration: keyword reverse
  Transfer into iteration: Not permitted
```

Nondeterministic Iteration   The nondeterministic conditional can be extended to form a nondeterministic iteration of the following form:

```
do
  when <condition-1> -> <statement-sequence-1>
  when <condition-2> -> <statement-sequence-2>
  ...
  when <condition-n> -> <statement-sequence-n>
od
```

As before, the choice of statement sequence to be executed will be made nondeterministically from among those whose guard conditions are true. The iterative form repeats as long as at least one guard condition is true and terminates whenever none are true. We see this form implemented for concurrent control in Chapter 18.

3.3.3 ▪ Unconstrained Control Statements

The most controversial of all control structures are those that are unconstrained — that is, permit branching to any program unit without restriction. These are generally known as `goto` constructs, and their use is of questionable value, as we discuss shortly. Nevertheless, all popular imperative languages, with the exception of Modula-2, provide a `goto` statement. In this section we examine this simple, yet powerful, control construct.

The general format of the `goto` statement in almost every language in which it is included is

```
goto <statement-label>;
```

FORTRAN contains alternative forms of the `goto`, but these are really just other ways of expressing a multialternative, `case`-like structure. SNOBOL permits a `goto` or two to be attached to every statement as a suffix.

The interesting issues and variations with `goto` constructs arise when the format of labels and the impact of scope are considered.

Statement Labels There is great variation in the way statement labels are formed. BASIC, for example, requires a label to be present for every statement. Other languages make labeling a statement optional. Optional statement labels are frequently separated from the statement by a colon. Ada is an exception, requiring that the label be enclosed between << and >>, because the colon is used in Ada to label iterations, as described earlier.

In order better to understand the use of labels and different languages' approaches, we return to the data object model that we used in Section 3.1. For our discussion here, we consider the data object to be a statement of the program that is bound at load time to the location in memory where the executable statement is stored. The approach most languages use toward labels is that illustrated by Figure 3.6. Here, the value is the element of the storage space where the instruction is located. This binding occurs at load time. The

FIGURE 3.6   **Statement Labels as Constants**

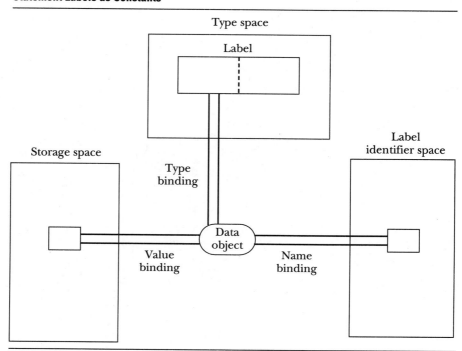

name binding occurs at compile time and binds the data object to an element of the label identifier space. This space may or may not be the same as the variable identifier space. In C and Ada, the label and variable identifier spaces are the same. But languages often select label identifiers from the space of integers, as in Pascal and FORTRAN. Another consideration is whether the label type binding is made explicitly through a label declaration (Pascal) or implicitly through attachment of the label identifier to a statement (C, Ada, and FORTRAN). When a label is declared, there are implications for the scope of the label, which we discuss later.

Figure 3.7 illustrates the use of label variables. The best example of this is found in PL/I, which permits the declaration of an identifier to be a label variable. That variable can be bound to any legal label constant as its value. This possibility permits such interesting activities as passing labels as parameters and forming arrays of labels. The languages SNOBOL and APL extend this idea even further by permitting calculated expressions to have their values assigned to labels. There is a price to be paid for this interesting extension — namely, the loss of program readability. We know that goto statements themselves can be detrimental to program readability, but when a single goto statement can branch to virtually any labeled statement — with the choice of statement dependent upon some nonlocal action — the read-

FIGURE 3.7   **Statement Labels as Variables**

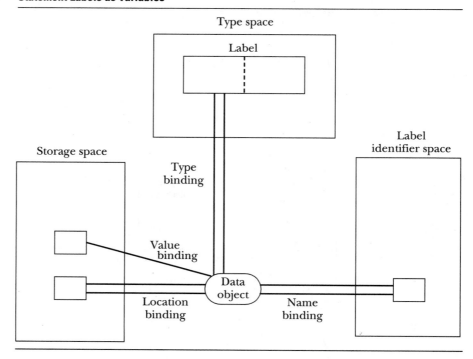

ability factor sinks to new lows. For this reason, the implementation of label variables is not included in most modern imperative languages.

Scope Issues There are several important issues related to the scope of labels. The first is the scope of the name binding to a labeled statement. In general, this follows the scoping rules for variables; that is, the binding holds in the present block and all contained blocks. Redefining a label identifier inside of a nested block, if allowed by a language, could result in the hole-in-scope problem as with variables.

To illustrate the preceding point, consider the following Ada fragment.

```
OUTER: declare
    . . .
      INNER: declare
          . . .
            <<INSIDE>> goto OUTSIDE;        --this is legal
          . . .
      end INNER;
    . . .
  <<OUTSIDE>> goto INSIDE;              --this is not legal
    . . .
end OUTER;
```

The `goto` in the `INNER` block is legal, because `OUTSIDE` is bound from the containing block. The `goto` in the `OUTER` block is not permitted, because `IN-SIDE` is bound only in the context of the `INNER` block. By the way, note that `OUTER` and `INNER` are block labels, whereas `INSIDE` and `OUTSIDE` are statement labels. It is illegal to use block labels in a `goto` statement.

One further type of scoping block can logically be defined for labels beyond those that apply to variables. This is the block of statements making up the body of a control structure. It is necessary to make these blocks scoping blocks for labels to prevent branching to the interior of a control structure's body without executing the test condition. For example, the following Ada fragment is illegal.

```
loop
  . . .
  <<INSIDE>>
  . . .
end loop;
  . . .
goto INSIDE    --illegal to branch into structure body
```

Similarly, branching to a statement inside the body of a conditional or any other iteration structure from outside that body is strictly prohibited. In defining the scope of labels, the bodies of control structures are thus treated the same as any other scoping block.

Another important observation can be made about the situation where a `goto` statement branches from inside a block to a statement in a containing block. This action is perfectly legal in most languages, but its implementation is not as simple as it might appear. Branching out of a block is actually a termination of that block and requires the removal of that block's activation record from the run-time stack. This action may require popping several activation records if the branch is out of several layers of nested blocks.

We are now able to summarize the unconstrained control structure of Ada.

```
Unconstrained Control Structure
Language: Ada

  goto statement ::= goto <label-name>
  label-name ::= <identifier>
  labeled-statement ::= {<<<label>>>} <statement>
  Declaration of label: implicit by its occurrence
  Scope of label: The unit in which it occurs and all
      containing units where unit is a block or a
      structure body.
```

The goto **Controversy**   The little goto statement has been the subject of a major controversy in the field of computer science initiated by Dijkstra (1968) and rekindled by Rubin (1987). This controversy is actually about programming practices rather than programming languages, but inasmuch as language has an impact on practice, programming languages have become a part of this discussion. We will limit our discussions to the impact that the presence of the goto statement has on the capabilities of a language.

Three facts about control structures are important considerations here:

1. *Simple conditionals and* goto *statements are sufficient to replace any control structures.* Each control structure that we discussed in this chapter can be replaced by a construct using only simple conditionals and goto statements. For example, the Pascal while construct of the form

```
while <condition> do
  <statement>;
```

can be replaced by

```
10: if <condition> then
          begin
            <statement>;
            goto 10;
          end;
```

Several exercises at the end of this chapter require you to replace other control structures with these two simple constructs.

2. *The two-alternative conditional and pretest loop constructs are sufficient to replace any control structure.* This result is far less obvious than the first, but it has been proved by Boehm and Jacopini (1966). One consequence of this result is that a language without a goto could duplicate the programs writ-

ten in a language containing the goto. In other words, there are no programs that require the use of a goto for their construction.

3. *The* goto *is the most powerful control structure.* This result has meaning only if the word *powerful* is defined. Kosaraju (1974) has proved that the goto is the most powerful in the sense that replacing a goto with other structures might require additional variables, whereas replacing other structures with a goto will never require additional variables. In this sense, programs expressed without the goto are more complex than those expressed with it.

What are the implications of these three results for programming languages? First, a programming language without a goto statement can express all the programs that can be expressed by the same language with a goto added. Second, there are situations where programs can be more simply represented by the use of a goto.

On the other hand, in the same way that powerful automobiles or powerful weapons give greater capability but are accompanied by greater danger, there is an increased danger with the use of the goto. This danger is in an increased ability to generate unreadable programs. Many computer scientists believe that the dangers of using the goto far outweigh the advantages inherent in its power. Programming language designers have reacted to this controversy by continuing to provide a goto statement, while at the same time providing a sufficiently rich set of weaker control structures to make the usage of the goto unnecessary. This presents the programmer with the final choice of whether to use the goto or not.

CHAPTER 3   Terms

data object	precedence
binding	type checking
storage space	strongly typed
location binding	dynamically typed language
compile time	statically typed language
load time	implicit type conversion
run time	type coercion
identifier space	explicit type conversion
name binding	type equivalence
type space	domain equivalence
type declaration	name equivalence
operator	declaration equivalence
monadic operator	anonymous type
dyadic operator	subtypes
prefix	derived type
infix	scalar data type
function	atomic data object
expressions	built-in type

user-defined type	dynamic storage allocation
integer type	extent
real type	activation record
fixed point	conditional control structure
floating point	conditional
mantissa	`if` statement
exponent	dangling else
Boolean type	case structure
short-circuit operators	nondeterministically
pointer type	guard
dangling reference	guarded command
garbage	iteration
dereference	nonterminating iteration
enumerated type	termination test
statement	continuation test
nested statement	pretest iteration
label	posttest iteration
block	in-test iteration
local binding	fixed-count iteration
nonlocal binding	iteration control variable (ICV)
lexical scoping	`goto`
static scoping	
hole-in-scope	
dynamic scoping	

C H A P T E R **3**   **Discussion Questions**

1. In what situations are location bindings made at run time?

2. What are some considerations in choosing between a more restrictive or less restrictive identifier space?

3. Languages that use prefix form for dyadic operators do not require parentheses. Why is this so?

4. Which, if any, of the three definitions of type equivalence form equivalence relations in the mathematical sense? Prove your answers.

5. Some languages permit the binding of type to a data object at run time. Discuss advantages and disadvantages of this strategy.

6. When programming in a language with both fixed-point and floating-point types, what considerations would be important in deciding which to use for a given data object?

7. Why would a language provide both the standard AND and a short circuit AND? When might the standard AND have a different effect?

8. What would be some uses of run-time binding of labels? What dangers would such a feature present?

9. Consider the parameter-passing mechanism of Pascal.
   a. Is the binding of actual to formal parameters a *static* or *dynamic* binding?
   b. Speculate how this mechanism would work if it was the opposite binding as your answer in part (a).

10. How would the usefulness of a language be limited if it contained no control structures?

11. Why do Pascal and Ada not permit the use of reals and string types in a `case` statement?

12. Why do you think Pascal's `repeat-until` uses an approach to blocking that differs from that of all other control structures in the language? What might be some negative consequences of this?

13. What are the advantages and disadvantages of Pascal's compound statement philosophy of blocking control structures?

14. Give an argument for permitting the modification of the ICV inside a loop body.

15. What are some reasons for requiring that labels be declared? What are some reasons for not doing so?

16. Consider the following Pascal code:

```
program GotoQuestion (input, output);
  label 99;
  procedure ReadUntil (match: integer);
    var potential: integer;
    begin
      while true do
        begin
          read(potential);
          if potential = match goto 99;
        end;
      end;
    begin
      ReadUntil(42);
99:   writeln('Got a 42!!')
    end.
```

Not only does the `goto` above "break" a loop, it also "breaks" a procedure by jumping outside of that procedure. Discuss the legality, advisability, and ramifications of using mechanisms such as this.

C H A P T E R **3**   Exercises

---

1. The language APL considers all operators to be of equal precedence and evaluated right to left. What would such a scheme evaluate for the following expressions? Rewrite each one in equivalent postfix form.
   a. `6 * 2 + 3`
   b. `2 + 3 * 6`

c. 4 - 2 - 1

d. 4 - 1 - 2

2. Consider the following declarations:

```
type S is INTEGER range 1..100;
type T is INTEGER range 1..100;
A,B:T;
C,D:S;
E,F:INTEGER range 1..100;
G,H:T;
```

Which variables are of equivalent type if the language uses each of the following?

a. Domain equivalence

b. Name equivalence

c. Declaration equivalence

3. There are 16 possible dyadic Boolean operators. These operators are constructed from the 16 possible combinations of results for the 4 possible operand combinations in filling in the following table:

```
Operand 1       Operand 2       Result
  TRUE            TRUE          _____
  TRUE            FALSE         _____
  FALSE           TRUE          _____
  FALSE           FALSE         _____
```

List them and indicate which of them will permit a short-circuit calculation.

4. **a.** Consider the following block definitions. For each block, determine the bindings of every bound name. Label each as local or global.

```
Program P;
  BLOCK B1;
    DECLARE A,B,C;
    BLOCK B2;
      DECLARE C,D;
      BLOCK B3;
        DECLARE B,D,F;
      BEGIN
        . . .
      END B3;
    BEGIN B2
      . . .
    END B2;
    BLOCK B4;
      DECLARE B,C,D;
    BEGIN B4
      . . .
    END B4;
  BEGIN B1
    . . .
  END B1;
END P;
```

b. Trace the contents of the stack of activation records for the following sample program written in our pseudolanguage. For each block, give the pair of integers used to locate each bound name.

```
PROGRAM P;
  DECLARE X,Y;
BEGIN P
  BLOCK A;
    DECLARE X,Y,Z;
  BEGIN A
    BLOCK B;
      DECLARE Y;
    BEGIN B
      BLOCK C;
        DECLARE X,Y;
      BEGIN C
        ...
      END C;
      BLOCK D;
        DECLARE Z;
      BEGIN D
        ...
      END D;
      ...
    END B;
  END A;
  BLOCK E;
    DECLARE Z;
  BEGIN E
    BLOCK F;
      DECLARE X;
    BEGIN F
      ...
    END F;
    ...
  END E;
  ...
END P;
```

5. Consider the following Pascal code:

```
program Question_5(input, output);
  type t = integer;
  var a,b,c: integer;

  procedure p1;
    var a: real;
    begin
      a := 1; b := 1; c := 1;
    end;

  procedure p2;
    var b: real; t: boolean;
```

```
    procedure p3;
       var a,c: real; t: real;
       begin
          a := 3; b := 3; c := 3;
           p1;
          end;
       begin
          a := 2; b := 2; c := 2;
        p3;
     end;

begin
  a := 0; b := 0; c := 0;
   p2;
end.
```

When execution of p1 begins, the calling structure will look like

main → p2 → p3 → p1

a. Using normal Pascal static scope rule, depict at each routine what variables are accessible. Use the notational convention

```
<var> of <proc name>
```

to denote <var> is accessible and that it is defined in <proc name>.

b. *Dynamic scope* determines the binding of a variable not declared in a block by its binding in the block that called the present block rather than by that of the containing block. Do the same thing you did for part a, but use dynamic scope rules instead of the static rules of Pascal.

6. Consider the following Pascal fragment and fill in the table as to legal (that is, type equivalent) assignments.

```
type t1 = 1..20;
      t2 = 5..10;
      t3 = record
              f1: boolean;
              f2: integer;
            end;
var a, b: t1;
    c: integer;
    d: t2;
    e: 1..5;
    f,g: t3;
    h,i: record
    f1: boolean;
    f2: integer;
  end;
```

Indicate the kind of equivalence between the two sides of the assignment statements in the following table:

		Structural	Name	Declaration
a := b;	:			
c := a;	:			
d := e;	:			
f.f2 := c;	:			
f := g;	:			
h := g;	:			
i := h;	:			

7. Fill in the table following the program with *L* if the statement number is legal and *I* if the statement number is illegal with respect to the kind of type equivalence specified.

```
    program Type_O_Rama(input, output);

    type T1 = array [1..10] of char;
         T2 = array [1..10] of T1;

    var a,b: T1;
        c: array [1..10] of array [1..10] of char;
        d: T2;
        e: char;
        f: T2;

    begin
{1}     a := b;
{2}     d[2] := a;
{3}     c := d;
{4}     d := f;
{5}     c[2][1] := e;
{6}     c[5] := b;
{7}     f := c;
    end.
```

	{1}	{2}	{3}	{4}	{5}	{6}	{7}
Domain Equivalence							
Name Equivalence							
Declaration Equivalence							

8. Upon completion of the following Pascal program, what is the value of a using (1) static scope rules, and (2) dynamic scope rules?

```pascal
program Question_8 (input, output);
  var a,b: integer;

  procedure p1;
    begin b := 4 end;

  procedure p2;
    var b: integer;
    begin a := 50; p1 end;

  begin
    b := 40;
    p2;
    a := b;
  end.
```

9. Consider the following code:

```pascal
program Question_9 (input, output);
  var a,b,c: integer;

  procedure p1;
    var b: integer;
    begin
      b := 4;
      a := a + b;
        {B}

    end;

  procedure p2;
    var b,c: integer;

    procedure p3;
      var a: integer;
      begin
        a := b;
        c := 14;
        p1;
      end;

    begin
      b := 10;
      c := 20;

        {A}

      p3;
    end;
```

```
procedure p4;
   begin
     p2;
   end;

begin
   a := 1; b := 2; c := 3;
   p4;
end.
```

a. Depict the identifiers accessible from p2 at point {A} using implicit, static scope rules.

b. Depict the identifiers accessible from p1 at point {B} using implicit, dynamic scope rules. Note that at point {B}, the calling structure is

main → p4 → p2 → p3 → p1

10. Operators that are defined on more than one type are called *overloaded operators*. Identify the operators that are overloaded in Pascal.

11. Show how a simple conditional and a goto can be used to simulate the actions of each of the following:

a. Two-alternative conditional (if-then-else)
b. Multialternative conditional (case)
c. Pretest iteration
d. Posttest iteration
e. Fixed-count iteration

12. For each of the following Pascal structures, solve the dangling else problem by indicating what will be printed when initially x is 10.

a.
```
if x>10 then
   x:=x+1;
   if x<12 then
      x:=x+1
else
   x:=x-1;
writeln(x);
```

b.
```
if x>10 then
   begin
      x:=x+2;
      if x<12 then
         begin
            x:=x-1;
         end
   end
else
   x:=x-2;
writeln(x);
```

13. Express the following Ada case structure as an if-elsif-else structure.

```
case x is
   when 1   => process1;
   when 2 | 4 => process2;
   when 6 | 9 => process3;
   when others => error;
end case;
```

14. Ada has no posttest iteration form directly built into the language. Design one that would remain consistent with Ada's other iteration constructs.

15. Design the syntax for a completely general iteration structure that permits both pretest and posttest and both continuation and termination logic. Write the EBNF for your construct. Does your answer permit more than one test for the same iteration?

16. Give examples of applications where each of the following are natural iteration forms:
    a. Nonterminating
    b. Termination, pretest
    c. Continuation, pretest
    d. Termination, posttest
    e. Continuation, posttest
    f. Termination, in-test
    g. Continuation, in-test

17. If neither an `exit` nor a `goto` statement were available in Ada, how might you simulate the action of an `exit` statement?

18. Give an illustration of the hole-in-scope problem for Ada labels.

19. Rewrite the following `for` loop as a `repeat` loop.
    ```
    for index := 10 downto -5 do something_or_other;
    ```

20. In Basic, the `on ... goto` statement evaluates an expression in much the same way a `case` statement does. For example, executing the statement
    ```
    25 ON (X) GOTO 100, 200, 300
    ```
    will cause the computer to jump to lines 100, 200, or 300 if X is either 1, 2, or 3. If X is none of these, no jump is done.
    a. Rewrite this statement as a `case` statement in Ada.
    b. Rewrite this statement as an `if` statement in Pascal.

C H A P T E R **3**   **Laboratory Exercises**

In Exercises 1–19, you are to work with a language or languages whose implementation you have available to you and determine the answer to the questions by constructing a sample program or programs and observing the results.

1. What is the definition of the identifier space for your language? What characters are allowed and in which positions? Is there a maximum identifier length? Are upper- and lowercase letters distinguishable?

2. What are the expression evaluation rules for your language? What are the operator precedences? Is left to right or right to left the direction among operators of equal precedence? Write the EBNF representation for these rules.

3. Does your language perform any implicit type conversions? What are they?

4. What does your language use for type equivalence, domain, name, or declaration?

5. If your language has a subtype capability, which of the three strategies is implemented when an expression of the parent type is assigned to a variable of

the subtype and the value of the expression is not within the domain of the subtype?

6. What is the domain of allowable integers in your language? What is the domain of allowable reals?

7. Does your language evaluate AND and OR with or without short-circuiting?

8. What happens when a pointer data object is deallocated while another data object is pointing to the same location?

9. What is the effect of assigning the same constant to two different enumerated types? Is it permitted? Are ambiguities discovered at compile time or run time?

10. Do blocks have a run-time location binding?

11. Does your language permit an unconditional branch into the block of statements executed under control of a conditional?

12. What types are permitted for the control expression of a case statement in your language?

13. How does your language react when an unspecified choice is evaluated for the expression controlling a case statement?

14. Does your language permit unconditional branching into or out of the body of an iteration?

15. What is the value of the ICV after completion of an iteration?

16. When is the final expression evaluated in a fixed-count iteration?

17. Does your language permit an ICV to be of a real type?

18. Does your language permit an iteration to have multiple exit tests?

19. Does your language permit modification of the ICV in the body of a fixed-count iteration?

In Exercise 20, you are to work with an implementation of the Pascal programming language that is available to you.

20. Pascal's version of type equivalence might be called "pseudostructural equivalence."

   a. Construct at least three tests that demonstrate Pascal's use of structural equivalence. Make the tests different (for example, using different data structures).

   b. Pascal does not use true structural equivalence, however. Find where it does not use structural equivalence to check for compatible types and provide at least two examples (again with different data structures).

· C H A P T E R · 4

Data
Aggregates

In addition to the fundamental data types introduced in Section 3.1, imperative programming languages have facilities for types, which are made up of aggregates of other types called **data aggregates**. This chapter examines these language capabilities, specifically, the aggregates array, string, record, file, and set.

Each of these aggregate types is examined from the following points of view:

1. *Declaration and binding* — In contrast to the data object bindings that we have seen previously, the bindings of interest in this chapter are the bindings of the aggregate type to its constituent types.

2. *Manipulation* — The fundamental operators on aggregate types are comparison and assignment. In addition, aggregate types need operators known as selectors, which convert from aggregate to constituent values, and constructor operators, which convert from constituent to aggregate values.

3. *Implementation* — The implementation of an aggregate type refers to special considerations given to the representation of aggregate structures in storage. Data compression, data organization, and indirect storage using pointers are important options in implementation.

Data aggregate types provided by a programming language are distinct from abstract data types constructed by the programmer from the simple and aggregate types of the language. We address language features related to data abstraction in Chapter 6.

4.1   Data Aggregate Models

First, we introduce five abstract models for representing data aggregation. These models will serve as useful tools in describing specific data aggregates. This classification of models is taken from Hoare (1972).

For the purpose of this section we use the notation that T_1, T_2, ... represent types, either simple or aggregate. These types are not necessarily distinct, so that T_1 and T_2 may represent the same type or different types. When an aggregate type T is defined in terms of other types, these other types are called **constituent types**. The values of an aggregate type are structures built from values of the constituent types.

We are also interested in the **cardinality** of a type. Simply stated, the cardinality of type T is the number of possible values of that type. Data types may have either finite cardinality or a denumerably infinite cardinality. The cardinality of an aggregate type is easily computed from the cardinality of its constituent types. We represent the cardinality of a type T by $C(T)$.

4.1.1 ▪ Cartesian Product

The **Cartesian product** type is constructed from a set of finite types and is defined as follows:

$$T_1 \times T_2 \times \ldots \times T_n = \{(t_1, t_2, \ldots, t_n) \text{ where } t_1 \in T_1, \ t_2 \in T_2, \ldots, t_n \in T_n\}$$

In words, the Cartesian product is the set of all possible tuples that can be formed by choosing one element from each of the n types participating in the product.

Consider the following example with $n = 3$ and finite types T_1, T_2, T_3.

```
T₁ = {1,2,3,4}
T₂ = {'A','B','C'}
T₃ = {true, false}
```

By our definition, the possible elements of type $T_1 \times T_2 \times T_3$ are

```
(1,'A',true)   (2,'A',true)   (3,'A',true)   (4,'A',true)
(1,'A',false)  (2,'A',false)  (3,'A',false)  (4,'A',false)
(1,'B',true)   (2,'B',true)   (3,'B',true)   (4,'B',true)
(1,'B',false)  (2,'B',false)  (3,'B',false)  (4,'B',false)
(1,'C',true)   (2,'C',true)   (3,'C',true)   (4,'C',true)
(1,'C',false)  (2,'C',false)  (3,'C',false)  (4,'C',false)
```

In general, the cardinality of a Cartesian product can be calculated by

$$C(T_1 \times \ldots \times T_n) = C(T_1) \bullet \cdots \bullet C(T_n)$$

It is not necessary for types participating in a Cartesian product to be either finite or distinct. For example, T_1 and T_2 could each be of type integer, in which case $T_1 \times T_2$ would be the set of all integer pairs.

The Cartesian product is the model that represents record structures in modern imperative languages.

4.1.2 ▪ Mapping

A **mapping** in its simplest form maps one type (called the **domain** type) into another type (called the **range** type). This mapping is defined such that each element of the domain type is mapped into one and only one element of the range type. A given element of the range type may be associated with several domain elements or may be associated with none through a mapping. Such a mapping can be represented by

$$M: T_1 \rightarrow T_2$$

where T_1 is the domain type and T_2 is the range type. Figure 4.1 illustrates this form of mapping. The mapping is finite in the sense that the domain type must consist of a finite number of elements.

A common representation of such a mapping that corresponds to the mathematical object known as function is a set of pairs of the form

$$\{ (d_1, r_1), (d_2, r_2), \ldots, (d_n, r_n) \}$$

where $\{d_i, i = 1, \ldots, n\}$ is the set of all distinct elements of the domain type and $\{r_i, i = 1, \ldots, n\}$ is a subset of the set of all elements of the range set and all r_i are not necessarily distinct. The cardinality of a mapping is given by

$$C(M:D \rightarrow R) = C(R)^{C(D)}$$

FIGURE 4.1   **Mapping from T_1 to T_2**

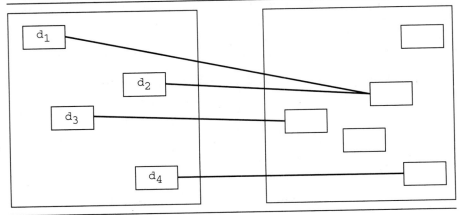

This model is commonly used to represent arrays, and in some languages it is also used for strings.

One special case of a mapping type occurs when the domain type is itself a Cartesian product type. Since the domain type must always be finite, it follows that all of the constituent types of the Cartesian product making up the domain must be finite as well. This form of the mapping type represents multi-indexed arrays and the application of the two preceding cardinality formulas yields

$$C(M:T_1 \times T_2 \times \cdots \times T_n \to T_{n+1}) = C(T_{n+1})^{C(T1) \cdot C(T2) \cdot \ldots \cdot C(Tn)}$$

4.1.3 ▪ **Discriminated Union**

A **discriminated union** type is constructed from two or more types in the following way:

$$T_1 \cup T_2 \cup \cdots \cup T_n = \{t \text{ where } t \in T_1 \text{ or } t \in T_2 \text{ or} \cdots \text{ or } t \in T_n\}$$

This statement says that an element of the discriminated union type may be an element of any one of the component types. The adjective *discriminated* appears because some value will be used to discriminate which of the n constituent domains is the presently active domain.

This model is not generally implemented in imperative languages in its pure form, but it is important in the construction of variant records. ALGOL 68 is a language where a pure discriminated union is present.

The discriminated union differs from the normal set union operator in that the values of the discriminated union type are distinct from the values of the constituent types and it must be possible to distinguish the constituent type from which a value originated. For example, suppose

$$T_1 = \{1,2,3\} \text{ and } T_2 = \{1,3,5\}$$

Then the discriminated union $T_1 \cup T_2$ is defined as

$$\{1 \text{ from } T_1, \ 2, \ 3 \text{ from } T_1, \ 1 \text{ from } T_2, \ 3 \text{ from } T_2, \ 5\}$$

Note that it is necessary to qualify those values in both of the constituent types to identify their original type. Under these assumptions, the cardinality of a discriminated union type is given by

$$C(T_1 \cup T_2 \cup \cdots \cup T_n) = C(T_1) + C(T_2) + \cdots + C(T_n)$$

This holds if two of the constituent types have a nonempty intersection — even if they are the same type.

4.1.4 ▪ **Sequence**

Unlike Cartesian product and mapping types, both of which are constructed from two or more other types, a **sequence** type is built from a single constituent type. The sequence type T^* constructed from constituent type T is defined as

$$T^* = \{(t_1, t_2, \cdots, t_n) \text{ where } t_1, t_2, \cdots, t_n \in T \text{ and } n > 0\}$$

In words, the space of the sequence type over constituent type T is the set of all sequences of elements from the space of T. The cardinality of the sequence type will always be infinite, even when the constituent type has finite cardinality.

4.1.5   ▪   Powerset

A **powerset** type is built from a single constituent type, as is a sequence type. It is defined as the set of all possible subsets of the elements in the constituent type. The powerset of constituent type T is denoted by 2^T. The constituent type may have either a finite or infinite cardinality. The cardinality of a powerset is given by

$$C(2^T) = 2^{C(T)}$$

Figure 4.2 gives a comparative illustration of the models introduced in this section. Careful study of these examples will aid you in understanding the concepts discussed here.

4.2   Arrays

Arrays are found in almost every imperative language and represent the oldest aggregate data structure. The **array** is based on the mapping model, where the domain type is the set of indices and the range is what is commonly called the type of the array. We use the terminology *domain type* and *range type* in our discussion.

4.2.1   ▪   Declaration and Binding

In the case of arrays, there are two types that must be bound to the array type, the domain and range. Consider, for example, the following Pascal array type declaration.

```
type A = array [1..10] of integer;
```

This general form permits the binding of both the domain (in this case `1..10`) and the range (in this case `integer`) to the array type A.

For implementation purposes, the domain type must be of finite cardinality. Early languages were quite restrictive in the permissible types for the domain, frequently limiting them to finite subranges of the integers starting at a given value, such as 0 or 1. More recent languages are much more flexible, permitting any finite range of an integer, character, or enumerated type.

Similarly, early languages restricted the range type to be a simple or scalar type. Again, more recent languages allow more generality in the range type so that any type, simple or aggregate, can be used. Because arrays themselves are thus included as possible range types, this provides one alternative for representing arrays with multiple indices. For example, Pascal permits the following declarations:

FIGURE **4.2** **Illustration of Mapping, Cartesian Product, Multiindexed Mapping, Discriminated Union, Sequence, and Powerset Models**

$T_1 = \{1,2\}$	$T_2 = \{true, false\}$	$T_3 = \{'A', 'B'\}$

Type	**Type Space**
Mapping $T_1 \rightarrow T_2$	$\{((1,true),(2,true)),((1,true),(2,false))$ $((1,false),(2,true)),((1,false),(2,false))\}$
Cartesian product $T_1 \times T_3$	$\{(1,'A'),(1,'B'),(2,'A'),(2,'B')\}$
Multi-indexed mapping $T_1 \times T_3 \rightarrow T_2$	$\{((1,'A',true),(1,'B',true),(2,'A',true),(2,'B',true)),$ $((1,'A',true),(1,'B',true),(2,'A',true),(2,'B',false)),$ $((1,'A',true),(1,'B',true),(2,'A',false),(2,'B',true)),$ $((1,'A',true),(1,'B',true),(2,'A',false),(2,'B',false)),$ $((1,'A',true),(1,'B',false),(2,'A',true),(2,'B',true)),$ $((1,'A',true),(1,'B',false),(2,'A',true),(2,'B',false)),$ $((1,'A',true),(1,'B',false),(2,'A',false),(2,'B',true)),$ $((1,'A',true),(1,'B',false),(2,'A',false),(2,'B',false)),$ $((1,'A',false),(1,'B',true),(1,'A',true),(2,'B',true)),$ $((1,'A',false),(1,'B',true),(1,'A',true),(2,'B',false)),$ $((1,'A',false),(1,'B',true),(1,'A',false),(2,'B',true)),$ $((1,'A',false),(1,'B',true),(1,'A',false),(2,'B',false)),$ $((1,'A',false),(1,'B',false),(1,'A',true),(2,'B',true)),$ $((1,'A',false),(1,'B',false),(1,'A',true),(2,'B',false)),$ $((1,'A',false),(1,'B',false),(1,'A',false),(2,'B',true)),$ $((1,'A',false),(1,'B',false),(1,'A',false),(2,'B',false))\}$
Discriminated union $T_1 \cup T_2 \cup T_3$	$\{1,2,'A','B',true,false\}$
Sequence T_1^*	$\{(1),(2),(1,1),(1,2),(2,1),(2,2),(1,1,1),\ldots$
Powerset 2^{T_1}	$\{\{\},\{1\},\{2\},\{1,2\}\}$

```
type ROW = array [1..10] of integer;
     TWOD = array [1..5] of ROW;
```

The aggregate type TWOD consists of five elements of type ROW, each of which contains 10 integers. In this case, the domain type of TWOD is the integer subrange 1..5 and the range type is the array type ROW. An alternative approach to multi-indexed arrays is considered later.

Pascal and many other imperative languages bind the domain type to the array aggregate at compile time. This restriction prevents the programmer from defining general procedures having array parameters of general domain, because the array type is bound to domain type at compile time. For example, consider the following Pascal declarations:

```
type ATYPE1 = array [1..10] of integer;
     ATYPE2 = array [11..20] of integer;
var A1:ATYPE1;
    A2:ATYPE2;
```

If we wish to find the mean of both A1 and A2, separate procedures are needed, because the formal parameters are bound to a type at compile time and that type must be fixed as either ATYPE1 or ATYPE2.

Ada addresses this situation by requiring the binding of the domain to only the base type at compile time but permitting the binding to a subrange of that base type at run time. This is called an **unconstrained array** definition.

To illustrate, consider the following Ada type declaration:

```
type VECTOR is array (INTEGER range < >) of FLOAT;
```

This declares VECTOR to be of type array with an unspecified integer subrange for its domain and range type FLOAT. In effect, this makes the subrange of the domain a parameter of type VECTOR rather than a part of its definition. The domain can then be bound at run time by the variable declaration

```
V : VECTOR (LO..HI);
```

where LO and HI are bound to their values in the containing block. A further use of the unconstrained array is in the passing of parameters. The unconstrained type is all that needs to be specified for the formal parameter, because it takes on the domain subrange of the actual parameter of the same type. This is discussed further in Chapter 5.

4.2.2 ▪ Manipulation

Several classes of operations on data aggregates are frequently provided by programming languages. We examine some of the more common ones here as they apply to arrays.

1. *Selection* — Indexing is the ubiquitous selection operation for arrays. It generates a range reference from the array identifier and a domain value. Two common delimiters used for expressing selection are parentheses and brackets. For example, the general form of selection in Pascal is

   ```
   <array-identifier> [ <domain-expression> ]
   ```

   whereas Ada uses the alternative

   ```
   <array-identifier> ( <domain-expression> )
   ```

   Another form of selection operator, known as the *slice*, selects a subarray. It accepts as operands the array and a subrange of the domain space of the array and returns the corresponding subset of the range. Ada contains this operation, and a slice is represented as an indexed reference, with the index expression replaced by a subrange specification. For example, a slice in Ada could be represented by

```
V(3..N)
```

The result of a slice operation is itself an array.

2. *Construction* — A construction operator in its simplest form accepts values from the range space as operands and constructs an array. A general form of such a constructor in Ada is

```
(<range-expression> {, <range-expression> } )
```

In this case, the first expression is assigned to the array element corresponding to the first domain value; the second, to the second; and so on. For example, a Boolean array of five elements could be represented by the array literal

```
(TRUE,FALSE,TRUE,TRUE,FALSE)
```

An extension to this positional association is to specify both the domain and the range values when building an array. The specification of subranges, alternatives, and others are possible in Ada. The following example illustrates all of these possibilities.

```
(1=>7.0, 5..12=>1.0, 3|15..17=>2.0, others=>0.0)
```

3. *Assignment* — When an assignment operator is defined for arrays, it is usually defined as an extension of the assignment operator for simple types. In general, this is of the form

```
<array-identifier> := <array-expression>;
```

The permissible expressions for the right side of the assignment depend on the allowable array operations within the language. A construction operator may be used in these expressions as well.

One issue here is the requirement for assignment compatibility. Although the requirement for identical ranges is obviously necessary, more flexibility can be provided for the domain. A language might require identical domains or, more flexibly, domains with the same cardinality for both operands of the assignment. This would determine, for example, whether A:=B is legal when the domain of A is 1..10 and the domain of B is 11..20.

4. *Composite operators* — **Composite operators** are the extension of operators defined on the range space to operators on arrays. The operands must be of the same cardinality for composite operators to be valid. The resulting array consists of components obtained from a component-by-component application of the operator on the range space.

For example, if

```
A =(1,2,3,4) and B =(5,9,7,1)
```

then

```
A + B = (6,11,10,5)
```

The composite operators applicable to an array depend on the type of the range. Numeric operators may apply if the range is numeric, logical operators if the range is Boolean, and so on.

5. *Aggregate operators* — **Aggregate operators** operate on elements of the array type as a whole. They are more complex than the element-by-element application of the a composite operator. An example of such an aggregate operator is the unary plus, defined as summing the component of an array. Then

```
+(1,4,12) = 17
```

Most languages have few operators of this type, although the language APL has an extensive set of such operators in addition to many composite operators.

6. *Attributes* — **Attributes** of an array are values that are derived from the array's structure. Four attributes provided by Ada are FIRST, LAST, RANGE, and LENGTH, which return the first element of the domain space, the last element of the domain space, the range of values in the domain space, and the cardinality of the domain space. Ada specifies the attribute of an element by

```
<identifier> ' <attribute-name>
```

For example, if array A is declared by

```
type ATYPE is array (integer range <>) of character;
A : ATYPE (4..12);
```

then A'FIRST is 4, A'LAST is 12, A'RANGE is 4..12, and A'LENGTH is 9.

7. *Comparison* — The comparison operators for equality and inequality can be defined in a natural way on two operand arrays with domains of identical cardinality. Ordered comparisons of arrays are also provided by some languages if the arrays have compatible range types. In the case of Ada, ordering comparisons represent comparison in lexicographic order.

Lexicographic order is an extension of the standard alphabetical order for character arrays. We define "less than" in lexicographic order as follows:

```
A <ₐ B ≡ if B is null then false
           else if A is null then true
           else if A(A'FIRST)=B(B'FIRST) then
             A(A'FIRST+1..A'LAST) <ₐ B(B'FIRST+1..B'LAST)
           else A(A'FIRST) < B'(B'FIRST)
```

In this recursive definition, the attributes A'FIRST and A'LAST refer to the first and last elements in the domain space of A. The symbol $<_A$ is used to distinguish the less-than operator for arrays from the less-than operator defined on the range space which is denoted by <.

4.2.3 ▪ Multi-indexed Arrays

As mentioned earlier, it is possible to define a **multi-indexed array** as an array whose range type is itself an array. The notation for expressing such arrays can become burdensome, however. Hence, most imperative languages provide a separate facility for defining this construct, a facility based on a different model.

We introduce this new model through the use of an example, which we can compare to the earlier model. Recall the example given by

```
type ROW = array [1..10] of integer;
     TWOD = array [1..5] of ROW;
```

This case results in the following two array structures:

type	domain	range
ROW	1..10	integer
TWOD	1..5	ROW

Selection reference to an element A of type TWOD is of the form

```
A[ROWNUM][COLNUM]
```

where ROWNUM is in 1..5 and COLNUM is in 1..10.

The other view of this structure in Pascal is through the type declaration

```
type TWOD2 = array [1..5,1..10] of integer;
```

In this case, a single array is defined, with the following structure:

type	domain	range
TWOD2	(1..5)×(1..10)	integer

Here, the domain is the Cartesian product of the two ranges and selection reference to A of type TWOD2 is of the form

```
A[ROWNUM,COLNUM]
```

This latter view is preferred because of its more convenient selection notation. The extension of this representation to n > 2 indices is a straightforward extension to a Cartesian product of n finite subrange spaces to form the domain.

4.2.4 ▪ Implementation

We represent the implementation of aggregate data structures in two parts, a descriptor and the data itself. The descriptor contains all the necessary information about the structure and a pointer to the data. We describe each type's implementation by giving the fields of the descriptor, the organization of the data storage, and algorithms for common operations such as selection.

The descriptor may be needed only at compile time if all components of the descriptor remain unchanged throughout the execution of the program. Frequently, a run-time descriptor is needed to permit more dynamic structures.

Figure 4.3 shows the descriptor for an array. With this descriptor, the selection of a location that contains the range value for a given domain value DV is calculated by

```
Range-Location + (DV - Domain-First)*Range-Size
```

FIGURE 4.3　　**Array Implementation**

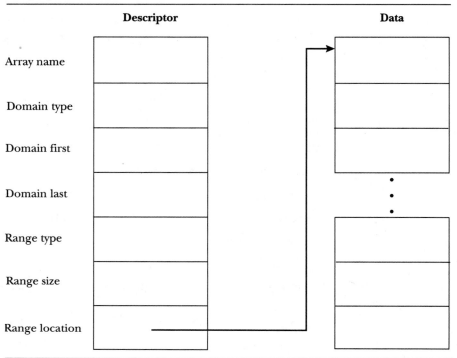

Range-Location is the location of the beginning of the array storage, Domain-First is the first value in the domain space, and Range-Size is the number of addressable locations occupied by each element of the array. This calculation assumes that either the domain is a subrange of the integers or (DV − Domain-First) is defined as the position number of DV in the Domain space minus the position of the element Domain-First. It also assumes that the array elements are stored in contiguous addressable locations.

This idea can be extended to doubly indexed arrays, as shown in Figure 4.4. The standard formula for calculating the location of the array element with indices DV_1 and DV_2 is

```
Range-Location + (DV₁ − Domain₁-First) *
        (Domain₂-Last − Domain₂-First + 1)*Range-Size
    + (DV₂ − Domain₂-First) * Range-Size
```

Here the first term added to Range-Location represents the number of locations skipped to pass over the first DV_1 − Domain$_1$-First rows, whereas the second term is the number of locations to skip over the first DV_2 − Domain$_2$-First columns in row DV_1. The assumption is that the array is stored by row, meaning that the first row is stored first, then the second, then the third, and

FIGURE 4.4   **Multi-indexed Array Implementation**

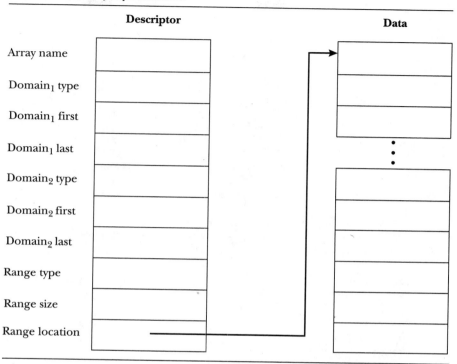

so on. Thus, the second index will vary the most rapidly as we progress through the memory locations of the data. This form of array storage is called **row major order**. In the case of A[1..5,4..7], the order of storage is

```
A[1,4],A[1,5],A[1,6],A[1,7],A[2,4],A[2,5],A[2,6],A[2,7],
A[3,4],A[3,5],A[3,6],A[3,7],A[4,4],A[4,5],A[4,6],A[4,7],
A[5,4],A[5,5],A[5,6],A[5,7]
```

The alternative order of storage is **column major order**, in which the first index varies most rapidly. Although row major order is the most common approach, FORTRAN is one well-known language that uses column major order.

Another factor in implementation of arrays is packing. The **packing** of array data refers to compressing the data into storage space that is smaller than the computer's addressable unit. Representing Boolean data with 1 bit or character data with 1 byte are examples of packing. If a computer has a 32-bit word, a Boolean array might fit into 1/32 of the storage space that would be required if it were stored unpacked.

The decision of whether to pack an array or not is based on a trade-off between saving storage space and saving time. Accessing packed data requires more complicated algorithms. This decision is usually made by the compiler,

although some languages, such as Pascal, permit the programmer to specify
when packing is desired.

4.2.5 ▪ **Arrays in Ada**

```
Arrays
Language: Ada
Definition
 1. Constrained array type definition
    array (<c-domain-type>{,<c-domain-type>}) of <range-type>
    where
    c-domain-type ::= <discrete-type> | <subrange>
 2. Unconstrained array type definition
    array (<u-domain-type>{,<u-domain-type>}) of <range-type>
    where
    u-domain-type ::= <type-name> range <>
 3. Definition of constraints on unconstrained type
    <unconstrained-array-name> (<subrange>{,<subrange>})
Manipulation
 1. Selection
    <array-identifier>(<index>{,<index>})
    where
    index ::= <domain-expression> | <domain-subrange>
 2. Construction
    (<component-association>{,<component-association>}
       [<other-association>])
    where
    component-association ::= [<choice>{| <choice>} =>]
                   <range-expression>
    choice ::= <domain-expression> | <domain-subrange>
    other-association ::= others => <range-expression>
 3. Assignment
    <array-identifier> := <array-expression>;
 4. Composite Operators
    and or xor not
    All apply to arrays with Boolean range
 5. Aggregate Operators
    &                 Catenation of arrays
 6. Attributes
    FIRST [(N)]   lower bound of Nth index subrange
    LAST [(N)]    upper bound of Nth index subrange
    RANGE [(N)]   Nth index subrange
    LENGTH [(N)] Number of elements in Nth index subrange
 7. Comparison
    =         True if all components are equal
    /=        True if at least one component not equal
    < <= > >= Lexicographic order tests
```

4.3 Strings

There are two different approaches taken by languages in the modeling of character strings. The first approach considers the strings as a special case of an array where the range type is type character. This approach, found in Ada and Pascal, uses the mapping model and provides the same operations for strings as for arrays.

There are a number of difficulties associated with the string-as-mapping model. First, the string, by its very nature, changes its size dynamically at run time. Array implementations usually fix the size of an array at compile time. Even those languages that permit run-time binding to size usually prevent that size from being dynamically changed once it is set. A second difficulty is that the operations that are commonly needed for strings are not available for arrays in general. Finally, the notation for expressing string constants is different than the notation used for expressing array constants.

For these reasons, it is advantageous to consider the alternative model of sequence for representing character strings. The primary advantage of a sequence is its dynamic and unlimited length property. BASIC and SNOBOL are two languages that use this approach.

4.3.1 ▪ **Declaration and Binding**

Because a string is of a dynamic nature, the declaration does not include a size restriction, except perhaps specifying some maximum size. When such a maximum is required, the compiler reserves storage space for the maximum number of characters, even though the actual size of the string can vary during run time up to that maximum. If no maximum is required, the binding of the string object to its location must be postponed until run time.

4.3.2 ▪ **Manipulation**

We will use the same general classes of operations here that we used for arrays, with attention to how they pertain to strings.

1. *Selection* — It is common for selection of characters from a string to involve the selection of several consecutive characters, known as a *substring*. Therefore, the most common selection operation is substring selection that requires two parameters: starting location and length or starting location and ending location. The latter form is equivalent to an array slice. Note that selection of a substring of length 1 is equivalent to a single-component selection, except that its type will be string rather than the constituent-type character.

2. *Construction* — Placing individual characters into a string is accomplished by placing the appropriate character sequence between quotation marks. The use of single or double quotes (' or ") is by far the most common option, and which is used depends on the syntax of the language.

3. *Assignment* — String assignment is usually provided as a direct extension of scalar assignment, using the same operator as well. Assignment to a string will dynamically change its size to the size of the assigned string.

4. *Composite operators* — These operators are not applicable to strings.

5. *Aggregate operators* — The most common aggregate operator is concatenation. This creates a new string consisting of the left operand string followed by the right operand string. The length function is another common aggregate operator. It has one operand — the string itself — and returns the number of characters in the string.

   Another frequently provided aggregate operator is a substring search function. The operands are the target string and a pattern string. The result is an integer specifying the position of the first occurrence of the pattern within the target.

6. *Attributes* — Although an ideal implementation for a string would not limit the length, it is often necessary to do so. When this is the case, the maximum length is an attribute.

7. *Comparison* — Comparison of strings is done according to lexicographic ordering.

4.3.3 ▪ Implementation

The implementation of strings is illustrated in Figure 4.5. The descriptor includes the length of the string plus a pointer to the first character. The string itself is frequently stored as a linked list to permit the length to grow without limit. The characters are typically blocked together to form each list element. In languages enforcing a maximum length, the implementation utilizes contiguous storage similar to that used in the implementation of arrays.

FIGURE 4.5   **Implementation of Strings**

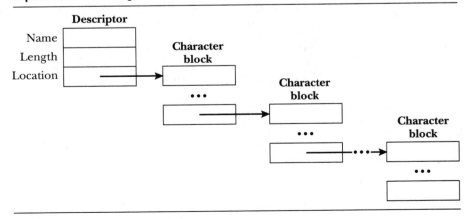

One additional consideration is that the dynamic nature of strings makes it necessary to reclaim string storage that is no longer in use through a technique known as **garbage collection**. We outline this process here:

1. All available, unused blocks for string storage are linked together into a list known as a *free list*.

2. As string storage is required, blocks are moved from the free list to the list for that string.

3. When the free list is nearly exhausted, the garbage collection process is activated. This process traces through the list of all current strings, marking each block encountered as "in use." It then recreates the free list by linking together all blocks not marked "in use."

4.3.4 • Strings in Ada

Ada takes a middle road between the mapping and sequence approaches to strings. Although it considers the string to be an array of characters, it provides array operators that facilitate string manipulation. For example, a concatenation operator is provided and comparison operators use lexicographic ordering. In addition, the representation of a string by inclusion of the characters within double quotes is equivalent to the usual array constructor, which encloses the elements in parentheses and separates them by commas. Therefore,

```
S := "A Test String";
```

is equivalent to

```
S := ('A',' ','T','e','s','t',' ','S','t','r','i','n','g');
```

Notice that string constants are distinguished from characters by the use of a double instead of a single quote. Therefore, `'A'` is a character, whereas `"A"` is a string consisting of one character.

Ada also provides a middle ground in the area of length binding. Like any other array, the Ada string can be bound to its domain space (and hence its size) by a run-time declaration. This is better than compile-time binding, but it falls short of the string ideal of binding at run-time assignment and permitting dynamic changes in the size of a string.

4.4 Records

The implementation of the Cartesian product model in a programming language is called a **record**, or *structure*. A record type is the Cartesian product of two or more other types, each of which may be simple or aggregate types themselves. The record type was first introduced in COBOL and is now available in all modern imperative languages.

4.4.1 ▪ Declaration and Binding

Record types are declared by specifying the name of the record type and, for each component of the record, the name and type of the component. For example, in Ada the simple form of a record declaration is

```
record
   <identifier-list> : <component-type> [:= <expression>];
  {<identifier-list> : <component-type> [:= <expression>];}
end record;
```

The bindings that occur are of the components to the record type and the component types and names to each component. All these bindings occur at compile time.

The expression being present in the preceding declaration causes run-time initialization of any data element of this component type or types to the value of the expression at the time the record element is declared. For example, if we have the declaration

```
type EXREC is record
                A : integer := 0;
                B : character := '*';
              end record;
```

then when a block is entered with the variable declaration

```
C : EXREC;
```

the components of C are initialized to 0 and '*'.

4.4.2 ▪ Manipulation

1. *Selection* — The selection of a component of a record is done by specifying the name of the record element and the component name. The form is commonly

   ```
   <record-identifier> . <component-name>
   ```

   although alternative notations can be used, such as in ALGOL 68, which selects by

   ```
   <component-name> of <record-identifier>
   ```

   Some languages, such as Pascal, permit a default specification of the record identifier within a block.

2. *Construction* — Record literals can be constructed in a manner similar to array literal construction, with a list of expressions either in the order of the components or paired with the component name. See the discussion of Ada records in a later section for a further description.

3. *Assignment* — Record assignment is of the usual form

   ```
   <record-identifier> := <record-expression>
   ```

   where both sides are of the same record type.

4. *Composite operators* — No composite operators are defined for records.

5. *Aggregate operators* — No aggregate operators are defined for records.

6. *Attributes* — The size of a record and its address are two attributes defined within Ada.

7. *Comparison* — Records of identical composition may be compared for equality and inequality.

4.4.3 ▪ Variant Records

Recall that a discriminated union model for a type consists of the union of all of the constituent types. It is discriminated by the presence of some component that determines which of the set of types is active at a given time.

Consider, for example, the discriminated union of the types T_1, T_2, T_3, T_4 with discriminant D having the type 1..4. Then the binding of a data object to a type occurs at run time, when the discriminant variable D is given a value. This is illustrated in Figure 4.6.

The implementation of this model in imperative languages is usually limited to its use in **variant records**. In this case, a part of a record is defined as a discriminated union of two or more other types. For example, the preceding situation could be written in Ada as

FIGURE *4.6* **Discriminated Union**

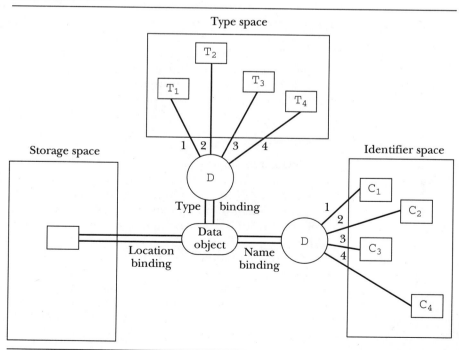

```
type T (D:integer) is record
  case D is
    when 1 => C1 : T1;
    when 2 => C2 : T2;
    when 3 => C3 : T3;
    when 4 => C4 : T4;
  end case;
end record;
```

The level of enforcement of the discriminated union varies from language to language. In most Pascal implementations, for example, all type checking occurs at compile time, so there is no enforcement at all. Any of the components C_i may be referenced at any point, regardless of the value of D. Ada, on the other hand, enforces the use of the **discriminant** by forcing all components of a record to be assigned using a record construction literal whenever the discriminant is assigned a new value. For example, assigning a value to C2 of a variable X of type T in the preceding example requires the statement

```
X := (D => 2, C2 => New_C2);
```

It is also possible to set the discriminant value to a permanent value in the declaration of a record. The declaration

```
X : T (D => 2);
```

restricts the variable X to the second variant definition throughout the extent of this variable.

In order to facilitate implementation, usually only one variant component is permitted within a record, and that component must be the last one. It is possible in Ada, however, for the variant component to itself end in a variant component, thus nesting variants to any level.

4.4.4 ▪ Implementation

Except for the variant part, a record descriptor can be easily constructed at run time, because all other components are of fixed size. The descriptor, as shown in Figure 4.7, contains the name and a pointer to the location of each component. Components are usually stored contiguously, as illustrated here, so the pointer to a component can be given as the offset from a base address.

The representation of a variant component of a record requires a different form. Figure 4.8 shows its format. Each alternative of the variant record is assumed to be of record type, so that a record descriptor is given for each alternative. Furthermore, the same storage is used for each alternative component, so that when a final mapping to data occurs, all components point to the same data area.

FIGURE 4.7   Record Implementation

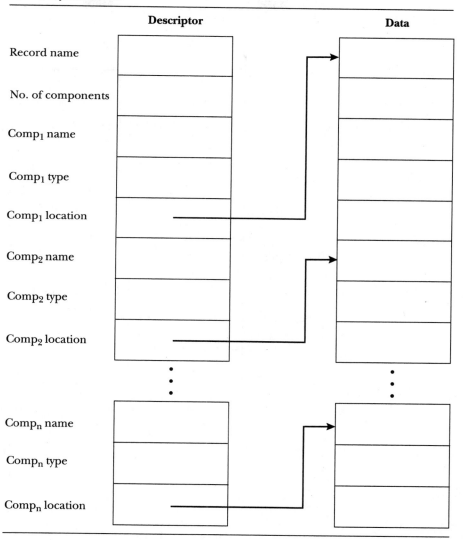

The nesting of data aggregates can occur at any level. When an aggregate is a component of another aggregate, the data pointer points to the descriptor of the aggregate rather than the data itself. An example of the implementation of a complex nested data aggregate is given in Figure 4.9. Note that all components of a record are stored contiguously, with the descriptor occupying that space if the component is an aggregate itself.

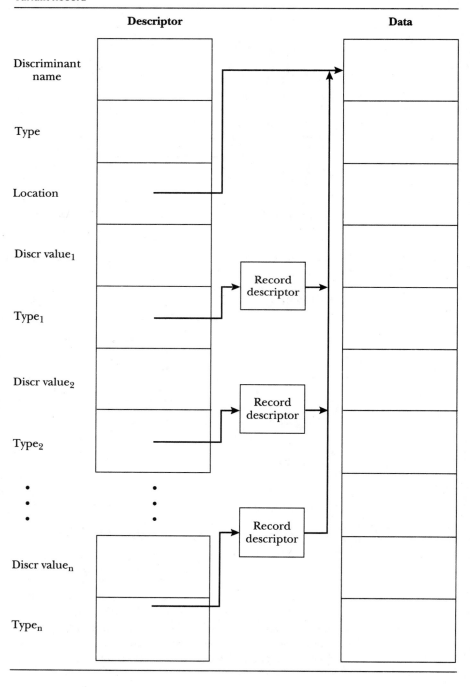

FIGURE *4.8*   **Variant Record**

FIGURE 4.9 **Nested Data Aggregates**

```
X : record;
   A : String;
   B : array (1..3) of character;
   C : integer;
   case D : 1..2 is
         when 1 => E : integer;
                   F : string;
         when 2 => G : real;
                   H : integer;
   end case;
end record;
```

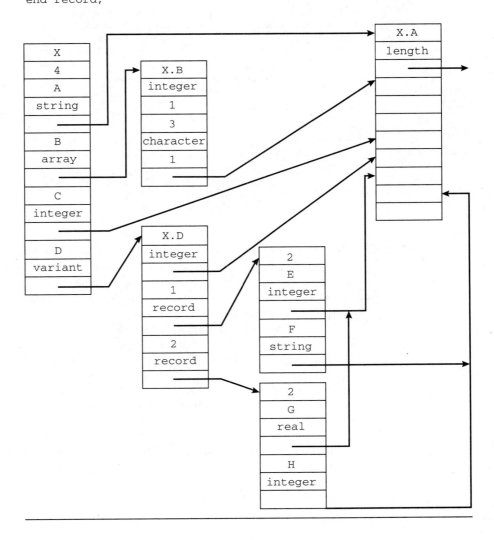

4.4.5 ▪ **Records in Ada**

The features of records in Ada are summarized in the following box.

```
Records
Language: Ada
Definition: record
            <component-list>
         end record;
   where
    <component-list> ::=
        <component-declaration>;{<component-declaration>;}
      | {<component-declaration>;} <variant-part>;
      | null;

    <component-declaration> ::=
    <identifier-list> : <subtype-declaration> [:= <expression>]
      <variant-part> ::=
         case <discriminant-name> is
            <variant>;
            {<variant>;}
            [others => <component-list>;]
         end case
    <variant> ::= when <choice> {|<choice>}=> <component-list>
     <choice> ::= <simple-expression> | <discrete-range>
```

4.5 Files

A second example of the sequence model of a data aggregate is the file. A **file** is a sequence of components of the same type, but unlike the string, whose components are always of character type, the file components may be of any type. A second distinguishing feature of the file is that it is typically stored in secondary storage rather than main storage.

Many languages do not define file as a type but rather treat it as a part of input/output processing. Pascal is one language that does take the approach of file as type, and we will base our brief discussion on the Pascal model for sequential files.

The declaration of a file in Pascal is of the form

```
file of <component-type>
```

This statement defines the type, and a separate facility is needed to bind the file to an actual physical file — a facility often provided by the operating system.

The set of Pascal operations on a file is limited to reset, rewrite, get, put, and component selection. The only component of a file that can be selected is the current one, which is accessible by `<file-name>^`. Other operations change the currently selected component. For example, `reset(<file-name>)` selects the first component of a file, and `get(<file-name>)` selects the next component after the current one.

When producing a file structure, `rewrite(<file-name>)` creates a blank structure and `put(<file-name>)` places the component presently in `<file-name>^` into the structure at the next position.

The most common operator on file type is end-of-file, which returns a Boolean that is true if no more components follow and is false otherwise.

4.6 Sets

Sets are the Pascal implementation of the powerset model. Sets are defined by

```
set of <component-type>
```

where the component type may be any finite subrange of integers, characters, or enumerated values. Possible elements of this type are all subsets of the elements in the defined base type of the set.

For example, with the Pascal declaration

```
type S = set of 1..4;
```

the set of possible values of type S is

```
{} {1} {2} {3} {4} {1,2} {1,3} {1,4} {2,3} {2,4}
{3,4} {1,2,3} {1,2,4} {1,3,4} {2,3,4} {1,2,3,4}
```

If the base type has cardinality C, the set type has cardinality 2^C.

The Pascal set constructor operation is denoted by enclosing those elements that are members of the set in brackets. For example, using the preceding definition of set type S, we can construct a set by

```
var X:S;
   ...
X := [1,2,4];
   ...
```

The `in` operator determines if an element is in the set or not. This makes possible statements such as

```
if 3 in X then ...
```

The common implementation of a set is with a Boolean array the size of the base set. A `true` in a position indicates that the corresponding element is included in the set, whereas a `false` indicates it is not. Figure 4.10 illustrates this representation.

FIGURE 4.10   **Boolean Array Representation of a Set**

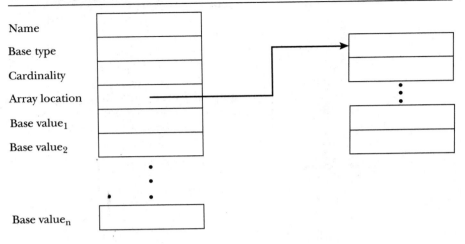

Name
Base type
Cardinality
Array location
Base value$_1$
Base value$_2$
Base value$_n$

Example: type S = Set of 1..4;
         var X : S;

X := [1,3];

Name	X	
Base type	Integer	True
Cardinality	4	False
Array location		True
Base value$_1$	1	False
Base value$_2$	2	
Base value$_3$	3	
Base value$_4$	4	

C H A P T E R **4**   **Terms**

data aggregate   mapping
constituent type   domain
cardinality   range
Cartesian product   discriminated union

sequence	row major order
powerset	column major order
array	packing
unconstrained array	garbage collection
composite operators	record
aggregate operators	variant record
attribute	discriminant
lexicographic order	file
multi-indexed array	

C H A P T E R *4*   Discussion Questions

1. What are the relative advantages and disadvantages in expressing a multi-indexed array as an array whose range is another array?

2. Why might the use of parentheses as index delimiters in a language be confusing?

3. Some languages permit nonhomogeneous arrays — that is, arrays whose components are not necessarily of the same type. What properties should a language have for such a structure to be compatible with the language, and how might such a structure be implemented?

4. Research the language APL. Examine the set of array operators built into that language and classify each as composite or aggregate.

5. How might you define A < B, where A and B are arrays, as a composite operator?

6. What is the value of having a type that is the union of types but not discriminated or where discrimination is not enforced?

C H A P T E R *4*   Exercises

1. Suppose type T_1 = {1,5,9} and T_2 = {a,b}.
   a. What is type $T_1 \times T_2$?
   b. What is type $T_2 \times T_1$?

2. Suppose type T_1 = {'a','test','to','see','if','you','know','how'} and T_2 = {0,1,2,3,4,5}. Define a mapping from T_1 to T_2 that maps a string into the number of characters it contains.

3. Suppose T_1 = {1,2} and T_2 = {true,false}.
   a. Define $T_1^* \times T_2^*$.
   b. Define $(T_1 \times T_2)^*$.
   c. Define $(2^{T_1})^*$.
   d. Define $2^{(T_1*)}$.

4. Extend the formula for computing the location of an element of a doubly indexed array to an array with N indices.

5. How would the formula for computing the location of an element of a doubly indexed array be changed if the array were stored in column major order?

6. Assume doubly indexed array A has domain (3..12) × (5..9), and each range element occupies two addressable storage cells. What is the address of each of the following if the array is stored beginning at location 1000 in row major order?

    a. A[3,5]

    b. A[12,9]

    c. A[7,5]

    d. A[8,7]

7. Construct a representation of the nested aggregate structures described below in a form similar to Figure 4.9.

    a. X : array (1..3) of record

    ```
                                A : integer;
                                B : array (Boolean) of character;
                                C : string;
                             end record;
    ```

    b. X : record

    ```
                  A : string;
                  case B: 1..2 is
                    when 1 => C : integer;
                                case D 0..1 is
                                   when 0 => E : real;
                                   when 1 => F : integer;
                                end case;
                    when 2 => G : Boolean;
                  end case;
               end record;
    ```

C H A P T E R 4   **Laboratory Exercises**

In the following exercises, you are to work with a language or languages whose implementation you have available to you and determine the answers to the questions by constructing a sample program or programs and observing the results.

1. When is the index of an array checked against its domain type?

2. When is the domain of a array bound to the array?

3. What types are permitted for the domain of an array?

4. What types are permitted for the range of an array?

5. Is array assignment permitted? How are arrays with different domains and the same cardinality handled?

6.   Is ordering defined on arrays? If so, how?

7.   Is there a maximum length enforced on strings? Is it user definable?

8.   If your language has variant records, is the discriminant selection enforced? Is assignment permitted to components not currently activated by the discriminant?

Procedural Abstraction

Among the most powerful of the tools contained in a programming language are those that allow procedural abstraction. An **abstraction** is a representation of an object that hides what could be considered as irrelevant details of that object, thus making use of the object easier. Procedural abstraction involves abstracting out the relevant details of a procedure from the irrelevant ones (Liskov and Guttag 1986). The two ways in which it does this — through parametric abstraction and through specification abstraction — are described in detail.

The syntax of procedure definition and invocation is examined. The environment in which a procedure operates is studied, with special attention paid to scope and binding of data objects.

Languages offer a variety of methods for passing parameters and these variations are described and compared. Whereas the common form for procedures serves as an abstraction of a statement, the value-returning procedure is an abstraction for an expression.

Some languages permit a further abstraction of procedures over parameter type through a technique called *overloading*. The concept of coroutines is introduced, and the procedure constructs that are found in the programming language Ada are summarized.

A language feature known as *exception handling*, where an abstract block of statements is invoked implicitly by the occurrence of a condition rather than explicitly by a call to a procedure, is examined and the approach used for exception handling in the programming language Ada is described.

5.1 Procedures as Abstractions

We have seen examples of abstraction in our earlier study. The record type, for example, is a low-level abstraction. This type permits the user to manipulate a record by name, ignoring the details such as component names and types when such details are irrelevant. Such an abstraction is useful when we wish to assign one entire record to another or pass an entire record as a parameter.

In this chapter we consider the procedure as an abstraction of a program unit into a simpler execution unit, such as a statement or an expression. In the course of making this abstraction, irrelevant details will be hidden from the user of the abstraction.

The advantages of using procedural abstractions are as follows:

1. Program units are simpler. This simplicity results in units that are easier to read, write, and modify. By hiding lower levels of detail, a unit can concentrate on a single task. This property is important in the implementation of top-down design.

2. Program units are independent. Abstraction permits the actions of a procedure to be independent from its use. Therefore, the program using the abstraction is not affected by the details of the abstraction's implementation.

3. Program units are reusable. A procedure, once defined, can be used within many different programming environments. This eliminates redundant programming effort and reduces errors.

In order to understand the role of procedural abstraction, recall the four levels of execution units described in Chapter 3. These execution units are expression, statement, block, and program, listed in increasing order of complexity, because a statement may contain several expressions, a block may contain several statements, and a program may contain several blocks. Procedural abstraction is, in effect, the representation of one execution unit by another one that is simpler. In practice, it is commonly the representation of a block by either an expression or a statement.

As an example, consider the following Pascal procedure:

```
procedure USELESS;
begin
  writeln('This is the result');
  writeln('of an execution');
  writeln('of procedure USELESS.');
end; {USELESS}
```

This defines USELESS to be a block of three statements that can be represented as a single statement, namely,

```
USELESS;
```

This abstracted statement can be used anywhere that a statement is appropriate. Similarly, a function in Pascal defines a block that can be represented as an expression.

Just as data types and objects, which are defined in Chapter 3, have various bindings, so do procedure types and objects. Figure 5.1 illustrates the bindings of a procedure type. The procedure type is bound to its name and its executable block by its declaration. These bindings both occur at compile time. Further bindings are introduced in later sections as they are required.

5.2 Procedure Definition and Invocation

The definition of the procedure specifies all the compile-time bindings that must occur. It is analogous to the definition of a data type. At this point, the two bindings that must be specified are name and executable block. For example, the simple form for Pascal is

```
procedure <procedure name>;
begin
  <procedure-block>
end;
```

FIGURE 5.1   Procedure Type

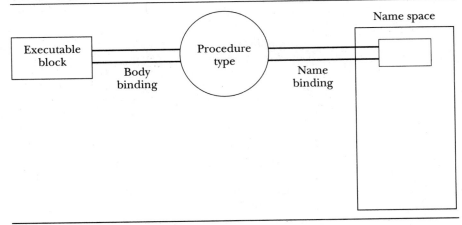

The invocation of a procedure is written as the procedure name, and it represents an abstract statement. This causes the executable block of statements associated with the procedure to be executed. In effect, it results in a further binding, the binding of the procedure object to an activation of the procedure. This binding, by its very nature, must occur at run time. A single defined procedure can have any number of activations at a given time. The activations of a procedure are similar to the variables of a given data type. Whereas the entrance of a block containing a declaration of a data variable creates a data object bound to the declared type, the invocation of a procedure creates the procedure object bound to the named procedure definition. This binding is illustrated in Figure 5.2.

This analogy between data types and procedures is very important. Consider the following examples. The statements

```
TYPE T is ...;
V1,V2 : T;
```

declare T to be a data type that is bound to its definition at compile time and V1 and V2 to be variables, or instances, of type T that are bound to their type and locations at run time, upon entry to the block in which they are declared. There may be many instances of the same type that are bound at run time.

Similarly, the declaration

```
PROCEDURE T is ...
```

declares T to be a procedure that is bound to its definition at compile time. Each invocation of T causes an activation of T that is created at run time. Each activation binds the procedure type T to an activation record in the same way that a variable declaration binds the object to its data type.

FIGURE 5.2   **Procedure Activation**

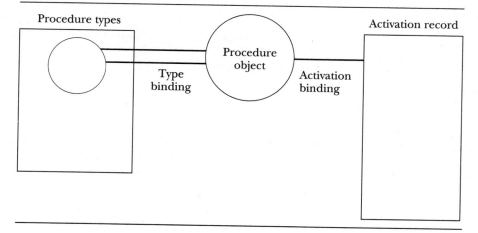

5.3 Procedure Environment

5.3.1 ▪ Activation Record

The invocation of a procedure results in the creation of an **activation record** for that procedure. The general form of the activation record consists of three parts: the local environment, the parameter environment, and a nonlocal environment pointer. The local environment contains all data objects that are defined locally inside this procedure. The parameter environment contains information about all data objects that are passed to and from the procedure. We postpone a detailed discussion of this environment until Section 5.4. The nonlocal environment pointer points to the activation record from which the present activation will inherit objects and their bindings. We call such inherited objects *nonlocal data objects.*

When a procedure is invoked, its activation record is pushed onto the **run-time stack** of activation records. When the procedure terminates, its activation record is popped off the run-time stack, making its invoking program unit the new top-of-stack activation record and, hence, the currently active program unit. Therefore, the run-time stack contains the activation records of all program units that are currently in the midst of execution. Only the unit whose activation record is on top of the stack is actually executing. The other units are suspended until all units above them in the stack are terminated and thus popped off the stack. To illustrate the use of activation records and the run-time stack, consider the Pascal program shown in Figure 5.3. The state of the run-time stack at each stage of execution is also found in this figure. Note that the invocation of a procedure causes an activation record to be placed on top of the stack; its termination pops off that activation record. Also note that recursion, as with procedure r, results in the stacking of multiple activation records of the same procedure. In this figure, no details are shown for the contents of the activation record. These are filled in later.

5.3.2 ▪ Local Environment

The **local environment** of a procedure includes the locally declared data objects. They are specified in the local environment section of the activation record. Also included in the local environment is a pointer to the next instruction to be executed in the procedure, known as the *return address pointer.* This pointer permits the activation record to store the location where execution will resume upon return from an invocation and allows multiple activations of the same procedure to specify different execution addresses.

One further category of information in the local environment is the temporary storage needed to retain data within expression evaluations. For example, execution of a procedure can be suspended by a function call in the middle of a statement. The parts of the expression that have already been evaluated need to be stored in the local environment so that they can be accessed when the invoked function returns control. This temporary storage is

FIGURE 5.3 **Sample Program and Status of Run-time Stack**

```
program p;
var i;

procedure q;
begin
   ...
end;

procedure r;
begin
   i:=i-1;
   if i>0 then
      r
   else
      q;
end;

procedure s;
begin
   r;
   q;
end;

begin --p
   i:=2;
   s;
end.
```

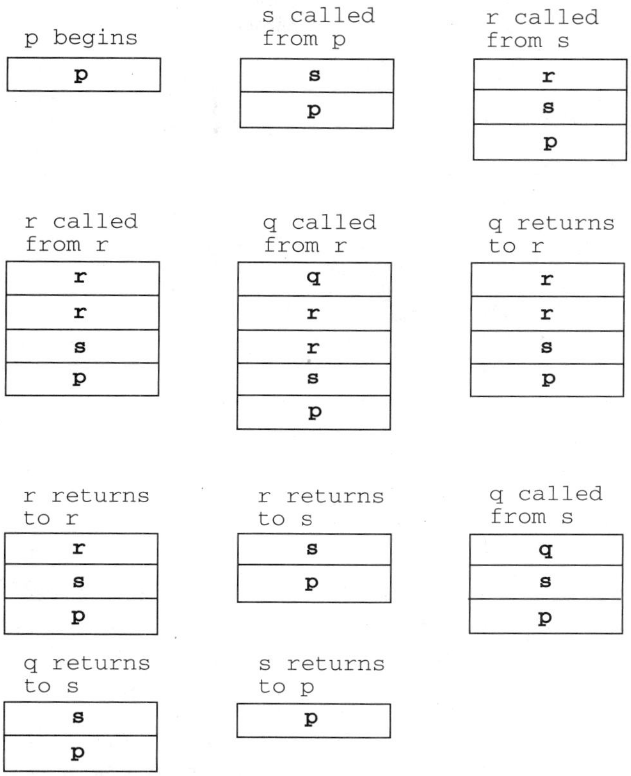

p begins
| p |

s called from p
| s |
| p |

r called from s
| r |
| s |
| p |

r called from r
| r |
| r |
| s |
| p |

q called from r
| q |
| r |
| r |
| s |
| p |

q returns to r
| r |
| r |
| s |
| p |

r returns to r
| r |
| s |
| p |

r returns to s
| s |
| p |

q called from s
| q |
| s |
| p |

q returns to s
| s |
| p |

s returns to p
| p |

highly implementation-dependent, so we do not mention it any further in our discussion.

If we extend the example of Figure 5.3 to add some local data objects and to show the contents of the local environment part of the activation record, we have the resulting Figure 5.4. The arrows in this figure represent the pointers to the next executable statement.

5.3.3 · Nonlocal Environment

Most imperative languages permit a procedure to access data objects other than those local to the procedure itself. The environment where these objects are bound is called the procedure's **nonlocal environment**. This environment can be represented in the procedure's activation record by a pointer to the activation record whose local and nonlocal environments will determine the nonlocal environment of the present activation record. In other words, when a data object is referenced whose name is not bound in the local environment, the nonlocal environment is next searched to satisfy the reference.

FIGURE **5.4**　　**Sample Program and Run-time Stack**

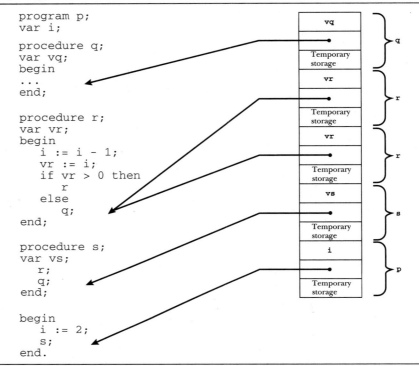

```
program p;
var i;

procedure q;
var vq;
begin
   ...
end;

procedure r;
var vr;
begin
   i := i - 1;
   vr := i;
   if vr > 0 then
      r
   else
      q;
end;

procedure s;
var vs;
   r;
   q;
end;

begin
   i := 2;
   s;
end.
```

The most common manner for defining the nonlocal environment is through **static scope**. In this case, the nonlocal environment of a procedure is inherited from the program unit in which the procedure is defined. Stated differently, any name used in a procedure but not bound within that procedure inherits the binding that the name has in the program unit that immediately contains the procedure. Note that this concept is identical to the static scope definitions of blocks that we introduced in Chapter 3.

We illustrate this static definition of nonlocal environments through the example in Figure 5.5. These bindings are completely specified at compile time, because they are determined by the placement of the procedures within the program itself. The procedures themselves are bound to their names in the same way as variables. Note, for example, that procedure r in Figure 5.5 is not a part of the nonlocal environment of procedure s, because it is not bound in s or in p, the containing unit of s.

Although the nonlocal environment of a procedure can be determined by type at compile time, it needs to be specified at run time in the activation record, because the procedure must refer to a specific activation record of the containing unit. Suppose the run-time stack for the program of Figure 5.5 has been constructed as in Figure 5.6. Here we specify only the nonlocal environment pointer. Each activation record points to the most recent activation

FIGURE 5.5   **Example to Illustrate Static Definition of Global Environment**

```
Program p;
var a,b,c : integer;

        procedure q;
        var a,c : integer;
            procedure r;
            var a : integer;
            begin {r}
                 {variables: a from r; b from p; c from q
                 procedures: q from p; r from q}
            end; {r}
        begin {q}
            {variables: a from q; b from p; c from q
            procedures: q from p; r from q}
        end; {q}
        procedure s;
        var b : integer
        begin {s}
            {variables: a from p; b from s; c from p
            procedures: q from p; s from p}
        end; {s}

begin {p}
    {variables: a,b,c from p
    procedures: q,s from p}
end. {p}
```

record of the containing program unit. Notice the importance of the phrase *most recent.* In the case of r in Figure 5.6, its containing unit is q, but q has two activation records on the run-time stack. The question is, to which version of q should r refer when accessing variable c? This is resolved by specifying the most recently invoked version — that is, the one whose activation record is nearest the top of the stack. The nonlocal environment pointers now form a linked list that specifies the nonlocal environment of a procedure. In Figure 5.6, the chain beginning at r goes through q and p. This means that if a reference is unresolved in r, the second activation of procedure q will next be interrogated, and if the reference is still unresolved, p will be tried. This chain represents the nesting of procedures within other program units in the physical code of the program.

A second natural approach to the binding of the nonlocal environment to a procedure is to use the environment of the program unit that invokes the procedure as that procedure's nonlocal environment. This technique is called **dynamic scope**, and the run-time stack in Figure 5.6 would be modified as shown in Figure 5.7 under the dynamic scope rule. Note that dynamic scope means that a procedure inherits as its nonlocal environment the environment of the program unit that invokes it and hence can be determined only at run time. On the other hand, with static scope the nonlocal environment is inherited from

FIGURE 5.6   **Global Environment — Static Scope Pointers**

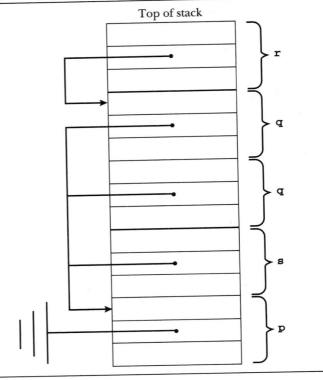

the program unit that physically contains the procedure, a relationship which can be determined at compile time, except for the case of multiple executions of that containing procedure, as described earlier. Note that although the illustrations in Figures 5.6 and 5.7 involve nested procedure calls, static and dynamic scope can cause different actions even when such nesting does not occur.

On initial observation, dynamic scoping seems to have several advantages over static scope. First, the nonlocal variable pointer could actually be eliminated altogether with dynamic scope, because the chain of activation records follows the physical ordering of the stack. In other words, the invoking unit is always the next one down the stack.

However, the dynamic nature of the environment proves to be a severe detriment to writing understandable programs, because the nonlocal environment of a procedure cannot be determined by examining the source code. Consider, for example, the program in Figure 5.8. A reference to variable a in procedure q could refer to variable a from p or variable a from r, depending on the point from which q is invoked. This problem greatly detracts from the understandability of the program and could be the source of great confusion. For this reason, static scope is the chosen method of defining a nonlocal procedure environment in most imperative languages.

FIGURE **5.7**   **Global Environment — Dynamic Scope Pointers**

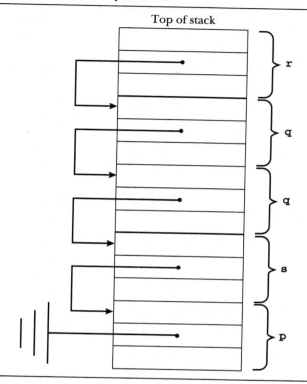

A third approach to nonlocal environments also has some merit. This approach involves disallowing them altogether, requiring the entire environment to be local or passed explicitly. The use of nonlocal environments is frequently discouraged, because it produces side effects. A **side effect** is the changing of the environment of a program unit without the change being specified in the code of that unit. An invoked procedure modifying a variable that it inherits in its nonlocal environment is an example of this.

No present imperative language takes the extreme position of eliminating the nonlocal environment altogether, but it would seem a worthy compromise lies in the approach taken by FORTRAN. Whereas languages such as Pascal, Ada, and Modula-2 require no declaration of objects in the nonlocal environment of a procedure, FORTRAN requires that nonlocal objects be declared in the procedure heading (for example, COMMON declarations). FORTRAN is actually forced into this by the fact that it does not require the declaration of local variables. Therefore, FORTRAN assumes a data object is local unless it is declared otherwise while the other languages assume it is nonlocal unless declared otherwise. A compromise might be to require that both local and nonlocal objects be declared, resulting in no implicitly bound objects.

FIGURE **5.8**   **Example Illustrating Dynamic Scope**

```
program p;
var a : integer

    procedure q;
    begin
        {variables: a from p or r
         procedures: q,r from p}
    end; {q}
    procedure r;
    var a : integer;
    begin
        {variables: a from r
         procedures: q,r from p}
        q;
    end; {r}

begin {p}
    {variables: a from p
     procedures: q,r from p}
    q;
end; {p}
```

5.4   Parameters

The third part of the procedure environment is the parameter part. The **parameters** are the means by which information is passed between the invoking and called units. We will categorize the parameters in three ways: (1) IN parameters, which are passed from the invoking unit to the procedure at the time of invocation, (2) OUT parameters, which are passed from the procedure to the invoking unit at the time of return, and (3) IN OUT parameters, which pass information both ways. The first two categories are restrictions of the third and are often included in languages to ensure the security of information. IN parameters are frequently referred to as parameters passed by value. IN OUT parameters are commonly called parameters passed by reference.

A parameter needs to be specified at two points: in the invoking unit and in the procedure definition itself. The specification in the invoking unit is called the **actual parameter**. It specifies the value to be sent for an IN parameter and the location to receive the returned value for an OUT parameter. This requires the actual parameter for an OUT or IN OUT parameter to be the name of an object that indicates a location where the result can be returned. An actual IN parameter can be any expression that results in a value of the desired type being passed.

A **formal parameter** is the specification of the parameter within the invoked procedure.

5.4.1 ▪ Parameter Association

In a procedure, the formal parameter is represented by a name that is referenced just like a variable within the procedure. It is also customary that the type of the parameter be specified in the procedure header by attaching a type to the formal parameter. Corresponding actual and formal parameters are required to be of the same type in a strongly typed language.

There are two modifications to this requirement that allow the formal parameter to be bound to a type at run time when the procedure is called. The more radical approach is to leave the formal parameter untyped and have it take on the type of the actual parameter. This is not compatible with compile-time type checking, however, because the type of the formal parameter in this situation is unknown at compile time. A less severe alternative is to permit an unconstrained array type for the formal parameter. The formal parameter then takes on the index constraints of the corresponding actual parameter at the time of invocation. This permits compile-time type checking to prevail, because the base type or range of the formal parameter array is specified in the procedure heading. Overloading and generics are other facilities for dealing with type correspondence and they will be discussed later.

There are two possible methods for associating actual and formal parameters. They are by position and by name. **Positional parameter association** is used by most imperative languages and simply associates the actual and formal parameters according to their relative positions in their parameter lists. **Named parameter association** requires that the name of the formal parameter be appended to the actual parameter in the invocation statement. Suppose that the following is the heading of an Ada procedure:

```
procedure TEST(A:in Atype; B:in out Btype; C out Ctype)
```

Then a call of TEST using positional association might be

```
TEST(X,Y,Z);
```

Here the actual parameters X, Y, and Z would be associated with formal parameters A, B, and C, respectively. A named association call might be

```
TEST(A=>X, C=>Z, B=>Y);
```

In this case, the formal parameter name is attached to the actual parameter to indicate association. Finally, Ada permits a mixture of the two, such as

```
TEST(X, C=>Z, B=>Y);
```

In the mixed association, positional can be used for all parameters up to the first named association, after which all remaining associations must be named.

One further association technique is the **default parameter association**. This permits the specification of default values for formal parameters in the procedure header. When an invocation is made with no actual parameter associated with the formal parameter, the default value is used. This is, of course, appropriate only for IN parameters.

5.4.2 ▪ IN Parameters

IN parameters can be implemented in two ways: as a reference or as a copy. When implemented as a reference, the location of the actual parameter is passed into the procedure and becomes the location of the formal parameter as well. In order to ensure that the formal parameter is not modified in the procedure, the compiler will check that it is never used in a context that might lead to modification. This includes appearing on the left side of an assignment and being used as an OUT or IN OUT actual parameter in the call to another procedure. In essence, the reference IN parameter is treated just like a named constant within the procedure.

The implementation of an IN parameter by copy requires that the formal parameter be treated as a local variable that is initialized to be equal to actual parameter value. The formal parameter can then be modified during procedure execution, but this will have no effect on the actual parameter's value. This model is the one used by default parameter passing in Pascal.

The copy implementation is less efficient in both time and storage space, especially when dealing with parameters of aggregate data types. In this case, duplicate storage needs to be reserved, and the time to copy the values of the actual to the formal parameter might be significant. The copy implementation does have the advantage of being more flexible, in that it permits modification of the formal parameter locally and may, therefore, reduce the need for local variables.

5.4.3 ▪ OUT Parameters

OUT parameters are the least frequently implemented of the three types, because they can usually be replaced with IN OUT parameters without any loss in utility or efficiency. Like IN parameters, OUT parameters can be implemented by reference or by copy. If implemented by reference, the location of the actual parameter is passed. In order to distinguish this mode from IN OUT, the compiler usually prevents access to such parameters in the procedure except for modification of the value. The actual parameter must be the name of a data object, and its value upon entry to the procedure must never be used inside the procedure.

Implementation by copy treats the formal parameter like a local variable whose initial value is undefined. At the termination of the procedure, the value of the formal parameter is then passed to the actual parameter. As with IN parameters, the copy implementation is less efficient when the parameter is of aggregate type.

5.4.4 ▪ IN OUT Parameters

As with IN parameters and OUT parameters, **IN OUT parameters** can be implemented by reference or by copy. Implementation by reference passes the location of the actual parameter to the formal parameter. There are no restrictions, then, on the use of the formal parameter inside the procedure. Pascal uses this model for its VARed parameters.

The IN OUT copy implementation combines the actions of IN and the OUT copy implementations. A local variable is created for the formal parameter and the actual parameter value is copied into the variable at the time of invocation. On termination of the procedure, the final value of the formal parameter is copied into the actual parameter location. The IN OUT copy implementation is commonly called **value-result parameter passing**.

The effects of these two implementations are the same except for the fact that implementation by reference causes immediate modification of the actual parameter each time the formal is modified, whereas implementation by copy delays any effect on the actual parameter until the termination of the procedure.

5.4.5 ▪ **Aliasing**

One problem that can arise in the passing of parameters and the use of nonlocal environments is **aliasing**. Aliasing is the ability to reference the same location by different names. To illustrate this problem, consider the Pascal program in Figure 5.9. Here the assignment statement in the procedure uses three data objects, X, A, and Y, where X and Y are formal parameters and A is a nonlocal variable. The call statement TEST(A,A) causes all three data objects to be bound to the same location, hence creating aliasing. This practice drives the understandability of the procedure to new lows and forces the programmer to depend on deeper levels of the language implementation. For example, the output from the program in Figure 5.9 depends on whether the VAR parameters of Pascal are implemented by copy or reference. The latter is the case, and the program prints

```
2 2 2
```

If a copy implementation were used by Pascal, which it is not, the program would print

```
1 2 1
```

because X and Y would have separate locations and A would not be changed until the procedure TEST terminates. Furthermore, because X would be 2 and Y would be 1 on termination of TEST and both would copy their values back into A, the order in which they are copied would affect the resulting value of A.

Aliasing can occur when nonlocal variables and formal parameters implemented by reference share the same location or when two actual parameters share the same location. Although implementing parameters by copy eliminates aliasing, it might still result in an ambiguity when two OUT or IN OUT actual parameters reference the same data object.

Some languages, such as Euclid, prevent aliasing by detecting situations that lead to it at compile time and, where that is impossible, generating runtime checks to detect its occurrence. Such testing generates a significant amount of overhead, usually too much for practical use.

```
program MAIN;

var A : integer;

        procedure TEST(var X,Y : integer);
        begin
             X := A + Y;
             writeln(A,X,Y);
        end;

begin
     A := 1;
     TEST(A,A);
end.
```

5.4.6 ▪ Procedures as Parameters

An additional feature available in some languages is the use of procedures as parameters. In specifying the formal procedure parameter, it is necessary that the types of all parameters to the procedure be specified as well, so that type checking can be performed when the formal procedure is called. Figure 5.10 shows a Pascal program that uses a procedure as a parameter. Procedure TEST-POS is called twice, the first time using E1 as the actual parameter procedure for formal parameter ERROR, and the second time using E2 as the actual parameter.

One confusing aspect of the Pascal implementation is that the formal procedure parameter must have formal parameter names expressed in its definition, whereas only the types of these parameters are used. This formal parameter name is MSG in Figure 5.10. Such formal parameters of formal procedure parameters have no meaning within the procedure but appear only as place holders so the parameter types can be specified.

A further consideration in the use of procedures as parameters is the information about them that must be passed into a procedure at invocation time. For a procedure, there are two items, the location of the executable code and a pointer to the nonlocal environment's activation record. These two items are all that are needed to create the activation record for the parametric procedure when it is invoked.

5.4.7 ▪ Name Parameters

A different form of parameter passing was implemented in the ALGOL 60 language. This form is called the **name parameter**, or parameters passed by name. Such parameters are implemented by the binding of the name of the actual parameter to the formal parameter on invocation of the procedure. This is conveniently visualized as a run-time textual substitution of the actual parameter name for the formal parameter within the procedure.

FIGURE 5.10   **Pascal Program to Illustrate Passing a Procedure as a Parameter**

```
program MAIN;

var A : real;

    procedure TESTPOS(X : real; procedure ERROR(MSG:String);
    begin
        if X <=0 then
          ERROR ('Negative X in TESTPOS');
    end;
    procedure E1 (M : STRING);
    begin
        writeln('E1 Error: ',M);
    end;
    procedure E2 (M : STRING);
    begin
        writeln('E2 Error: ',M);
    end;
    begin
        readln (A);
        TESTPOS(A,E1);
        TESTPOS(A,E2);
    end.
```

Name parameters behave identically to IN OUT parameters implemented by reference as long as the name of the actual parameter remains bound to the same location throughout the execution of the procedure. This may not be the case, however, especially when an actual parameter is an array element. Consider the procedure

```
procedure swap(a,b: integer);
var temp:integer;
begin
  temp := a;
  a := b;
  b := temp;
end;
```

If we assume that the formal parameters a and b are name parameters, then in the program

```
program main;
var i:integer;
    m:array [1..100] of integer;
    ...
begin
  ...
  swap(m[i],i);
  ...
end.
```

the call to swap will yield a different result than if the parameters were IN OUT. Because the names of m[i] and i are passed, the procedure, after textual substitution, will be executed as

```
temp := m[i];
i := temp;
m[i] := i;
```

The index i in the third line will be modified by the assignment in the second line, resulting in the destination location of the final assignment being different from the location referenced on the right-hand side of the first assignment.

Another anomaly occurs with name parameters when one of the actual parameter's names is the same as a local variable of the procedure. Suppose our main program that calls swap is

```
program main;
var i,temp:integer;
    . . .
begin
  . . .
  swap(i,temp);
  . . .
end.
```

Name parameter passing results in the execution of

```
temp := temp;
i := temp;
temp := i;
```

Confusion results because there are two data objects bound to the name temp in this procedure, one local to the procedure and the other local to the calling program unit. Each reference to temp in the execution of swap must be resolved to one of these objects. The method used by ALGOL 60 is to bind name parameters to the data object to which the corresponding actual parameter name is bound in the invoking program unit. In the case of our example, the two objects named temp would be referenced according to

```
temp_swap := temp_main;
i := temp_swap;
temp_main := i;
```

Here the subscripts are used to differentiate the references to the two objects bound to the name temp.

Because of the problems just described and the difficulty in implementing name parameters, they have not been provided in imperative languages since ALGOL 60.

5.5 Value-Returning Procedures

The second level of procedural abstraction is realized by **value-returning procedures (VRPs)**, which are commonly known as *functions*. These represent blocks that are abstractions of expressions and return a single value of their defined type.

In the definition of a VRP, one additional piece of information needs specification: the type of the value returned. Some languages label such procedures as functions and others label them as procedures and differentiate them from statement abstractions by appending a type to be returned. For example, in Pascal, the definition of a VRP is written as

```
function F(X:XType; Y:YType) : ResultType;
```

whereas Modula-2 defines the same VRP with

```
procedure F(X:XType; Y:YType) : ResultType;
```

Other than the use of the words *function* and *procedure*, the two definitions are identical. The Modula-2 form emphasizes that a VRP is nothing more than a procedure that returns a value. When a VRP is invoked, it is placed into the same context in the invoking program that any expression of the same type might occupy.

Within the VRP, there are two common methods employed to specify the value which is to be returned. The first, used by Pascal, is to create a pseudovariable in the local environment that is bound to the name of the VRP. The pseudovariable differs from a variable in the sense that it is not declared within the VRP and it can only be modified and not accessed within the VRP. It may never appear as a variable on the right-hand side of an assignment statement, for example. The value stored in that variable on termination of the VRP is the value returned to the invoking program. This method requires that a data object for the return value be added to the local environment part of the activation record of the VRP.

The second approach, exemplified by Ada, is to use a RETURN statement with an expression following the word RETURN. When this statement is executed, the expression is evaluated, the VRP is terminated, and the value of the expression is returned as the value of the VRP.

One further consideration with VRPs is the mode permitted for the parameters. There is no difficulty in implementing the same three modes (IN, OUT, IN OUT) as used in standard procedures. The side effects of using OUT or IN OUT parameters in VRPs are not desirable, however, because an expression, which the VRP abstracts, should not change any values in the environment.

5.6 Overloading

Overloading of procedures permits two or more procedures to have the same name if they can be distinguished by the number or type of their parameters or, in the case of a VRP, by the type of the return value. Such overloading permits procedures that perform the same operation on different parameter types to be called by the same name. The use of this feature is discussed further in Chapter 6 under data abstraction.

The language Ada provides a good example of procedure overloading. Figure 5.11 shows an example of the use of this facility. Here the VRP F is overloaded. The five different definitions of F are distinguished by the types of the parameters, the number of parameters, the order of the parameters, and the type of the returned value.

5.7 Coroutines

A variation of the procedure that is implemented in some programming languages is the coroutine. Whereas a procedure, when invoked, executes from the beginning of its body to the end, a **coroutine** executes from the point

FIGURE 5.11   **Example of Overloading in Ada**

```
procedure MAIN is
     R : FLOAT := 0.0;
     I : INTEGER := 0;
     function F(X : FLOAT) return INTEGER is
     begin
          return 1;
     end F;
     function F(X : INTEGER) return INTEGER is
     begin
          return 2;
     end F;
     function F(X : FLOAT; Y : INTEGER) return INTEGER is
     begin
          return 3;
     end F;
     function F(X : INTEGER ; Y : FLOAT) return INTEGER is
     begin
          return 4;
     end F;
     function F(X : INTEGER) return FLOAT is
     begin
          return 5.0;
     end F;
 begin --MAIN
     put (F(R)); --Prints 1
     put (F(I)); --Prints 2
     put (F(R,I)); --Prints 3
     put (F(I,R)); --Prints 4
     R := F(I);
     put (INTEGER (R)); — Prints 5
end MAIN;
```

where it last suspended execution up to the next instruction that suspends its execution. In other words, a procedure, when invoked, has its entire body executed, whereas a coroutine may have only a portion of its body executed before it is suspended. The relationship between a coroutine and its invoking body is illustrated in Figure 5.12.

The pseudolanguage model that we will use in our description considers coroutines to be variables to which an executable body can be bound. In this way, several coroutine variables can be bound to the same executable body at the same time and therefore be in the midst of execution. All but at most one will be suspended at any time, because only one coroutine alternative can be actively executing. Also, for our model, we will assume that the bodies to which coroutines are bound are described as parameterless procedures. We will specify the declaration of coroutine variables through statements of the form

```
C : COROUTINE;
```

Four basic coroutine operations are included in our model. The first is CREATE, which binds the coroutine variable to a parameterless procedure body. Its general form is

```
CREATE <coroutine-variable-name> FROM
       <parameterless-procedure-name>
```

FIGURE 5.12   **Coroutine Execution**

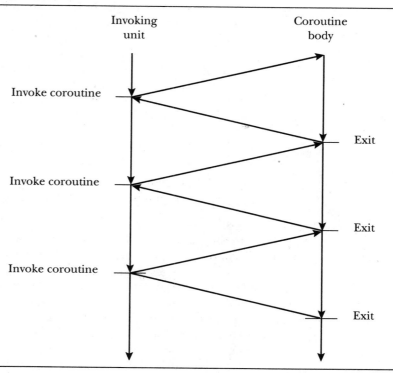

The CREATE statement creates an activation record for the coroutine and binds it to its name and procedure body. It also sets the current execution location in the activation record to the beginning of the procedure.

The DELETE statement deletes the activation record associated with its coroutine variable parameter. Its general form is

DELETE <coroutine-variable-name>

A coroutine is invoked through the RESUME statement, which is of the form

RESUME <coroutine-variable-name>

This sets the invoking unit pointer in the called coroutine to point to the invoking unit and begins execution of the coroutine at its present execution location.

A coroutine in execution may RESUME another coroutine or may return to the point from which it was invoked. The latter action is accomplished through an EXIT statement of the form

EXIT

This suspends execution of the present coroutine and returns to the invoking unit at the statement immediately following the invocation.

The implementation of coroutines requires some modification to our previous stack model of activation records. Because coroutines do not follow the procedure-call protocol, their activation records can be deleted in any order, independent of the order in which they were created. Therefore, the activation records of all coroutines defined in a program unit will form a linked list rather than a stack. Furthermore, the invoking unit of a coroutine must be explicitly identified within the coroutine's activation record. Coroutines will inherit as their nonlocal environment the environment of the activation record in which they are defined. Therefore, the activation record of a coroutine must include the following fields, in addition to its local environment:

Name of coroutine

Pointer to current execution location of coroutine

Pointer to invoking activation record

Pointer to defining activation record

Pointer to next coroutine activation record in linked list

Furthermore, the activation record of the invoking unit must contain a pointer to the list of coroutines that the unit has defined. Figure 5.13 illustrates this implementation model through a detailed example. In this figure, execution unit A creates two coroutines, C1 and C2, from the procedures P1 and P2. For each step of the execution, a box is provided that displays the pertinent code of each of the three program modules, and a box representing each activation record is located beneath its associated module. Those components of the activation record that are current instruction pointers always point to the instruction in the preceding code. Similarly, pointers to activation records point to the appropriate activation record boxes.

FIGURE **5.13**   **Illustration of Coroutine Activation Records**

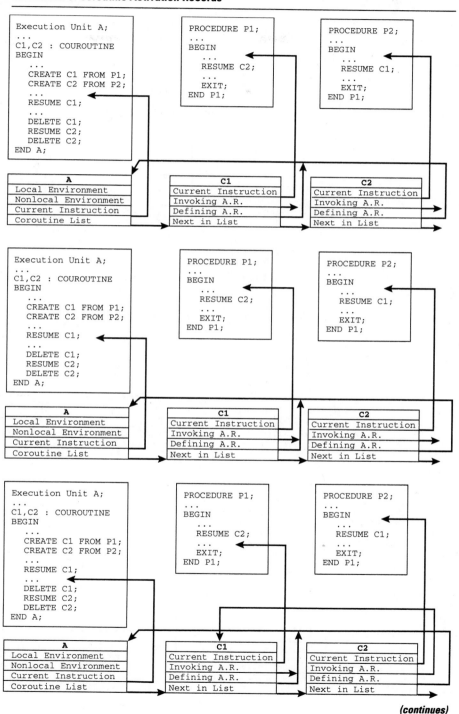

(continues)

FIGURE 5.13   (cont.)

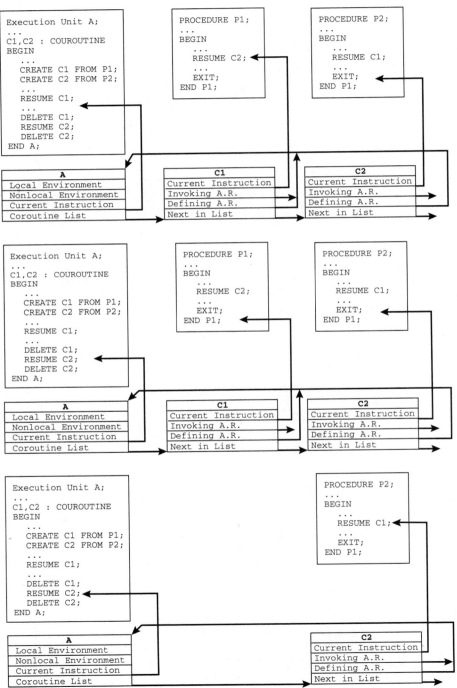

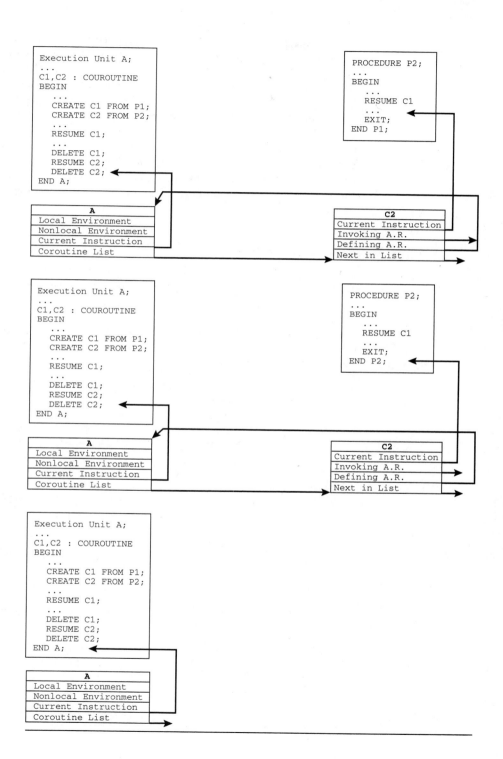

Figure 5.14 shows an example of a coroutine written in the language ACL, a coroutine language designed by Marlin (1980). ACL is a derivative of Pascal that adds two features: (1) coroutines and (2) explicit scope rules. The ACL code in Figure 5.14 is a mutation where the explicit scope rules have been ignored in order to illustrate the coroutine concept.

In this program, the code between `initbegin` and `initend` is executed when the `create Count` statement causes an instance of `Count` to be allocated. The `return` statement in `Count` causes a return from the coroutine, but on the next call to `Count`, execution begins at the statement immediately following the `return` statement. Figure 5.15 shows the output generated by the program in Figure 5.14. In Chapter 7, we see how coroutines are implemented in Modula-2.

5.8   Procedures in Ada

Ada splits the definition of a procedure into two parts, its declaration and its body. These can be specified either separately or together. The declaration defines the name of the procedure, the order, names, default values, and types of the parameters, and the type of the return value if the procedure is a VRP. The body of the procedure must include all the information that the

---

FIGURE 5.14   **Example of Coroutines in ACL**

```
program Counter (input, output);
    coroutine Count;
        var i, counter : integer;
        initbegin {started only when instance is allocated}
            counter := 0;
        initend;
    begin {started any time a call is made}
            for i := 1 to 5 do begin
                counter := counter + 1; writeln(counter:1);
            end;
            return;
            for i := 1 to 5 do begin
                counter := counter + 1; writeln(counter:1)
            end;
            return;
    end;
var C : instance of Count;
begin
    C :=create Count;
    call C;
    writeln('Halfway through');
    call C;
    delete C;
end.
```

FIGURE **5.15** **Output Generated by ACL Program in Figure 5.14**

```
1
2
3
4
5
Halfway through
6
7
8
9
10
```

declaration does plus the declaration of local data objects and the statements that make up the procedure. In the absence of a separate declaration, the body serves as the procedure declaration as well.

When a procedure is called in Ada, actual parameters may be associated with formal parameters by position or name. Overloading is permitted as described in Section 5.6. Parameters of functions must be of IN mode.

The syntax of Ada procedures is given in the accompanying box.

```
Procedures
Language: Ada

procedure declaration ::=
    procedure <identifier> [<formal-part>]
  | function <identifier> [<formal-part>] return <type>

formal-part ::= (<parameter-spec> {;<parameter-spec>})

parameter-spec ::= <identifier-list> : <mode> <type> [:= <expression>]

mode ::= in | out | in out

procedure-body ::= <procedure-declaration> is
                [<local-declarations>]
            begin
                <sequence-of-statements>
            end [<procedure-name>];

procedure-call ::= <procedure-name> [<actual-part>]

actual-part ::= (<parameter-association> {,<parameter-association>})

parameter-association ::= [<identifier>=>]<expression>
```

5.9 Exceptions

An **exception** is a condition that requires some immediate action on the part of the program. Such a condition might be an error, such as arithmetic overflow or index out of range, or it might be an abnormal or rarely occurring condition that is not considered an error. An example of such a condition is end-of-file. An additional type of exception is the modification of a specified storage location. This latter type of exception is useful for the purpose of debugging.

Conditions that are considered to be exceptions are said to be **synchronous**, meaning that they arise at predictable places in the program. For example, overflow will occur only when arithmetic is being done, index out of range will occur only when an array is being accessed, and end-of-file will occur only when a file is being read. This distinguishes exceptions from conditions that are **asynchronous** — that is, that may occur at any time. A user-generated interrupt or a device-ready signal are examples of asynchronous conditions. These asynchronous conditions are more appropriately handled by the concurrency features of a language, because they are generated by some concurrently executing process.

Procedures, as we have described them, are invoked through an explicit call that calls the procedure into execution and suspends execution of the invoking unit. This situation is illustrated in Figure 5.16. On completion of the procedure, the invoking unit is resumed from the point of invocation.

Procedures invoked implicitly by the occurrence of an exception are called **exception handlers**. As with a procedure call, exception handling results in suspension of execution of the invoking unit. Two different actions are possible on termination of the exception handler: resumption of the in-

FIGURE 5.16   Procedure Execution

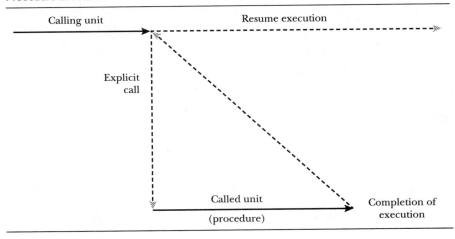

voking unit, as with procedures, or termination of the invoking unit. These two approaches are illustrated in Figure 5.17a and b.

When exceptions occur, a block of statements is invoked implicitly — that is, without an explicit call. This feature is the distinguishing feature of exceptions. The same effect could be obtained through explicit calls by including conditional calls to the handling routines. For example, a statement could be placed before each array access of the form

```
if index>index_max or index<index_min then
    out_of_range_handler;
```

FIGURE 5.17   **Exception Handling**

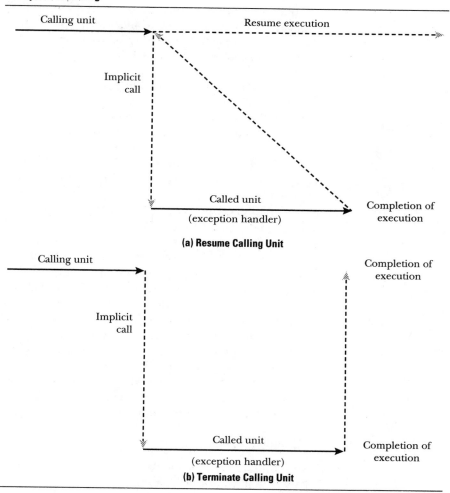

(a) Resume Calling Unit

(b) Terminate Calling Unit

Such frequently recurring statements would detract from the understandability of the program, however. Therefore, implicit invocation is desirable.

Not all imperative languages contain a facility for exception handling. Among the commonly used languages, only PL/I and Ada include this feature. Several lesser-known languages — among them CLU, MESA, and CHILL — contain features that support exception handling. Our discussion in this section will focus on the general approach rather than on a single language's implementation. In Section 5.10 the Ada approach is described.

5.9.1 ▪ Raising Exceptions

Due to the implicit nature of the invocation of exception handlers, no special syntactic features are required for their invocation. The implicit invocation of an exception is commonly referred to as **raising the exception**. Most languages do, however, provide a facility for the explicit invocation of exceptions as well. This facility is in the general form of a RAISE statement and consists of a keyword such as RAISE, followed by the name of the exception. This convention permits the program artificially to raise a built-in exception in order to invoke the exception handler at that point even without the associated condition occurring.

In addition to the built-in exceptions provided by a language, the language may also permit user-defined exceptions. Such exceptions can be declared like any other data object and will exist within the scope of their declaration. User-defined exceptions must be raised explicitly, because they have no associated condition. These exceptions thus behave much like procedures and may even be permitted to accept parameters. The major difference between user-defined exceptions and procedures lies in the flow of control on termination of the invoked unit. Procedures will always return to the point immediately after the point of invocation, whereas an explicitly invoked exception handler may proceed differently. The possibilities are discussed shortly.

A language might permit the **enabling** and **disabling** of exceptions. Whether these conditions are permitted is a philosophical decision that the language designers must make. Suppression of an exception through disabling might be of value when testing for the exception is expensive in time and space and the value of the resulting reliability is not worth that cost to the programmer. Index-bound testing for arrays is an example of an exception whose cost might exceed its value in some circumstances. In these cases, some languages permit specified exceptions to be disabled in the scope of a program unit. This suppression occurs at compile time and prevents the generation of the code needed to implement the exception.

5.9.2 ▪ Handling Exceptions

Exception handlers are blocks of statements that are bound to an exception. Figure 5.18 illustrates the bindings of exceptions. For built-in exceptions, the name binding is a permanent part of the language. User-defined exceptions

FIGURE 5.18   **Exception Object**

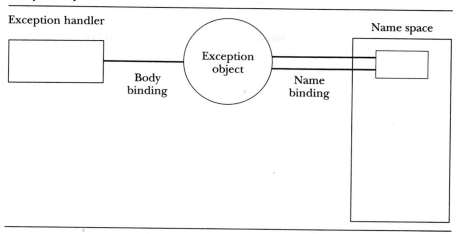

are bound to their name at the point of declaration, and that binding holds within the scope of that declaration.

The binding of the exception to its exception handler can follow either one of two models. First, the binding can be patterned after data object-name bindings within program units. In this case, the exception-handling block is bound to the exception in the scope of a program unit through a declaration attached to that unit. A redefinition of the exception handler in a contained unit will temporarily interrupt that binding, giving an exception version of a hole-in-scope.

The second model is similar to the data object-value binding, in which statements executed within the block can modify the exception–exception handler binding.

To illustrate these two models, consider the pseudocode illustrations in Figures 5.19 and 5.20. In Figure 5.19, exceptions are declared, and they are separately assigned handlers in the declaration section of the program unit. The binding of a handler to an exception holds throughout the scope of the unit. The handler for exception E1 is redeclared in procedure B, introducing a hole-in-scope for the H1 handler within B. Here we see that the name binding E1 holds throughout A, although the handler binding changes within B. This model is implemented in Ada, as we shall see in the next section.

The second model is illustrated by Figure 5.20. Here the handler is not bound to the exception by a declaration, but rather by an executable statement. The statement we create to do this, the SET HANDLER statement, acts much like an assignment statement by binding an exception handler to an exception at run time. A difficulty with this second model is illustrated by the example. The environment of the call effects the binding of the handler. In Figure 5.20, exceptions E1 and E2 have different initial bindings for the two invocations of B. This model is implemented in PL/I.

FIGURE 5.19   **Illustration of Model 1 Exception Binding**

```
procedure A
  E1, E2 : exception;
  handler E1 is
    <H1 Block-of-statements>
  handler E2 is
    <H2 Block-of-statements>
  procedure B;
    E3 : exception;
    handler E1 is
      <H4 Block-of-statements>
    handler E3 is
      <H3 Block-of-statements>
    begin --B
      <B Block-of-statements>
      -- E1 handler is H4
      -- E2 handler is H2
      -- E3 handler is H3
    end --B
  begin --A
    -- E1 handler is H1
    -- E2 handler is H2
    B;
  end; --A
```

The flow of control upon completion of the exception handler is a rather complex issue. There are four alternative approaches here:

1. Terminate the program unit that invoked the exception, returning to that unit's invoking unit.
2. Terminate the program unit that invoked the exception as in (1) and raise the same exception in the unit's invoking unit.
3. Resume execution of the program unit that invoked the exception by retrying the statement or expression where the exception occurred.
4. Resume execution of the program unit that invoked the exception at the point immediately following the statement where the exception occurred.

Languages may determine which of the above alternatives will be used through one of the following policies:

1. Use the same default alternative on completion of all exceptions.
2. Each exception type will have a given default completion alternative associated with it, but different built-in exceptions may have different default actions.
3. The language includes constructs for specifying the completion alternative within the exception handler.

FIGURE **5.20**   **Illustration of Model 2 Exception Binding**

```
procedure A;
  E1, E2 : exception;
procedure B;
  E3 : exception;
begin --B
  -- E1 handler is H1 (first call) or H4 (second call)
  -- E2 handler is H2 (first call) or H5 (second call)
  set handler E3 to
    <H3 Block-of-statements>
  -- E3 handler is H3
  ...
  set handler E1 to
    <H4 Block-of-statements>
  -- E1 handler is H4
  ...
end; --B
begin --A
  set handler E1 to
    <H1 Block-of-statements>
  -- E1 handler is H1
  set handler E2 to
    <H2 Block-of-statements>
  -- E2 handler is H2
  ...
  B;
  -- E1 handler is H4
  ...
  set handler E2 to
    <H5 Block-of-statements>
  -- E2 handler is H5
  B;
end; --A
```

A related issue is the raising of an exception for which no handler has been defined. In this case, there may either be a default handler associated with every exception whose handler has not been explicitly defined or the exception may be propagated.

Exception propagation occurs as follows. If an exception is raised when no handler is specified, it terminates the program unit that raised the exception and raises the same exception in the unit that invoked the current unit. The same exception — which is now raised in the invoking unit — may have a defined handler in that unit, in which case the handler is executed. If there is no handler there, that unit will be terminated, and the same exception will be raised in its invoking unit. Thus, an unhandled exception will continue to propagate up levels of the dynamic invocation tree until it reaches a unit where it is handled. If it reaches the root of the tree and still is not handled, a default handler will be executed, resulting in the root unit being terminated.

Another way of dealing with unhandled exceptions is to permit the programmer to specify a default handler that will be invoked when any exception is raised that has no defined handler in the present context.

5.9.3 ▪ Implementation

The implementation of an exception depends on its type and the way it is specified in the language. The implementation of exception raising can be performed by hardware interrupts in some cases, operating system traps in others, and compiler-generated code inserted into the program in others. Which technique is used for a given exception depends upon the hardware and software capabilities of the system on which the language is implemented.

In terms of the activation record, a list of built-in and user-defined exceptions is included as a part of the activation record of each program unit. Each exception entry in the table includes a pointer to the associated handler if one is defined in the present program unit. When an exception is raised, the table is searched for the appropriate exception name, and if it is found, a branch is made to the code for the associated handler. If no handler is specified, either a default handler is executed or the exception is propagated. If the exception is not found in the list of defined exceptions, a search of the nonlocal environment through the static pointer chain can proceed just as with other data objects, if that is the action prescribed by the language.

Exception propagation is implemented by terminating the presently active program unit, popping its activation record off the run-time stack, and raising the same exception in its invoking unit, which is represented by the present top-of-stack activation record. This propagation will continue down the dynamic chain until an activation record is found that handles the exception.

The implementation of the exception handler depends on the action taken upon completion of the handler. Handlers that resume execution of the invoking unit can be implemented just like procedures with activation records of their own. Handlers that terminate the invoking unit are typically implemented like a `goto` within the same unit, with a return from the active unit executed at the completion of the handler causing the present activation record to be popped off the run-time stack.

5.10 Exceptions in Ada

Ada has five built-in exceptions. These exceptions are listed next, along with a brief description of each:

CONSTRAINT_ERROR is raised when a range, index, or discriminant constraint is violated, a variant record component is not available under the current discriminant values, or an access value is unreachable.

NUMERIC_ERROR is raised if the result of a numeric operation is outside the range of its type.

PROGRAM_ERROR is raised when an unavailable program unit is invoked.

STORAGE_ERROR is raised when storage that is dynamically allocated is not available.

TASKING_ERROR is raised when an error occurs during the concurrent execution of tasks.

Further exceptions are supported by system-provided packages such as the TEXT_IO package.

User-defined exceptions are also provided in Ada. Their declaration is similar to that of any other data object, with the type name being EXCEPTION. The scope of user-defined exceptions follow normal scope rules for data objects as well. User-defined exceptions must be raised explicitly by a RAISE statement. Built-in exceptions can be raised explicitly through a RAISE statement, in addition to being raised implicitly through the occurrence of the specified exception.

Exception handlers in Ada can be attached to either blocks, procedures, or functions. In addition, tasks, which are discussed in Chapter 18, may also have handlers attached. The syntax of the exception handler is shown in the following box. The choice of OTHERS labels the handler for any exceptions that are not otherwise specified. The operation of the handler differs according to where in the program unit the exception is raised. There are two possible cases:

1. If the exception is raised during execution of the body of the unit, then: If the unit has a handler defined for the raised exception, the handler is executed, the unit is terminated, and control is passed to the invoking unit at the point of a normal return. If the unit has no handler for the raised exception, the unit is terminated as with a return or exit, and the same exception is raised in the invoking unit at the point of return.

2. If the exception is raised in the declarations of a unit or during the execution of an exception handler, then the unit is terminated as with a return or exit and the same exception is raised in the invoking unit at the point of return.

A RAISE statement without a specified exception may appear only within an exception handler. It causes the original precipitating exception to be reraised within the invoking unit.

Exceptions may be suppressed in Ada, but suppression is defined on checks rather than the entire exception. Each exception type has a set of checks that are eligible for suppression. For example, CONSTRAINT_ERROR has the checks ACCESS_CHECK, DISCRIMINANT_CHECK, INDEX_CHECK, LENGTH_CHECK, and RANGE_CHECK. Any or all of these can be suppressed through the use of the statement

```
pragma SUPPRESS <check-identifier>
```

which must appear in the declarative part of the program unit to which it is applied.

The syntax for exceptions in Ada is given in the accompanying box.

```
Exceptions
Language: Ada
Exception declaration ::= <identifier-list> : exception;
Raise-statement ::= raise [<exception-name>];
Position of exception handlers:
  program-unit ::= <declarations>
              begin
                <body>
              exception
                <exception-handler>
              end
Exception-handler-part ::= <exception-handler>{exception-handler}
              [others => <sequence-of-statements>]
Exception-handler ::= when <exception-name> { | <exception-name>}
                      => <sequence-of-statements>
```

C H A P T E R **5**   **Terms**

abstraction
activation record
run-time stack
local environment
nonlocal environment
static scope
dynamic scope
side effect
parameters
actual parameter
formal parameter
positional parameter association
named parameter association
default parameter association
IN parameter
OUT parameter

IN OUT parameter
value-result parameter passing
aliasing
name parameter
value-returning procedure (VRP)
overloading
coroutine
exception
synchronous
asynchronous
exception handler
raising the exception
enabling
disabling
exception propagation

C H A P T E R **5**   **Discussion Questions**

1. State some advantages of dynamic scope over static scope in defining the nonlocal environment of a procedure.

2. Give the relative advantages and disadvantages of disallowing nonlocal environments in procedures.

3. It is stated in the text that IN and OUT parameters are both special cases of IN OUT parameters. What would be the result if only IN OUT parameters were available? Would it matter whether they were implemented by reference or by copy?

4. One type that can be passed as a parameter that was ignored in this chapter is the label. Discuss some of the difficulties that might arise if label passing is permitted.

5. In this chapter it was suggested that nonlocal data objects be declared in a program unit. An extension of this would be to specify in the declaration the name of the program unit whose binding is to be used for every nonlocal object. What are some difficulties with this approach?

6. When procedure parameters can be associated by name as in Ada, some would argue that all parameters should be associated in this way, because it provides greater clarity than the positional association. Do you agree?

7. Some languages provide multiple entry points into the same procedure that are called by different names and may have different parameters associated with them. What are the benefits and dangers of such a feature?

8. List some exceptions for which each of the four policies for flow of control after exception handling would be appropriate.

   a. Terminate program unit and return to invoking unit.
   b. Terminate program unit and raise same exception in invoking unit.
   c. Resume execution by retrying statement where exception was raised.
   d. Resume execution immediately after statement where exception was raised.

9. In Ada, exception suppression occurs at compile time rather than run time. What advantage would run-time suppression provide? What difficulties would it present in implementation?

C H A P T E R **5** **Exercises**

---

1. Consider the following code:

```
program Exercise1 (input, output);
  var a,b,c: integer;

  procedure p1 ([MODE] a,b: integer);
    begin
      a := a * b;
      if (c/b)=a then a:=0 else a:=100;
    end;
```

```
procedure p2 ([MODE] a,b: integer);
  begin
    a := a - b;
    if a=c then p1(b,a) else p1(a,b);
  end;

begin
  a := 1; b := 5; c := 10;
  p2(c,b);
end.
```

Give the values of a, b, and c from the main program after execution when each of four parameter passing modes are used for [MODE] in Exercise1. As a reminder, the parameter passing modes are

IN implemented by copy

OUT implemented by copy

IN OUT implemented by reference

IN OUT implemented by copy

2. Consider the following code:

```
program Exercise2 (input, output);
  var a,b: integer;
      c,d: real;
  procedure p1;
    var d: real;
        x: Boolean;
    begin
      {****** HERE!!!! ******}
    end;
  procedure p2;
    var b,c: real;
    procedure p3;
      var x,b: real;
      begin
        a := 1; p2; x := a; p1
      end;
    begin
      if a=0 then p3 else p1
    end;
  begin
    a := 0; p2; p1;
  end.
```

At the point marked {****** HERE!!!! ******}, give the activation record structure of the run-time environment the first time p1 is called. Note that the calling sequence is

```
        main → p2 → p3 → p2 → p1
```

3. Consider the following Pascal code:

```
program Exercise3 (input, output);
  var limit: integer;
  function Summation ([MODE] lim: integer): integer;
    var s: integer;
    begin
      s := 0;
      while lim > 0 do
        begin
          s := s + limit;
          limit := limit - 1;
        end;
      Summation := s
    end;
  begin
    limit := 6;
    writeln('Sum of 1 through 6 is ', Summation(limit))
  end.
```

Which parameter mode would cause the function Summation to have an infinite loop? Explain your answer.

4. Consider the following program:

```
program Exercise4 (input, output);
  var a,b,c: integer;
      d: Boolean;
  procedure p1(var q:Boolean; var r, s:integer);
    begin
      if d then r := 100 else r := 200;
      s := s / a;
    end;
  procedure p2(var x,y: integer; var z: boolean);
    begin
      x := 15; y := x + a; z := (x<a);
      p1(z,y,x);
      z := (x<a);
    end;
  begin
    a := -1; b := -1; c := -1; d := true;
    p2(a,b,d);
  end.
```

Using call by value-result semantics as the parameter-passing mode, what
would the final values of the variables in the main program be at program
termination?

5. Write a program that would be described by the activation record structure in Figure 5.21. Indicate where the execution would have to be suspended to produce the structure. The following is the format of the activation records:

local vars
parameters
return addr
static pointer
dynamic pointer

It is assumed that the static and dynamic pointers point to the containing modules according to the static and dynamic scope rules, respectively.

6. Describe how a general `while` loop could be simulated by exceptions as they are implemented in Ada.

CHAPTER 5   Laboratory Exercises

1. Write a program that determines whether IN parameters are implemented by reference or by copy.

2. Write a program that determines whether OUT parameters are implemented by reference or by copy.

3. Write a program that determines whether IN OUT parameters are implemented by reference or by copy.

4. If your language implements OUT or IN OUT parameters by copy, determine whether parameters are copied left to right or right to left on completion of a procedure.

5. Write a program that shows whether parameters of a VRP can be OUT or IN OUT in your language.

6. The sieve of Eratosthenes is an interesting algorithm for computing prime numbers. It is an example of an inherently concurrent problem, but it is adaptable to coroutines.

   Let's suppose we have a set of activations that all do the following:

   a. Read a number from an input stream.
   b. Print this first number.
   c. Activate a new routine and pass that activation all numbers from the input stream that are not divisible by the first number.

   Each activation becomes a *filter*. If we have a main process that generates all integers (in some range), activates a filter, and passes this stream of integers

FIGURE **5.21**   **Activation Record Structures for Exercise 5**

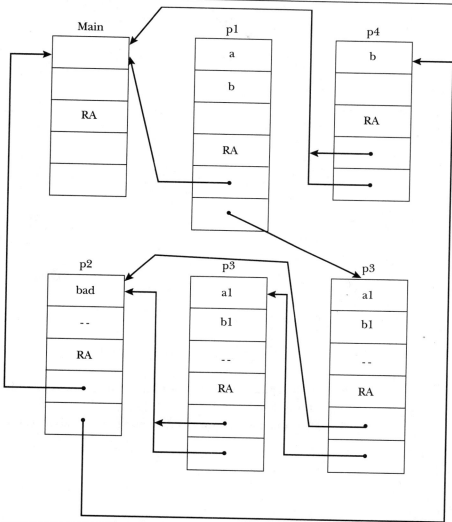

on to this filter, we get the configuration found in Figure 5.22. The first number in each filter is prime; the rest are filtered out or passed on. This situation makes for an interesting program because it features (1) an inherently nonprocedural problem and (2) an elegant solution. You are to design a solution to the sieve of Eratosthenes in pseudo-ACL. Design and specify the solution using coroutine semantics as we have sketched them in this chapter.

7. For each built-in exception in your language, generate a situation that will raise it.

FIGURE 5.22   Illustration of Filters in Laboratory Exercise 6

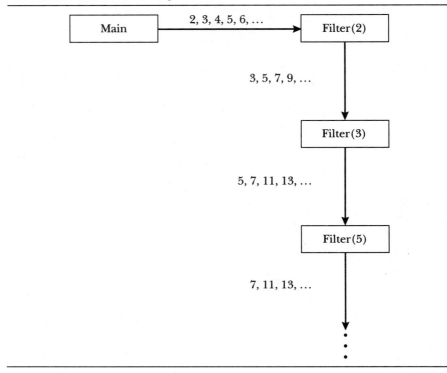

8. Write a binary search procedure using exceptions instead of controlled iteration statements.

9. Determine what happens if an exception is raised within an exception handler.

Data Abstraction

6.1 ▪ Abstract Data Types
6.2 ▪ Encapsulation
6.3 ▪ Parameterization
6.4 ▪ Monitors
6.5 ▪ Data Abstraction in Ada

In Chapter 5, the idea of procedural abstraction was introduced. This concept permits the abstraction of higher-level execution units to lower-level ones. Two important properties of this abstraction are encapsulation and parameterization. **Encapsulation** refers to the isolation of the operational details of a procedure from the environment where it is used. In particular, the invoking unit does not need to know the algorithms, data structures, or any other details of the procedure. **Parameterization** refers to the ability to create a generalized abstraction that has the flexibility to perform a variety of activities based on the values of parameters. For example, a sort procedure will typically have parameters representing the array and its size. This provides the procedure with sufficient generality to sort any array of any size.

In this chapter, we apply this same abstraction principle to data types. We have already discussed how aggregate data types can be abstracted to simple data types through the use of arrays and records and how some languages, such as Ada, permit the parameterization of attributes such as the domain of arrays. In this chapter we extend our consideration to abstract data types, which include the data type and the operations defined on that data type. The idea of encapsulation for data types — that is, separating the detailed description from the usage of the type — is introduced, and an extension of the concept of parameterization of types is applied to the abstract data types. Special abstract data type definitions, called *monitors*, which permit the specification of concurrent processes, are discussed, and the implementation of abstract data types in the programming language Ada is described.

6.1 Abstract Data Types

An **abstract data type** is defined as a collection of data structures and operations abstracted into a simple data type. As an example, consider an abstract data type (ADT) called bst, which represents a binary search tree. It will consist of objects that belong to the class binary search tree along with a set of useful operations that could be performed on such a tree. Some possible operations with their associated parameters are as follows:

```
initialize_tree(tree:out bst);
—Initialize tree to be empty

empty(tree:in bst):boolean;
—return true if tree is empty and false
—otherwise

root(tree:in bst):item_type;
—returns the value of the item at the root
— of tree. An exception is raised if tree
— is empty.

left_subtree(tree:in bst):bst;
—returns the binary search tree that is the
— left subtree of the root of tree. An
— exception is raised if tree is empty.

right_subtree(tree:in bst):bst;
—returns the binary search tree that is the
— right subtree of the root of tree. An
— exception is raised if tree is empty.

insert_in_tree(item:in item_type,tree:in out bst);
—inserts item into tree at the correct
— position.
```

These definitions are given in a pseudolanguage, which, though similar to Ada, does not exactly follow the syntax of any actual programming language.

This abstract data type could then be used to define and manipulate binary search trees without knowledge of the data structure used to represent bst or the algorithms used to implement the operations. For example, a procedure could be written to count the number of nodes in a bst as follows:

```
procedure count_nodes(tree:in bst):integer is
begin
  if empty(tree) then
    return 0;
  else
    return count_nodes(left_subtree(tree)) +
           count_nodes(right_subtree(tree)) + 1;
  end if;
end count_nodes;
```

The important point here is that the objects of an abstract data type can be used without any knowledge of their implementation. All operations on elements of the ADT must be part of the abstract data type. No other operations on the ADT are permitted.

There are two major purposes for the use of abstract data types. The first is the independence of the use of the abstract data type from its implementation, which permits modification of the implementation without affecting the execution units where the abstract data type is used. The second purpose is maintaining the integrity of the abstract data type by restricting access to the operations provided. For example, if the binary search tree were implemented using pointers, it would not be possible for an execution unit using bst to destroy the binary search tree structure of a bst object, because the unit does not have direct access to the data involved.

In the following sections we see how languages implement this important feature. In so doing, we continue to illustrate data abstractions through the use of a pseudolanguage.

6.2 Encapsulation

There are two approaches to the definition of an abstract data type. The first is an extension of the type definition to include the definition of operations. For example, Figure 6.1 illustrates the implementation of bst in our pseudolanguage using this approach. Here we see the definition of type bst is divided into three parts. The export section indicates those operations that are to be visible to the unit that uses the bst data type. The structure section defines the data type itself and corresponds to the normal definition of a data type. The local section defines all nonexported objects — including data types, variables, and procedures — that are a part of the implementation but that are completely hidden from units outside of this definition. The bst ADT defined in Figure 6.1 exports the six procedures defined earlier, defines the structure as a pointer to an element of type node, and locally defines the type node and the bodies of the six procedures. Because type node is defined in the local section, it is not directly available to external units but must be accessed through the bst type.

The second approach to defining an ADT is more general in that it can be used to define entities other than an ADT as well. It consists of a collection of

FIGURE 6.1   **ADT Definition by Type**

```
type bst is
  export: initialize_tree,
          insert_in_tree,
          empty,
          root,
          left_subtree,
          right_subtree;
  end export;

  structure: access node;
  end structure;

  local: type node is record
                root_item : item_type;
                left : bst;
                right : bst;
              end node;

    procedure initialize_tree(tree:in out bst) is
      tree:=NIL;
    end initialize_tree;

    procedure empty(tree:in bst) return Boolean is
      return (tree=NIL);
    end empty;

    procedure left_subtree(tree:in bst) return bst is
    begin
      if tree=NIL then
      raise bst_error;
    else
      return tree.left;
    end left_subtree;

    procedure right_subtree(tree:in bst) return bst is
    begin
      if tree=NIL then
        raise bst_error;
      else
        return tree.right;
    end right_subtree;

    procedure insert_in_tree(item:in item_type;
                             tree:in out bst) is

    begin
      if tree=NIL then
        tree := new node(item,NIL,NIL);
```

```
        else if item < tree.root_item then
          insert_in_tree(item,tree.left);
        else
          insert_in_tree(item,tree.right);
      end insert_in_tree;

      procedure root(tree:in bst) return item_type is
      begin
        if tree=NIL then
          raise bst_error;
        else
          return tree.root_item;
      end root;
  end local;
```

object definitions divided into two classes: those that are to be visible to external units and those that are not visible. When this format is used to define an ADT, the ADT itself is included as one of the exported objects defined within the collection of visible definitions, as opposed to the separate `structure` section it was given in the first approach.

Figure 6.2 sketches how our example might look using this collection approach. Here the `bst` is defined as an exported type, but its definition is deferred to the local section. This indicates that `bst` is to be visible outside; that is, objects can be bound to this type, but its implementation is to be hidden. Thus, in this case outside reference to `bst.root_item` is not permitted, because the structure of `bst` is not known beyond the local environment.

FIGURE 6.2 **ADT Definition by Collection**

```
collection binary_search_tree is

export: type bst is private;
        procedure initialize_tree(tree:in out bst);
        procedure empty(tree:in bst) return Boolean;
        procedure left_subtree(tree:in bst) return bst;
        procedure right_subtree(tree:in bst) return bst;
        procedure insert_in_tree(item:in item_type;
                                  tree:in out bst);
        procedure root(tree:in bst) return item_type;

local:  type bst is access node;
        type node is record
              root_item : item_type;
              left : bst;
              right : bst;
            end node;
        procedure initialize_tree(tree:in out bst) is
        ...
```

(continues)

```
        procedure empty(tree:in bst) return boolean is
        ...
        procedure left_subtree(tree:in bst) return bst is
        ...
        procedure right_subtree(tree:in bst) return bst is
        ...
        procedure insert_in_tree(item:in item_type;
                                 tree:in out bst) is

        ...
        procedure root(tree:in bst) return item_type is
        ...
end local;
```

This approach can be used to define multiple types within a single collection or, if no types are in the export section, simply to export a collection of procedures.

In either case, the definition has two major parts: information that is visible to an external program unit and information that is hidden. The visible information may be variables, constants, procedure-call templates, type definitions, or type names. The hidden information may include the definition of types that are named in the visible section, bodies of procedures whose call templates are listed in the visible section, and complete definitions of local objects such as variables, types, and procedures.

Some languages permit a block of code to be included in the hidden section that is to be executed to initialize a variable whenever one is declared to be of the specified abstract data type. This code could, for example, replace the `initialize_tree` procedure in Figure 6.1 and, therefore, eliminate the necessity of calling that procedure before a variable of type `bst` can be used. Some languages also include a termination block of code that is executed whenever the defining unit of an ADT variable is exited. In the case of the ADT in Figure 6.1, a block that recovered the storage used for the tree would be an appropriate termination block.

Another feature that some languages add to an ADT environment is the implementation of local variables as **own variables**. These variables, although known locally only to the ADT, retain their values from one activation of ADT procedures to the next.

6.3 Parameterization

The parameterization of data types was introduced in Chapter 4, where the bounds on the domain of an array were considered as parameters. In this section, we extend this idea by permitting much broader parameterization of aggregate types.

For example, with our binary search tree ADT defined in Figures 6.1 and 6.2, a likely candidate for parameterization would be `item_type`. This would permit the same ADT to represent binary trees, where the nodes are of any defined type that is specified by an actual parameter.

To implement this, an additional section to specify parameters is required in the ADT definition. Figure 6.3 shows modifications of Figure 6.1 and 6.2 that could specify this feature.

Binding actual parameters to formal parameters is accomplished differently by the two different forms of expressing ADTs. The type definition form can simply use parameterized type names in variable declarations — for example,

```
A : bst(real);
B : bst(small_array);
C : bst(string);
D : bst(employee_record);
```

The collection form requires **instantiations** of the collection for each parameter set applied, which means that the parameterized collection is just a shell. When the parameters are filled in, actual collections are created or instantiated. For example, constructs like the preceding ones could be expressed by

```
collection bst_real is bst(real);
collection bst_small_array is bst(small_array);
collection bst_string is bst(string);
collection bst_emp_rec is bst(employee_record);
```

FIGURE 6.3   **ADT Definitions with Parameters**

Type Definition from Figure 6.1

```
    type bst is

        parameters:
            type item_type;
        end parameters;

        export:
            . . .


Collection Definition from Figure 6.2

    collection binary_search_module is

        parameters:
            type item_type;
        end parameters

        export:
            . . .
```

Then the preceding variable declarations would be replaced by

```
A : bst_real.bst;
B : bst_small_array.bst;
C : bst_string.bst;
D : bst_emp_rec.bst;
```

In this case, because four actual collections are created containing the type bst, when one of the types is used, it must be prefixed by the appropriate collection name. This rule applies not only to types but to all visible objects defined in the instantiated collections.

Objects other than types could be defined parametrically in the use of ADTs. For example, a procedure or an operation could be a parameter to the definition of an ADT. In the binary_search_tree definition, we have assumed that the operation < makes sense for the parameterized type item_type. If, however, item_type is a record or an array, this operation has no built-in definition. Therefore, such types are invalid as actual parameters as our definition now stands despite the fact that in practice, nodes of a binary tree are frequently records.

One way to handle this problem is to change < to a function and have that function passed as a parameter when the collection is instantiated. Figure 6.4 illustrates the definition of collection binary_search_tree under this assumption, showing only the changes from Figure 6.2. Value returning procedure LESS_THAN is a formal parameter to our collection that compares two values of item_type.

FIGURE 6.4   **ADT Definition with Operator Parameter**

```
collection binary_search_tree is


   parameters:
     type item_type;
     procedure LESS_THAN(A,B:item_type):boolean;
   end parameters;

   export:
          . . .
   end export;

   local:
          . . .
        else if LESS_THAN(item,tree.root_node) then
          . . .
         else if LESS_THAN(item,tree.root_node) then
          . . .
   end local;
```

LESS_THAN takes on the usual definition for numeric or string types. For example, for type float the following function would be appropriate:

```
function LESS_THAN_FLOAT(X,Y : in float) return boolean is
begin
   return (X < Y);
end LESS_THAN_FLOAT;
```

For arrays or records, a more complex definition might be necessary. Suppose we wish to define two orders on employee_record type as follows:

```
function LESS_NAME(X,Y : in employee_record) return boolean is
begin
   return X.NAME < Y.NAME;
end LESS_NAME;

function LESS_ID(X,Y : in employee_record) return boolean is
begin
   return X.ID < Y.ID;
end LESS_ID;
```

Then we could instantiate two different collections with the statements

```
collection bst_by_name is bst(employee_record,LESS_NAME);
collection bst_by_id is bst(employee_record,LESS_ID);
```

and declare the variables

```
X : bst_by_name.bst;
Y : bst_by_id.bst;
```

Then X is a binary tree of employee records ordered by the name field of the record, and Y is a binary tree of employee records ordered by the id field.

If a language permits the overloading of procedures, then the use of procedures as parameters is avoidable if procedure names are chosen appropriately. This enforces a restriction on the execution unit using the ADT that we would rather avoid — namely, the requirement of using a specific name for the given procedure. This result requires external knowledge of the name used within the ADT definition. In the case of our preceding example, if all types that are actual parameters corresponding to item_type have a LESS_THAN procedure defined appropriately for them, then LESS_THAN need not be passed as a parameter, because overloading assumes the appropriate LESS_THAN is chosen for each type.

A further extension of this idea is to permit operators such as < to be given overloaded definitions. Then artificial functions would not be necessary to redefine operators for types where the operator is already built in. Note that such overloading also precludes the use of two different orderings on the same type, as we did with employee_record earlier.

6.4   Monitors

One strategy for concurrent processing is the use of a **monitor**. In this section we examine the monitor as an encapsulation similar to that used in defining ADTs. The purpose of the monitor is to guarantee mutual exclusion in data access and/or processing among concurrently executing processes.

A monitor is similar to the collection that we defined earlier in this chapter in that it contains an encapsulated set of procedures and data objects. In its most restrictive form, a monitor might permit only one of its procedures to be in execution at a time. Because these procedures are called by concurrent processes and all manipulation of shared data is encapsulated inside the monitor, it is guaranteed that no two processes will access the shared data concurrently. In the example in Figure 6.5, written in an Ada-like pseudolanguage, two exported procedures are provided, addup and store. The monitor differs from a collection as defined before in that these procedures are candidates for overlapping execution by concurrent processes. If this occurs, the first procedure invoked prevents any further invocations of procedures in the monitor from proceeding until the initial one is terminated. The rejected invocations are placed on a queue and are successively permitted to proceed one execution at a time, when the currently executing invocation terminates. This structure guarantees that data of a type defined locally in the monitor can be accessed by only one process at a time, thus ensuring mutual exclusion.

This form of concurrency control may be overly restrictive for some applications. For this reason, a more flexible type of monitor is permitted by some languages that allows more than one process to execute procedures from the monitor concurrently, but provides some synchronization mechanism that these procedures can use among themselves. This situation results in all synchronization occurring within monitor procedures, in order to encapsulate synchronization as well as data and procedures. Procedures within this more flexible monitor are therefore able to execute concurrently.

6.5   Data Abstraction in Ada

The programming language Ada contains extensive data abstraction capabilities. The **package** is the basic data abstraction construct and follows the model of the collection construct from Section 6.1. The package includes almost all the features described in the previous sections, including public and private declarations, initialization statements, information hiding, and parameterization of types.

6.5.1   ▪   Package Definition

The definition of a package in Ada is divided into two parts: the **package specification** and the **package body**. Each of these is, in turn, divided into two parts. The specification has a visible and a private part, whereas the body has

FIGURE **6.5**   **Example of Restrictive Monitor**

```
monitor restrict is

    parameters:
         type item_type;
         lower,upper : integer;
    end parameters;

    export:
         type restricted_array is private;
         procedure addup(A:in restricted_array) result
           item_type;
         procedure store(VALUE:in item_type;
                         LOCATION:in integer;
                         A:in out restricted_array);
    end export;

    local:
         type restricted_array is array [lower..upper] of
           item_type;
         procedure addup(A:in restricted_array) result
           item_type is
         begin
           ...
         end addup;
         procedure store(VALUE:in item_type;
                         LOCATION:in integer;
                         A:in out restricted_array) is
         begin
           A[location] := VALUE;
         end store;
    end local;
```

a declarative and an executable part. The body may also contain exception handlers, but we will not consider that feature in our discussion.

The general form of the specification of an Ada package is

```
package <identifier> is
  <visible-declarations>
[private
  <private-declarations>]
end [<identifier>];
```

The identifier specifies the package name and, if an identifier is included with the end statement, it must match the identifier following package. The visible declarations declare those objects of the package that are visible outside the package. These may include variables, types, procedures, and functions. In the case of procedures and functions, only the header is given here. The body of these entities must be written in the package body. Declarations in the private section of the visible part specify properties of visible objects that are not to be visible outside the package. This concept is further discussed later.

The body of a package is declared after its specification. It defines all entities that are completely local to the package as well as the bodies of all procedures and functions, both visible and local. Its form is

```
package body <identifier> is
  <declarative-part>
[begin
  <sequence-of-statements>]
end [<identifier>];
```

Again, the identifiers must both match those found in the corresponding specification. The declarative part contains the bodies of all visible procedures and functions as well as the bodies of all local procedures and functions — that is, those used inside the package but not visible there. It also contains declarations for any local types and variables. Variables declared in the package body and used in subprograms defined in the package body, retain their values from one invocation of a package subprogram to another, and hence have a location binding that spans the activation of the execution unit in which the package is declared. The sequence of statements in the executable part of a package body specifies an initialization procedure that is executed when the execution unit containing the package's definition is first activated. This can be used to initialize local variables, for example.

Figure 6.6 shows an example of an Ada package. In this package, the function `random` and the integer variable `seed` are visible to the execution unit that uses this package. The three variables that are declared locally in the package body retain their values from one call of `random` to the next. The visible variable `seed` retains its value as well. The difference between a visible variable such as `seed` and the other local variables is that `seed` can also be accessed and changed by an external execution unit. The function `get_time_in_seconds` is local, because it is not included in the package specification but only in the package body. This means that it is not usable by any external execution unit.

Packages containing no body may be specified. Such packages simply provide a set of declarations to the external execution unit. Procedures and functions cannot be included in such bodyless packages. An example of such a package is given in Figure 6.7. It defines the type `employee_record`, and the inclusion of this package would make this data type available to an external execution unit.

6.5.2 ▪ Private Types

Frequently, an abstract data type is created inside a package that needs to be visible outside the package as a type, but the actual structure of the type needs to be hidden from the external unit. This prevents the user of the package from manipulating objects of this type directly, enforcing the use of the encapsulated operations. In Ada, this capability is provided through the use of **private types**.

FIGURE 6.6 **Ada Package for Random-Number Generation**

```
package rng is
  function random return float;
  seed:integer;
end rng;

package body rng is
  modulus: integer :=65536;
  mult: integer := 13849;
  addon: integer := 56963;

  function random return float is
  begin
    seed := (seed*mult+addon) mod modulus;
    return float(seed)/float(modulus);
  end random;

  function get_time_in_seconds return integer is
  begin
    ...
  end get_time_in_seconds;

begin
  seed := get_time_in_seconds mod modulus;
end rng;
```

A visible type whose definition is to be hidden is declared to be `private` in the visible part of the specification of the package. Its full definition is then given in the private part of the specification. Any additional declarations needed to fully determine the private type are also included in the private part, such as the type definitions for components of the private type.

Consider the example in Figure 6.8. A private type will have its full definition specified within the body of the package for which it is declared. Outside of the package body, the structure of the type is unknown, although its name is visible. The only operations permitted outside the package on a private type are assignment, tests for equality and inequality, and visible operations defined by the package.

FIGURE 6.7 **Ada Package without a Body**

```
package employee is
  type employee_record is record
        name : string(1..20);
        id : integer;
        address : string(1..20);
        pay_rate : float;
      end record;
end employee;
```

FIGURE **6.8**   **Ada Package Specification Using Private Type**

```
package binary_search_tree is
   type bst is private;
private
   type bst is access node;
   type node is record
           root_item : item_type;
           left : bst;
           right : bst;
         end record;
end binary_search_tree;
```

In the example from Figure 6.8, if a variable `tree` is of type `bst`, then `tree.root_item` would be legally accessible within the package body but not in an external execution unit, because the internal structure of type `bst` would not be visible.

A further restriction can be applied in Ada if a type is declared to be `limited private`. These types behave just like `private` types except even assignment and equality/inequality tests are disallowed outside the package. Only operations defined in the package body are permitted on `limited ▪ private` types.

6.5.3 ▪ Using Packages

A package in Ada either can be included in the unit containing the execution unit in which it is used or can be placed in a user library. If it is placed in a library in compiled form, it is made available to an execution unit by appearing in a `with` statement of the form

```
with <package-name>;
```

Visible names in a package must be preceded by a prefix indicating the package name when used within an external unit. It is possible to remove this requirement through a `use` statement. This statement has the form

```
use <package-name>;
```

and permits access to visible objects in the package without use of the prefix. Consider the package defined in Figure 6.8. If a program using this package declared the variable `tree` to be of type `bst`, the declaration would be

```
tree:binary_search_tree.bst;
```

If a `use` clause were present, the prefix would be unnecessary. Therefore,

```
use binary_search_tree;
tree:bst;
```

is equivalent to the previous declaration of `tree`. Of course, if there are several visible objects with the same name whose identity cannot be otherwise determined by context, a prefix might still be necessary.

6.5.4 ▪ **Generic Packages**

Ada permits the parameterization of packages through the use of a construct known as the **generic package**. The language also permits generic procedures and functions, but we do not discuss them here.

The general form of a generic package declaration is

```
generic
  <declaration-of-formal-parameters>
<package-specification>
```

The formal parameters for an Ada generic package may be data objects, types, or subprograms. These formal parameters may be used naturally within the package specification and body. The generic package does not, however, create an actual package but rather a template for a set of packages. When actual parameters are provided for the formal parameters, an instantiation occurs, creating an actual package. Many actual packages can be created from a single generic package. The construct for creating or instantiating a package from a generic is

```
package <package-name> is new <generic-name> [(<actual-
  parameter-list>)];
```

The best way to get a feel for the use of generics is to consider an example. Figure 6.9 is a generic package for the binary search tree. The two parameters for this generic are the type of the items in the tree and the definition of the operator function <. The latter is necessary because item_type will not necessarily have a built-in < operator. This will permit, for example, the use of record types for item_type as long as an appropriate < is defined for the record and is used as the actual parameter. The default definition of formal parameter < given by the <> box means that if the formal parameter item_type has an operator already defined by <, that operator can be inherited by the package if the second actual parameter is omitted.

FIGURE *6.9*   **Ada Generic Package Definition**

```
generic
  type item_type is private;
  with function "<" (A,B:item_type) return boolean is <>;
package binary_search_tree is
  type bst is private;
  procedure initialize_tree(tree:out bst);
  function empty(tree:in bst) return boolean;
  function left_subtree(tree:in bst) return bst;
  function right_subtree(tree:in bst) return bst;
  procedure insert_in_tree(item:in item_type; tree:in out bst);
  function root(tree:in bst) return item_type;
```

(continues)

FIGURE 6.9   (cont.)

```
private
  type node is record
                root_item:item_type;
                  left,right:bst;
      end record;
  type bst is access node;
end;

package body binary_search_tree is

  bst_error:exception;

  procedure initialize_tree(tree:out bst) is
  begin
    tree:=NULL;
  end initialize_tree;

  function empty(tree:in bst) return boolean is
  begin
    return tree=NULL;
  end empty;

  function left_subtree(tree:in bst) return bst is
  begin
    if tree=NULL then
      raise bst_error;
    else
      return tree.left;
    end if;
  end left_subtree;

  function right_subtree(tree:in bst) return bst is
  begin
    if tree=NULL then
      raise bst_error;
    else
      return tree.right;
    end if;
  end right_subtree;

  procedure insert_in_tree(item:in item_type; tree:in out bst) is
  begin
    if tree=NULL then
      tree:=new node'(item,NULL,NULL);
    elsif item < tree.root_item then
      insert_in_tree(item,tree.left);
    else
      insert_in_tree(item,tree.right);
    end if;
  end insert_in_tree;
```

```
      function root(tree:in bst) return item_type is
      begin
        return tree.root_item;
      end root;

  end binary_search_tree;

  package bst_integer is new binary_search_tree(integer);
```

Figure 6.10 shows some sample instantiations of this generic package. The instantiation of bst_integer does not require a second parameter, because < is already defined for integer type. The two packages bst_name and bst_id require explicit functions for the second actual parameter. Notice that the two instantiations use the same item_type (employee_record) but different < functions, one ordering the tree on the component name and the other on the component id.

Trees might then be declared in an execution unit in which all three packages are instantiated by

```
tree1 : bst_integer.bst;
tree2 : bst_name.bst;
tree3 : bst_id.bst;
```

FIGURE 6.10   **Instantiations of Package binary_search_tree Defined in Figure 6.9**

```
function less_id(A,B:in emp_rec) return boolean is
begin
  return A.id<B.id;
end less_id;

function less_name(A,B:in emp_rec) return boolean is
pos:integer;
begin
  pos := A.name'first;
  loop
    exit when pos > A.name'last;
    exit when A.name(pos) /= B.name(pos);
    pos:=pos+1;
  end loop;
  if pos>A.name'last then
    return FALSE;
  else
    return A.name(pos)<B.name(pos);
  end if;
end less_name;

package bst_name is new
  binary_search_tree(emp_rec,less_name);
package bst_id is new binary_search_tree(emp_rec,less_id);
```

Notice that prefixes were required on these type names, because all three instantiated packages define a type `bst`. In addition, the tree initialization procedures could then be invoked by

```
initialize_tree(tree1);
initialize_tree(tree2);
initialize_tree(tree3);
```

In this case, prefixes are not required because the version of `initialize_tree` can be determined by the type of its actual parameter.

C H A P T E R **6**   **Terms**

encapsulation	package
parameterization	package specification
abstract data type	package body
own variables	private type
instantiation	own variable
monitor	generic package

C H A P T E R **6**   **Discussion Questions**

1. What are the advantages and disadvantages to the use of the type definition form compared to the collection form of defining ADTs?

2. Although parameterized ADT definitions are a very interesting concept, their implementation can force other, perhaps undesirable, constraints on a compiler and run-time system. An implication of the implementation of generic packages in Ada is that binding of generic packages is dynamic — that is, packages must now be instantiated. This, in turn, makes the resolution of overloading a run-time process, not a static one.

   a. Why does dynamic instantiation force dynamic overloading resolution?
   b. Why are these implementation constraints unfortunate?
   c. Can you dream up any way around these constraints? You may restrict the semantics of the language as you think about this one.
   d. Can you think of any other implications of generic implementation?

3. Consider the concepts of *encapsulation* and *parameterization* discussed at the beginning of this chapter. How well does the Ada package mechanism implement these concepts?

4. What would be some considerations in implementing a monitor?

C H A P T E R **6**   **Exercises**

1. What would be possible parameters for each of the following ADTs?
   a. Stacks
   b. Polynomials

    c. Strings

    d. Sets

2. Consider the following Ada package specification:

```
generic
   size: integer;
   type set_type is private;
package SET_PACK is
   type set is private;
   function new_set return set;
   procedure add(s: in out set; item: in set_type);
   function member(s: in set; item: in set_type) return boolean;
   procedure delete(s: in out set; item: in set_type);

   private
      type set is array (1..size) of set_type;
end SET_PACK;
```

The package implements a set ADT. Use this package to provide solutions to the following:

a. Declare two sets, `intset` and `floatset`, that are sets of 100 integers and 50 floats, respectively. Do this problem with and without the `use` statement. Does it make a difference?

b. Using your declarations, write code fragments to add `10` to the `intset` and `1.5` to the `floatset`. Do this problem with and without the `use` statement. Does it make a difference?

c. Add a new function, call it `member`, that checks to see if two distinct elements are in a set (takes three arguments). Is `member` a permissible name? (*Hint:* Yes it is. Why?) What does the argument list look like?

3. Consider the ADT specification below. STRINGS_PACK is an Ada generic package.

```
generic
   string_length: integer;
   type string_range is private;
package STRINGS_PACK is
   type string is private;
   procedure assign(str1: out string; str2: in string);
   procedure append(str: in out string; c: in character);
   procedure concat(str1: in out string; str2: in string);
   function index(str: in string; c: in character) return
      integer;
   private
      type string is array(1..string_length) of string_range;
end STRINGS_PACK;
```

a. Write a section of Ada code that will declare a string of only capital letters of maximum size 100 characters long and will initialize it to some value. Assume that the preceding package is declared separately from and external to the code you will write.

(*Hint:* The statement

```
type XYZ is range ('A'..'Z');
```

declares a type XYZ of capital letters.)

b. Redo part a, but use different statements/declarations so that you can use an alternate notation to make the references to the preceding package/modules.

4. Consider the following generic stack ADT:

```
generic
    size: positive;  -- "positive" means integers > 0
      type item is private;
  package stack_adt is
      type STACK is limited private;
      function initialize return STACK;
      procedure PUSH (stk: in out STACK; it: in item);
      function POP (stk: in out STACK) return item;
      private
         type table is array (1..size) of item;
         type STACK is record
                           top: range 1..size := 0;
                           element: table;
                       end record
      end stack_adt;
```

Write the type declarations for a stack of 200 integers (call it `int_stack`) and 100 booleans (call the type `bool_stack`).

5. Now consider the following declarations (based on your answer to Exercise 4):

```
istk: int_stack.STACK;
jstk: int_stack.STACK;
bstk: bool_stack.STACK;
i: integer;
```

Identify the following statements as legal or illegal, and explain your answer:

a. `istk := initialize;`
b. `PUSH(istk, 10);`
c. `i := int_stack.POP(istk);`
d. `if istk = jstk then`
      `    int_stack.PUSH(jstk,20);`
   `endif;`

6. Design a generic ADT for trees. That is, design an ADT that could be used to design a binary tree, a binary search tree, or a tree with three children at each node, all by changing the instantiation parameters. (*Hint:* Expand your thinking about what can be the instantiation paramaters to a generic ADT.)

C H A P T E R *6* Laboratory Exercises

1. Design and implement an abstract data type for rational numbers.
2. Implement an abstract data type for stacks.
3. Implement an abstract data type for polynomials. Use parameters if available.

An Example Language: C

In Chapters 3 through 6 we discussed the characteristics of imperative languages. Throughout this discussion, the languages Ada and Pascal have served as our primary examples. In this and the following chapter, we present detailed descriptions of two other modern imperative languages, Modula-2 and C, for comparison purposes. These two languages were chosen for their widespread use and for the variety of language properties they exhibit.

The description of C in this chapter is not intended to be complete. For a complete description the reader is referred to the defining document (Kernighan and Ritchie 1988). The present discussion focuses on the facilities and approaches C takes that are different from those of Ada, described earlier.

Included at the end of the chapter in Listing 7 is a complete program written in C. Excerpts from this program are used throughout this chapter to illustrate many of the principles of this language.

7.1 Philosophy and Approach

The programming language C was developed about 1972 by Dennis Ritchie as a part of the UNIX operating system. It was designed to be a lower-level language with emphasis on generality and economy of expression. It includes a rich set of control structures and operators. It is much more lenient with types than Ada or Modula-2, because it widely accepts type coercion. Its operators and pointer capabilities give the programmer access to lower-level machine facilities, making C a useful language in which to write systems programs.

The philosophy of C is to provide the programmer with as much power as possible to control the execution of a program and to encourage compactness of expression.

7.2 Information Binding

7.2.1 ▪ Data Objects

The language C defines its identifiers to be **case sensitive**, which means that the two identifiers IDName and IdName are distinct identifiers in the language. C is quite lenient with respect to type coercion. Operands of various scalar types may be mixed within C expressions. Predetermined implicit conversion rules are applied so that the expression may be evaluated.

Named constants are handled as **compile-time variables**. This convention means that every occurrence of the constant name within the program text is replaced by the associated constant before compilation. The declaration is, therefore, considered a substitution to be made by the preprocessor rather than a C statement as such and has as its scope the compilation unit. Lines 10–16 of Listing 7 show examples of this.

C has a rich set of operators that extend far beyond those normally found in an imperative language. A few of the more noteworthy are described here. Among the monadic operators, the increment and decrement operators are the most interesting and useful. The increment operator is signified by ++ and can be written either before or after a numeric identifier. When written before, it indicates that 1 will be added to the operand before it is used in the expression; when written after, it shows that 1 will be added after it is used. For example, if variable A has an initial value of 1, the statement

```
B = (++A) + 1;
```

results in B having a value of 3 and A having a value of 2. The statement

```
B = (A++) + 1;
```

causes both B and A to be bound to the value 2, because the value 1 (A's value before being incremented) is used for A in the expression. The operator -- works in a similar manner for decrementing.

In harmony with its goal of facilitating low-level access, C also has operators for shifting bits and performing logical bit operations.

The assignment operator, which is an equal sign (=) in C, is a value-returning operator. The value returned is the value evaluated for the right-hand side of the assignment. For example, the first of the preceding statements could also be written

```
B = (A = A + 1) + 1;
```

This format permits multiple assignments to be placed within a single statement.

Additional operators can be combined with the assignment operator to form another compactly expressed assignment. For example,

```
A += B;
```

means

```
A = A + B;
```

In its most general form, this type of assignment is

```
<expression-1> <op>= <expression-2>
```

where expression-1 may be a numeric variable or pointer expression, expression-2 may be any arithmetic expression, and op may be any diadic numeric operator.

Another interesting operator in C is the conditional operator that accepts three operands. Its general form is

```
<expression-1> ? <expression-2> : <expression-3>
```

The result of the operation depends on the value of expression-1. If expression-1 is nonzero, the result is the value of expression-2. If the result of expression-1 is zero, the result of the operation is expression-3. For example, the statement

```
a = d ? 1/d : 0;
```

sets a to zero if d is zero and sets a to 1/d if d is not zero.

C supports named types through the use of a TYPEDEF statement. The declaration of a variable to be of a specified type is given by the type name followed by the variable name. There is no subtype capability provided. TYPEDEF does not create any new types but rather defines a compile-time synonym for an existing type. Therefore, types so defined are completely interchangeable with their defined equivalents. Line 30 of Listing 7 contains an example of TYPEDEF.

7.2.2 ▪ Scalar Data Types

C supports a variety of numeric data types, including integer types SHORT INT, INT, LONG INT, and UNSIGNED, and floating-point types FLOAT and DOUBLE. In addition, the language includes a character type CHAR.

Boolean type does not exist in C. Instead, all relational and logical operations have integer results that are 1 if true and 0 if false. Similarly, the operands for logical operators are required to be numeric expressions, where 0 is considered false and any nonzero value is true. The relational operators in C are <, >, <=, >=, ==, and !=. Note the use of == for equality comparison. This practice is often troublesome for novice C programmers, who may want to use the assignment operator incorrectly where comparison is intended. The logical operators are !, &&, and || for not, and, and or, respectively.

Pointer types are very powerful constructs in C. When declared, objects of pointer type are indicated by preceding the name with an asterisk. For example,

```
int *x;
```

binds the name x to a pointer to a data object of integer type.

C has an extensive set of operators on pointer objects. We do not discuss them all here, but we briefly illustrate two of the more important ones. In order that we might illustrate C's pointer operators, consider the following declarations:

```
int *p;
int x;
```

These statements declare p to be a pointer to an integer and x to be an integer. The monadic * operator, when applied to a pointer object, returns the object to which the operand points. In this case, the assignment statement

```
*p = x;
```

causes the integer data object pointed to by p to be assigned the same value as the integer data object named by x. The inverse of the * operator is the & operator, which returns the address of the data object that is its operand. Using this operator, the assignment

```
p = &x;
```

causes the value of the pointer object named by p to be the address of the integer object named by x. Pointers are used extensively in C to work with arrays and pass parameters. We will describe these uses in later sections.

Line 175 of Listing 7 illustrates several of these concepts. This statement results in string s2 being copied into string s1. First note that the iteration will be repeated until the enclosed expression is zero, because zero corresponds to false. That expression will be zero when the source value *s2++ is zero. *s2 refers to the character pointed to by s2, and it is zero when the end of the string is reached, because ASCII zero signifies end-of-string. Therefore, for each repetition of the iteration, the location pointed to by s1 is filled with the character pointed to by s2, and both pointers are incremented by 1 after the assignment is completed. This action accomplishes the desired copy operation.

7.2.3 ▪ Execution Units

Statements in C may have labels. The label may be any legal identifier, and its attachment to a statement serves as an implicit declaration. The label is separated from the statement body by a colon. The semicolon is used as a statement terminator in C.

C permits the definition of blocks that are delimited by braces ({}). These blocks serve as the scope of control structures, scope of procedural abstraction, and scope of binding. Declarations occurring at the beginning of such a block specify run-time bindings that are in effect until the execution of the block is completed. Hole-in-scope occurs for names that duplicate those of externally bound objects.

A further unit of execution in C is the **source file**. Declarations that occur at the beginning of a source file define bindings that will hold throughout that file, with the possible exception of hole-in-scope. A declaration preceded by the word `extern` makes visible a data object of that name that is defined in a different source file. The source files can be compiled separately and thus serve as units of compilation, in addition to being scope-defining units. Lines 125–176 of Listing 7 illustrate such a source file. Three `extern` declarations referencing this file are given in lines 36–38, making visible the three functions `compare_strings`, `read_strings`, and `copy_string`.

7.3 Control Structures

7.3.1 ▪ Conditional Structures

The general form of the two-alternative conditional in C is given by

```
if (<expression>)
  <statement-block>;
[else
  <statement-block>;]
```

The expression may be of any type. The first statement block is executed if the expression evaluates to a nonzero value. If it evaluates to zero and an `else` clause is present, the statement block associated with the `else` clause is executed. The example given previously, namely,

```
a = d ? 1/d : 0;
```

can be rewritten as follows using the condition structure:

```
if (d)
  a = 1/d;
else
  a = 0;
```

The statement block can either be a single statement or a sequence of statements delimited by braces ({}). A multi-alternative `if` statement is not built in to C but must be simulated using nested two-alternative statements in the same manner as in Pascal. Lines 54–66 of Listing 7 contain a nested `if` statement.

C also provides a case-type conditional called the **switch statement**. Its general form is

```
switch (<selector-expression>) {
    {case <expression> : [<sequence-of-statements>]}}
    [default : <sequence-of-statements>]
}
```

This statement has several interesting features. First, the selector expression is always interpreted as integer with type coercion occurring when a noninteger expression is provided. Each `case` expression can specify just one value. When a case expression is matched, the statement sequences for that and all following `cases` are executed. In order to block the execution of the following cases, a `break` statement must be used to terminate the statement sequence. Notice that the sequence of statements may be null. This will still result in the remaining statement sequences being executed.

Consider the following example:

```
switch (i) {
    case 0:
    case 2:
    case 4: printf("1");
    case 6:
    case 8: printf("2");
            break;
    case 1:
    case 5: printf("3");
    case 7:
    case 3: printf("4");
    default: printf("5");
}
```

The following output would result from each of the given values of i:

```
Value of i        Output
    0               12
    1               345
    2               12
    3               45
    4               12
    5               345
    6               2
    7               45
    8               2
    9               5
```

7.3.2 ▪ Iterative Structures

The C language has a rich set of iterative structures. Its pretest iteration is of the form

```
while (<expression>)
  <statement>;
```

As usual, the expression is of integer type with zero meaning false and nonzero meaning true. The statement could be a block enclosed in braces. The posttest iteration takes the form

```
do
  <statement>;
while <expression>;
```

The meaning here is obvious, and the iteration body is always executed at least once.

In-test iterations are implemented through use of the `break` and `continue` statements within the body of an `if` statement located inside the iteration. The **break statement** causes an immediate branch to the statement following the end of the innermost active iteration body. The **continue statement** causes the next repetition of the innermost iteration to begin.

To illustrate, consider the following C iteration:

```
x = 0;
while (x < 5)
{ if (++x == 3)
    break;
  printf("%d",x);
}
```

This fragment will print

```
1 2
```

whereas the fragment

```
x = 0;

while (x < 5)

{if (++x == 3)

   continue;

 printf("%d",x);

}
```

will print

```
1 2 4 5
```

The fixed-count iteration construct of C is more powerful than those found in most other languages. It implements a generalized loop with an initialization action, modification action, and continuation condition. The general form is

```
for (<initial-expression>;<continuation-expression>;
  <modification-expression>)
  <statement>;
```

This form is equivalent to the following sequence of statements:

```
<initial-expression>;
while (<continuation-expression>) {
  <statement>;
  <modification-expression>;
}
```

The typical fixed-count iteration, which modifies an iteration variable i from low to high, is written

```
for (i=lo; i<=high; i++) ...
```

The preceding iteration, used to illustrate the continue statement, can be written equivalently as

```
for (x = 1; x <= 5; x++)
  {if (x == 3)
    continue;
  else
    printf("%d",x);
  }
```

7.3.3 ▪ Unconstrained Control Structures

C includes a goto statement that performs an unconditional branch to the statement whose label is after the word goto. C deals with all labels as if they were constants and does not support the use of label variables.

7.4 Data Aggregates

7.4.1 ▪ Arrays

Arrays in C are restricted in their domain to integer subranges from zero to some positive integer. The declaration of an array is of the form

```
<range-type> <array-name> [[<num-of-elements>]]
            [={<list-of-initial-values>}];
```

For example, the declaration

```
int name[10]={6,4,8,9,2,7,17,21,16,8};
```

declares name to be an array with domain 0..9 and range integer. The number of elements may be omitted if it can be determined from the initialization list or if the array is a formal parameter.

Specific elements of the array can be selected via indexes contained in brackets. Apart from initialization, there is no construction operation. There are no assignment, composite, or aggregate operators for arrays in C. The attribute of the size of an array in bytes is given by the sizeof operator. Multi-indexed arrays are declared by specifying more than one domain size. For example

```
int c[3][5][4];
```

is a three-indexed array whose domain space is

```
0..2 x 0..4 x 0..3
```

Only the first bound of a multi-indexed array can be omitted when the array is declared as a formal parameter.

One unique feature of C with respect to arrays is that an array is always represented by a pointer to its first element. In other words, if a is an array, then *a and a[0] are the same object. This use of pointers to implement arrays is quite useful when arrays are passed as parameters, as we shall see later.

7.4.2 ▪ Strings

C supports string constants for use in output but has no direct support for string type. String constants in output are enclosed in double quotes, whereas character constants are enclosed in single quotes. Strings are simulated in C through arrays of characters. The convention is to include the null character (ASCII value 0) to mark the end of string. Listing 7 contains an illustration of the way strings can be implemented using arrays in C. The standard function library of C, stdio, contains several functions that can be used to manipulate strings. These are described later.

7.4.3 ▪ Records

Records in C are called **structures**. The general form of a structure-type declaration is

```
struct <structure-name> {
  {<component-type> <component-name-list>;}
};
```

Structure variables are declared by

```
struct <structure-name> <variable-name-list>;
```

The selection operator for C is the period so that selection is given by

```
<structure-variable-name> . <structure-component>
```

In addition, an operator is provided in C that permits reference to a component of a record that is pointed to by a pointer data object. This operator is -> and is defined in such a way that A -> B means the component B of the record pointed to by pointer variable A. In other words, A -> B is equivalent to (*A).B. The initial values of a structure can be provided by a list enclosed in braces, but no other form of construction is available. For example, the following specifies initial values for the structure variable R of structure type T:

```
struct T {
  int A;
  int B[3];
  char C;
};
```

```
struct T R = {12,{1,1,1},'A'};
```

Variant records are implemented in C through use of the union construct. **Unions** are identical to structures in their declaration and operators. The difference between the two is that a union's components all occupy the same storage area, whereas a structure's components occupy different storage areas. Therefore, the union is essentially an undiscriminated variant that permits the same storage area to be multiply bound to data objects. No associated tag is permitted with unions.

The use of structures and pointers for constructing linked lists is illustrated in lines 25–31 of Listing 7. Here the structure person is defined in lines 25–29 with three components: a character string name, an integer age, and next, which is a pointer to another element of type person. Line 30 defines namelist to be a type that is a pointer to an element of type person, and line 31 defines two variables, head and current, to be variables of type namelist and initializes both of them to NULL.

7.5 Procedural Abstraction

7.5.1 ▪ Definition and Invocation

Every procedure in C returns a value and hence is a function. The form for function definition in C is

```
[<func-type>] <func-name> [(<formal-par-name>
                            {,<formal-par-name>})]
```

The type of the return value of the function, when its specification is omitted from the definition, is integer by default. Line 144 of Listing 7 is an example definition where the type specification int is present, but optional. A void function type indicates no value is returned. See line 47 of Listing 7.

When a function is invoked, C gives considerable flexibility in the types of the actual parameters. The types are declared immediately following the function definition statement. This is discussed in more detail later. All type conversions that are defined for assignments are also permitted when converting from actual to formal parameters.

7.5.2 ▪ Procedure Environment

Within a C function, there are four types of storage classes: automatic, register, external, and static.

Automatic class variables are declared within the function by placing the word `auto` in front of the declaration. This state is the default if no storage class is specified. `Auto` represents a local data object whose storage is allocated upon each call to the function and deallocated upon termination. The prefix `register` is functionally identical to `auto` but alerts the compiler to the fact that the data object is used frequently and the use of storage for the object may be optimized, if possible, through the use of registers. This prefix defines the **register class**.

Data objects are declared to be **external class** by preceding their declaration with the word `extern`. This prefix indicates that the data object is nonlocal and must have been defined in a separate file.

Data objects are declared **static class** by preceding their declaration with the word `static`. Data objects of this class have as their scope of name binding the function in which they are declared, but their location binding holds from the first invocation of the function until the end of program execution. This class of data object retains its value from one invocation of the procedure to the next, because it keeps its location binding. We have previously referred to such variables as `own` variables.

Nesting of procedures is not permitted in C, so there is no inherited procedure environment.

7.5.3 ▪ Parameters

The declarations of type for C formal parameters are listed after the template for the function call in the function definition. Positional association of parameters is used. See, for example, line 145 of Listing 7.

Actual parameters may be of different types than their corresponding formal parameters. A type conversion is made to the type of the formal parameter.

The only mode used by C is `IN` implemented by copy. This means that although formal parameters may be modified within a function, no change can occur to the actual parameters. The ability of C to manipulate pointers easily gives the programmer a natural way to simulate the reference implementation of parameter passing. The idea is to pass a pointer to the parametric data object as the actual parameter and dereference the formal parameter with the monadic * operator whenever it is used. For example, the following C function would double the value of its lone parameter:

```
void twice (v)
    int *v;
    {
    *v = *v * 2;
    }
```

Here the formal parameter v is declared to be a pointer to an integer. When the parameter is used, it is preceded by the referencing operator to indicate the integer pointed to by v. This function could be invoked as follows:

```
...
int i;
...
twice(&i);
...
```

Here, the address of the integer variable i is passed as the actual parameter.

Arrays deserve special attention, because arrays in C are always represented by a pointer. Therefore, arrays will naturally be passed by reference. The size of a singly indexed array that is a formal parameter need not be specified. Similarly, the size of the first index of a multi-indexed array need not be specified, but all other index sizes must be. The following procedure zeros the first Asize entries of an array of arbitrary size.

```
void zeroarray (Asize, A)
    int Asize, A[];
    {
    int i
    for (i=0; i<Asize; i++)
      A[i] = 0;
    }
```

Functions in C may be passed as parameters to other functions through a feature that permits the definition of pointers to functions. As an example, the following function adds the N terms resulting from applying an arbitrary function to the first N integers.

```
sum(N, F)
  int N;
  int (*F) ();
{
  int i,s
  s=0;
  for (i=1; i<=N; i++)
    s = s + (*F)(i);
  return s;
}
```

Here the parameter F is declared as a pointer to a function indicated by the empty parentheses following its declaration. This declaration also indicates the function pointed to by F returns an int. Note that the function is called by invoking (*F).

The following main program can now be used to add the squares of the first 10 integers.

```
main()
{
  int square();
  printf("%d \n",sum(10,square));
}
square(i)
  int i;
{
  return i*i;
}
```

7.5.4 ▪ Value-Returning Procedures

Values may be returned in C functions through a return statement, which has the form

```
return <expression>;
```

See lines 149–152 of Listing 7 for an example.

Functions may return only scalar types in C. Pointers are included as a scalar type, however, so pointers to arrays and structures are permitted as function return types as in lines 157–163 of Listing 7. The type returned by the function is included before the name in the call template of its definition. If no type is indicated, int type is assumed by default.

7.6 Data Abstraction

7.6.1 ▪ Encapsulation

Encapsulation in C is handled through use of source files as modules and through extern and static declarations of variables that are nonlocal to source files. Objects that are declared static within a source file are hidden from other source files. There is no provision for exporting the name of a data aggregate while hiding its constituent components. Therefore, this mechanism is not true data abstraction.

Communication between source file modules is through objects that are defined in one module and then declared as extern in a source file that needs to import them. Therefore, nonlocal objects — that is, objects declared outside of any execution block that are declared static — are local to the source file. Those declared extern are imported. Those declared with neither are candidates for being exported. Objects communicated may be functions, variables, or constants. Types are not exportable but must be redefined in each source file module where used.

7.7 Common Library Functions

Some facilities are not built into C but are so commonly included in standard libraries that they are considered a part of the language. The standard library is made available in a source file by including the line

```
#include <stdio.h>
```

This action provides several different classes of library functions, three of which are described in this section.

7.7.1 ▪ Input/Output Functions

Formatted input/output is available in C. The format is specified by the use of a conversion control string, which indicates how the data are to be formatted. The general form of a conversion control string is

```
%[-][<width>[.<precision>]] <conversion-code>
```

The percent symbol (%) indicates the beginning of a conversion control string. The minus sign (–) specifies that the data are to be left-justified in the field rather than right-justified, which is the default. The width field is an integer that specifies the field width, whereas the precision field indicates the number of places after the decimal for a float or double value. The conversion code indicates the type of the object to be converted. A list of conversion codes is found in Figure 7.1.

When used for output, the format string may contain any number of format conversion strings embedded within a longer character string. For example,

```
"The answer to problem %2d is %6.1f feet.\n"
```

specifies output that includes two values to be formatted, an integer and a floating point.

Special characters can also be embedded in this longer string. The most commonly used of these are \n for newline character and \t for tab character. The standard input/output functions are printf and scanf, and we describe them in some detail.

FIGURE 7.1 **Conversion Code Characters for C Standard Input/Output**

d	Integer in decimal
o	Integer in unsigned octal
x	Integer in unsigned hexadecimal
u	Integer in unsigned decimal
ld	Long integer in decimal
c	Single character
s	Character string
f	Floating-point number in decimal notation
e	Floating-point number in exponential notation
g	Floating-point number using shorter of %f and %e

The general form of a call to `printf` is

```
printf("<control-string>",{expression})
```

where the number of conversion codes included in the `control-string` must be the same as the number of occurrences of `expression`. For example, a `printf` to use the previous control string would be

```
printf("The answer to problem %2d is %6.1f feet.\n",n,ft);
```

The function `scanf` provides formatted input and its general form is similar to that of `printf`, namely,

```
scanf("<control-string>",{pointer});
```

Note that the arguments to `scanf` must be pointers to the data objects that are being input. The `control-string` for `scanf` will frequently contain only conversion control strings without width. This permits natural boundaries of input fields (such as spaces, newlines, or tabs) to be recognized as field delimiters. Widths can be included to restrict the input field to a specific size.

Variations of these two functions exist to write and read from files (`fprintf`, `fscanf`) and to memory (`sprintf`, `sscanf`). In addition, string and character I/O functions are available.

7.7.2 ▪ String-Handling Functions

Four functions are provided to facilitate string handling in C. These functions duplicate the operations of some of the functions in Listing 7, but these functions were defined there instead of imported from the library to provide a more complete demonstration of C programming.

The first function is `strcat`, which takes two strings as arguments and returns with the second argument string concatenated on the end of the first.

The function `strcmp` also takes two string arguments and compares them, returning zero if the two strings are identical, a positive integer if the first is larger than the second in lexicographic order, and a negative integer if the second is larger than the first. In Listing 7, `compare_strings` in lines 140–152 accomplishes the same task using a different coding scheme for the result.

The function `strcpy` accepts two string arguments and copies the first to the second. It is virtually identical to `copy_string` in lines 164–176 of Listing 7.

Finally, the function `strlen` accepts a single string argument and returns the integer length of that string. It could be written as follows:

```
int strlen (s)
  char *s;
{int len;
 for (len=0; s[len]!=0; len++);
 return (len);
}
```

7.7.3 ▪ **Memory-Allocation Functions**

Three functions are included in C to facilitate memory allocation. The sizeof function accepts one argument, which may be either a type or a variable, and returns an integer specifying the number of bytes used to represent the argument.

Memory is allocated through the use of the malloc function, which has a single integer argument specifying the number of bytes requested. This function then returns a pointer to the block of memory allocated to the program. The function free releases the memory previously allocated by malloc.

The following fragment illustrates the use of these three functions:

```
char *s
...
s = malloc(sizeof(float) * 100);
...
free(s);
...
```

C H A P T E R **7** **Terms**

case sensitive	structure
compile-time variable	union
source file	automatic class
switch statement	register class
break statement	external class
continue statement	static class

C H A P T E R **7** **Discussion Questions**

1. The power of the operators in C permits compact expression of many processes. What are advantages and disadvantages of this compactness?

2. How do types defined by TYPEDEF in C functionally differ from types declared in Ada?

C H A P T E R **7** **Exercises**

1. Indicate the equivalent Ada statement or statements corresponding to each of the following C statements:

   a. C++;
   b. C = (++C) + (D--);
   c. A = (B += 2) - 1;
   d. C = (A > B)?A++ : A--;
   e. C = (A > B)?++A : --A;

2. Given the following C declarations:

```
int *X, *Y;
int I,J;
```

Indicate the actions resulting from each of the following statements:

a. `X = I;`
b. `X = &I;`
c. `*X = I;`
d. `X = Y;`
e. `*X = *Y;`
f. `I = *X;`
g. `J = &I;`

3. Indicate Ada equivalents for each of the following C constructs:

a.
```
switch (x) {
      case 4:
      case 6: t=6;
              break;
      case 8: t=12;
      case 10:x=t+1;
              break;
      case 2: t=t-1;
      default:x=0;
  }
```

b.
```
while (x) {
      x=x-1;
      q=q/2;
  }
```

c.
```
do {
      c=c+1;
      x=x/2;
   }
   while (x>0);
```

d.
```
for (x=0; x<10; x=x+h)
   t=t-x;
```

4. Think about the size of various data elements you can represent through C. Predict the sizes of the following:

```
short
int
long
char
unsigned char
float
double
```

5. Why does the word "FALSE" never print in the sequence below?

```
x = 2;
y = 5;
if (x = y) {
   printf("TRUE\n");
} else {
   printf("FALSE\n");
}
```

6. What values are assigned to the variable "x" in the statements below? Assume the following declarations:

```
int x=5, y=10, z=25;
float a=3.1415, b=5.0;
```

   a. x = y;
   b. x = z/10;
   c. x = (float)z/10/b;
   d. x = (float)(x/10/b);
   e. a = z / b / 2;
   f. a = (int) b / 2;
   g. x = (char)b * 10 + 100;
   h. a = (char)y + 10 * (int)b;

C H A P T E R **7** **Laboratory Exercises**
_____

Write programs for each of the following exercises in C.

1. Write procedures to perform both quicksort and bubble sort, and write a calling program that performs an analysis of the timing for the two sorts by producing timings for the sorting of 100, 200, 400, and 800 elements.

2. Write a set of procedures to perform arithmetic on integers that are 100 decimal digits long.

3. Examine the predictions or estimates you made in Exercise 4. The "sizeof" function prints the size of a structure or type in bytes. Use this function to verify your estimates.

4. Write a C program to determine the largest integer possible on the machine in your lab. (*Note:* A program using an integer that is too big will probably not crash! Think about what it may do instead.)

(continues)

LISTING 7

```
1   /********************************************************************
2         Chapter 7 example written in C
3       Read and sort information on people.
4       See notes along the way about the oddities of C syntax.
5   *********************************************************************/
6   /*
7   * Constant definitions. Note (1) enumerated type values are just
8   * constants, and (2) we have no Booleans: TRUE and FALSE are integers.
9   */
10  #define NULL 0
11  #define Max_Name_Length 128
12  #define EQUAL 1
13  #define GREATER_THAN 2
14  #define LESS_THAN 3
15  #define TRUE 1
16  #define FALSE 0
17  /*
18  * Here is a definition for the NEW function on pointers.
19  */
20  #define NEW(A)    ((A *) malloc(sizeof(A)))
21  /*
22  * Type declarations. The "person" record/struct and named type to
23  * denote it.
24  */
25  struct person {
26          char name[Max_Name_Length];
27          int age;
28          struct person *next;
29  } ;
```

```
30   typedef struct person *namelist;

31   namelist head = NULL, current = NULL;

32   /*
33    * These declarations are necessary to use the external "string"
34    * package of definitions.
35    */

36   extern int compare_strings();
37   extern char *read_string();
38   extern void copy_string();

39   /***********************************************************************/
40   /*
41    * "read_info" reads in a sequence of name/age pairs and adds them to
42    * a linked list, modifying the global "head" and "tail" variables.
43    * The reading terminates when a name of "done" is entered. The procedure
44    * takes no arguments.
45    * --> Note "atoi" is a C library function that converts Ascii to Integer.
46    */

47   void read_info()
48   {
49       char    *str;
50       namelist tmp;

51       do {
52           printf("Enter name: ");
53           str = read_string();

54           if (compare_strings(str, "done") != EQUAL) {
55               tmp = NEW(struct person);
56               if (head == NULL) {
57                   head = tmp;
58               } else {
59                   current->next = tmp;
60               }
```

```
61            current = tmp;
62            copy_string(current->name, str);
63
64            printf("Enter age: ");
65            str = read_string();
66            current->age = atoi(str);
67        }
68     } while (compare_strings(str, "done") != EQUAL);
69     /*
70      * "sort_info" implements a simple bubble sort. A little work is needed
71      * to keep the pointers straight. It takes no arguments.
72      */
73     void sort_info()
74     {
75         int changed=TRUE; /* initialized every time proc is called! */
76         namelist prev, curr, tmp;
77
78         while (changed) {
79             changed = FALSE;
80             prev = NULL;
81
82             /*
83              * Note that the "for" loop has an empty third component. This
84              * is handled by the last statement in the block. Still the "for"
85              * construct makes for neat while loop shorthand.
86              */
87             for (curr=head; curr->next != NULL; ) {
88                 if (compare_strings(curr->name,curr->next->name)==GREATER_THAN) {
89                     changed = TRUE;
90                     tmp = curr->next;
91                     curr->next = tmp->next;
92                     tmp->next = curr;
93                     if (prev == NULL) {
94                         head = tmp;
                        } else {
                            prev->next = tmp;
```

```
 95                }
 96            }
 97            prev = curr;
 98            if (curr->next != NULL) curr=curr->next;
 99        }
100    }
101 }

102 /*
103  * "print_info" simply follows the links through the list and prints
104  * what it finds. It uses the "printf" C call, provided by I/O libraries.
105  * No arguments.
106  */
107 void print_info()
108 {
109    namelist curr;
110    int index = 0;

111    printf("\nPerson list: \n");
112    for (curr=head; curr != NULL; curr=curr->next)
113        printf(" #%d is %s, age %d<n", ++index, curr->name, curr->age);
114 }

115 /*
116  * MAIN PROGRAM! Short and sweet.
117  */
118
119 main()
120 {
121    read_info();
122    sort_info();
123    print_info();
124 }

125 /**********************************************************************
126  * string.c -- a separately-compiled collection of string routines.
127    Implemented: compare_strings, read_string, copy_string
```

(continues)

```
128        Note these routines are quite short. This is because arrays are
129    manipulated through pointers -- which are manipulated as integers
130    with "+" operations. Remember an ASCII 0 (\0) terminates strings.
131    ******************************************************************/
132    /*
133     * Constant definition. Note these are the same definitions contained
134     * in the main module, repeated out of necessity here.
135     */
136    #define Max_Name_Length 128

137    #define EQUAL 1
138    #define GREATER_THAN 2
139    #define LESS_THAN 3

140    /*
141     * "compare_strings" compares string"s1" to string "s2" and returns the
142     * appropriate constant.
143     */
144    int compare_strings(s1, s2)
145    char *s1, *s2;
146    {
147        while (*s1 == *s2) {
148            if (*s1 == '\0') return EQUAL;
149            s1++; s2++;
150        }
151        if (*s1 < *s2) {return LESS_THAN;} else {return GREATER_THAN;}
152    }

153    /*
154     * "read_string" reads a string from the keyboard. Made simple by the
155     * C library call "gets".
156     */
157    char *read_string()
158    {
159        char str[Max_Name_Length];
```

```
160        gets(str);
161        return str;
162
163    }

164    /*
165     * "copy_string" copies string "s2" to string "s1" (in the spirit of
166     * "s1 := s2"). Incredibly short because of C's compact notation.
167     * The single statement assigns, increments pointers, and returns the
168     * ASCII value of the assigned character in one line. When an ASCII 0
169     * is copied, a 0 is returned from the assignment, and the "while" will
170     * terminate.
171     */

172    void copy_string(s1, s2)
173    char *s1, *s2;
174    {
175        while (*s1++ = *s2++) ;
176    }
```

· C H A P T E R · 8

An Example Language:
Modula-2

8.1 ▪ Philosophy and Approach
8.2 ▪ Information Binding
8.3 ▪ Control Structures
8.4 ▪ Data Aggregates
8.5 ▪ Procedural Abstraction
8.6 ▪ Data Abstraction

8.1 Philosophy and Approach

Modula-2 is the third in a series of languages developed by Niklaus Wirth. The first, Pascal, was designed to be used as a teaching language, with its goals being language simplicity and support for structured programming concepts. The second language in the series was Modula, which was based on Pascal but was intended for use in programming real-time dedicated systems. It added features for concurrency and data abstraction. Modula-2, the third language in the sequence, combines some of the capabilities of both its predecessors and is intended to serve as a general-purpose programming language. Its extensive data abstraction features facilitate the development of large software projects. Modula-2 is also proposed by some as a replacement for Pascal as the primary teaching language.

The philosophy of Modula-2 is to encourage programming that is structured, modular, and understandable. It retains the block structure of Pascal and adds the concept of modules for encapsulation.

8.2 Information Binding

8.2.1 ▪ Data Objects

Like C, the identifiers in Modula-2 are case sensitive. This feature has been the source of many complaints from programmers who have become accustomed to languages like Pascal and Ada, which are not case sensitive.

Modula-2 does not permit type coercion. This feature implies that any mixing of types requires the use of an explicit type-conversion function. In particular, reals and integers may not be freely mixed in expressions. Neither may a real variable be assigned an integer expression value.

Constant declarations in Modula-2 may include expressions that involve previously defined constants. In addition to the usual types, Modula-2 also supports types called WORD and ADDRESS. These two types are provided to permit access to low-level features of the computer system. Data objects of type WORD refer to an addressable unit of storage. Assignment is the only permissible operator. The size of a WORD data object is implementation dependent. Type-transfer functions are required for moving data to and from other types to type WORD.

The type ADDRESS is a generic pointer variable that can specify the address of any data object and is operationally compatible with all pointer types and with type CARDINAL (the nonnegative integers).

Modula-2 permits the definition of a subrange type of any scalar type. This subrange type is then operationally compatible with its parent type without the use of a type conversion function. Modula-2 supports type declarations. Type equivalence in Modula-2 is based on structural equivalence.

8.2.2 ▪ Scalar Data Types

Modula-2 supports the numeric types INTEGER, CARDINAL, and REAL. CARDINAL is the set of nonnegative integers and shares operators with INTEGER type. The two types are assignment compatible but not compatible with respect to other operators.

Modula-2 also provides a Boolean type. In the evaluation of Boolean expressions, the operators AND and OR are treated as short-circuit operators. There are no corresponding operators that force evaluation of both operands.

Pointer types are declared as

```
POINTER TO <type>;
```

The dereferencing of the pointer object is done through the ↑ operator. For example, ↑x specifies the data object pointed to by pointer variable x. Allocation and deallocation of storage to a pointer variable are done through use of the NEW and DISPOSE procedures. NEW does not specify the type of object allocated, because that is implied by the type of the parameter to NEW, nor does NEW include any capability for initializing the object allocated. User-defined types may be enumerated in a manner similar to that used by Pascal.

8.2.3 ▪ Execution Units

The statement is the most elementary execution unit in Modula-2. Because Modula-2 has no unconditional branch instruction, statement labels are unnecessary and hence are not a part of the language definition. Like Pascal, Modula-2 uses the semicolon as a statement separator.

Blocks, as units of scope binding, do not exist in Modula-2. Modula-2 separates the concept of object binding and object visibility through the use of modules. Although modules are discussed in further detail under data abstraction and procedures are discussed under procedural abstraction, let us look at these two execution units with respect to binding and visibility at this point.

A procedure in Modula-2 has the following general form:

```
PROCEDURE <procedure-name> (<parameter-list>) [:<type>];
  [<local-declarations>]
BEGIN
  <statement-sequence>
END <procedure-name>;
```

When a procedure is called, ignoring the parameters for now, the following occurs:

1. All locally declared objects have their bindings enforced.
2. All bound objects in the containing environment whose names do not conflict with local bindings are inherited.
3. All modules declared locally in the procedure have their object bindings enforced and their bodies executed.
4. Finally, the procedure body itself is executed.

Therefore, the procedure serves as the basic unit of binding with inherited visibility from its containing procedure. When a procedure completes its execution, all local bindings are released.

A module serves as a unit of visibility rather than a unit of binding. The general form of the module is

```
MODULE <module-name>;
  {[FROM <module-name>] IMPORT <identifier-list>];}
  {EXPORT [QUALIFIED] <identifier-list>;}
  [<local-declarations>]
BEGIN
  <statement-sequence>
END <module-name>;
```

The **import** list specifies those objects declared in other modules that are to be visible in this module. The **export** list specifies those objects that are declared locally in this module but that are to be made visible to other modules through the other modules' import lists. The visible objects in a module are those that are locally declared plus those that are imported. The issue of qualifying the imported objects by the name of their defining module involves details beyond the scope of our present discussion.

A module's local objects are bound at the time its containing procedure is called. In addition, its body is executed at the time of the containing procedure's call, before the procedure's body is executed. A module not contained in a procedure is considered to be a main program module, and the beginning of execution of the program is considered the procedure call. Its body is the main program's execution body, and an export list is not permitted in a main program module. When another module name is included in the import list, then all that module's locally defined objects are made visible to the present module.

The use of blocks for delimiting control structures is handled by the use of special reserved words as delimiters in Modula-2. This process is described in the later discussion of control structures. Modules may also be used as compilation unit blocks. Lines 126–233 of Listing 8 illustrate the definition of a module.

8.3 Control Structures

8.3.1 ▪ Conditional Structures

Modula-2 has the following general form for the multialternative conditional:

```
IF <boolean-expression> THEN
  <sequence-of-statements>
{ELSIF <boolean-expression> THEN
  <sequence-of-statements>}
[ELSE
  <sequence-of-statements>]
END;
```

The blocks for the scope of the conditional are implied by the required use of the termination keywords ELSIF, ELSE, and END. These words replace the BEGIN-END blocks of Pascal. The use of semicolons in the last statement in each sequence is optional, because Modula-2 uses the semicolon as a statement separator. It is not prohibited before the ELSE, as is the case with Pascal, because the required END delimiter makes the interpretation clear.

Modula-2 also has a CASE statement. Its general form is

```
CASE <expression> OF
  <alternative-list> : <sequence-of-statements> {|
  <alternative-list> : <sequence-of-statements>}[|
  ELSE
    <sequence-of-statements>]
END;
```

The symbol | is used to separate each block of statements from the following alternative list. The selector expression can be of any discrete scalar type. The alternatives are comma-separated lists of values, expressions, or subranges of a type compatible with that of the selector expression. Duplicate values in the alternative lists are not permitted, but the alternatives do not need to be exhaustive of the selector type. A run-time error will occur, however, if the selector expression ever evaluates to an expression not found among the alternatives and no ELSE clause is included.

8.3.2 • Iterative Structures

Modula-2 has a nonterminating iteration structure of the form

```
LOOP
  <sequence-of-statements>
END;
```

Its pretest iteration is of the form

```
WHILE <condition> DO
  <sequence-of-statements>
END;
```

Its posttest iteration is of the form

```
REPEAT
  <sequence-of-statements>
UNTIL <condition>;
```

Modula-2 also has an in-test iteration that is implemented by including an EXIT statement within the scope of a LOOP-END iteration. The EXIT statement causes a branch to the statement following the END of the innermost active iteration.

The fixed-count iteration for Modula-2 is of the form

```
FOR <variable> := <expression> TO <expression>
  [BY <expression>] DO
  <sequence-of-statements>
END;
```

The index variable must be of a discrete type, making indexing by reals illegal in this context. All expressions must be of the same type as the index variable and the expressions are evaluated once at the initialization of the iteration.

8.4 Data Aggregates

8.4.1 • Arrays

Modula-2 binds an array to its domain and range at compile time. The selection operator is an index contained in brackets. Assignment of arrays is permissible if the arrays are of the same type as defined by named type equivalence. No composite or comparison operators are available for arrays. Modula-2 has one array attribute referenced by the function HIGH, which returns the highest index in the domain of the array.

Multi-indexed arrays are declared in a manner similar to Pascal, except that each index domain is enclosed in a separate set of brackets — for example

```
VAR a : ARRAY [1..10][1..20] OF REAL;
```

Elements of such an array can be referenced by either `a[i][j]` or `a[i,j]`.

8.4.2   ▪   Strings

Modula-2 has no formal string type, but strings are defined as arrays of type `CHAR` with domain `0..n-1` for some positive integer `n`. String constants may be enclosed in single or double quotes. String variables are assignment compatible with string constants. A string is terminated by the first null character in the array. Modula-2 then provides a utility module called `Strings`, which includes procedures to assign one string to another, insert or delete substrings, find the position of the first occurrence of a substring within a string, concatenate two strings, find the length of a string, and compare two strings lexicographically. The `Strings` module also defines the type `STRING` by

```
TYPE STRING = ARRAY [0..80] OF CHAR;
```

Listing 8 contains a rudimentary string module. This module was used in this example instead of the utility module `Strings` to illustrate Modula-2 concepts.

8.4.3   ▪   Records

Modula-2 has a standard record aggregate type. Selection of a component is via the period operator. The form of selection is

```
<record-name> . <record-component-name>
```

Literal record construction is not provided. Assignment of records is defined by the normal assignment operator. The general form of record declaration in Modula-2 is

```
RECORD <record-name>
  {<component-name-list> : <component-type>;}
END;
```

Modula-2 permits any number of record variants to be placed anywhere within a record. The syntax of a variant construct is

```
CASE [<tag-component>] : <tag-type> OF
  <expression-list> : {<component-name>:<type>;}
 {| <expression-list> : {<component-name>:<type>;}}
END;
```

Modula-2 provides no enforcement of the variants, permitting reference to any of the alternative components regardless of the value of the tag component. When the tag component name is omitted, even the pretense of a tag field is removed.

Another feature of Modula-2 records, inherited from Pascal, is the implementation of a WITH statement that specifies default record prefixes within its scope. Its general form is

```
WITH <record-name-list> DO
  <sequence-of-statements>
END;
```

Within the contained statement sequence, reference to components of any records whose names are listed in the WITH statement do not require the record name as a prefix.

8.4.4 ▪ Sets

Sets are fully implemented as a type in Modula-2. The declaration of a set is given by

```
SET OF <type>
```

The base type of a set must be Boolean type, character type, integer type, an enumeration type, or a subrange type. The cardinality of the base type is limited to some implementation-dependent finite number. Modula-2 has a predefined set type known as BITSET, which is the set of integers from 0 to b - 1, where b is the number of bits per memory word in the system. This permits objects of this type to be represented by a bit vector stored in a single word of memory.

Modula-2 supports the set operators of union (+), intersection (*), difference (−), and symmetric difference (/). In addition, predicates are provided to test for element inclusion (IN), set equality (=), set inequality (< >), subset (<=) and superset (>=).

8.5   Procedural Abstraction

8.5.1 ▪ Definition and Invocation

Modula-2 permits the abstraction of both a statement and an expression through the same procedure construct. Its general form of definition is

```
PROCEDURE <proc-name> [({[VAR] <par-name-list>:<type>})]
                                              [:<proc-type>]
```

The parameter list may be empty, in which case no parentheses need to be included. If a procedure type is included, the procedure is a function that abstracts an expression. If it is not included, the procedure abstracts a statement. See lines 37 and 159 of Listing 8 for example definitions.

The invocation of a procedure is specified by the procedure name, followed by a list of actual parameters separated by commas and enclosed in parentheses.

8.5.2 ▪ Procedure Environment

Modula-2 procedures may declare their own local data objects. These data objects are allocated memory at run time, with the binding to a storage location occurring at the time of procedure invocation. These local objects have their storage deallocated upon completion of procedure execution.

Data objects whose scope contains the procedure definition are nonlocal variables with respect to the procedure. In general, the scope rule for Modula-2 is that the scope of a data object binding is the procedure in which it is declared and all contained procedures that do not have a redeclaration of the same name.

8.5.3 ▪ Parameters

Modula-2 permits only positional association of parameters. The type of each formal parameter follows its appearance in the defining statement. Formal and actual parameter type matching is strictly enforced at compile time. The default mode for parameters is IN implemented by copy. IN formal parameters may, therefore, be modified within a procedure without affecting the value of the corresponding actual parameters. The IN OUT mode is indicated by placing the keyword VAR in front of the formal parameter declaration in the defining statement. It is implemented by reference.

One important feature of Modula-2 is the ability to include an open array as a formal parameter. An **open array** is an array whose declaration does not contain a domain definition. The formal parameter then assumes the domain of the corresponding actual parameter array. The procedure definition in line 179 of Listing 8 illustrates this.

Modula-2 implements the use of procedures as parameters by permitting the definition of procedure types by specifying the mode and type of all of its parameters. The general form of a procedure type declaration is

```
TYPE <type-name>=PROCEDURE ([[VAR] <type-identifier>
         {, [VAR] <type-identifier>}]) [:<type-identifier>];
```

Such procedure types may then be used as the types for formal parameters to procedures. This action enforces the requirement that the actual and formal procedures match in parameter order, in mode and type, and in result type.

8.5.4 ▪ Value-Returning Procedures

Modula-2 signifies that a procedure returns a value by placing a colon followed by a type name after the procedure invocation template. The return value is specified in a RETURN statement of the form

```
RETURN <expression>;
```

See the function in lines 159–166 of Listing 8. A procedure that does not return a value can still include a RETURN statement without an expression, which signifies immediate termination of the procedure execution. Both parameter modes are permissible for function parameters. There is no restriction on the type that can be returned by a function.

8.5.5 ▪ Coroutines

Modula-2 supports coroutines for alternate execution of units. Variables may be declared to be of type PROCESS. A variable of **process type** can be bound to a procedure through a call to the library procedure NEWPROCESS. Eligible procedures for this binding must be parameterless. Control is then transferred from one process to another via a call to the TRANSFER library procedure. The form of this call is

```
TRANSFER(OLD, NEW);
```

where OLD and NEW are both process variables. The present execution unit will be suspended and its execution state stored in the PROCESS variable OLD. Execution of the process whose state is identified by process variable NEW will then begin from its previously suspended state. It will begin execution from the start of the process procedure if that process has not been executed since NEWPROCESS was called for it. When any process completes execution, all currently suspended processes, as well as the initiating execution unit, are also terminated.

8.6 ▪ Data Abstraction

8.6.1 ▪ Encapsulation

Modula-2 supports data abstraction through modules. A **module** is a separate compilation unit that consists of two parts, definition and implementation, each of which must be in a physically different file. The **definition module** contains IMPORT and EXPORT statements and definitions of objects that are to be exported. Exported objects may be procedures, types, variables, or constants. Procedures whose identifiers are in the export list must have their call template included in the definition module. Types whose identifiers are in the export list must appear in a type declaration in the definition module, but the definition of the type may or may not appear in that type declaration, depending on whether the definition of the type is to be visible to or hidden from the modules that import that type. Hidden definitions are important in data abstraction. Variables and constants in the export list must be fully defined through declarations in the definition module. A main program module is a module containing no export list. Lines 126–139 of Listing 8 show a definition module.

The import list in the definition module contains the module names and corresponding identifiers that need to be visible for use in declarations in the definition module. Imported items needed only in the implementation module may be declared through an IMPORT statement there. The listed identifiers must be in the export list of their originating modules. The general form of the IMPORT statement is

```
FROM <module-name> IMPORT <identifier-list>;
```

Another form of the IMPORT statement is

```
IMPORT <module-name-list>;
```

This latter IMPORT statement makes all exported objects of the named modules visible to the present module but requires that all such objects be referenced through qualified identifiers of the form

```
<module-name> . <imported-identifier>
```

After the IMPORT and EXPORT statements, the definition module contains declarations (incomplete in the case of procedures and types with hidden implementation) of all exported objects.

The **implementation module** contains complete definitions of any procedures and hidden types that are exported from the module. In addition, definitions of any types, constants, variables, and procedures that are local to the module are included. Variables that are local to the module are own variables, retaining their location binding throughout the active life of the module. After all declarations, a further execution unit may be specified, contained within BEGIN and END. This is the initialization unit that is executed when the module is first imported by another module.

8.6.2 ▪ Parameterization

The format parameter type ARRAY OF WORD is compatible with any actual parameter type, and the function HIGH applied to a data element of this type will yield the size in words of the element. Unlike Ada, Modula-2 creates one executable unit that accepts any type rather than instantiating a separate unit for each specific type.

C H A P T E R **8**   **Terms**

import	module
export	definition module
open array	implementation module
process type	

C H A P T E R **8**   **Discussion Questions**

1. C and Modula-2 use quite different philosophies with respect to type coercion. Which philosophy do you prefer and why?

2. Modula-2 uses different constructs for specifying blocks for control structures, scope of binding, and procedural abstraction. C uses the same construct for all three. Discuss the relative advantages of these two approaches.

C H A P T E R **8** **Exercises**

1. Using the `if` and `loop` statement constructs in Modula-2, construct equivalents to the following statements.
   a. `WHILE x < y+2 DO x := x + 2 END;`
   b. `FOR i := 1 TO 50 BY 3 DO`
      `total := total + arr[i];`
   `END;`
   c. `REPEAT`
      `x := x + 2;`
      `y := y - 1;`
   `UNTIL x > y;`
   d. `WHILE zm(a,b) < x DO`
      `FOR i := zm(a,b) TO x DO`
         `xrr[a,b] := xrr[a,b] + x;`
         `a := a + b - 2;`
      `END;`
   `END;`

2. Pascal and Modula-2 are quite similar in many respects. Find points where they differ. Write code to illustrate the differences. (*Hint:* Modula-2's use of the `BEGIN` and `END` keywords differs from their use in Pascal.)

3. Pointers in Modula-2 differ from pointers in C, especially in declaration.
   a. Explain the declaration "`char **p[20]`" from C.
   b. Write a code fragment in Modula-2 that declares the same pointer structure as in (a).
   c. Explain which style you prefer.

4. Think about the size of various data elements you can represent through Modula-2. Predict the sizes of the following:

   ```
   WORD
   BYTE
   CARDINAL
   INTEGER
   CHAR
   ```

5. Consider the following generic stack ADT written in Ada (see Chapter 6 exercises):

   ```
   generic
         size: positive; -- ``positive'' means integers > 0
            type item is private;
         package stack_adt is
            type STACK is limited private;
            function initialize return STACK;
            procedure PUSH (stk: in out STACK; it: in item);
            function POP (stk: in out STACK) return item;
            private
               type table is array (1..size) of item;
   ```

```
type STACK is record
                        top: range 1..size := 0;
                        element: table;
                end record
    end stack_adt;
```

Write this specification as a parameterized stack module in Modula-2.

6. Based on your specification above, write the declarations for
    a. a stack of 100 integers
    b. a stack of 200 booleans
    c. a stack of 100 stacks, each a stack of 100 integers

7. For each of the type casts as follows in C (from Chapter 7, Exercise 6), write
    the corresponding statement in Modula-2. Are the results the same?

```
int x=5, y=10, z=25;
float a=3.1415, b=5.0;
```

   a. x = y;
   b. x = z/10;
   c. x = (float)z/10/b;
   d. x = (float)(x/10/b);
   e. a = z / b / 2;
   f. a = (int) b / 2;
   g. x = (char)b * 10 + 100;
   h. a = (char)y + 10 * (int)b;

C H A P T E R **8** **Laboratory Exercises**

Write programs for each of the following exercises in Modula-2.

1. Write procedures to perform both quicksort and bubble sort, and write a
    calling program that performs an analysis of the timing for the two sorts by
    producing timings for the sorting of 100, 200, 400, and 800 elements.

2. Write a set of procedures to perform arithmetic on integers that are 100 dec-
    imal digits long.

3. There is no sizeof operator in Modula-2 as in C. However, devise a way to
    test your predictions from Exercise 4. Then use this method to verify your
    answers to Exercise 4.

4. Write a program that counts from 1 to 100 by 2. This is simple, but write the
    identical programs in Pascal and C. Compare your solutions.

5. Write a MAZE module, using all the descriptions from Chapter 7, exercises 5
    and 6.
    a. First, design the module. What is the data representation? What is the set
    of operations?
    b. Now implement the module. Are the data representations sufficient? Is
    the set of functions sufficient?
    c. Now test the module.

(continues)

LISTING 8

```
 1    (*********************************************************
 2        Chapter 8 example written in Modula-2

 3        Read and sort information on people.
 4        See notes along the way about Modula-2 syntax.

 5    **********************************************************)

 6    MODULE Sorter;

 7    (*
 8    * Start off with importing the external routines we will need. The first
 9    * module imported is the user-written string module. This module contains
10    * the string definition and the comparison values (EQUAL, etc.).
11    *)

12    FROM string IMPORT compare_strings, read_string, copy_string,
13                       string, compare_values;
14    FROM InOut IMPORT WriteString, WriteLn, WriteInt, ReadInt;
15    FROM Storage IMPORT ALLOCATE, DEALLOCATE;

16    (*
17    * Type declarations. The "person" record and a named type to denote it.
18    *)
19    TYPE namelist = POINTER TO person;
20         person = RECORD
21                     name: string;
22                     age: INTEGER;
23                     next: namelist;
24                  END;
```

```
25    (*
26    *  Variables used below.
27    *)
28
29    VAR head: namelist;
30
31    (**********************************************************)
32    (*
33    * "read_info" reads in a sequence of name/age pairs and adds them to
34    * a linked list, modifying the formal parameter "head".
35    * The reading terminates when a name of "done" is entered.
36    *
37    *)
38
39    PROCEDURE read_info(VAR head: namelist);
40
41    VAR str, done_string: string;
42        tmp, curr: namelist;
43
44    BEGIN
45        done_string := 'done';
46        LOOP
47            WriteString("Enter name: ");
48            read_string(str);
49
          IF compare_strings(str, done_string) <> EQUAL THEN
              NEW(tmp);
              IF head = NIL THEN
                  head := tmp
```

(continues)

```
50              ELSE
51                  curr^.next := tmp
52              END;
53              curr := tmp;
54              copy_string(curr^.name, str);

55              WriteString("Enter age: ");
56              ReadInt(curr^.age)
57          END;
58          IF compare_strings(str, done_string) = EQUAL THEN EXIT END
59      END
60  END read_info;

61  (*
62   * "sort_info" implements a simple bubble sort. A little work is needed
63   * to keep the pointers straight. It takes one arguments, "head".
64   *)

65  PROCEDURE sort_info(VAR head: namelist);

66      VAR changed: BOOLEAN;
67          curr, prev, tmp: namelist;

68      BEGIN
69          changed := TRUE;
70          WHILE changed DO
71              changed := FALSE;
72              prev := NIL;
73              curr := head;
```

```
74          WHILE curr^.next <> NIL DO
75              IF compare_strings(curr^.name, curr^.next^.name) = GREATER_THAN THEN
76                  changed := TRUE;
77                  tmp := curr^.next;
78                  curr^.next := tmp^.next;
79                  tmp^.next := curr;
80                  IF prev = NIL THEN
81                      head := tmp
82                  ELSE
83                      prev^.next := tmp
84                  END
85              END;
86              prev := curr;
87              IF (curr^.next <> NIL) THEN curr := curr^.next END
88          END
89      END
90  END sort_info;

91  (*
92   * "print_info" simply follows the links through the list and prints
93   * what it finds.
94   *)

95  PROCEDURE print_info(head: namelist);
96
97      VAR curr: namelist;
98          index: INTEGER;
99
100 BEGIN
101     WriteLn();
```

(continues)

```
102         WriteString("Person list: "); WriteLn();
103         index := 0;
104         curr := head;

105         WHILE curr <> NIL DO
106           index := index + 1;
107           WriteString(" #");
108           WriteInt(index,1);
109           WriteString(" is ");
110           WriteString(curr^.name);
111           WriteString(", age ");
112           WriteInt(curr^.age,1);
113           WriteLn();
114           curr := curr^.next
115         END
116       END print_info;

117    (*
118     * MAIN PROGRAM! Short and sweet.
119     *)

120    BEGIN
121       head := NIL;

122       read_info(head);
123       sort_info(head);
124       print_info(head)
125    END Sorter.
```

```
126    (*****************************************************************
127    Definition module for the external string routines.
128    This is the only file the main program sees when it is compiled.
129    ****************************************************************)

130    DEFINITION MODULE string;

131    EXPORT QUALIFIED compare_strings, read_string, copy_string,
132                     string, compare_values;

133    CONST Max_Name_Length = 128;
134    TYPE compare_values = (EQUAL, GREATER_THAN, LESS_THAN);
135         string = ARRAY [0..Max_Name_Length] OF CHAR;

136    PROCEDURE compare_strings (s1, s2: ARRAY OF CHAR) : compare_values;
137    PROCEDURE read_string (VAR str: ARRAY OF CHAR);
138    PROCEDURE copy_string (VAR s1, s2: ARRAY OF CHAR);

139    END string.

140    (*****************************************************************
141    string.mod -- the implementation module for the external string routines.

142    See the definition module for global definitions.

143    Because of Modula-2's strong typing, these routines are rather lengthy.
144    Note that an end-of-string character is inserted at the end of each
145    string -- an ASCII 0 like in C.
146    ****************************************************************)
```

(continues)

```
147      IMPLEMENTATION MODULE string;

148      (*
149      * Import necessary file I/O routines....
150      *)

151      FROM InOut IMPORT Read, ReadLn, EOL, Done;

152      CONST EOS = 0C; (* End-of-string mark *)

153      (*
154      * Below are two local (private) routines for this module: MIN returns
155      * minimum of its two integer arguments and LENGTH returns the integer
156      * length of its string argument.
157      * --> Note that only this module can "see" these definitions.
158      *)

159      PROCEDURE MIN (i1, i2: INTEGER) : INTEGER;
160          BEGIN
161              IF i1 <= i2 THEN
162                  RETURN i1
163              ELSE
164                  RETURN i2
165              END
166          END MIN;

167      PROCEDURE length (s: ARRAY OF CHAR) : INTEGER;
168          VAR index: INTEGER;
169          BEGIN
170              FOR index := 0 TO HIGH(s) DO
```

```
171            IF s[index] = EOS THEN RETURN index END
172         END;
173         RETURN HIGH(s)+1
174     END length;

175  (*
176   * "compare_strings" compares string"s1" to string "s2" and returns
177   * appropriate "compare_value" constant.
178   *)

179  PROCEDURE compare_strings(s1, s2: ARRAY OF CHAR)  : compare_values;
180     VAR index, minimum_length: INTEGER;
181     BEGIN
182        minimum_length := MIN(length(s1), length(s2));
183        index := 0;
184        WHILE (s1[index] = s2[index]) AND (index <= minimum_length) DO
185           IF (index = length(s1)) AND (index = length(s2)) THEN RETURN EQUAL END;
186           index := index + 1
187        END;
188        IF (index <= length(s1)) AND (index <= length(s2)) THEN
189           IF s1[index] < s2[index] THEN
190              RETURN LESS_THAN
191           ELSE
192              RETURN GREATER_THAN
193           END
194        ELSE
195           IF index < length(s1) THEN
196              RETURN GREATER_THAN
197           ELSE
198              RETURN LESS_THAN
```

```
199              END
200          END
201      END compare_strings;

202  (*
203   * "read_string" reads a string from the keyboard, inserting an end-of-string
204   * mark after it.
205   *)

206  PROCEDURE read_string (VAR str: ARRAY OF CHAR);
207      VAR index: INTEGER;
208          ch: CHAR;
209      BEGIN
210          index := 0;
211          LOOP
212              Read(ch);
213              IF ch = EOL THEN (* end of the line? *)
214                  ReadLn();
215                  EXIT
216              END;
217              str[index] := ch;
218              index := index + 1
219          END;
220          str[index] := EOS
221      END read_string;

222  (*
223   * "copy_string" copies string "s2" to string "s1" (in the spirit of
224   * "s1 := s2"). Amounts to an array copy.
225   *)
```

```
226     PROCEDURE copy_string (VAR s1, s2: ARRAY OF CHAR);
227        VAR len, index: INTEGER;
228        BEGIN
229           FOR index := 0 TO length(s2) DO
230              s1[index] := s2[index]
231           END
232        END copy_string;

233     END string.
```

![gray banner]

An Overview of a Functional Model

The programming language model that is introduced in this chapter is based on the mathematical concept of function, which is a mapping from a domain set to a range set. When this concept is used as a model for programs, the domain is the set of all possible inputs, and the range is the set of all possible outputs.

Functions are precisely defined and analyzed. The concept of functional programming is introduced, and languages that implement that paradigm are described. A brief review of the development of functional languages is presented, the FP programming language is introduced, and an evaluation of functional languages in comparison with imperative programming languages is provided.

9.1 Introduction to the Functional Language Model

The functional language model implements the functional paradigm of computing. This paradigm considers a program to be a mathematical function. A formal definition of mathematical functions and their mapping into functional languages is given later in this chapter. The basic idea is that a function is a black box that is provided with a number of inputs, called parameters, and produces a single output, called a result. What is done to obtain the result is unknown and unspecified to the user of the function.

For functions to be useful, they must be defined and invoked. The definition of a function needs to include a prototype of the way it is invoked, including the identification of the function and the identification of its parameter(s). The meaning of identification as used in the preceding sentence depends upon the nature of the functional language. In a strongly typed language, identification includes both a name and a type, where the type of the function itself is the type of the value it returns. In a language that is not strongly typed, only the name is required to identify a parameter, because type will be determined at run time.

The parameters of a function correspond to its inputs, and the function name itself refers to its output, or return value. In addition to the invocation prototype, the definition needs to specify the action of the function — that is, the way the parameters are transformed into a result. In the functional paradigm, the only way that a function's actions can be specified is through the invocation of another function.

The invocation of a function is specified by the name of the function to be invoked plus a list of values to be supplied for the parameters of the function. The parameters themselves may be given as constant values or the results of other function invocations.

To clarify the concepts just discussed, consider a function for evaluating one root of the quadratic equation $ax^2 + bx + c$. Algebraically, the calculation of such a root is specified by

$$x = \frac{-b + \sqrt{b^2 - 4ac}}{2a}$$

In a functional language, assuming all entities are of type real, our function might be defined as follows:

```
Function name: oneroot
Parameters: a,b,c all real
Return value: real
Definition:
      div(add(neg(b),sqrt(sub(sqr(b),mult(4,mult(a,c))))),
         mult(2,a))
```

Notice that this assumes that the functions div, add, neg, sqrt, sub, sqr, and mult already exist. Here the result of an invocation of function oneroot with three parameters is defined to be the result of the invocation of another function (div), with two parameters that are the results of invocations of the functions add and mult, and so on.

In order for this process to work, a language of the functional model must contain a set of functions that are predefined within the language. These functions are called *primitive functions*. In the case of the oneroot function, the seven functions used in its definition might all be primitive functions for a language. On the other hand, some of the functions, like sqr, might be non-primitive and defined in terms of invocations of other functions.

A key property of functional languages is that there are no variables and, correspondingly, no assignment statements. Imperative languages employ a modifiable state of data objects, which consists of variables whose values change at run time. In the functional model, no such state exists. Parameters, although they are named and used like variables, are never changed. They are given a value at the beginning of function execution, and that value never changes. In that way, they behave more like named constants.

A final feature of the functional model is that function parameters and return values may themselves be functions. This feature is often referred to as treating functions as first-class values. A functional language includes some of these functions of functions, also called functional forms, among its primitive set of functions.

Control structures in a functional language are expressed as functional forms. For example, a conditional control structure might be expressed as a function with three functional parameters, where a call is of the form

```
conditional(f₁,f₂,f₃)
```

The meaning of this functional form is that if f_1 is evaluated to true, f_2 will be evaluated as the result of function conditional. Otherwise, f_3 will be evaluated as the result of conditional. Of course, such a function needs an appropriate set of parameters to be properly evaluated.

Functional languages frequently build in some appropriate data aggregation facility, often a list, that permits multiple data objects to be considered as a single object. This feature is especially useful in dealing with the single-output restriction of functions, permitting the single-return result to be an aggregate of many values.

9.2 Functions

A **function** has three basic components: domain, range, and definition. The **domain** is the set of objects to which the function can be applied, the **range** is a set containing all objects that can result from an application of the function, and the **definition** is a specification of how a range element is determined from a domain element. A fourth, optional, component of a function is its name.

For example, if we wish to define a function called *double*, we could specify its four components as follows:

Domain: set of integers

Range: set of integers

Definition: $x + x$, where x is an element from the domain

Name: double

In mathematical notation, we would write this function definition as

```
double(x) = x + x
```

and specify the domain and range by

```
double : integer → integer
```

The mathematical notation for the application of a function to a specific domain value is the name of the function followed by the domain value enclosed in parentheses. For example, function `double` applied to 2 is written as

```
double(2)
```

Several points need to be made about this notation. First, it makes naming a function a requirement, because the name is a required part of the function's application. Second, note that the function definition includes the operator *plus*, which is in reality a function itself. A more consistent functional notation for x + y would be + (x,y), to indicate + is a function with domain the set of integer pairs and range the set of integers.

For our future discussion of functions, we will introduce a notation different from the traditional mathematical one for the definition and application of functions. This form of expressing functions is known as the **lambda expression**, after the Greek letter used as a part of the notation. It was developed by Alonzo Church (1941).

The new form of function definition is

```
[<function name>≡]  λ<list of domain element names>.<definition>
```

For our function double, the definition is

```
double ≡  λx.x+x
```

The fact that the name specification is optional permits the definition of a function without assigning that function a name.

In addition, the application of a function now has a completely different form from its definition. The lambda expression form for function application is

```
<function specifier> : <domain value>
```

The function specifier could be either a name or the definition of a function. Given the preceding definition of `double`, this function could be applied to domain value 2 by

```
double : 2
```

or, equivalently, by

```
λx.x+x : 2
```

As an example of a function with a composite domain, consider the `max` function, which could be defined by

```
max : integer × integer → integer
max ≡   λx,y. if x>y then x else y
```

Note that, for our purposes, the definition can be specified in any form as long as any domain tuple maps into a unique range value. The application of the function max is then written, in lambda format, as

```
max : <4,2>
```

where the angle brackets are used to enclose the components of a multicomponent domain.

The definition of functions can frequently include the application of other functions. For example, the absolute value function can be defined as

```
abs ≡ λ x . max:<x,-x>
```

The mechanics of the application of a function are straightforward. Each name appearing in the domain list of the definition is bound to the positionally corresponding value in the function application. These names are referred to as **bound variables**. In the case of the abs function just defined, its application specified by

```
abs : 6
```

would result in 6 replacing x in the definition of abs, yielding

```
max : <6,-6>
```

This application of max would then result in x being replaced by 6 and y by –6 in the max definition, giving

```
if 6>-6 then 6 else -6
```

which would evaluate to the value 6. We can represent this application more compactly by

```
abs : 6                    ⇒
max : <6,-6>               ⇒
if 6>-6 then 6 else -6  ⇒
6
```

One further feature is the ability to compose two functions to form a new function. For example, suppose we wish to construct a function that returns the absolute value of twice the given domain value. In mathematical notation, we can write

```
f(x) = abs(double(x))
```

In our lambda expression notation, we define such **function composition** by a new operator. This operator defines a new function from two previously defined functions through composition. The function f defined by the composition of abs and double is defined in lambda notation by

```
f ≡ abs ∘ double
```

This means that an application of f is equivalent to successive applications of double and abs.

To see how composition behaves during its application, study the application description:

```
f : -3                          ⇒
abs : double : -3               ⇒
abs : -3 + -3                   ⇒
abs : -6                        ⇒
if -6>6 then -6 else 6  ⇒
6
```

Composition is an example of what we will call a **functional form**, namely, a function whose domain is a tuple (possibly a singleton) of functions and whose range is also a function. For example, composition takes two functions as domain values and results in a third function, which is the composition of the original two.

9.3   Functional Programming

To a certain degree all programming can be thought of as functional in nature; that is, programs can be considered as representations of functions. The input given to the program corresponds to the functional parameters, whereas the output corresponds to the result of the function. Functional programming carries this idea to the most fundamental level of program construction.

Whereas imperative programming is based on the sequential modification of some internal machine state or store, functional programming builds programs from other programs, always considering the programs as black boxes, with no consideration for the sequence of activities that must be performed or for the progression of internal states of the data store during the computation.

The key property of a functional program is **referential transparency**. This property refers to the ability to call a function without producing side effects — that is, without changing the internal state of the computations. A function that exhibits referential transparency depends only upon its parameters and effects only its return value. In languages such as Ada, the use of nonlocal variables or file operations destroys referential transparency.

The main value of this referential transparency is in enhancing our ability to reason about a program, either formally or informally, because the complete description of the function's activity is specified by its definition, with no other intervening factors.

A second property of functional programming is the treatment of functions as **first-class objects**. This property means that functions are treated like any other object in the language. In particular, it means that functions can be used as parameters and return values of other functions.

9.4 Functional Programming Languages

Functional programming languages are languages that are intended to support the functional paradigm of programming. Such languages have six major components.

1. *A set of primitive functions* — Primitive functions are basic functions that are built into the language and that can be used as the fundamental building blocks for all functions which can be constructed.

2. *A set of functional forms* — Functional forms are functions that accept functions as parameters. If functions are first-class objects in a language, the set of built-in functions might include a set of build-in functional forms. Otherwise, functional forms might be provided separately or given as operators instead of functions. Functional forms are useful for constructing new functions from functions that are already defined.

3. *The application operator* — The application operator is a special functional form that takes as parameters a function and a set of parameter values and returns the result of applying the function to the parameters.

4. *A set of data objects* — Data objects in a functional language typically consist of some atomic type of object and the ability to construct some form of aggregate object from atoms and other aggregate objects. Languages use different models for constructing aggregates: FP uses sequences, LISP uses lists, APL uses arrays.

5. *Binding of names to functions* — This binding is the only form of permanent binding provided in a purely functional language. Most languages compromise on the issue of referential transparency, however, and provide some form for binding names to data objects.

6. *Implicit storage management* — Because functional languages do not provide facilities for directly modifying the state of the storage for a computation, the management of the store must be handled implicitly. This typically includes implicit dynamic storage allocation and garbage collection.

An additional issue that frequently arises in functional languages is **lazy function evaluation**. This refers to a strategy that eliminates unnecessary evaluations of functions and includes two substrategies: (1) postponing evaluation of a function until it is needed, and (2) eliminating the reevaluation of the same function more than once.

As an illustration of these two strategies, consider the following FP function:

```
if g(f(x)) then m(f(x)) else n(f(x))
```

This is an `if-then` construct, and if it is evaluated strictly, it requires six function evaluations. Lazy evaluation, however, would reduce this to only two function evaluations, because `f` would need to be evaluated only once (thanks to referential transparency) and only one of the two functions `m` and `n` would need to be evaluated.

9.5 History of Functional Languages

A detailed discussion of the evolution of functional languages is given in Hudak (1989). We briefly summarize this evolution here. LISP was the first functional language, developed by John McCarthy in the late 1950s for artificial intelligence applications. LISP is discussed in detail in Chapter 10. Dialects of LISP, such as Logo and Scheme, have also become heavily used.

APL, although not designed to be a functional language, has some strong functional characteristics. APL contains both the assignment statement and statement sequencing as fundamental nonfunctional features, but it contains enough powerful operators to permit functional definition of programs as well. It differs from Lisp in its introduction of an expanded alphabet to express operators, its use of infix rather than prefix notation, and its use of arrays rather than lists as the fundamental data structure. Although it contains several functional forms in its language definition, APL fails to treat functions as first-class objects and does not have referential transparency.

In his 1978 Turing Award lecture, John Backus defined the class of functional programming languages called FP. The purpose of his paper was to define and advocate functional programming. FP followed the APL model of introducing an extensive set of functional forms. Because of its defining role in functional programming, we introduce FP in Chapter 9.

The language Standard ML, or SML, was designed by a team in the United Kingdom in the mid-1980s. It is described in Milner et al. (1990) and Wikstrom (1987). Combining the features of two earlier languages, ML and Hope, its main feature is its strong type facility. This permits the definition of abstract data types as well as overloading and polymorphism. The latter term is a defining property of the object-oriented paradigm and is defined in Chapter 14.

Several more recent functional programming languages have been based on the λ-calculus of expressions. The most prominent of these are Miranda and Haskell.

9.6 FP: A Pure Functional Language

9.6.1 ▪ Introduction

In this chapter we introduce a language developed by Backus (1978) called FP, which is designed to embody the pure form of a functional programming system. Backus actually defines a general class of functional languages and then specifies one language of that class as an example. That example language is FP.

The general class of languages has four basic components. When all these components are defined, a particular functional programming language is determined. These components are

1. a set of atomic objects, from which a more general set of objects can be constructed;

2. an application operation that applies a function to an object;

3. a set of primitive functions, each of which maps objects into objects and cannot be defined in terms of other functions;

4. a set of functional forms, where a functional form is defined as a function that maps a sequence of functions and objects into a new function.

The language FP is a member of this class of languages, and it is described next by a specification of each of these four components.

9.6.2 ▪ Basic Components

Objects   The set of objects for any language in the class of functional languages is defined as the set of atomic objects, sequences of objects, and an undefined object denoted by $\perp$. In BNF notation, an object is

```
object ::= ⊥ | <defined-object>
defined-object ::= <atom> | <object-sequence>
object-sequence ::= < <defined-object> {,<defined-object>} >
```

The set of atomic objects for the FP language consists of nonempty sequences of characters made up of digits, uppercase letters, and other special symbols that are not used by the notation of FP. The character $\varnothing$ is used to represent the empty sequence and is considered to be both an atom and a sequence. The special atoms T and F are used to represent true and false.

Some example objects are

```
⊥ A C12 12 <4,A,B> <7,<A,B>,20>
```

Application Operation   The application of a function to an object is expressed by the function specifier, followed by a colon, followed by the object specifier. The function specifier might be either a function name or the definition of a function. Note that a function can only be applied to a single object, but that object can be a sequence of objects, thus permitting more complex domains.

The following are examples of functions applications:

```
max:<4,2>        +:<3,7>        cat:<<4,A>,<C,D>>
```

Primitive Functions   The set of primitive functions defined for FP can be divided into four groups, each of which we describe individually. The functions are defined in Figure 9.1 by a three-column table. The first column contains a generalized application of the function, followed by $\equiv$, followed by a description of the meaning of the generalized application. The second column contains an English description of the function. The third column contains a sample application and its result separated by $\equiv$.

FIGURE 9.1   Primitive Functions of FP

Simple Selection and Structure

$i:\langle x_1,\ldots,x_n\rangle \equiv x_i$	selection of ith component	$2:\langle a,\langle b,c\rangle,d\rangle \equiv \langle b,c\rangle$
$tl:\langle x_1,\ldots,x_n\rangle \equiv \langle x_2,\ldots,x_n\rangle$	selection of tail subsequence	$tl:\langle a,\langle b,c\rangle,d\rangle \equiv \langle\langle b,c\rangle,d\rangle$
$cons:\langle x,\langle x_1,\ldots,x_n\rangle \equiv$ $\quad \langle x,x_1,\ldots,x_n\rangle$	construct a sequence from an object and another sequence	$cons\langle a,\langle b,c\rangle\rangle \equiv \langle a,b,c\rangle$
$length:\langle x_1,\ldots,x_n\rangle \equiv n$	length of a sequence	$length\langle a,\langle b,c\rangle,d\rangle \equiv 3$
$id:x \equiv x$	identity function	$id:a \equiv a$

Arithmetic (defined only for numeric sequences)

$+:\langle x,y\rangle \equiv x + y$	addition	$+:\langle 4,2\rangle \equiv 6$
$-:\langle x,y\rangle \equiv x - y$	subtraction	$-:\langle 4,2\rangle \equiv 2$
$\times:\langle x,y\rangle \equiv x \times y$	multiplication	$\times:\langle 4,2\rangle \equiv 8$
$\div:\langle x,y\rangle \equiv x \div y$	division	$\div:\langle 4,2\rangle \equiv 2$
$>:\langle x,y\rangle \equiv$ T if x>y $\quad$ F otherwise	greater than	$>:\langle 4,2\rangle \equiv$ T

Boolean (result is T or F)

$atom:x \equiv$ T if x atom	test for atom	$atom:\langle a,b\rangle \equiv$ F
$null:x \equiv$ T if x is ϕ	test for null sequence	$null:\langle a,b\rangle \equiv$ F
$eq:\langle x,y\rangle \equiv$ T if x=y	test for equality	$eq:\langle a,a\rangle \equiv$ T
$and:\langle x,y\rangle \equiv$ T if both are T	and	$and:\langle T,F\rangle \equiv$ F
$or:\langle x,y\rangle \equiv$ T if one is T	or	$or:\langle T,F\rangle \equiv$ T
$not:x \equiv$ T if x is F	not	$not:F \equiv$ T

Complex Selection and Structure

$distl:\langle y,\langle x_1,\ldots,x_n\rangle\rangle \equiv$ $\quad \langle\langle y,x_1\rangle,\ldots,\langle y,x_n\rangle\rangle$	distribute left	$distl:\langle a,\langle b,c,d\rangle\rangle \equiv$ $\quad \langle\langle a,b\rangle,\langle a,c\rangle,\langle a,d\rangle\rangle$
$distr:\langle\langle x_1,\ldots,x_n\rangle,y\rangle \equiv$ $\quad \langle\langle x_1,y\rangle,\ldots,\langle x_n,y\rangle\rangle$	distribute right	$distr:\langle\langle b,c,d\rangle,a\rangle \equiv$ $\quad \langle\langle b,a\rangle,\langle c,a\rangle,\langle d,a\rangle\rangle$
$apndl:\langle y,\langle x_1,\ldots,x_n\rangle\rangle \equiv$ $\quad \langle y,x_1,\ldots,x_n\rangle$	append left	$apndl:\langle a,\langle b,c,d\rangle\rangle \equiv$ $\quad \langle a,b,c,d\rangle$
$apndr:\langle\langle x_1,\ldots,x_n\rangle,y\rangle \equiv$ $\quad \langle x_1,\ldots,x_n,y\rangle$	append right	$apndr:\langle\langle b,c,d\rangle,a\rangle \equiv$ $\quad \langle b,c,d,a\rangle$
$tlr:\langle x_1,\ldots,x_n\rangle \equiv$ $\quad \langle x_1,\ldots,x_{n-1}\rangle$	tail right	$tlr:\langle a,b,c\rangle \equiv \langle a,b\rangle$
$ir:\langle x_1,\ldots,x_n\rangle \equiv x_{n-i+1}$	ith from the right	$2r:\langle a,b,c,d\rangle \equiv c$

In the case of each function, the function applied to ⊥, the undefined object, results in the undefined object. In addition, if the structure of the object to which a function is applied makes application of the function impossible, the result is also the undefined object. For example, because the function tl requires a sequence for its application,

```
tl : A ≡ ⊥
```

Functional Forms The FP language includes seven functional forms, as defined in Figure 9.2. A functional form creates a new function from a tuple of elements. These elements may be functions or objects. The functional form for constant is the only one defined here that has an object parameter. It creates a function equal to the constant value of the object. Several functional forms require one of their parameters to be a special function that returns T or F in order for the function result to be defined. If the function provided is not of this form, the result is undefined. For example,

```
(+ → tl ; tlr) : <6,4> ≡ ⊥
```

is invalid, because this functional form requires a Boolean function for its initial parameter, and + is not Boolean — that is, it does not always return either T or F.

One further notation is introduced into our language to permit the binding of a name to a function. The form of this construct is

```
Def l ≡ r
```

where l is some function identifier that is not already bound to a definition and r is a definition of the function. Therefore, it is possible, for example, to construct all the comparison functions from >. These definitions are

FIGURE 9.2 **Functional Forms in FP**

$$f_1 \circ f_2 : x \equiv f_1 : (f_2 : x) \qquad \text{composition} \qquad 2 \circ tl : <a,b,c,d> \equiv c$$
$$\overline{n} \equiv n \qquad \text{constant} \qquad \overline{1} \equiv 1$$
$$[f_1, \ldots, f_n] : x \equiv <f_1 : x, \ldots, f_n : x> \qquad \text{construction} \qquad [+, \times, \overline{2}] : <3,2> \equiv <5,6,2>$$
$$\alpha f : <x_1, \ldots, x_n> \equiv <f : x_1, \ldots, f : x_n> \qquad \text{apply-to-all} \qquad \alpha + : <<3,1>, <5,3>,$$
$$<6,6>> \equiv <4,8,12>$$
$$/f : x \equiv x_1 \text{ if } x = <x_1> \qquad \text{insertion} \qquad /+ : <2,4,3,7> \equiv 16$$
$$\qquad f : <x_1, /f : <x_2, \ldots, x_n>> \text{ otherwise}$$
$$(p \to f;g) : x \equiv f : x \text{ if } p : x = T \qquad \text{condition} \qquad (> \circ [1,2] \to - ; +) : <5,3> \equiv 2$$
$$\qquad g : x \text{ if } p : x = F$$
$$(\text{while } p \ f) : x \equiv x \text{ if } p : x = F \qquad \text{while} \qquad (\text{while atom} \circ \overline{1} \ tl):$$
$$<a,b,<c,d>,e> \equiv <<c,d>,e>$$
$$\qquad (\text{while } p \ f) : (f : x) \text{ if } p : x = T$$

```
Def geq ≡ or ∘ [>,eq]
Def leq ≡ not ∘ >
Def lss ≡ not ∘ geq
Def neq ≡ not ∘ eq
```

Programs in FP are then function definitions, and the execution of a program corresponds to the application of the function to an object. The program input is the object to which the function is applied, and the output is the object resulting from the function application. The preceding four function definitions are, therefore, examples of programs as well as functions that can be used in the construction of other functions.

9.6.3 • Examples

In this section we examine four function definitions that illustrate the spirit of functional programming in FP.

Example 1: Factorial   The factorial function can be written with the aid of three auxiliary functions. The first tests its atomic parameter for the zero value. Its form is

```
Def eq0 ≡ eq ∘ [id, 0̄]
```

The second function decrements its atomic parameter by 1. It is given by

```
Def dec ≡ - ∘ [id, 1̄]
```

The third function determines whether its atomic parameter is positive:

```
Def pos ≡ gtr ∘ [id, 0̄]
```

With these three functions and from the recursive definition of factorial, given by

```
factorial(x) = 1                     if x=0
               x * factorial(x-1)    if x>0
               undefined             if x<0
```

we can construct the FP factorial function:

```
Def fact ≡ (eq0 → 1̄;(pos → × ∘ [id,fact ∘ dec];⊥))
```

Note that the first condition function form has as its else part another conditional form. Also observe the recursive nature of this definition.

Consider the application of fact specified by

```
fact : 3
```

This result is calculated by

```
fact : 3                               =>
× ∘ [id,fact ∘ dec] : 3                =>
× : <3,fact:2>                         =>
× : <3,× ∘ [id,fact ∘ dec]:2>          =>
× : <3,×:<2,fact:1>>                   =>
```

```
X : <3,X:<2,X ∘ [id,fact ∘ dec]:1>>                    =>
X : <3,X:<2,X:<1,fact:0>>>                             =>
X : <3,X:<2,X:<1,0>>>                                  =>
X : <3,X:<2,X:<1,1>>>                                  =>
X : <3,X:<2,1>>                                        =>
X : <3,2>                                              =>
6
```

Example 2: Append The second example function appends two sequences — for example,

```
append : < <a,b,c>,<d,e> > ≡ <a,b,c,d,e>
```

We again construct an auxiliary function to make the `append` function easier to express. This auxiliary function will take the first component of the right sequence and move it to become the last component of the left sequence — in other words,

$$\texttt{moveleft} : <<x_1,...,x_n>,<y_1,...,y_m>> \equiv$$
$$<<x_1,...,x_n,y_1>,<y_2,...,y_m>>$$

This expression says that the left sequence of the result is constructed by appending the first component of the second sequence to the right end of the left sequence. Furthermore, the right sequence of the result is the tail of the original right sequence. In FP, this is written

```
Def moveleft ≡ [apndr ∘ [1,1 ∘ 2],tl ∘ 2]
```

To see how this expression works, examine the following example application sequence:

```
moveleft : <<a,b>,<c,d>>                               =>
[apndr ∘ [1,1 ∘ 2],tl ∘ 2] : <<a,b>,<c,d>>             =>
<apndr ∘ [1,1 ∘ 2] : <<a,b>,<c,d>>,tl ∘ 2:<<a,b>,<c,d>>>   =>
<apndr : <<a,b>,c>>,<d>>                               =>
<<a,b,c>,<d>>
```

The construction of the append function is now accomplished by repeatedly moving one component left until the second sequence is null. This is written in FP as

```
Def append ≡ 1 ∘ (while  not ∘ null ∘ 2   moveleft)
```

This expression says, While the second parameter is not null, move one component from the second to the first sequence; then select the first parameter from this result.

A sample application is shown here, step by step:

```
append : <<a,b,c>,<d,e>>                               =>
1 ∘ (while not ∘ null ∘ 2   moveleft):<<a,b,c>,<d,e>>   =>
1 ∘ (while not ∘ null ∘ 2   moveleft):<<a,b,c,d>,<e>>   =>
1 ∘ (while not ∘ null ∘ 2   moveleft):<<a,b,c,d,e>,φ>   =>
1 : <<a,b,c,d,e>,m>                                    =>
<a,b,c,d,e>
```

Example 3: Database Retrieval　　Suppose that a database is represented as a sequence of key/record pairs and, given a key, that we wish to construct a function that will return the corresponding record from the database sequence. For example, a small database might be represented by

```
<<371489622,<BOSS,BIG>>,
 <274379811,<MANAGER,MIDDLE>>,
 <374921488,<WORKER,WILLING>> >
```

Then, an application of our `search` function would result in

```
search : <<...>,374921488> ≡ <WORKER,WILLING>
```

where `<...>` represents the database sequence just defined.

We construct this `search` function from a function select that, when applied to a key/record pair and a key value, returns the one component sequence consisting of the record if its key matches the second parameter and returns the null sequence otherwise. Symbolically, we can represent the action of this function by

$$\text{select} : <<k_i,r_i>,k> \equiv \begin{array}{l} <r_i> \text{ if } k=k_i \\ \emptyset \quad \text{ otherwise} \end{array}$$

The function can be expressed in FP by

```
Def select ≡ (eq ∘ [2,1 ∘ 1] → tl ∘ 1 ; ∅)
```

This says that the result is the tail of the first component (the record) if the second component (key value searched for) equals the first component of the first component (key value of pair). Otherwise, the function $\emptyset$ is a constant function that always returns the object $\emptyset$, the null sequence.

With this function defined, we can construct search:

```
Def search ≡ (/append) ∘ (α select) ∘ distr
```

The `distr` function pairs the `search` value with each key/record pair using `distr`. The (α select) applies `select` to all these components, resulting in a one-element sequence containing the record where the `search` value matches the key or a null sequence when there is no match. The application of `/append` then appends all the resulting sequences together. If there is more than one matching key, this function will result in a sequence of all the corresponding records.

The following steps through an example application of search:

```
search:<<<1,A>,<2,B>,<3,C>>,2>                                      =>
(/append) ∘ (α select) ∘ distr:<<<1,A>,<2,B>,<3,C>>,2>             =>
(/append) ∘ (α select):<<<1,A>,2>,<<2,B>,2>,<<3,C>,2>>             =>
(/append):<select:<<1,A>,2>,select:<<2,B>,2>,select:<<3,C>,2>>=>
(/append):(∅,<B>,∅>                                                =>
append:<∅, (/append):<<B<,∅>>                                       =>
append:<∅,append:<<B>, (/append):<∅>>>                             =>
```

```
append:<φ,append:<<B>,φ>>                                              =>
append<φ,<B>>                                                          =>
<B>
```

Example 4: Quicksort   Our final example is a sort function that, when applied to a sequence, will return the components of the original sequence in ascending order. As with all versions of quicksort, the hard part is partitioning the sequence. We first derive the function

```
partition:<x₁,...,xₙ> ≡ <<all xᵢ≤x₁>,x₁,<all xᵢ>x₁>>
```

We will use four auxiliary functions to construct `partition` in FP. The first is `pairup` which pairs up the first component of the parameter with each of the remaining components. Symbolically, we have

```
pairup : <x₁,...,xₙ> ≡ <<x₁,x₂>,...,<x₁,xₙ>>
```

In FP we write this

```
Def pairup ≡ distl ∘ [1,tl]
```

The second auxiliary function uses a sequence of pairs to construct a sequence of all of the second elements that are less than or equal to their corresponding first elements. Symbolically, this function is

```
keep_le : <<x₁,y₁>,...,<xₙ,yₙ>> ≡ <all yᵢ≤xᵢ>
```

In FP, this is written

```
Def keep_le ≡ (/append) ∘ α(geq → 2; φ)
```

Similarly, all second elements that are greater than their corresponding first elements would be returned by

```
Def keep_gt ≡ (/append) ∘ α(lss → 2; φ)
```

Finally, the first element of the first pair is returned as the single component of a sequence by

```
Def keep_x ≡ tlr ∘ 1
```

To illustrate these last three functions, consider their actions when applied to the sequence

```
<<4,2>,<4,6>,<4,7>,<4,3>>
```

The results would be

```
keep_le : <...> ⟹ <2,3>
keep_gt : <...> ⟹ <6,7>
keep_x  : <...> ⟹ <4>
```

With these definitions, we can construct `partition` as follows:

```
Def partition ≡ [keep_le,keep_x,keep_gt] ∘ pairup
```

Consider the following example application of `partition`:

```
partition:<7,9,4,12,2,10>                                      =>
[keep_le,keep_x,keep_gt] ∘ pairup:<7,9,4,12,2,10>              =>
[keep_le,keep_x,keep_gt]:<<7,9>,<7,4>,<7,12>,<7,2>,<7,10>> =>
<<4,2>,<7>,<9,12,10>>
```

The `sort` function can now be constructed recursively from the result of `partition` by appending the sorted first component to the second component and the sorted third component. To stop the recursion, a test needs to be made for the trivial sequences that contain one or zero components. Our final FP function definition for quicksort is

```
Def sort ≡ (leq ∘[ length 1] → id;
                (/append ∘ [sort ∘ 1 ,2,sort ∘ 3] ∘ partition)
```

To better understand how this works, consider the illustration of `sort`, where for convenience we do not completely expand the recursive calls.

```
sort:<7,12,4,9,2,10>                                            =>
(/append) ∘ [sort ∘ 1 ,2,sort ∘ 3] ∘ partition:<7,12,4,9,2,10>  =>
(/append) ∘ [sort ∘ 1 ,2,sort ∘ 3]:<<4,2>,<7>,<12,9,10>>        =>
(/append):<<2,4>,<7>,<9,10,12>>                                 =>
<2,4,7,9,10,12>
```

9.7 Evaluation of Functional Programming Languages

When compared to imperative languages, functional languages offer several advantages. Because the structure of the program is related to the computation rather than the machine, it is easier to construct programs for problems that are functional in nature. Contributing to the efficiency of learning and using functional languages is the fact that their syntactic structures are much simpler than those of imperative languages.

The referential transparency of functional languages means that the order of function evaluations is irrelevant to the computation. This permits functional languages to easily be used for concurrent processing, because function applications may be applied in any order without concern for dependencies in the computation. The referential transparency also makes it easier to reason about the correctness of a program, because the correctness of any function is unaffected by side effects of other computations.

There are also disadvantages to functional languages. The functional approach means that efficient execution of programs is more difficult, because the structure of the program differs significantly from the structure of the machine on which it is run. Functional languages also require more extensive notation, which results in either long, complex expressions, as in LISP, or a cumbersome alphabet, as in APL or FP.

Perhaps the most significant drawback to functional languages is the fact that many programmers find it difficult to think in the functional paradigm. It is believed by advocates of functional languages that this is a consequence of programmers first learning programming with an imperative language. Many, such as Abelson et al. (1985), have designed introductory courses around the functional paradigm to address this issue.

C H A P T E R *9* Terms

function	function composition
domain	functional form
range	referential transparency
definition	first-class objects
lambda expression	lazy function evaluation
bound variables	

C H A P T E R *9* Discussion Questions

1. What do you see as advantages of programming in the functional paradigm? What are disadvantages?

2. What extensions would you add to the functional model to make it easier to use? How would these affect the integrity of the model?

3. Discuss how a sort algorithm would look different in a functional language. Choose a sort (say, an exchange (bubble) or a quicksort) and depict it in both imperative and functional paradigms.

4. Discuss the types of problems that are best suited for functional program solutions.

5. Discuss features of imperative program control in functional terms. Can iteration be represented in a functional form? Can recursion be implemented functionally? How are concepts like variables or run-time binding handled?

6. Can you find programming language concepts that are better suited for the imperative paradigm than the functional?

7. What are some primitive functions that might be added to the FP collection?

8. What are some functional forms that might be added to the FP collection?

9. Which features of FP would be difficult to implement? Which features would be easy?

10. Think about data structuring that is not available in FP. Why might this be? Why are records or arrays not possible in FP? Could you "emulate" an array or a record?

11. Specifically, why are pointers not a concept that functional languages in general (and FP in specific) implement?

1. Write lambda expressions for the following functions typically found on calculators:

    x^2

    square root

    the slope of a line

    pound-to-kilogram conversion

    Fahrenheit to Celsius conversion

2. For each of the functions expressed in Exercise 1, show a demonstration application.

3. Define a lambda expression to compute $ax^2 + by + z$. Show an application for $a = 2$, $b = 3$, $x = 4$, $y = 6$, and $z = 9$.

4. Express a functional composition — that is, a function of a function as a lambda expression.

    Exercises 5–7 all deal with binary search trees as implemented in FP.

5. Describe a method of structuring sequences in FP that could be used to depict a binary search tree. You may assume the value stored in each node is an integer. State any other assumptions you make, should you make any. *Remember:* There are no pointers in FP, and your data structuring facilities are restricted to atoms and sequences.

6. Using your structuring method for Exercise 1, you are to write three functions, `create`, `search`, and `insert`. The function `create` should simply return an empty tree. The function `search` should take an integer value and a tree for arguments and return a 1 if that argument is in the tree and a 0 if it is not. The function `insert` should take an integer value and a tree as arguments, insert that value into the tree, if that value does not already exist in the tree, and returns the resulting tree. *Note:* The `search` and `insert` definitions must be those for a binary search tree, not simple sequential versions that take advantage of your particular sequence construction.

7. Demonstrate that your functions written for Exercise 2 really work by evaluating your functions on examples and showing that such evaluation yields the proper results. Show at least one example of `create` and two examples each of `search` and `insert`.

8. Examine the following FP function:

    ```
    def func /+ ∘ α1
    ```

    Write a function in Pascal, C, or Ada that computes the equivalent return value.

9. Examine the following code fragment:

```
function totaler (A: array of integer): integer;
    begin
        for i := 1 to 10 do
            total := total + A[i]*2;
        totaler := total+A[1];
    end;
```

Write a fragment that has the same functionality in FP. Instead of an array as an argument, you may assume a list structure of at least 10 integers.

C H A P T E R *9* Laboratory Exercises

1. Consider a list to be a list of integers implemented in Ada as a linked list. Implement the following FP primitive functions as Ada functions:
    a. `function selection( i : integer; 1 : list) return integer;`
    b. `function tail(1 : list) return list;`
    c. `function cons(x : integer; 1 : list) return list;`
    d. `function length(1 : list) return integer;`
    e. `function id(x : integer) return integer;`

2. Implement the complex selection and structure functions of FP in Ada.

3. In a language such as Pascal or C++ that allows the passing of functions as parameters, implement the functional forms of FP.

Scheme: A Functional-Oriented Language

10.1 ▪ Basic Components
10.2 ▪ Function Definition
10.3 ▪ Examples
10.4 ▪ Comparison of Scheme to FP

The programming language LISP adheres more closely to the functional model than any other language in general use. LISP was developed by John McCarthy in 1960 to facilitate work on the list data structure. The language was designed so that programs in LISP are lists themselves, and it is based on the functional model, complete with lambda expressions and recursion. Over the years, LISP has been the favorite language among researchers in the field of artificial intelligence.

There is no single established standard version of LISP, but one that has emerged recently as important in the field of education is Scheme. Scheme was developed at MIT by Sussman and Steele (1975) and is an improvement over earlier dialects of LISP in that it uses static scope and treats functions as first class objects. Scheme is the dialect of LISP that we will discuss in this chapter, where we study features of Scheme in comparison to the functional model established by FP. We also introduce features of Scheme that lie outside of that functional model.

10.1 __Basic Components__

10.1.1   ▪   __Objects and Evaluations__

As with FP, Scheme permits two types of objects, atoms and lists. **Atoms** are represented by strings of nonblank characters. Those atoms that are represented by numeric characters are called *numeric atoms* and admit to the application of a set of numeric functions. Other atoms may be enclosed in double quotes and are considered string atoms. Atoms that are neither numeric nor string are called identifier atoms. Sample atoms are

```
28
-14.292
"A string"
x
anAtom
```

A **list** is represented by a sequence of atoms and lists separated by blanks and enclosed in parentheses. It corresponds to the sequence in FP. Examples of Scheme lists are

```
( x y z)
(+ 14 12)
(x (a b c) () )
```

The special list () that contains no elements is the empty list. As in FP, the empty list is considered both an atom and a list. It is alternatively referred to as *nil.*

Every expression in Scheme lends itself to an evaluation. In this text, we will indicate the result of expression evaluation by printing the expression on one line with the result of the expression evaluation indented on the following line.

The rule for evaluating an expression is as follows:

1. If the expression is a numeric or string atom, it evaluates to itself — for example,

```
27
   27
2.25
   2.25
"A string"
   "A string"
```

2. An atom that is an identifier is bound to a function or a numeric or string atom and evaluates to the value to which it is bound. For example, assuming the appropriate bindings have been made via methods to be described later, the following are results of identifier evaluations:

```
X
    27
Name
    "Joseph"
sort
    #PROCEDURE SORT
```

3. A list is treated as a function evaluation with the first element evaluating to the function and the remaining elements of the list serving as its parameters. We will examine this evaluation later.

10.1.2 ▪ Implementation Model

The **cell model** is commonly used to view the implementation of lists in Scheme. In the cell model, a list is represented by a linked list of cells. The data component of each cell is a pointer to the corresponding atom or list, and the pointer element points to the next element in the list. The last element in a list points to nil. Figure 10.1 shows several sample lists represented by the cell model. Using conventional Scheme notation, a pointer to `nil` is indicated by a diagonal line in our diagram.

Scheme uses special terminology for the two components of each cell. The data part is known as the **CAR** component and the pointer part is called the **CDR** component. These terms are a consequence of the historical names used for the registers in which these components were stored in the original implementation of LISP. CAR stands for Contents of Accumulator Register, and CDR stands for Contents of Decrement Register. In actuality, the CAR is a pointer to the first element of the list and the CDR is a pointer to the cells that represent the remainder of the list.

10.1.3 ▪ Functions

In order to enforce the property that functions are represented by lists, Scheme requires the special notation for expressing function applications known as the **S-expression**. Its general form is

```
(<function-name> <first-parameter> ... <last-parameter>)
```

In words, a function application is represented by a list whose first element is an atom expressing the function's name and whose remaining elements are atoms or lists representing the parameters to the function. For example, 6 is added to 9 by the S-expression

```
(+ 6 9)
    15
```

More complex evaluations can be specified by groupings of function applications — for example,

```
(+ (* 3 4) (* 6 7))
    54
```

FIGURE **10.1**   **Cell Model Representation of Lists**

(a b c)

(a (b c (d) e))

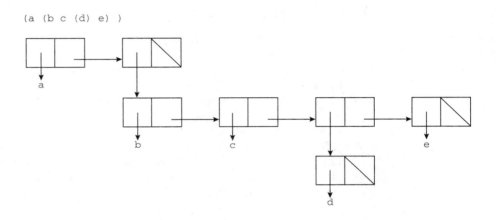

((a b) nil)

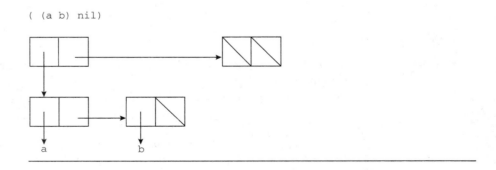

10.1.4 ▪ Built-in Functions

Functions in Scheme are either built in or user-defined. We discuss the way the user can define functions later. In the present section we describe several of the most important built-in functions.

Because the Scheme interpreter considers every S-expression to be a function to be evaluated, if Scheme wishes to consider an S-expression as data and prevent its evaluation, this desire must be specified with a special function called `quote` — for example,

```
(quote (+ 2 3))
    (+ 2 3)
```

indicates to the Scheme interpreter that the list

```
(+ 2 3)
```

is to be considered as a three-element list rather than be evaluated and regarded as the atomic element 5. Because atoms are considered as elements to be evaluated in a way that will be explained later, the quote function may also be applied to them to inhibit their evaluation — for example,

```
(quote a)
    a
```

Due to the frequency with which the function `quote` is applied, it is usually abbreviated by a single quote mark. For example, the preceding expressions can be written

```
'(+ 2 3)
    (+ 2 3)
'a
    a
```

The quote function will be applied to a function's actual parameters when they are to be considered as data rather than other functions to be evaluated.

Two other commonly used functions are `car` and `cdr`, named after the two components of the cell in the cell model. These functions both take a list as their only parameter, the `car` returning the first element of that list and the `cdr` returning the list parameter with the first element removed. In other words, the `car` returns the element to which the CAR component points and `cdr` returns the element to which the CDR component points — for example,

```
(car '(a b c))
    a
```

Applying the `cdr` function to the same list gives

```
(cdr '(a b c))
    (b c)
```

Note that this result of the `car` is an atom, because the first element of the list (a b c) is an atom. The result of the `cdr` is always a list. Neither of these functions is defined when its parameter is an atom or nil. Further examples of applications of `car` and `cdr` are shown here and are numbered for convenience:

1. `(car '((a b) c d))`

```
    (a b)
```

2. `(car '(a))`

   `a`

3. `(cdr '((a b) c))`

   `(c)`

4. `(cdr '(a))`

   `nil`

5. `(car (cdr '(a b c)))`

   `b`

6. `(car '(cdr (a b c)))`

   `cdr`

The last two examples are of special interest. In example 5, because the list to which `car` is applied is not quoted, it is evaluated before the `car` function is applied. Therefore, this expression is equivalent to

`(car '(b c))`

because `(b c)` is the `cdr` of `(a b c)`. In example 6, the `car` function is applied to the two-element list

`(cdr (a b c))`

because the preceding quote inhibits evaluation. The `car` of this list is the atom `cdr`.

The `car` and `cdr` functions are the two fundamental list functions for taking a list apart. The `cons` function is the fundamental function for constructing a list. It takes two parameters, the first becoming the `car` of the result and the second, the `cdr` — for example,

`(cons 'a '(b c))`

   `(a b c)`

In contrast, if the first parameter is a list, then we have

`(cons '(a) '(b c))`

   `((a) b c)`

The inverse relationship of `cons` with `car` and `cdr` is illustrated by the rule that

`(cons (car X) (cdr X))`

is X for any list nonempty list X.

Scheme recognizes the atom `#t` to have the meaning *true* when used in the context of logical results. The meaning *false* is associated with `#f`.

In this context, a **predicate** is a function whose result is always either `#t` or `#f`. For example, function `atom?` returns `#t` if its parameter is an atom and `#f` if it is not. Consider the following:

```
(atom? 'a)
    #t
(atom? '(a))
    #f
(atom? '(a b))
    #f
```

Another commonly used predicate is `equal?`, which tests its two parameters for equality, where the parameters can be atoms or lists. In addition, comparison predicates exist that apply to numeric atoms, namely, =, >, and <.

One further construct is used to abbreviate the composition of `car` and `cdr` applications. For example,

```
(cdr (cdr (car '((a b c)(d e)))))
```

can be abbreviated as

```
(cddar '((a b c)(d e)))
    (c)
```

There are two ways to represent conditional control within Scheme. In adherence to the functional nature of the language, both are expressed as functions.

The first takes the general form of an `if-then-else` by application of the `if` function. Its general form is

```
(if <predicate>
    <expression-1>
    <expression-2>)
```

If the predicate evaluates to anything but `#f`, the `if` function is the evaluation of `expression-1`. If the predicate evaluates to `#f`, the `if` function is the evaluation of `expression-2`. For example,

```
(if (= n 0)
    0
    (/ 1 n))
```

evaluates to `0` if n is zero and to `1/n` if n is not zero.

A second conditional is the `cond` function, which has the form

```
(cond (<test-1> <result-1>)
      (<test-2> <result-2>)
      ...
      (<test-n> <result-n>)
)
```

The `cond` function evaluates the test clause until one is found that is not `nil`. The value of the corresponding result clause is then returned as the value of the `cond` function. If all test clauses are `nil`, the value of the `cond` function is nil. In this sense it acts like an `if-elsif-elsif-····-endif` type of construct. Illustrations of the application of `cond` are shown in future examples.

10.1.5 ▪ Nonfunctional Built-in Functions

Although Scheme is developed around the functional model, several features are included that are in violation of that model. Most notably, the ability to bind identifiers to values permits side effects, because the evaluation of a function may be different when different bindings hold. Therefore, all functions that establish such bindings are in violation of the strict functional model.

The binding of names to values occurs in Scheme through the `let` function. The general format of this function is

```
(let ((name-1 expression-1)
      (name-2 expression-2)
           . . .
      (name-n expression-n))
  expression-n+1)
```

This function first binds each specified name to the value of its corresponding expression. The value of the function is then the result of the evaluation of the final expression, with the appropriate values substituted for the names.

Consider the following example:

```
(let ((n 2)
      (m 3))
  (+ n m))
     5
```

The `let` function can be used to avoid redundant function evaluations. For example, the function call

```
(* (+ 2 4) (+ 2 4))
```

results in the same addition occurring twice. This can be reduced to a single evaluation by using

```
(let ((sum (+ 2 4))
  (* sum sum))
```

The `let` assumes that all bindings are done simultaneously. In other words, the binding made in one expression cannot be used in a later expression. This dependence can be enforced, however, with the `let*` function. In the case of `let*`, the bindings occur sequentially, and earlier bindings can be used in later ones. The difference between `let` and `let*` is illustrated in the following:

```
(define a 1)
        a
(let ((a 2)
```

```
        (b a))
    (+ a b))
       3
(let* ((a 2)
       (b a))
    (+ a b))
       4
```

10.2 Function Definition

In the previous section we introduced a number of built-in functions. In this section we discuss how to construct user-defined functions in Scheme. This construction is done through the define function. The general form of this function-defining function is

```
(define (<function-name>
         <parameter-1> ... <parameter-n>)
        <function-body>
)
```

Therefore, function define takes two parameters. The first is a list with first element being the function identifier and the remaining elements being atomic formal parameter names. The second element is the expression that is to be evaluated when the function is called. The atomic function name is returned as the result of the function define, but the primary result of the define application is the side effect that binds the function identifier with the function definition provided in the body. Parameters are used as local variables in the function body.

Consider the following example:

```
(define (length list)
    (cond ((atom? list) 0)
          ((null? list) 0)
          ( else       (+ 1 (length (cdr list)))))
    )
)
```

This function counts the number of elements in its formal parameter. Note the use of the conditional and recursion in the body of the function. The function length can now be called by the form

```
(length '(a b (c d)))
    3
```

Functions in Scheme can also be defined without binding them to a name. This is done through the use of lambda expressions. The general form is

```
(lambda (<parameter-1> ... <parameter-n>)
        <function-body>
)
```

This expression defines the specified function but, rather than binding it to a name, makes the function available for an application without naming it. For example, the preceding call to length could be replaced by the lambda expression application shown here:

```
((lambda (list)
        (cond ((atom? list) 0)
              ((null? list) 0)
              ( else          (+ 1 (length (cdr list))))) 
        )
 )  `(a b (c d))
)
   3
```

Notice the equivalence of this to the lambda notation introduced in Chapter 9.

The parameters within function calls act as parameters implemented by copy. Therefore, if we are given the function f defined by

```
(define (f test)
       ((define test () )
        (null? test)
        )
)
   f
```

the nil value to which the formal parameter is set will have no effect on the corresponding actual parameter in the calling environment. The function will always return nil, however. This fact is illustrated by the following sequence of evaluations:

```
(define x `a)
     x
(f x)
     #t
x
     a
```

Note that the formal parameter test does change during the evaluation of function f, but the associated actual parameter x is unaffected. In addition, all nonparametric variables used in a function definition are considered global to the defining environment in Scheme. Some LISP dialects use dynamic scoping by allowing the function to inherit the variable name bindings of the calling environment.

The function f defined here illustrates another important point about Scheme function definitions. A function body may contain any number of evaluations. In the situation where there is more than one, only the result of the last evaluation is returned as the value of the function.

10.3 Examples

The best way to understand the true power of the Scheme language is through the use of examples. In order to observe the correspondence to the FP model, the examples found in Chapter 9 will be implemented in Scheme.

Example 1: Factorial A simple function to evaluate factorial in Scheme is defined by

```
(define (factorial x)
           (cond ((< x 0) () )
                 ((= x 0) 1)
                 (else    (* x (factorial (- x 1)))))
           )
)
```

Here the negative parameter is considered illegal and hence returns `nil`. The function is called by a form such as

```
(factorial 6)
   720
```

Example 2: Quicksort Our quicksort program in Scheme makes use of two functions, `keep_le` and `keep_gt`, similar to auxiliary functions of the same name defined in our FP version. Both of these functions accept two parameters, the first of which is a numeric atom and the second of which is a list of numeric atoms. The function `keep_le` returns a list of all elements in the second parameter that are less than or equal to the first parameter. The function `keep_gt` performs similarly, but it returns a list of elements greater than the first parameter. These two functions are defined in Figure 10.2.

With these definitions, the quicksort function can be defined as in Figure 10.2. Here the built-in function `append` is used to concatenate two lists into a single list.

Example 3: Stacks To implement stacks in Scheme, we represent the stack by a list, with the first element of the list being the top element of the stack. The three fundamental stack functions are then defined by

```
empty : stack → #t   if stack is empty
                 #f   if stack is not empty
push  : stack,element → newstack where newstack is stack with
                    element on top
pop   : stack → (element,newstack) where element is the top
                    and newstack with top removed
```

The function `pop` returns a list consisting of the element popped off of the stack and the resulting stack after the element is popped. This action is necessary, because a function can return only a single value. We get around this by returning the two values as the components of a single list.

FIGURE 10.2   **Quicksort in Scheme**

```scheme
(define (keep_some f)
      (lambda (x slist)
          (cond ((null? slist)      () )
                ((f (car slist) x) (cons (car slist)
                                          ((keep_some f) x
                                           (cdr slist))))
                ( else             ((keep_some f) x (cdr slist)))
          )
      )
)

(define (leq x y) (if (> x y) #f #t))

(define keep_gt (keep_some >))

(define keep_le (keep_some leq))

(define (quicksort slist)
              (if (null? slist)
                        ()
                    (append (quicksort (keep_le (car slist) (cdr slist)))
                            (cons (car slist) (quicksort (keep_gt
                              (car slist) (cdr slist))))
                    )
              )
)
```

Our function definitions are found in Figure 10.3. The empty and push functions are direct applications of the null? and cons built-in functions. The pop function is constructed via a conditional, which returns nil if the stack is empty to indicate an improper pop operation. If the stack is not empty, pop is the application of a built-in Scheme function called list. This function is similar in operation to cons, except that it makes a list with its first parameter as the first element, its second as the second, and so on, for any number of parameters provided. To illustrate, consider the following examples:

```scheme
(list 'a '(b c))
    (a (b c))
(cons 'a '(b c))
    (a b c)
```

Example 4: Attribute Lists   We assume that we have objects that are described by lists of pairs, the first element of each pair being the name of an attribute and the second being the value of that attribute associated with the given object. Although Scheme has built-in functions that implement the insertion

FIGURE **10.3**   **Stack Implementation in Scheme**

```
(define (empty? stack)
        (null? stack)
)

(define (push stack element)
        (cons element stack)
)

(define (pop stack)
        (if ((empty? stack)
              nil
              (list (car stack) (cdr stack)))
        )
)
```

and retrieval of attribute values, we will write our own here for illustrative purposes. As an example, a student object might be represented by the list

```
((lastname Smith) (firstname Sam) (class FR) (sex M))
```

We provide three functions for use with such attribute lists, specified by

```
addattr : attr-list,attr-name,attr-value → new-attr-list
            adds a name/value pair to the attribute list
remattr : attr-list,attr-name → new-attr-list
            removes the first pair with attr-name from attr-
            list
getattr : attr-list,attr-name → attr-value
            retrieve the value paired with attr-name in
            attr-list
```

The preceding functions are defined in Scheme in Figure 10.4. Both `remattr` and `getattr` illustrate the use of recursion to perform a list search. Note the similarities between this search and the database search on a key field implemented in FP.

10.4 Comparison of Scheme to FP

10.4.1 ▪ Departures from the Functional Model

Scheme departs from the functional model established by FP in two fundamental ways:

1. The use of the imperative model concept of variable, permitting names to be bound to values during a function evaluation.

FIGURE **10.4**   **Attribute Lists in Scheme**

```
(define (addattr alist aname avalue)
          (cons (list aname avalue) alist)
)

(define (remattr alist aname)
          (cond ((null? alist)                     ())
                ((equal? (caar alist) aname)  (cdr alist))
                ( else                             (cons (car alist)
                                                    (remattr (cdr alist) aname)))
          )
)

(define (getattr alist aname)
        (cond ((null? alist)                     ())
              ((equal? (caar alist) aname)  (cadar alist))
              ( else                             (getattr (cdr alist) aname))
        )
)
```

2. The ability of Scheme to specify the sequential execution of functions, as illustrated by the `let*` function. This was not included among the functional forms provided by FP.

As an example of sequential execution, let us modify function `getattr` of Figure 10.4 to retrieve a list of all attribute values associated with a given attribute name, assuming that several name/value pairs could have the same associated name part — for example,

```
((lastname,Smith) (firstname Sam) (brother Joe) (brother
  Charles))
```

A retrieval for attribute name "brother" applied with this list as an actual parameter, should result in

```
(Joe Charles)
```

The function `getall` — defined in Figure 10.5 — accomplishes this through the use of sequential function applications. The `let` function is used here, employing local binding of identifiers.

Function `getall` uses two local variables, `rest` and `result`. Inside the `let*` two functions are applied sequentially to calculate these variables. The result of the function is the `cons` of these two.

10.4.2 ▪ **Functional Forms in Scheme**

Within Scheme, functions are treated as first-class objects, which means they can be used as parameters to functions and returned as the value of a func-

FIGURE **10.5**   **Function** `getall` **in Scheme**

```
(define (getall alist aname)
       (let* ((rest (if (null? alist)
                              ()
                              (getall (cdr alist) aname)))
               (result (if (equal? (caar alist) aname)
                              (cadar alist)
                              () )))
          (cons result rest)
       )
)
```

tion. This gives Scheme the power to express the FP functional forms, and we will duplicate them in this section.

For example, consider the following Scheme function:

```
(define (composition f g)
       (lambda (x) (f (g x))
       )
)
```

This function accepts two functions, f and g, as parameters, and the result is a third function defined by the lambda expression, which is the composition of f and g. This new function can then be applied as follows:

```
((composition car car) `((a b) c))
       a
((composition cdr car) `((a b) c))
       (b)
```

Another example is the apply-to-all functional form, which is defined in Scheme by

```
(define (apply-to-all f)
  (lambda (list)
    (if (null? list)
        nil
        (cons (f (car list)) ((apply-to-all f) (cdr list)))
    )
  )
)
```

Some applications of this function are

```
((apply-to-all car) `((a b) (c d) (e f)))
       (a,c,e)
((apply-to-all atom?) `(a (b c) (d e) f))
       (#t #f #f #t)
```

The remaining functional forms are defined in Figure 10.6.

FIGURE 10.6 **Scheme Equivalence to FP Functional Forms**

```
(define (construction flist)
  (lambda (x) (if (null? flist)
                  ()
                      (cons (eval (cons (car flist) (list
                       (quote x))) user-initial-environment)
                            ((construction (cdr flist)) x))
                      )
                )
  )
)

(define (insertion f)
   (lambda (list)
       (if (null? (cdr list))
           (car list)
           (f (car list) ((insertion f) (cdr list)))
       )
   )
)

(define (condition p f g)
       (lambda (x)
              (if (p x) (f x) (g x))
       )
)

(define (while p f)
   (lambda (x)
     (if (p x)
       ((while p f) (f x))
       x
     )
   )
)
```

CHAPTER 10 Terms

atom
list
cell model
CAR
CDR
S-expression
predicate

CHAPTER 10 Discussion Questions

1. As discussed in this chapter, Scheme goes beyond the functional model in several ways. What are the advantages of doing this? What are the disadvantages?

2. Think about data structuring in Scheme. In considering Discussion Question 1, several facilities in Scheme that go beyond the functional model were discussed. Are records or arrays possible in Scheme? How would you implement something like a stack or a tree in Scheme?

3. Would pointers be useful in Scheme? Why or why not?

4. Both functions and data are expressed in the form of an S-expression in Scheme. Why might this be useful?

5. How does the concept of abstract data type apply to Scheme?

6. LISP dialects like Scheme are preferred by many computer scientists. For example, artificial intelligence researchers prefer LISP for applications like planning systems and game playing strategy developers. Discuss the features of LISP that make it desirable for these applications.

C H A P T E R **10**   Exercises

1. Examine the following FP function (from the exercises for Chapter 9):

    ```
    def func /+ ∘ α1
    ```

    Write a Scheme function that correctly implements this FP function.

2. Consider the depiction of a LISP S-expression given in Figure 10.7. If the structure is the value of "lst," what is the value of

    ```
    (cdaadr lst)
    ```

3. Write the Scheme code necessary to add the following structure to "d," as in Figure 10.8.

FIGURE 10.7

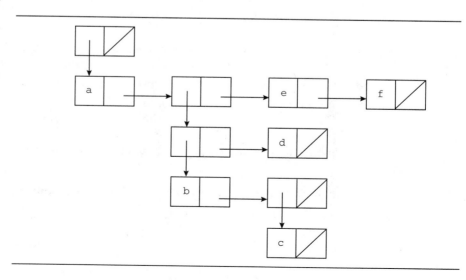

FIGURE **10.8**

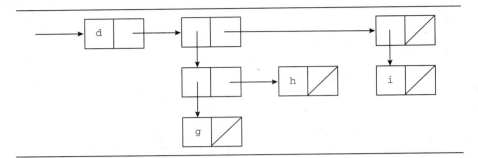

4. Using the cell model of Scheme, depict (that is, draw) the list

   `((b c) (x (y z)))`

5. Using only the functions car, cdr, cond, and itself (that is, recursively), write a Scheme function called rev that takes a list and returns a list that is a reversed version of the original.

6. Using the cell model for Scheme, depict the internal representation of the following lists:

   a. `(a (b c) d e (f))`
   b. `(a b (c (d e) f))`
   c. `(a b (c) d (e f))`

7. Examine the following code fragment (from Chapter 9):

```
function totaler (A: array of integer): integer;
    begin
        for i := 1 to 10 do
            total := total + A[i]*2;
        totaler := total+A[1];
    end;
```

   Write a fragment that has the same functionality in Scheme. Instead of an array as an argument, you may assume a list structure of at least 10 integers.

8. Convert the database example given in the FP discussion to Scheme.

9. Recall the BST implementation in FP, illustrated in Exercises 5 through 7 of Chapter 9. Using the same version of a BST, write Scheme functions to implement a BST of this type.

10. Recall the Chapter 9 exercise where we represented a 3 x 3 matrix in FP as

    `<<1,2,3>,<4,5,6>,<7,8,9>>`

    Now, let's do the same for Scheme. We can represent this matrix as list of lists:

    `( (1 2 3) (4 5 6) (7 8 9) )`

    or row-by-row order.

a. Write a Scheme function to sum the items in a column. Call the function

```
(column matrix 2)
```

where `matrix` is the matrix as a list and 2 is the column to sum.

b. Write a Scheme function that sums all numbers in a matrix. Call this

```
(summation matrix)
```

where `matrix` is the matrix to be summed up as a list.

C H A P T E R 10   Laboratory Exercises

1. This exercise involves the implementation of a heavily recursive program that implements a solution in Scheme to the *n-queens problem.*

The *n*-queens problem is a classic combinatorial problem where the object is to place *n* queens on an $n \times n$ chessboard so that no two can "attack" each other, that is, so that no two of them are on the same row, column, or diagonal. An iterative algorithm that computes a solution to the *n*-queens problem is as follows:

```
algorithm NQUEENS(n);
  var n,c,r:integer; board:boardtype;
  begin
    board:=newboard;
    c:=0; r:=1;
    while r>0 do
      c:=c+1;
      mark(board,c,r);
      while c≤n and not goodplace(board,c,r) do
        unmark(board,c,r);
        c:=c+1;
        mark(board,c,r);
      endwhile;
      if c≤n then
        if r=n then
          print("Solution found");
          exit;
        else
          r:=r+1;
          c:=0;
        endif;
      else
        r:=r-1;
        c:=place(board,r);
        unmark(board,c,r);
      endif;
    endwhile;
  endalgorithm
```

The preceding algorithm requires a few notes. First, note that board is defined in terms of boardtype, which is not specified. Note as well that board is manipulated by three functions: newboard, which initializes the board representation to an empty board, mark, which places a queen on board at column c and row r, and unmark, which removes the queen at column c and row r on board. Finally, note that the function goodplace is undefined. This function determines if a queen placed on column c and row r on board can be attacked. You must also provide implementation for a function called place which takes a board and a row as arguments, and returns the column in which the row's queen is placed.

You are to implement a recursive solution to the n-queens problem in Scheme. As a guide, follow these steps:

- Rewrite the preceding algorithm so that it is defined recursively and is phrased as functionally as possible.

- Design a data structure (using Scheme lists and atoms) to represent the board. Then write the supporting routines newboard, mark, and unmark.

- Write the function goodplace in terms of the data structure just designed.

- Finally, write the function NQUEENS. This function should take one argument, the number of queens in the problem, and produce some indication of where the queens are placed. For example, you might print an entire board or simply an indication of row and column placement of queens.

You should also keep these points in mind:

- For a given n, there are many solutions to the n-queens problem. Your program needs to find only one.

- You may alter the number and type of arguments used in the functions in the description of the preceding NQUEENS algorithm. Of course, you may introduce your own functions.

- The function NQUEENS must take only one argument, however.

2. Verify your answer to Exercise 9 by implementing the BST specification in Scheme. Example output from this type of implementation is shown below:

```
1 ]=> (define tree1 (insert `() 50))
;Value: tree1
 1 ]=> tree1
;Value: (() 50 ())
 1 ]=> (define tree2 (insert (insert tree1 20) 70))
 ;Value: tree2
 1 ]=> tree2
 ;Value: ((() 20 ()) 50 (() 70 ())))
```

3. Consider (again) the following FP function:

```
def func = /+ ∘ α1
```

Write a Scheme function to compute the equivalent return value.

ML: A Typed Functional Language

11.1 ▪ Features of ML
11.2 ▪ Examples
11.3 ▪ Comparison of ML to FP

A different approach to the implementation of the functional paradigm is represented by the language ML. **ML** stands for **meta language**, and it was developed at the University of Edinburgh by a team headed by Robin Milner. Its original purpose was to find and perform proofs in a formal logical system. The full definition of the original language is given by Gordon et al. (1979).

ML proved to be useful as a general-purpose language and was developed as such by the team at Edinburgh. A standardization effort took place in the early 1980s, incorporating some of the ideas from the functional language HOPE, a language developed by Burstall et al. (1980). This resulted in the definition of Standard ML, or SML. This definition was published by Milner et al. (1990). Standard ML is the version of the language that we describe in this chapter.

11.1 Features of ML

11.1.1 ▪ Types

A primary difference between ML and Scheme is the former's use of strict typing. All items in ML are bound to a type, and that binding persists for the life of the item. Type is so important in ML that it is reported as a part of each function application. As with Scheme, we indicate the results of function evaluations by showing the ML syntax followed by the report returned by ML on a separate line, indented and in italics. For example, a simple function evaluation in ML is

```
5 + 2;
  val it = 7 : int
```

This indicates that the application of the built-in infix function + results in a value 7 of type int that is stored in a scratch variable called it, the recipient of all function evaluations not explicitly assigned elsewhere. All statements are terminated by a semicolon, as indicated by this example.

We contrast the preceding function call to the following:

```
5.0 + 2.0;
  val it = 7.0 : real
```

The difference here is that the + operator, which is overloaded in ML, is taken to be real addition, because the operands are expressed as real constants.

ML does not permit the mixture of types, which requires type conversion. When this is attempted in ML, the result looks like the following:

```
5.0 + 2;
  Error: operator and operand don't agree
```

All functions are strictly typed in both their parameters and their results. A function is defined by the keyword fun — for example,

```
fun double(x) = 2*x;
  val double = fn : int -> int
```

This statement says that the identifier double has been bound to a function that takes one int parameter and results in a single int return value. The types associated with this function are inferred by ML, because it is nowhere stated that either the parameter or the return types are int. The inference was made in this case from the presence of the int constant 2 in the definition. Consider, in contrast, the function definition

```
fun double(x) = x + x;
  Error: overloaded variable cannot be resolved: +
```

Here there is no clue for ML to use in determining the type of the function, because the operator + applies to both int and real operands. The specification of any single element may be enough for ML to infer correctly all types in the function definition — for example,

```
fun double(x:int) = x + x;
  val double = fn: int -> int
```

Here ML is able to determine the type of the result, because the type of the parameter is specified. Similarly, specifying the type of the result completely specifies all types for the function, as in

```
fun double(x):int = x + x;
  val double = fn: int -> int
```

Functions that are user defined can be applied by writing their names, followed by the value or values that specify their parameters. The function double, defined previously, can therefore be applied in the following ways:

```
double 5;
  val it = 10 : int
double(5);
  val it = 10 : int
double(5.0);
  Error: operator and operand don't agree
```

In the last case, ML objects to being given a parameter of incorrect type.

Functions can be applied to function results as well — for example,

```
double(double(3));
  val it = 12 : int
```

There are four atomic types in ML: int, real, bool, and string. Common operators are provided with each of these types.

Identifiers can be bound to values through statements beginning with the keyword val — for example,

```
val x = 2;
  val x = 2 : int
val y = 2*x;
  val y = 4 : int
val z = x-y;
  val z = ~2 : int
```

Note that although ML is very strict about typing, an identifier is not bound to a type but rather to a value (plus its associated type), and the rebinding of the same identifier to a value of a different type is allowed, as in

```
val x = 2;
  val x = 2 : int
val x = 2.0;
  val x = 2.0 : real
val x = "a string";
  val x = "a string" : string
```

We have seen that the binding of an identifier to a function is accomplished by use of the fun keyword. An alternative form uses the val keyword to bind the identifier to a value that is a function, which is one way that functions are treated as first-class values in ML — for example,

```
val double = fun x : int => x + x;
  val double = fn : int -> int
```

The use of the `fn` keyword to indicate a value is a function is identical in concept to the λ-notation. It permits the application of a function without the function being named. As an example, consider

```
(fun x:int => x+x)(2);
  val it = 4 : int
```

Functions that require several alternative specifications can be defined in two ways in ML. Consider factorial, for example, which can be written

```
fun factorial(n) = if n = 0 then 1
                               else n*factorial(n-1);
  val factorial = fn : int -> int
```

This form of function specification permits a sequence of alternative conditions, each followed by its corresponding return value, given in an `if-else if-···=else` form. If there are more than two alternatives, they might be specified as follows:

```
fun sign(x) = if x>0 then "+"
              else if x=0 then "0"
              else "-";
  val sign = fn : int -> string
```

Another way of specifying alternative definitions is by specifying parameters that match patterns. In this manner, `factorial` could be written

```
fun factorial(0) = 1
  | factorial(n) = n*factorial(n-1);
  val fact = fn : int -> int
```

This definition searches alternative patterns for parameters until one is found that matches the parameters in the actual function application. The same approach can be used to generate the `sign` function:

```
fun sign(0) = "0"
  | sign(1) = "1"
  | sign(~1) = "-"
  | sign(x) = sign(x div abs(x));
  val sign = fn : int -> string
```

This last example also illustrates that ~ is used for specifying negative numbers. The built-in functions `div` and `abs` are used to divide integers and compute the integer absolute value.

Thus far we have avoided functions that accept more than one parameter, but these functions are handled easily in ML. Consider the following function, which returns a string that is a repetition of its first parameter the number of times indicated by its second parameter:

```
fun repeat(s,n) = if n=0 then ""
                  else s^repeat(s,n-1);
  val repeat = fn : string * int -> string
```

The domain of the function is listed as `string * int`. This notation indicates that it is the Cartesian product of the two types, `string` and `int`. The string operator `^` is used for concatenation. The preceding function can be applied to a pair of values, as indicated:

```
repeat("ab",5);
  val it = "ababababab" : string
```

11.1.2 ▪ Lists

List constants in ML are enclosed in brackets, and elements are separated by commas. Using that notation, we illustrate the fact that lists must be homogeneous by the following sequence of examples:

```
[1,2];
  val it = [1,2] : int list
[1,2.0];
  Error: operator and operand don't agree
[1,2,3];
  val it = [1,2,3] : int list
[1,[2,3]];
  Error: operator and operand don't agree
[[1],[2,3]];
  val it = [[1],[2,3]] : int list list
```

These examples illustrate that a list is permitted as a list element only if all other elements are lists of the same type.

There are several important built-in list operators and functions, which we illustrate here. The built-in functions `hd` and `tl` correspond to `car` and `cdr` from Scheme. Therefore,

```
hd([1,2,3]);
  val it = 1 : int
tl([1,2,3]);
  val it = [2,3] : int list
hd([1]);
  val it = 1 : int
tl([1]);
  val it - [] : int list
hd([]);
  uncaught exception Hd
tl([]);
  uncaught exception Tl
```

The last two examples display the exception feature of ML, which we describe later.

ML employs the operator `::` to accomplish the job of Scheme's `cons` function — for example,

```
"a" :: ["b","c"];
  val it = ["a","b","c"] : string list
```

A second infix operator that applies to lists is the append operator, denoted
by @ and illustrated by

```
[1,2,3] @ [4,5];
  val it = [1,2,3,4,5] : int list
```

A prefix function `rev` is also defined to reverse a list.

```
rev[1,2,3];
  val it = [3,2,1] : int list
```

It is convenient to define list functions via patterns, particularly using the
`::` operator to define a pattern on the list parameter. For example, if we wish
to construct the recursive function for summing all the elements in a list, we
could write it as

```
fun sum(nil) = 0
  | sum(first::rest) = first + sum(rest);
  val sum = fn : int list -> int
```

Here the first pattern is the `nil`, or empty, list, which sums to zero and serves
as the recursion stopper for this function definition. In the second pattern,
`first` matches the head of the parameter list and `rest` matches the tail.

11.1.3 ▪ Parametric Polymorphism

ML does not require that parameters to function be bound to a type when
there is nothing in the function definition which requires such a binding. In
this case, binding can be postponed until function application when the type
of the actual parameter can be used to infer types for each evaluation. This
ability to define functions independently of the types of their parameters is
called **parametric polymorphism**.

As a first example of this ability, consider the following function, which
accepts a list as a parameter and returns the same list with the last element
removed:

```
fun allbutlast(nil) = nil
  | allbutlast(x::nil) = nil
  | allbutlast(x::y) = x :: allbutlast(y);
  val allbutlast = fn : 'a list -> 'a list
```

Notice the interesting new notation in the type description of `allbutlast`.
This description indicates that the function accepts as its parameter a list of
type `'a` and returns a list of the same type. The notation `'a` indicates that the
type of the list is unrestricted, but the fact that it is used for both the parameter and the return value indicates that they must be lists of the same type. As
an illustration, consider the following calls to `allbutlast`:

```
allbutlast([1,2,3,4]);
  val it = [1,2,3] : int list
```

```
allbutlast(["a","b","c"]);
  val it = ["a","b"] : string list
allbutlast([[1,2],[3,4],[5],[6,7]]);
  val it = [[1,2],[3,4],[5]] : int list list
```

Such polymorphism is possible only when there is nothing in the function definition that restricts the type. For example, the similar function that returns the smallest value in a list is not legally defined.

```
fun smallest(nil) = nil
  | smallest(x::nil) = [x]
  | smallest(x::y) = if x<hd(smallest(y)) then [x]
                                else smallest(y);
  Error: overloaded variable cannot be resolved: <
```

The problem here is the use of the operator <, which applies to three different types (int, real, string) and does not apply to other types. Therefore, the type of element in the parametric list is required to define which < is to be used in the definition of the function smallest. A definition that works for list of type int is

```
fun smallest(nil):int list = nil
  | smallest(x::nil) = [x]
  | smallest(x::y) = if x<hd(smallest(y)) then [x]
                                else smallest(y);
  val smallest = fn : int list -> int list
```

In this definition, the result of the function is bound to type int list, giving the < operator a unique specification.

Let us examine one more function to illustrate parametric polymorphism. The function reversepair accepts a pair of parameters and returns the same pair in the reverse order:

```
fun reversepair(x,y) = (y,x);
  val reversepair = fn 'a * 'b -> 'b * 'a
```

Several new concepts are introduced by this function. First, it shows that functions in ML can return multiple results. In this case, two results are returned as a tuple. Tuples are enclosed by parentheses and are distinct from lists, which are enclosed by square brackets. Tuples have Cartesian product types. This function also illustrates that more than one unspecified type can occur in the same function definition. Here the two parameters x and y are not bound to a type, so the variable type specifications 'a and 'b are used. The fact that these names are distinct says that not only are x and y not bound to a type in the function definition, but when they are bound during an application of this function, they need not be bound to the same type. The following applications of this function illustrate this:

```
reversepair(1,"a");
  val it = ("a",1) : string * int
```

```
reversepair([1,2],5.5);
  val it = (5.5,[1,2]]) : real * int list
reversepair(1,5);
  val it = (5,1) : int * int
```

11.1.4 ▪ Datatypes

ML permits the user to define enumerated types and discriminated union types, both through the use of the keyword datatype. We first illustrate enumerated types:

```
datatype honor = none | CumLaude | MagnaCumLaude
                     | SummaCumLaude;
  datatype honor
     con CumLaude : honor
     con MagnaCumLaude : honor
     con SummaCumLaude : honor
     con none : honor
```

This enumerated datatype can be used in any further function definition, as well as in the definition of other datatypes. For example, a function that converts a grade-point average to honors is given by

```
fun computehonor(gpa:real) = if gpa>=3.87 then SummaCumLaude
                        else if gpa>=3.6 then MagnaCumLaude
                        else if gpa>3.3 then CumLaude
                        else none
  val computehonor = fn : real -> honor
```

The construction of discriminated union types is made possible through the same construct. As an example, we construct a data type that is a discriminated union of int and int list. This construction is accomplished by

```
datatype listorint = alist of int list
                     | anint of int;
  datatype listorint
     con alist : int list -> listorint
     con anint : int -> listorint
```

Notice that functions named alist and anint have been created that convert from the types int list and int into listorint type. Therefore, these functions can be used to construct objects of this new type — for example,

```
alist([1,2]);
  val it = alist [1,2] : listorint
anint(16);
  val it = anint 16 : listorint
```

Functions can now be defined that detect the actual type of a parameter and perform the appropriate action. A function to sum objects of type listorint is constructed as follows:

```
fun sum(anint(x)) = x
  | sum(alist(nil)) = 0
  | sum(alist(x::y)) = x+sum(alist(y));
  val sum = fn : listorint -> int
```

When this function is applied, its parameter must be of one of the acceptable types. Consider the results of the following applications:

```
sum(alist([1,2,3]));
  val it = 6 : int
sum(anint(12));
  val it = 12 : int
sum([1,2,3]);
  Error: operator and operand don't agree
```

We close our discussion of the ML datatype definition with an illustration of how enumerated and discriminated types can be mixed and how the type variables can be used in the definition of types. We construct a representation of a binary tree over an unspecified type as follows:

```
datatype 'a binarytree = empty
            | node of 'a * ('a binarytree) * ('a binarytree);
  datatype 'a binarytree
    con empty : 'a binarytree
    con node  : 'a * 'a binarytree * 'a binarytree
```

Here the `binarytree` datatype has two alternative definitions: `empty`, an enumerated value, and `node`, a type that is the Cartesian product of three types. The specification of `'a` immediately after the keyword `datatype` indicates that `'a` will be considered as a type parameter for this type definition.

Using the above definition for `binarytree`, a tree of any type can be constructed. For example, a simple tree of integers is constructed by

```
val tree = node(0,node(5,node(3,empty,empty),
                          node(7,empty,empty)),
                  node(15,node(12,empty,empty),
                          empty)));
```

This represents the binary tree

```
            9
          /   \
         5     15
        / \   /
       3   7 12
```

A function to search such a binary tree for a given value is

```
fun search(x,empty) = false
  | search(x,node(root,left,right)) = search(x,left) orelse
                                      x=root orelse
                                      search(x,right);
  val search = fn : ''a * ''a binarytree -> bool
```

Note that this function performs the search via an in-order traversal. The binary tree `tree` constructed before can be searched by applications of the function `search`, such as

```
search(5,tree);
  val it = true : bool
search(17,tree);
  val it = false : bool
```

The general nature of the `binarytree` datatype can be illustrated by the following sequence in ML, which creates a binary tree of strings and uses the same `search` function to search that tree.

```
val tree2 = node("nine",node("five",node("three",empty,empty),
                                     node("seven",empty,empty)),
                   node("fifteen",node("twelve",empty,
                                       empty)),empty));
search(tree2,"nine");
  val it = true : bool
search(tree2,"four");
  val it = false : bool
```

11.1.5 ▪ Exceptions

Another very useful feature of ML is the inclusion of exceptions, which can be raised at any point in a function application. For example, when we constructed the function `allbutlast`, we returned an empty list when an empty list was the parameter, even though the function should be undefined in that case. A more appropriate action might be to raise an exception when that situation occurs. The revised version of the function is

```
exception EmptyParameter;
  val EmptyParameter : exception
fun allbutlast(nil) = raise EmptyParameter
  | allbutlast(x::nil) = nil
  | allbutlast(x::y) = x::allbutlast(y);
  val allbutlast = fn : 'a list -> 'a list
```

Then, calling this function with an empty parameter gives

```
allbutlast(nil);
  uncaught exception EmptyParameter
```

Exceptions can be handled in the environment where a function raising the exception is called — for example,

```
fun tryab1(aList) = (allbutlast(alist),"good")
                handle EmptyParameter => (nil,"no good");
  val tryab1 = fn : 'a list -> 'a list * string
```

```
tryabl([1,2,3]);
  val it = ([1,2],"good") : int list * string
tryabl([]);
  val it = ([],"no good") : 'a list * string
tryabl([1.0]);
  val it = ([],"good") : real list * string
tryabl(allbutlast(["a"]));
  val it = ([],"no good") : string list * string
```

As in Ada, unhandled exceptions are propagated up to the calling environment.

11.1.6 ▪ First-Class Functions

ML treats functions as first-class objects, permitting them to be used as parameters and return values in function definitions. This powerful feature is implemented in a very natural way, as illustrated by the following function:

```
fun twice(f) = fn x => f(f(x));
  val twice = fn : ('a -> 'a) -> 'a -> 'a
```

The function `twice` returns a function that is the application of the parametric function `f` to its parameter twice. For example, this function can be applied to factorial as follows:

```
val twinfact = twice(factorial);
  val twinfact = fn : int -> int
twinfact(3);
  val it = 720 : int
```

Note that the function `twice` is polymorphic in that it applies to functions on any type. Applying it to a list function gives

```
val twintail = twice(tl);
  val twintail = fn : 'a list -> 'a list
twintail([1,2,3,4]);
  val it = [3,4] : int list
twintail(["a","b","c"]);
  val it = ["c"] : string list
```

This function can even be applied to itself:

```
val twintwice = twice(twice);
  val twintwice = fn : ('a -> 'a) -> 'a -> 'a
val quadtl = twintwice(tl);
  val quadtl = fn : 'a list -> 'a list
quadtl([1,2,3,4]);
  val it = [] : int list
```

Further examples of higher-order functions are found later, when FP functional forms are duplicated in ML.

11.2 Examples

In this section we develop ML functions that correspond to the example programs presented earlier in FP and Scheme.

Example 1: Factorial   Although a factorial function was presented earlier in this chapter, we include another version here that raises an exception when the parameter is negative.

```
exception NegativeParameter;
    exception NegativeParameter
fun factorial(n) = if n< 0 then raise NegativeParameter
                   else if n=0 then 1
                   else n*factorial(n-1);
  val factorial = fn : int -> int
```

Example 2: Quicksort   The approach used to construct quicksort in Scheme can be duplicated in ML. We construct the functional form `keep_some`, which keeps only those elements of a list for which an application of f results in a true value.

```
fun keep_some(f) = fn(x,alist) => if alist=nil then nil
    else if f(hd(alist),x) then
                hd(alist)::(keep_some(f))(x,tl(alist))
    else (keep_some(f))(x,tl(alist));
  val keep_some = fn : (''a * 'b -> bool) ->
                       'b * ''a list -> ''a list
```

Next we construct two functions to which `keep_some` can be applied. At this point we restrict ourselves to type `int`.

```
fun gtr(x,y:int) = x>y;
  val gtr = fn : int * int -> bool
fun leq(x,y:int) = x<=y;
  val leq = fn : int * int -> bool
```

We can now define two versions of `keep_some`, one for `gtr` and one for `leq`.

```
val keep_gt = keep_some(gtr);
  val keep_gt = fn : int * int list -> int list
val keep_le = keep_some(leq);
  val keep_le = fn : int * int list -> int list
```

Quicksort can now be constructed from these two functions.

```
fun quicksort(nil)=nil
  | quicksort(x::y)=quicksort(keep_le(x,y)) @
                  [x] @
                  quicksort(keep_gt(x,y));
  val quicksort = fn : int list -> int list
```

In order to modify quicksort to apply to different types, new definitions of gtr and leq must be constructed and keep_gt, keep_le and quicksort must be reinstantiated, using the same definitions as before.

```
fun gtr(x,y:string) = x>y;
  val gtr = fn : string * string -> bool
fun leq(x,y:string) = x<=y;
  val gtr = fn : string * string -> bool
val keep_le = keep_some(leq);
  val keep_le = fn : string * string list -> string list
val keep_gt = keep_some(gtr);
  val keep_gt = fn : string * string list -> string list
fun quicksort(nil) = nil
  | quicksort(x::y) = quicksort(keep_le(x,y))@
                      [x] @
                      quicksort(keep_gt(x,y));
  val quicksort = fn : string list -> string list
```

ML also contains more advanced data abstraction features, which permit a better generic definition of functions such as quicksort, but those are beyond the scope of the present discussion.

Example 3: Stacks   We will again use lists as the representation for stacks, with the first element of the list representing the top element. Our three stack operations are then defined as follows:

```
fun empty(nil)=true
  | empty(x) = false;
  val empty = fn : 'a list -> bool
fun push(stack,element) = element::stack;
  val push = fn : 'a list * 'a -> 'a list
exception PopEmpty;
  exception PopEmpty
fun pop(nil) = raise PopEmpty
  | pop(x::y) = (x,y);
  val pop = fn : 'a list -> 'a * 'a list
```

Example 4: Attribute Lists   We implement attribute lists in ML as a list of 2-tuples. This approach is used rather than the list of lists used in Scheme because a list of lists in ML would require the attribute name and the attribute value to be of the same type. This requirement exists because of the homogeneous nature of ML lists. To facilitate this approach, we need an auxiliary function that extracts the first element from a 2-tuple.

```
fun first(x,y) = x;
```

```
val first = fn : 'a * 'b -> 'a
```

Next we construct the three attribute list functions.

```
fun addattr(attlist,aname,avalue) = (aname,avalue)::attlist;
   val addattr = fn:('a * 'b) list * 'a * 'b->('a * 'b) list
fun rmattr(nil,aname) = nil
  | rmattr(x::y,aname) = if first(x)=aname then
                                          rmattr(y,aname)
                        else x::rmattr(y,aname);
   val rmattr = fn : (''a * 'b) list * ''a -> (''a * 'b) list
fun getattr(nil,aname) = nil
  | getattr(x::y,aname) = if first(x)=aname then
                                          x::getattr(y,aname)
                        else getattr(y,aname);
   val getattr = fn: (''a * 'b) list * ''a -> (''a * 'b) list
```

11.3   Comparison of ML to FP

11.3.1 ▪ Departures from the Functional Model

ML is similar to Scheme in its departures from the functional model of FP. The use of variables that create a side effect, in the sense of modifying some permanent store, is implemented by means of references in ML. References correspond to pointer variables.

Furthermore, sequential execution is also possible in ML. This idea is illustrated by the following function, which prints a count from its parametric value down to 1.

```
fun count_down(0) = print("\n")
  | count_down(n) = (print(n);
                     print(" ");
                     count_down(n-1));
   val count_down = fn : int -> unit
count_down(10);
   10 9 8 7 6 5 4 3 2 1
   val it = () : unit
```

The built-in print function is used to produce printed results. Functions such as print, which have no result but exist for their side effects, are said to return type unit. In the case of the definition of count_down, three statements are collected into a sequential block, and they are enclosed in parentheses.

11.3.2 ▪ Functional Forms in ML

Although ML has some of the functional forms of FP built in as operators or functions, we derive definitions for all of them in this section to illustrate the way ML treats functions as first-class objects.

We begin with composition, which is directly defined by

```
fun composition(f,g) = fn x => f(g(x));
  val composition = fn : ('a -> 'b) * ('c -> 'a) -> 'c -> 'b
```

Note how the types are inferred in this definition. This function can be applied directly to any pair of functions, with the domain of the first matching the range of the second. Some examples are

```
composition(factorial,factorial)(3);
  val it = 720 : int
composition(hd,tl)([1,2,3]);
  val it = 2 : int
```

This functional form is also built in to ML in the operator o. Therefore, the preceding action application could also be written

```
(hd o tl)([1,2,3]);
  val it = 2 : int
```

The constant functional form, which produces a function that always returns the same constant value, is written as

```
fun constant(n) = fn y => x;
  val constant = fn : 'a -> 'b -> 'a
```

The construction functional form applies a list of functions to a single common parameter, producing a list of results. This form is expressed in ML by

```
fun construct(flist) fn x => if length(flist)=0 then nil
            else (hd(flist))(x)::construct(tl(flist))(x);
  val construct = fn : ('a -> 'b) list -> 'a -> 'b list
```

This expression can be applied in the following way:

```
(construct([sqrt,exp,ln,sin]))(2.0);
  [1.414213,7.389056,0.693147,0.909297] : real list
```

The apply_to_all functional form applies a single function to a list of domain values. It is provided in ML as the built-in function map but can also be constructed as follows:

```
fun apply_to_all(f) = fn x => if x=nil then nil
                      else f(hd(x))::apply_to_all(f)(tl(x));
  val apply_to_all = fn : (''a -> 'b) -> ''a list -> 'b list
```

The insertion functional form takes as its parameter a two-parameter function. When applied to a list of this type, insertion constructs a result that cumulatively applies the parametric function to elements from the list, with applications going from right to left. The ML version of the insertion functional form is

```
fun insertion(f) = fn x => if length(x)=1 then hd(x)
                      else f(hd(x),insertion(f)(tl(x)));
  val insertion = fn : ('a * 'a list -> 'a list) -> 'a list
                      -> 'a list
```

If we wish to apply this to an arithmetic operator such as + or −, we first need to convert the operator from infix to prefix (called nonfix by ML) form. This is done by writing

```
nonfix +;
  nonfix +
3+4;
  Error: operator is not a function
+(3,4);
  val it = 7 : int
```

We can now apply + using `insertion`:

```
insertion(+)([1,2,3,4,5]);
  val it = 15 : int
nonfix -;
  nonfix -
insertion(-)([1,2,3,4]);
  val it = ~2 : int
```

The final application illustrates that `insertion` applies its function from right to left.

The `condition` functional form is implemented by a direct application of the `if` in ML.

```
fun condition(p,f,g) = fn x => if p(x) then f(x)
                                        else g(x);
  val condition = fn ('a -> bool) * ('a' -> 'b) *
                  ('a -> 'b) -> 'a -> 'b
```

When defining the `while` functional form, we will use the name `newwhile`, because `while` is a reserved word in ML.

```
fun newwhile(p,f) = fn x => if p(x) then
                              (newwhile(p,f))(f(x))
                            else x;
  val newwhile = fn : ('a -> bool) * ('a -> 'a) -> 'a -> 'a
```

CHAPTER 11 Terms

ML   parametric polymorphism
meta language

CHAPTER 11 Discussion Questions

1. What are some advantages to ML's strict typing over the more relaxed view of types taken by Scheme? What are some disadvantages?

2. Functions in ML can be defined using the `fun` keyword or the `val` keyword. Which do you think is better and why?

3. ML lists must be homogeneous, whereas Scheme's lists may be heterogeneous. What are some advantages to each of these strategies?

4. Compare the exception handling feature of ML with that of Ada.

5. Compare the functional forms of FP to those of which ML is capable. Where do they differ? Why do they differ?

C H A P T E R **11**   Exercises

1. What is the type of each of the following ML expressions? If the expression is illegal because of type, explain why.

   a. `6+2;`
   b. `6/2;`
   c. `6 div 2;`
   d. `fun d(x,y) = x+y;`
   e. `fun e(x,y) = x+1;`
   f. `fun f(x) = x::x;`
   g. `fun g(x) = x::[x];`

2. The function `repeat` was defined in this chapter using the `if-then-else` construct of ML. Create a pattern-matching definition for the same function.

3. The following functions were defined in this chapter using the pattern-matching construct of ML. Create `if-then-else` definitions for each of them.

`sum(x:intlist)`	`sum(x:listorint)`
`allbutlast`	`search`
`smallest`	`empty`
	`pop`

4. Construct a function that applies to two parameters of type `listorint` in the following way:

`add(x,y) = x+y`	if x and y are both integers
`add(x,y) = [x+y_1...x+y_n]`	if x is an integer and $y=[y_1...y_n]$
`add(x,y) = [x_1+y...x_n+y]`	if $x=[x_1...x_n]$ and y is an integer
`add(x,y) = [x_1+y_1...x_n+y_n]`	if x and y are both lists

5. Verify that all of the primitive functions of FP can be constructed in ML by providing ML definitions for each of them.

6. Construct the following functional form in ML:

   ```
   prod(f,g):x = (f(x),g(x))
   list_to_list([f_1...f_n]):[x_1...x_n] = [f_1(x_1)...f_n(x_n)]
   ```

7. Examine the following code fragment (from Chapter 9):

   ```
   function totaler (A: array of integer): integer;
        begin
            for i := 1 to 10 do
                total := total + A[i]*2;
            totaler := total+A[1];
        end;
   ```

   Write a fragment that has the same functionality in ML. Instead of an array as an argument, you may assume a list structure of at least 10 integers.

8. Recall the Chapter 9 (and 10) exercise where we represented a 3×3 matrix in FP as

    ```
    < <1,2,3>,<4,5,6>,<7,8,9> >
    ```

    Now, let's do the same for ML. We can represent this matrix as list of lists,

    ```
    [[1, 2, 3], [4, 5, 6], [7, 8, 9]]
    ```

    or with row-by-row order.

    a. Write an ML function to sum the items in a column. Compare this to the functions you wrote for FP and Scheme.

    b. Write an ML function that sums all numbers in a matrix. Compare this to what you wrote for FP and Scheme. Specifically, compare how you used functional forms in FP and ML versus the method in which you combined functions in Scheme.

C H A P T E R **11**   **Laboratory Exercises**

---

1. Construct a set of string functions in ML as specified:

`charinstring(n,s)`	returns the *n*th character in string s
`position(s1,s2)`	returns the integer position of the leftmost occurrence of s1 in s2; empty if not found
`count(s1,s2)`	returns a count of the number of times s1 occurs in s2
`wordcount(s)`	returns a count of the number of words in s, where a word is defined as any sequence of letters delimited by non-letters, beginning of string, or end of string

2. Construct a set of functions in ML that will simulate complex arithmetic by accepting as parameters and returning as values pairs of reals to represent complex numbers.

`realpart(c)`	returns the real part of complex number c
`imagpart(c)`	returns the imaginary part of c
`cadd(c1,c2)`	returns c1+c2
`csub(c1,c2)`	returns c1-c2
`cmult(c1,c2)`	returns c1*c2
`cdiv(c1,c2)`	returns c1/c2
`cabs(c)`	returns the real number that is the modulus of c

3. Construct a discriminated union data type that can be either `real` or `int` and define `add(x,y)` over this type to perform the correct addition no matter what the base types of the two parameters and to return a `real` result.

4. Construct a set of functions to perform binary search tree functions on the `binarytree` type defined in this chapter. Functions should include

    ```
    insert(x,bst)    delete(x,bst)    printinorder(x,bst)
    ```

5. Consider the NQUEENS problem from Chapter 10. Write this algorithm, using the same steps, in ML. Compare the efforts in both cases. Did functionality give you advantages or disadvantages? Did typing give you advantages or disadvantages?

An Overview of the Logic-Oriented Model

The logic-oriented model is introduced in this chapter. It is briefly described, then discussed in more detail through the use of a hypothetical language, LP. The implementation of the basic-oriented model in database query languages is illustrated, using the language SQL as an example. (The language Prolog is described as an implementation of the logic-oriented model in Chapter 13.)

12.1 Introduction to the Logic Language Model

The logic model for programming languages permits the expression of programs in a form similar to symbolic logic. This process is essentially the same as writing a program that proves a theorem. In order to understand how this works, let us examine how a theorem is proved.

First, a theorem must be proved from a set of facts that are accepted as true. These are called **axioms** in mathematics. The statement to be proved is then considered a goal, and the given information is manipulated using rules of logical inference until the goal statement is demonstrated to be true.

A program written using a programming language of the logic model consists of a set of axioms and a goal statement, both expressed in the syntax of the language. The rules of inference are then applied to determine whether the axioms are sufficient to ensure the truth of the goal statement or not. The manner in which the rules of inference are applied to derive the goal from the axioms is not expressed in the language but is assumed to occur automatically. In this way, programs written in the logic model express a goal and the facts from which this goal is to be derived but do not express the method by which this derivation takes place. The method may be produced by the execution of the program if the goal is derivable.

As an example, consider the logic model approach to finding the greatest common divisor of 16 and 56. We first state the axioms that define the greatest common divisor:

```
Axiom 1: gcd(N,0) = 1 for all N ≥ 1.
Axiom 2: gcd(N,M) = gcd(M,N mod M) for N ≥ 1 and M ≥ 1.
Goal: gcd(56,16)
```

The axioms state a definition of the greatest common divisor, and the goal is the result we wish to derive. This is the entire program in a logic model language. It is unnecessary for the programmer to express how the program should go about determining the validity of the goal statement.

In contrast to the imperative model — where the programmer must describe how a problem is solved — under the logic model, the programmer describes the goal, and the system searches for a solution in the form of a proof that verifies that goal.

12.2 A Pure Logic Language

In this section we define a pure logic model programming language that we call *LP*. This language is a representation of Horn clauses from logic and is based on a similar language described by Hogger (1984). We will keep our discussion of formal logic to the minimum needed to understand the actions of the logic programs that can be written in LP. In addition, we use notation and terminology that is convenient for understanding but not necessarily consistent with that used in formal logic. For more formal discussions of logic languages, see Kowalski (1979) or Genesereth and Ginsberg (1985).

12.2.1 ▪ Basic Components

An **object** is the most basic component of LP and can be any specific object at all. It might be a number, a person, a set of books, a program, a list of names, a sequence of characters, or anything that can be conceptually abstracted into a single item. Note that an object can be composite in nature such as the list, set, or sequence just mentioned. The meaning of an object is completely determined by its use within the program — that is, through its logical relationships with other objects. In the pure logic model, there is no binding of type to an object.

An individual object in LP is represented by a sequence of characters that begins with an uppercase letter or a digit. We will use the convention that any sequence of digits represents a number object that corresponds to the sequence interpreted as a decimal integer. This can be done without violating the typeless property of the logic model, because such objects are assumed to carry with them the entire set of arithmetic relations that are necessary to define them.

Relations represent some quality, attribute, or relationship of one or more objects. Relations are given names that begin with an uppercase letter and are expressed by the relation name, which is followed by a list of object names separated by commas and enclosed in parentheses. Some examples of relations are

```
FATHER(TOM,JANE)
LARGER(2,1)
MALE(ROBERT)
COST(CAR1,17246)
```

A variable in LP is represented by a sequence of characters beginning with a lowercase letter. A variable, when used in the context of a relation, indicates that the relation holds for all objects in the space of objects that are defined. For example, the relation

```
SAME_AGE(x,x)
```

indicates that every object is related to itself by the relation SAME_AGE.

A program written in LP may contain three kinds of statements — a goal, facts, and rules — all terminated with a period. The program must contain exactly one goal, but it may include any number of facts and rules. A goal is expressed by a question mark followed by a fact. There are two types of goals, depending on whether the embedded fact contains any variables or not. A goal with no variables is simply a request to determine whether the stated fact can be derived as true from the facts and rules present in the program. For example,

```
?FATHER(JOHN,SUE).
```

will result in TRUE if JOHN can be derived to be the father of SUE according to the facts and rules given and will result in FALSE if this relation cannot be derived. Note that we do not say the relation is "not true." Rather, it cannot be derived as true from the information present in the program.

The second form of a goal, that containing one or more variables, requests that all object tuples be listed if, when substituted into the embedded fact for the corresponding variables, they cause the fact to be derivably true. For example, the goal

```
?FATHER(x,SUE).
```

might return the result

```
x = JOHN
```

Furthermore, the goal statement

```
?ADJACENT(x,CALIFORNIA).
```

might return

```
x = OREGON
x = NEVADA
x = ARIZONA
```

and

```
?COMPLETED(JOHN,course,grade).
```

might return

```
course = CS100  grade = A
course = CS200  grade = B
course = MA110  grade = B
course = EN200  grade = C
```

A **fact** is a relation between objects and indicates that the given relation does indeed hold. For example,

```
FATHER(JOHN,SUE).
```

states that JOHN is the father of SUE. If a fact contains variables, then the fact holds for all objects in the object space of this program. For example,

```
FEMALE(person).
```

specifies that all objects that are used within the containing program have the property FEMALE. Similarly,

```
KNOWS(x,BARB).
```

indicates that the relation KNOWS holds between all objects and BARB.

Finally, a rule consists of two parts, a fact that is the conclusion of the rule and a list of facts that form the hypotheses. The general form is

```
c if h₁,h₂,...,hₙ for n>0
```

The meaning of such a rule is that fact c is derived to be true if facts $h_1, h_2, \ldots, h_n$ are all derivably true. For example, the rule

```
PARENT(JOHN,SUE) if FATHER(JOHN,SUE).
```

states that JOHN is a parent of SUE if JOHN is a father of SUE. Furthermore, the use of variables is common in the case of rules in order to generalize the rule to hold for all possible objects. The preceding rule could be generalized to

```
PARENT(x,y) if FATHER(x,y).
```

There may be many ways of deriving the same fact, and thus the same conclusion might be present in many rules. For example,

```
PARENT(x,y) if MOTHER(x,y).
```

would also be appropriate.

Finally, some examples of rules containing multiple hypotheses are

```
MOTHER(x,y) if PARENT(x,y),FEMALE(x).
GRANDMOTHER(x,y) if MOTHER(x,z),PARENT(z,y).
```

Note that in the last example, the variable z is used in the hypotheses even though it does not appear in the conclusion. Such a variable is used to tie together facts in the hypotheses. This last rule could be stated: x is a GRAND-MOTHER of y if x is the MOTHER of z and z is the PARENT of y for some z. In other words, a variable found only in the hypotheses of a rule is handled differently from one appearing in the conclusion. To further define this difference, if variables $x_1, x_2, \ldots, x_n$ are used in the conclusion and variables $y_1, y_2, \ldots, y_m$ are used in the hypotheses but not in the conclusion, the rule

$$c(x_1, x_2, \ldots, x_n) \text{ if } h(x_1, x_2, \ldots, x_n, y_1, y_2, \ldots y_m).$$

is interpreted as

For all objects $x_1, x_2, \ldots, x_n$, c holds if there exist objects $y_1, y_2, \ldots, y_m$ such that h holds.

Figure 12.1 shows the BNF definition of our LP language.

Example Program in LP In this section we will develop an extensive example program in our new LP language to illustrate how programming takes place under the logic model. This program consists of the description of relations between people, machines, types of hardware, and types of software. The eventual objective of our program will be to determine if a given person can run a specific software product.

FIGURE 12.1 **BNF Representation of LP**

```
program   ::=   <goal>
                {<rule> | <fact>}

fact      ::=   <constant> | <variable> |
                <relation-name> ( <fact> {,<fact>} )

rule      ::=   <fact> if <fact> {,<fact>}

goal      ::=   ?<fact> .

constant  ::=   <uppercase letter> {<character>} |
                <digit> {<character>}

variable  ::=   <lowercase letter> {<character>}

relation-name   ::=   <uppercase letter> {<character>}
```

Our example includes five types of objects, described in Figure 12.2, and five relations, described in Figure 12.3. Figure 12.4 lists a set of facts in LP syntax that are a part of the program. In particular, this figure defines specific relations among the objects considered by the program using the three relations TYPE, RUNS, and ACCESS. The other two relations, CAN_RUN and CAN_USE, are relations that are defined by rules rather than facts. Rules for the example program are given in Figure 12.5. The first rule, which defines CAN_USE, can be stated in words as follows:

For all objects p and sw, p can use sw if there exists an object mach such that p has access to mach and mach can run sw.

This statement indicates that the relation CAN_USE holds between two objects if an object can be found that satisfies both facts on the right-hand side of the rule.
For example, the goal

```
?CAN_USE(SUE,BASIC).
```

FIGURE 12.2 **Objects Used in Example Program**

```
Machines (mach) = {IBMPC,MAC}

Software (sw)    = {SPREADSHEET,PASCAL,BASIC,SMALLTALK}

Hardware (hw)    = {MACH1,MACH2,MACH3}

Memory Size (mem1,mem2) in Kbytes = set of integers

Person (p)       = {SUE,JERRY,SAM}
```

FIGURE 12.3 **Relations Used in Example Program**

```
RUNS(hw,sw,mem)
    The hardware hw runs software sw if it has at
    least mem Kbytes of memory.

SPEC(mach,hw,mem)
    Machine mach is of type hw and has memory size
    mem.

ACCESS(p,mach)
    Person p has access to machine mach.

CAN_RUN(mach,sw)
    Machine mach can run software sw.

CAN_USE(p,sw)
    Person p can use software sw.
```

FIGURE 12.4   **Facts for Example Program in LP**

```
F1:   SPEC(MACH1,IBMPC,320)
F2:   SPEC(MACH2,MAC,1000)
F3:   SPEC(MACH3,IBMPC,640)
F4:   RUNS(IBMPC,SPREADSHEET,500)
F5:   RUNS(IBMPC,BASIC,128)
F6:   RUNS(IBMPC,PASCAL,256)
F7:   RUNS(MAC,BASIC,200)
F8:   RUNS(MAC,SMALLTALK,1000)
F9:   ACCESS(SUE,MACH1)
F10:  ACCESS(JERRY,MACH3)
F11:  ACCESS(SAM,MACH1)
F12:  ACCESS(SAM,MACH2)
```

FIGURE 12.5   **Rules for Example Program in LP**

```
R1:   CAN_USE(p,sw) if ACCESS(p,mach),
                       CAN_RUN(mach,sw)

R2:   CAN_RUN(mach,sw) if SPEC(mach,hw,mem1),
                          RUNS(hw,sw,mem2),
                          GEQ(mem1,mem2)
```

will be satisfied if there is some object mach for which both ACCESS(SUE,mach) and CAN_RUN(mach,BASIC) are satisfied. By examining the facts in Figure 12.4, we see that the only mach for which the first fact is satisfied is MACH1. For the remaining subgoal, we may then assume that mach is MACH1, because that is the only object that satisfies the first subgoal. This process is referred to as **binding** the variable mach to MACH1. The second clause of the rule is itself a rule, namely, CAN_RUN. Because mach has to be MACH1 to satisfy the first subgoal, we now need to determine if CAN_RUN(MACH1,BASIC) is satisfied. This will be satisfied if all three of the subgoals for CAN_RUN are satisfied for some specific objects mem1, mem2, and hw. In our case, the three subgoals will be

```
SPEC(MACH1,hw,mem1).
RUNS(hw,BASIC,mem2).
GEQ(mem1,mem2).
```

The relation GEQ requires further explanation, because it is not defined elsewhere in the program. This relation is assumed to be built into our LP language with a specific meaning for all pairs of objects. The relation will hold whenever the first object is greater than or equal to the second object. If both objects are numeric, a numeric comparison is assumed. If one or both of the objects contain nonnumeric characters, an alphabetical comparison is assumed. The first two subgoals can be matched by rules found in our program (Figure 12.4), with the third matched by the definition of GEQ:

```
SPEC(MACH1,IBMPC,320).
RUNS(IBMPC,BASIC,128).
GEQ(320,128).
```

with variable bindings hw=IBMPC, mem1=320, and mem2=128. Therefore, the rule

```
CAN_RUN(MACH1,BASIC).
```

is satisfied; hence, so is the original goal

```
CAN_USE(SUE,BASIC).
```

Figure 12.6 illustrates the preceding process using a derivation tree. In this tree, each rule becomes a parent node for all the subgoals on its right-hand side. Variables that are bound are indicated by assignments labeling the edges of the tree. This tree shows the path by which the goal is verified, but it does not indicate the method by which this is done. We will examine this process later.

The goal just considered contained no variables and hence was either satisfied or not satisfied. The more complex form of a goal — that containing one or more variables — asks for all tuples of objects that, when substituted

FIGURE 12.6   **Derivation Tree**

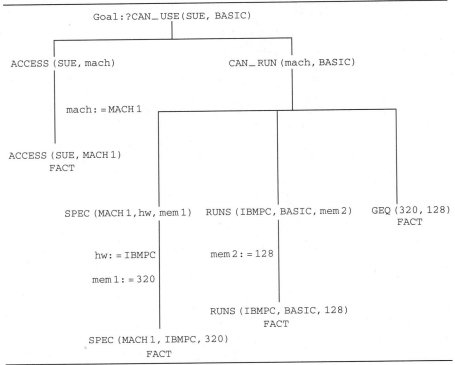

for the variables, satisfy the goal. For example, our example program might have as its goal

```
?CAN_USE(SUE,x).
```

This goal is asking for all objects that represent software products that SUE can use. After some examination, we could deduce that the rules in Figure 12.4 yield two possible values of x,

```
x = BASIC
x = PASCAL
```

12.2.3 ▪ The Process of Deduction

At the heart of our logic programming language LP is a processor commonly known as the **inference engine**, whose role is to take all the provided facts and rules and derive new facts from them. In particular, in the context of our LP language, the inference engine is asked to derive new facts based on the goal that is given. In this section, we will study how the inference engine operates.

The two primary operations used by an inference engine to derive new facts from given facts and rules are resolution and unification. **Resolution** says that if we are given two rules, with a given fact f on the left-hand side of one rule and f also on the right-hand side of the other rule, a new rule can be derived whose left-hand side consists of the union of the two left-hand sides with f removed and whose right-hand side consists of the union of the right-hand sides with f removed. Stated in generality, the two rules

```
f if a₁,a₂,...,aₙ
g if f,b₁,b₂,...,bₘ
```

resolve to the new rule

```
g if a₁,a₂,...,aₙ,b₁,b₂,...,bₘ
```

If you follow the logic of these statements carefully, you will be able to verify that the result of resolution is logically valid.

Consider the following example of resolution. Suppose we are given

```
PLAY_BALL(x) if NOT_RAINING,NOT_WORKING(x).
NOT_WORKING(x) if WEEKEND.
```

We can derive the following new rule by resolution over the relation NOT_WORKING(x):

```
PLAY_BALL(x) if NOT_RAINING,WEEKEND.
```

Notice that this is a valid logical deduction from the two given rules, which will always be the case for resolution, because it is verifiably valid by rules of logic.

A special case of resolution arises when we observe that a fact is a degenerate occurrence of a rule. For example, the fact

```
CSMAJOR(HARRY).
```

is a special case of the rule

```
CSMAJOR(HARRY) [if anything].
```

The "if anything" is enclosed in brackets in the preceding rule to indicate that it need not be present and is included only to illustrate that a fact is a special case of a rule.

If this new rule is resolved with the rule

```
INVITE(HARRY) if CSMAJOR(HARRY),SENIOR(HARRY).
```

the result will be

```
INVITE(HARRY) if [anything,]SENIOR(HARRY).
```

or, equivalently,

```
INVITE(HARRY) if SENIOR(HARRY).
```

Similarly, if the two rules had been

```
CSMAJOR(HARRY) [if anything].
INVITE(HARRY) if CSMAJOR(HARRY).
```

then resolution would yield the fact

```
INVITE(HARRY) [if anything].
```

Therefore, resolution can be used to derive a new rule from two rules or from a rule and a fact or to derive a new fact from a rule and a fact.

Unification is the derivation of a new rule from a given rule through the binding of variables. For example, the rule

```
INVITE(x) if CSMAJOR(x),SENIOR(x).
```

would unify to the new rule

```
INVITE(HARRY) if CSMAJOR(HARRY),SENIOR(HARRY).
```

under the binding of HARRY to the variable x.

The derivation of new facts, including goal facts, can be expressed through a sequence of resolutions and unifications. Consider, for example, the derivation of the goal

```
?CAN_USE(SUE,BASIC).
```

which is illustrated in Figure 12.6. As a series of resolutions and unifications, it might be derived as follows:

```
Unify R1 with sw=BASIC,p=SUE,mach=MACH1
    R3: CAN_USE(SUE,BASIC) if
                ACCESS(SUE,MACH1),CAN_RUN(MACH1,BASIC).
Unify R2 with mach=MACH1,sw=BASIC,mem1=320,mem2=128
    R4: CAN_RUN(MACH1,BASIC) if
```

```
                                SPEC(MACH1,IBMPC,320),
                                RUNS(IBMPC,BASIC,128),
                                GEQ(320,128).
    Resolve R3 with F9
       R5: CAN_USE(SUE,BASIC) if CAN_RUN(MACH1,BASIC).
    Resolve R4 with F1
       R6: CAN_RUN(MACH1,BASIC) if RUNS(IBMPC,BASIC,128),
                                    GEQ(320,128).
    Resolve R6 with F5
       R7: CAN_RUN(MACH1,BASIC) if GEQ(320,128).
    Resolve R7 with assumed fact for GEQ
       F13: CAN_RUN(MACH1,BASIC).
    Resolve R5 with F13
       F14: CAN_USE(SUE,BASIC).
```

12.2.4 ▪ Implementation Considerations

You may have observed that we have said nothing about how the inference engine decides which unification or resolution to perform next in the derivation of a goal. This omission has been intentional, because that is part of the "how" in the solution of the problem that we have attempted to avoid in our logic model. The programmer simply states the goal, facts, and rules in LP, and the inference engine determines the satisfiability of the goal. It is fine to consider the program as independent of the implementation of the inference engine when working with a hypothetical language such as LP, but, in practice, efficiency considerations usually require some knowledge of the implementation. The development of an appropriate derivation of a goal usually requires a search for the appropriate sequence of unifications and resolutions, and the choice of strategy used in that search might determine whether the derivation is accomplished in a reasonable amount of time or not. In some cases, an unwisely chosen search strategy could lead to a nonterminating search that never finds a valid derivation, even when one is possible.

The derivation of a goal can proceed in either of two ways. First, all possible resolutions and unifications could be performed until the goal is derived. This process has the disadvantage that many irrelevant facts and rules will be derived before the desired goal appears. In fact, because there may be an infinite number of derivable facts and rules, the desired goal may never be derived.

The more useful approach is to start with the goal and work backward by identifying facts and rules from which the goal can be derived. In particular, this backward process can occur in two ways: the expansion of a goal by applying a rule and the reduction of a goal by applying a fact.

First, let's examine expansion by applying a rule. At any point, our goal will be a list of facts, all of which must be satisfied for the goal to be satisfied. We will represent facts by uppercase letters and assume that our present goal is

```
?A,B,C.
```

If a rule is present that can be unified with fact A — that is, if the conclusion of the rule is the same as fact A when a variable is bound to an object — then the goal can be expanded according to that rule. For example, suppose the rule

```
A if D,E,F.
```

is present in the program. Then the original goal can be expanded to

```
?D,E,F,B,C.
```

This process is valid, because ?A,B,C can be derived if ?D,E,F,B,C can be derived from the application of the preceding rule.

Note that this process can be summarized by

```
A and (A if D,E,F) → D,E,F.
```

where the B and C parts of the goal are simply carried along as additional sub-goals. This process is the reversal of the resolution that would occur if the arrow went the other way. In other words, because we are starting with the goal and working backward, each step is a reversed derivation step.

The second type of step — reduction using a fact — is the elimination of one of the facts in the goal because that fact matches a fact given in the program, possibly after the binding of one or more variables. For example, if the goal is

```
?A,B,C.
```

and the fact A is given in the program, then this goal can be reduced to

```
?B,C.
```

Thus, ?A,B,C can be derived if ?B,C can be derived, because A is a given fact.

Now we can apply this backward process to our derivation of ?CAN_USE(SUE,BASIC) examined earlier.

1. ?CAN_USE(SUE,BASIC).   /R1/p=SUE,sw=BASIC

2. ?ACCESS(SUE,mach),CAN_RUN(mach,BASIC).   /F9/mach=MACH1

3. ?CAN_RUN(MACH1,BASIC).   /R2

4. ?SPEC(MACH1,hw,mem1),RUNS(hw,BASIC,mem2),GEQ(mem1,mem2).

                                              /F1/hw=IBMPC,mem1=320

5. ?RUNS(IBMPC,BASIC,mem2),GEQ(320,mem2).   /F10/mem2=128

6. ?GEQ(320,128).   /success

The logical argument then follows that if goal 6 is satisfied, then so is goal 5, if goal 5 is satisfied, then so is goal 4, and so on. Because goal 6 is a verified fact, the original goal (goal 1) is also satisfied.

In the preceding derivation, this process went more smoothly than we have a right to expect. To illustrate a possible difficulty, consider the goal

```
?CAN_USE(JERRY,SPREADSHEET).
```

Our process can proceed as before:

1. ?CAN_USE(SAM,SPREADSHEET).   /R1/p=JERRY,
                                                        sp=SPREADSHEET

2. ?ACCESS(SAM,mach),CAN_RUN(mach,SPREADSHEET).

                                                     /F12/mach=MACH2

3. ?CAN_RUN(MACH2,SPREADSHEET).   /R2

4. ?SPEC(MACH2,hw,mem1),RUNS(hw,SPREADSHEET,mem2),GEQ(mem1,mem2).

                                                     /F2/hw=MAC,mem1=1000

5. ?RUNS(MAC,SPREADSHEET,mem2),GEQ(1000,mem2).

Now the first subgoal at step 5 cannot be satisfied. This does not mean, however, that the original goal cannot be satisfied, because careful examination of the problem will indicate that it can be. This difficulty arises because at step 2, both F10 and F11 apply, and we made the wrong choice for completing our derivation. Had we chosen F11, we would have been successful.

This points to the necessity, in implementing this derivation process, of backing up to try other alternatives whenever we fail to satisfy a subgoal. The process that we outline here will back up, one level at a time, until we reach a level where there is an alternative choice for satisfying the leading subgoal. If no such level exists, the search is completed and the derivation fails. This backing-up process is especially necessary when the original goal contains variables, so that all bindings of the variables must be found that lead to successful derivations. The derivation of the goal ?CAN_USE(x,SPREADSHEET) utilizing the backing-up process just described is illustrated in Figure 12.7. Notice that at each step the first goal (subgoal) in the list is either expanded by a rule or satisfied by a fact; in the case where neither can occur, the process backs up to the immediately preceding set of subgoals, where it searches for matches beyond those already tried.

FIGURE 12.7 **Derivation of Goal Using Backtracking**

```
1. ?CAN_USE(x,SPREADSHEET)                               R1/sw:=SPREADSHEET
2. ?ACCESS(x,m),CAN_RUN(m,SPREADSHEET)                   F9/x:=SUE,m:=MACH1
3. ?CAN_RUN(MACH1,SPREADSHEET)                           R2
4. ?SPEC(MACH1,hw,m1),RUNS(hw,SPREADSHEET,m2),GEQ(m1,m2) F1/hw:=IBMPC,m1:=320
5. ?RUNS(IBMPC,SPREADSHEET,m2),GEQ(320,m2)               F4/m2:=500
6. ?GEQ(320,500)                                         Fails
5. ?RUNS(IBMPC,SPREADSHEET,m2),GEQ(320,m2)               Fails
4. ?SPEC(MACH1,hw,m1),RUNS(hw,SPREADSHEET,m2),GEQ(m1,m2) Fails
3. ?CAN_RUN(MACH1,SPREADSHEET)                           Fails
2. ?ACCESS(x,m),CAN_RUN(m,SPREADSHEET)                   F10/x:=JERRY,m:=MACH3
3. ?CAN_RUN(MACH3,SPREADSHEET)                           R2
4. ?SPEC(MACH3,hw,m1),RUNS(hw,SPREADSHEET,m2),GEQ(m1,m2) F3/hw:=IBMPC,m1:=640
5. ?RUNS(IBMPC,SPREADSHEET,m2),GEQ(640,m2)               F4/m2:=500
6. ?GEQ(640,500)                                         success/x:=JERRY
5. ?RUNS(IBMPC,SPREADSHEET,m2),GEQ(640,m2)               Fails
4. ?SPEC(MACH3,hw,m1),RUNS(hw,SPREADSHEET,m2),GEQ(m1,m2) Fails
```

(continues)

```
3.  ?CAN_RUN(MACH3,SPREADSHEET)                                       Fails
2.  ?ACCESS(x,m),CAN_RUN(m,SPREADSHEET)                               F11/x:=SAM,m:=MACH1
3.  ?CAN_RUN(MACH1,SPREADSHEET)                                       R2
4.  ?SPEC(MACH1,hw,m1),RUNS(hw,SPREADSHEET,m2),GEQ(m1,m2)  F1/hw:=IBMPC,m1:=320
5.  ?RUNS(IBMPC,SPREADSHEET,m2),GEQ(320,m2)                           F4/m2:=500
6.  ?GEQ(320,500)                                                     Fails
5.  ?RUNS(IBMPC,SPREADSHEET,m2),GEQ(320,m2)                           Fails
4.  ?SPEC(MACH1,hw,m1),RUNS(hw,SPREADSHEET,m2),GEQ(m1,m2) Fails
3.  ?CAN_RUN(MACH1,SPREADSHEET)                                       Fails
2.  ?ACCESS(x,m),CAN_RUN(m,SPREADSHEET)                               F12/x:=SAM,m:=MACH2
3.  ?CAN_RUN(MACH2,SPREADSHEET)                                       R2
4.  ?SPEC(MACH2,hw,m1),RUNS(hw,SPREADSHEET,m2),GEQ(m1,m2) F2/hw:=MAC,m1:=1000
5.  ?RUNS(MAC,SPREADSHEET,m2),GEQ(m1,m2)                              Fails
4.  ?SPEC(MACH2,hw,m1),RUNS(hw,SPREADSHEET,m2),GEQ(m1,m2) Fails
3.  ?CAN_RUN(MACH2,SPREADSHEET)                                       Fails
2.  ?ACCESS(x,m),CAN_RUN(m,SPREADSHEET)                               Fails
1.  ?CAN_USE(x,SPREADSHEET)                                           Fails
```

For example, after the first failure at goal 6, the process backs up to goal 5, where an alternative to m=500 is required. None being found, the process backs up to goal 4, where an alternative to hw=IBMPC and m1=320 is required. Again, none is found, so the process backs up to goal 3. Because goal 3 causes no variables to be bound, it is not possible to try other alternative bindings here, so the process immediately backs up to goal 2. At goal 2, a match can be found other than x=SUE, m=MACH1. The next such match being x=JERRY,m=MACH2, these bindings are made and the process proceeds forward once again. You can trace the rest of the process through Figure 12.7.

In summary, the language LP can be implemented through a simple process of reverse resolution and unification that results in the generation of subgoals from the original goal. Because there may be several alternative subgoals generated by a given goal, the process may require **backtracking** to try all possible substitutions. This process can become quite time-consuming in practice, and the efficiency of the process can be affected by the order in which alternatives are considered.

Furthermore, in the case of recursive rules — that is, rules whose right-hand side contains the same relation as is expressed on the left-hand side — the order of search can determine whether the derivation will terminate or not. For example, consider the following addition to our example LP program. First, we add the new relation WRITTEN_IN, where

WRITTEN_IN(x,y) means software x is written in language y.

Then, a simplified new rule can be added to our program:

CAN_RUN(mach,sw) if CAN_RUN(mach,l),WRITTEN_IN(sw,l).

Now, if we add the fact

WRITTEN_IN(SPREADSHEET,PASCAL).

and assume that our new rule for CAN_RUN is attempted before any other rule for CAN_RUN in our program search space, we generate the following derivation:

1. `?CAN_RUN(x,SPREADSHEET).`

2. `?CAN_RUN(x,1),WRITTEN_IN(SPREADSHEET,1).`

3. `?CAN_RUN(x,1'),WRITTEN_IN(1,1'),WRITTEN_IN(SPREADSHEET,1').`

.
.
.

This example illustrates that the order in which rules and facts are matched in the derivation can have a major impact on the result. In a pure logic programming environment, such as LP, the assumption is made that if there is a valid derivation, the system will find it and that the order in which rules and facts occur is irrelevant. In practice, this concept is very difficult to implement, and actual languages do perform their searches for derivations in a way that is dependent on the order of declarations in the program.

12.3 Database Query Languages

One popular implementation of the logic model for a programming language is the query language of a relational database management system. In order to illustrate the correspondence between a relational query language and the logic model, we first introduce the fundamentals of a relational database management system. Then we describe a relational query language, SQL, and, finally, we detail the query language–logic model correspondence.

12.3.1 ▪ Relational Database Management Systems

The fundamental entity of a relational database management system is the **relation**, which can be viewed as a table of rows and columns, where each row, called a **tuple**, represents an object, and each column, called an **attribute**, represents a property of the object. For example, Figure 12.8 represents the relation STUDENT, where each tuple is a single student and each column is an attribute that students have. This particular table has four tuples, representing four students, and five attributes, NAME, CLASS, SEX, MAJOR, and AGE.

A database consists of one or more relations. Data are manipulated, stored in the tables, and retrieved from the tables via commands written in a **query language**. Many tools are provided for the organization of the data for effi-

FIGURE 12.8 **Relation** STUDENT

	Attributes			
NAME	CLASS	SEX	MAJOR	AGE
Sue	SR	F	Math	21
John	JR	M	English	20
Jerry	FR	M	History	18
Sally	FR	F	Physics	17

cient data entry, efficient retrieval, and formatting of reports and screens, but because these tools are not pertinent to our purposes here, we will not discuss them. Our focus is on the query language as it applies to the logic model for programming languages.

12.3.2 ▪ Query Language SQL

SQL is the most commonly used relational query language. Many features of SQL are omitted from our discussion, because our intent here is to illustrate its basic adherence to the logic model. The fundamental features described in this section are those required to create relations, add tuples to relations, define views, and selectively retrieve information from relations.

First, the creation of a relation is specified by a CREATE statement. The creation in SQL of the relation STUDENT shown in Figure 12.8 is accomplished by the statement

```
CREATE STUDENT (NAME    CHAR(20,
                CLASS   CHAR(2),
                SEX     CHAR(1),
                MAJOR   CHAR(10),
                AGE     INTEGER
```

The CREATE statement consists of the word CREATE followed by the name of the relation and the list of attributes, with each attribute's name and type specified. When a relation is created, it is assumed to be empty, containing no tuple.

Tuples can be added to a relation through the INSERT statement. One simple form of such a statement is

```
INSERT INTO STUDENT (NAME,CLASS,SEX,MAJOR,AGE)
             VALUES ('Sue','SR','F','Math',21)
```

This statement includes the name of the relation, the list of attribute names, and a list of values that correspond positionally to the attributes named.

To illustrate views and retrievals in SQL, we need to define a second relation, ATHLETE, in our database. This relation contains three tuples and two attributes and is shown in Figure 12.9. It is assumed that tuples in STUDENT and ATHLETE represent the same person when their NAME attribute values are identical.

Retrievals are ways of specifying tables of data that are to be returned to the user. For example, one might wish to find the names of all students older than 20. Such a retrieval is expressed in SQL by

FIGURE 12.9   **Relation** ATHLETE

```
    Attributes
NAME    SPORT
John    Swimming
Sally   Soccer
Joe     Baseball
```

```
SELECT NAME
     FROM STUDENT
     WHERE ABE > 20
```

Here, the word SELECT is followed by the name of the attribute to be retrieved, the word FROM is followed by the name of the relation from which retrieval takes place, and WHERE is followed by a condition that is used to make the selection.

It is possible to retrieve more than one field using the SELECT statement. In the preceding example, if we want the ages and names of students to be retrieved, we could write

```
SELECT NAME, AGE
     FROM STUDENT
     WHERE AGE > 20
```

We can also base the retrieval on more than one relation. Suppose we wish to retrieve the names and ages only of students who are also athletes. We could do this with

```
SELECT STUDENT.NAME, STUDENT.AGE
     FROM STUDENT, ATHLETE
     WHERE STUDENT.NAME = ATHLETE.NAME
```

The qualifiers need to be placed on NAME and AGE after SELECT because there are two relations involved in the retrieval. Therefore, attribute names need to specify the relation from which they are to be retrieved.

In addition, the condition for retrieval can be a complex logical expression. If we wish to retrieve the names and ages of all students who are athletes and older than 20, we can write

```
SELECT STUDENT.NAME, STUDENT.AGE
     FROM STUDENT, ATHLETE
     WHERE STUDENT.NAME = ATHLETE.NAME AND STUDENT.AGE > 20
```

A view in SQL is conceptually the same as a relation, consisting of tuples and attributes. A view, however, is not actually found within the storage of the computer. Rather, it is derived from existing relations and the definition of the view. For example, the view STUDENT_ATHLETE can be created by the statement

```
CREATE VIEW STUDENT_ATHLETE
     AS SELECT STUDENT.NAME, STUDENT.AGE, ATHLETE.SPORT
         FROM STUDENT, ATHLETE
         WHERE STUDENT.NAME = ATHLETE.NAME
```

This view has three attributes, two selected from STUDENT and one selected from ATHLETE. The rule for forming tuples is that tuples are formed only when the NAME field of STUDENT equals the NAME field of ATHLETE. Therefore, view STUDENT_ATHLETE consists of the two tuples shown in Figure 12.10. Views can then be used as if they were actual tables in retrievals. For example, all student-athletes older than 20 could be retrieved by

FIGURE **12.10**   **View** STUDENT_ATHLETE

```
Attributes
NAME    AGE    SPORT
John    20     Swimming
Sally   17     Soccer
```

```
SELECT NAME, AGE
      FROM STUDENT_ATHLETE
      WHERE AGE > 20
```

The contents of the hypothetical table associated with a VIEW change automatically as its constituent tables are modified.

Many other facilities are present in SQL, but those described here are sufficient for the purposes of the following section in showing how SQL adheres to the logic model of a programming language.

12.3.3   ▪   SQL as a Logic Language

Most logic model capabilities can be specified in SQL through the INSERT, VIEW, and SELECT facilities. For example, the assertion of facts corresponds directly to the insertion of tuples into a relation, with the tuple defining an occurrence of a relation just like a fact does. A view is the SQL way of defining a rule, because it is the creation of a relation that is formed through logical manipulation of other relations. Finally, the SELECT query in SQL corresponds to a goal in the logic model, with the variables in the goal corresponding to the retrieved attributes of the view.

To illustrate this correspondence, we return to the logic model program given in Figures 12.2 through 12.5. Its expression in SQL is found in Figure 12.11.

We next show how goals can be duplicated by retrievals in SQL. Consider the goal

```
?can_use(Sue,Spreadsheet).
```

In SQL, this can be accomplished by the retrieval

```
SELECT PERSON,SW
      FROM CAN_USE
      WHERE PERSON = 'Sue' AND SW = 'Spreadsheet'
```

Goals involving variables in the logic model are even more easily implemented in SQL. For example,

```
?can_use(x,Spreadsheet).
```

is expressed in SQL by

```
SELECT PERSON
      FROM CAN_USE
      WHERE SW = 'Spreadsheet'
```

FIGURE *12.11*   **SQL Expression of Logic Program in Figures 12.2–12.5**

```
CREATE TABLE RUNS (MACH CHAR(5),
                   SW CHAR(11)),
                   MEM INTEGER);
CREATE TABLE SPEC (MACH CHAR(5),
                   HW CHAR(5),
                   MEM INTEGER);
CREATE VIEW CAN_RUN
        AS SELECT SPEC.MACH,RUNS.SW
           FROM SPEC,RUNS
           WHERE SPEC.HW=RUNS.HW AND
                 SPEC.MEM>=RUNS.MEM;
CREATE VIEW CAN_USE
        AS SELECT ACCESS.PERSON,CAN_RUN.SW
           FROM ACCESS,CAN_RUN
           WHERE ACCESS.MACH=CAN_RUN.MACH;
INSERT INTO SPEC (MACH,HW,MEM)
        VALUES ('MACH1','IBMPC',320);
...
```

and the two-variable goal

```
can_use(x,y).
```

is expressed by

```
SELECT PERSON, SW
     FROM CAN_USE
```

SQL and other relational query languages have some strong limitations as representatives of the logic model. First, the definition of relations binds each attribute to a specific type, in violation of the typeless definition of objects in the logic model. The use of views is also much more limited than the construction of rules, particularly when rules are recursively defined. Views in SQL may not be defined in terms of themselves. Similarly, multiple definitions of the same rule can lead to some complex logical manipulation and the creation of auxiliary views in SQL.

C H A P T E R *12*   **Terms**

axiom

object

relation

fact

binding

inference engine

resolution

unification

backtracking

relation

tuple

attribute

query language

CHAPTER **12**   **Discussion Questions**

1. The logic language model separates the statement of the problem from the method used to solve it. What are the advantages and disadvantages of this approach?

2. To write programs for other paradigms — for example, the imperative paradigm — you would use a design method like top-down design. How does the logical paradigm change your problem-solving methodology? What type of method would be useful for logical programming?

3. "Programs" in a logical programming environment consist of sets of facts and rules and follow-up queries or goals that are solved by the inference engine. Evaluate the types of problems you could solve with this approach. What types of problems are best suited for logical programming?

4. Following up on Question 3, how would you guess that programs are "debugged" in a logical programming environment? Are bugs easier or harder to spot than with imperative or functional programs, for instance?

5. Discuss the usefulness of the principles of resolution and unification in everyday logic. Give examples of their application.

6. Does SQL use resolution or unification? In what way?

7. Describe the implementation restrictions on the inference engine that might have to be applied with SQL.

CHAPTER **12**   **Exercises**

1. Give the result of applying resolution and unification to the following groups of clauses.

   a. A(t) if B,C(t)
      B if D,E
   b. A(t) if B(t),C(t)
      C(X) if D(X),E
   c. A(t) if B(t),C(t)
      C(X)
   d. A(t) if B(t),C(t)
      B(X) if D(X)
      C(t) if D(t)
   e. A if B(t)
      B(t) if C(X),D(t)
      C(t) if B(t),E(t)
      E(X)
   f. A(X) if B(Y),C
      B(t) if C,D(t)
      D(Y) if A(Y),E

2. Construct logical goals and rules for `prime(X)` that will verify that `X` is a prime number (for an unbound `X`).

3. Using the facts and rules given in Figures 12.4 and 12.5, construct the derivation tree of each of the following:

    a. `CAN_USE(JERRY,PASCAL).`
    b. `CAN_USE(SAM,SMALLTALK).`

4. Consider the facts and rules from Figures 12.4 and 12.5. Which of the following goal definitions determine if one could maintain software on a particular machine?

    a. `can_maintain(P,SW) if`
    `     can_use(P,SW), written_in(SW,L), knows(P,L).`
    b. `can_maintain(P,SW) if`
    `     access(P,M), written_in(SW,L), can_run(M,SW).`
    c. `can_maintain(P,SW) if`
    `      written_in(SW,L), can_use(P,SW), knows(P,L).`
    `knows(P,L) if access(P,L).`
    d. `can_maintain(P,SW) if`
    `      written_in(SW,L), can_use(P,SW), knows(P,L).`
    `knows(P,L) if access(P,L), runs(M,L,Mem).`

5. Derive the following goals using backtracking. Your answers should be given in a manner similar to Figure 12.7.

    a. `CAN_USE(SAM,x).`
    b. `CAN_USE(x,BASIC).`
    c. `CAN_RUN(x,y).`

6. Given the facts and rules of Figures 12.4 and 12.5, why does the query

    `CAN_USE(JERRY,SMALLTALK)`

    fail?

C H A P T E R 12   Laboratory Exercises

1. Write a program that is a parser for the LP grammar described in Figure 12.1.

2. Write a program to perform resolution. Assume that facts are represented by a single uppercase letter and the rule is input as the letter for the consequence fact followed by the letter for the hypothesis facts. For example, the rule

    `F if A,B,C`

    is input to the program as

    `FABC`

    Your program is to input two rules of this form and output the rule derived by resolution. Note that the order in which the hypothesis facts appear in the input is arbitrary.

13

Prolog: A Logic-Oriented Language

13.1 ▪ Syntax of Prolog
13.2 ▪ Nonlogic Model Features of Prolog
13.3 ▪ Example Programs in Prolog

Prolog is a language that is based very closely on the logic model described in Chapter 12. It was created in 1972 by Alain Colmerauer in Marseilles, France. Since its creation, it has been extensively used in computer science research in Europe and has been adopted as the core language of the Japanese Fifth Generation Project. It is of particular interest to the artificial intelligence community, where it has found most of its applications. This chapter briefly describes the syntax of this language, comparing it to the logic model, and presents many examples of Prolog.

13.1 Syntax of Prolog

Prolog exists in many different forms, because no standards have been observed in its implementations. We will fix our consideration on one version, which is commonly known as the Clocksin and Mellish version of Prolog and is defined in their book (1987). Other versions of Prolog have similar syntax.

There are several purely syntactic differences between Prolog and LP. First of all, the names of objects and relations begin with lowercase letters in Prolog, whereas the names of variables begin with uppercase letters. A goal is preceded by ?- instead of just a question mark. The conclusion of a rule is separated from the hypotheses by :- instead of the word *if.*

Figure 13.1 shows the program described in Section 12.2.2 as it is written in Prolog. Another syntactic difference is evident in the use of the built-in relation GEQ from LP, which is expressed as an infix operator in Prolog, where all arithmetic operators and all comparison operators are expressed in infix notation.

13.2 Nonlogic Model Features of Prolog

There are a number of features of Prolog that violate the spirit of the logic model. These generally provide imperative capabilities, which permit a more useful or efficient implementation of the logic model in practice.

The first variance is that the order of search for a derivation is in the order that the rules and facts are entered in the program. This order does make the efficiency and the termination of derivations dependent on the ordering within the program and, as discussed in Section 12.2, is in violation of the strict logic model, where all "how" information is excluded.

The most famous of the nonlogic features of Prolog is the **cut**. The purpose of the cut is to control backtracking during the derivation process. Therefore, it is very much a part of the "how" related to a program. As an illustration of the use of the cut, let us add a second rule for can_run to our Prolog program, namely, the one corresponding to the rule introduced in

---

FIGURE 13.1   **Prolog Program for Logic Model Program in Figures 12.2–12.5**

```
F1:    spec(mach1,ibmpc,320).
F2:    spec(mach2,mac,1000).
F3:    spec(mach3,ibmpc,640).
F4:    runs(ibmpc,spreadsheet,500).
F5:    runs(ibmpc,basic,128).
F6:    runs(ibmpc,pascal,256).
F7:    runs(mac,basic,200).
F8:    runs(mac,smalltalk,1000).
F9:    access(sue,mach1).
F10:   access(jerry,mach3).
F11:   access(sam,mach1).
F12:   access(sam,mach2).
F13:   written_in(spreadsheet,pascal).

R1:    can_use(P,SW)  :- access(P,M),
                           can_run(M,SW).
R2:    can_run(M,SW)  :- spec(M,HW,Mem1),
                           runs(HW,SW,Mem2),
                           Mem1>=Mem2.
R3:    can_run(M,SW)  :- written_in(SW,L),can_run(M,L).
```

Section 12.2 regarding the fact that one software product can be written in the language of another. If we make a more intelligent choice for the order of the two clauses in the hypothesis, our two rules are

```
can_run(MACH,SW)  :- spec(MACH,HW,MEM1),
                     runs(HW,SW,MEM2),
                     MEM1 >= MEM2.
can_run(MACH,SW)  :- written_in(SW,L),
                     can_run(MACH,L).
```

If we run the corresponding program with the goal

```
?-can_use(X,spreadsheet).
```

we will obtain the following output:

```
X = sue
X = jerry
X = jerry
X = sam
```

Notice that `jerry` is derived twice, indicating that the program is doing some unnecessary work. Let's see why this happened. The object 'jerry' will satisfy `can_use` once because `jerry` has access to `mach3`, which can run a spreadsheet directly. But the goal can also be derived from the second rule for `can_run`, because Pascal can run on `mach3` as well and the spreadsheet is written in Pascal.

The cut is considered as a subgoal that is universally satisfied, but that cannot be backed up over. It then stands as a one-way gate for the subgoal-generation process, which, once passed, cannot be backed through.

In the preceding example, the first rule for `can_run` could be rewritten with the cut as follows:

```
can_run(MACH,SW)  :- spec(MACH,HW,MEM1),
                     runs(HW,SW,MEM2),
                     MEM1 >= MEM2,
                     !.
```

After the first three subgoals are satisfied, the cut is then satisfied as well, completing the derivation of `can_run`. After the entire derivation is completed, the cut then prevents the backing-up process from trying other alternatives for `can_run`, so unnecessary checking is avoided, because it is irrelevant how many ways a computer `can_run` a software product.

The goal

```
?-can_use(X,spreadsheet)
```

will now find only one derivation for each of the three people; the derivation process is displayed in Figure 13.2. The derivation process, when backing up to a cut, will automatically produce a failure for all subgoals that have arisen since the generation of the subgoal that contains the cut.

FIGURE 13.2 **Derivation of a Goal in Prolog using Cut**

```
1. ?-can_use(X,spreadsheet).                                      R1/SW:=spreadsheet
2. ?-access(X,M),can_run(M,spreadsheet).                          F9/M:=mach1,X:=sue
3. ?-can_run(mach1,spreadsheet).                                  R2
4. ?-spec(mach1,HW,M1),runs(HW,spreadsheet,M2),M1>=M2,!.          F1/HW:=ibmpc,M1:=320
5. ?-runs(ibmpc,spreadsheet,M2),320>=M2,!.                        F4/M2:=500
6. ?-320>=500,!.                                                  Fails
5. ?-runs(ibmpc,spreadsheet,M2),320>=M2,!.                        Fails
4. ?-spec(mach1,HW,M1),runs(HW,spreadsheet,M2),M1>=M2,!.          Fails
3. ?-can_run(mach1,spreadsheet).                                  R3
4. ?-written_in(spreadsheet,L),can_run(mach1,L).                 F13/L:=pascal
5. ?-can_run(mach1,pascal).                                       R2
6. ?-spec(mach1,HW,M1),runs(HW,pascal,M2),M1>=M2,!.              F1/HW:=ibmpc,M1:=320
7. ?-runs(ibmpc,pascal,M2),320>=M2,!.                             F6/M2:=256
8. ?-320>=256,!.                                                  satisfied
9. ?-!                                                            Skip backup because of cut -
5. completed                                                     satisfied  X=sue
4. ?-written_in(spreadsheet,L),can_run(mach1,L).                 Fails
3. ?-can_run(mach1,spreadsheet).                                  Fails
2. ?-access(X,M),can_run(M,spreadsheet).                          F10/X:=jerry,M:=mach3
3. ?-can_run(mach3,spreadsheet).                                  R2
4. ?-spec(mach3,HW,M1),runs(HW,spreadsheet,M2),M1>=M2,!.          F3/M1:=640,HW=ibmpc
5. ?-runs(ibmpc,spreadsheet,M2),640>=M2,!.                        F4/M2:=500
6. ?-640>=500,!.                                                  satisfied
7. ?-!                                                            Skip backup because of cut -
3. completed                                                     satisfied  X=jerry
2. ?-access(X,M),can_run(M,spreadsheet).                          F11/X:=sam,M:=mach1
3. ?-can_run(mach1,spreadsheet).                                  R2
4. ?-spec(mach1,HW,M1),runs(HW,spreadsheet,M2),M1>=M2,!.          F1/HW:=ibmpc,M1:=320
5. ?-runs(ibmpc,spreadsheet,M2),320>=M2,!.                        F4/M2:=500
6. ?-320>=500,!.                                                  Fails
5. ?-runs(ibmpc,spreadsheet,M2),320>=M2,!.                        Fails
4. ?-spec(mach1,HW,M1),runs(HW,spreadsheet,M2),M1>=M2,!.          Fails
3. ?-can_run(mach1,spreadsheet).                                  R3
4. ?-written_in(spreadsheet,L),can_run(mach1,L).                 F13/L:=pascal
5. ?-can_run(mach1,pascal).                                       R2
6. ?-spec(mach1,HW,M1),runs(HW,pascal,M2),M1>=M2,!.              F1/HW:=ibmpc,M1:=320
7. ?-runs(ibmpc,pascal,M2),320>=M2,!.                             F6/M2:=256
8. ?-320>=256,!.                                                  satisfied
9. ?-!                                                            Skip backup because of cut -
5. completed                                                     satisfied  X=sam
4. ?-written_in(spreadsheet,L),can_run(mach1,L).                 Fails
3. ?-can_run(mach1,spreadsheet).                                  Fails
2. ?-access(X,M),can_run(M,spreadsheet).                          F12/X:=sam,M:=mach2
3. ?-can_run(mach2,spreadsheet).                                  R2
4. ?-spec(mach2,HW,M1),runs(HW,spreadsheet,M2),M1>=M2,!.          F2/HW:=mac,M1:=1000
5. ?-runs(mac,spreadsheet,M2),1000>=M2,!.                         Fails
4. ?-spec(mach2,HW,M1),runs(HW,spreadsheet,M2),M1>=M2,!.          Fails
3. ?-can_run(mach2,spreadsheet).                                  R3
```

(continues)

```
4.  ?-written_in(spreadsheet,L),can_run(mach2,L).          F13/L:=pascal
5.  ?-can_run(mach2,pascal).                                R2
6.  ?-spec(mach2,HW,M1),runs(HW,pascal,M2),M1>=M2,!.        F2/HW:=mac,M1:=1000
7.  ?-runs(mac,pascal,M2),M1>=M2,!.                         Fails
6.  ?-spec(mach2,HW,M1),runs(HW,pascal,M2),M1>=M2,!.        Fails
5.  ?-can_run(mach2,pascal).                                R3
6.  ?-written_in(pascal,L),can_run(mach2,L).               Fails
5.  ?-can_run(mach2,pascal).                                Fails
4.  ?-written_in(spreadsheet,L),can_run(mach2,L).          Fails
3.  ?-can_run(mach2,spreadsheet).                           Fails
2.  ?-access(X,M),can_run(M,spreadsheet).                   Fails
1.  ?-can_use(X,spreadsheet).                               Fails
```

Prolog also includes relations called `asserta` and `assertz`, which add new facts to the beginning or end of the search list. These **relations**, when included within a rule, imply that the logical derivation will actually change the facts. In pure logic programming, the derivation should have no effect on the set of facts that hold. Similarly, the relation retract, which removes a fact from the collection, is not a part of the logic model for the same reason.

Prolog also provides input and output facilities. By the structure of the language, these must be specified within a derivation through the testing of built-in rules as subgoals. For example, the goal of the form `read(Variable)` will bind the variable to the next data value appearing in the input stream. A more direct assignment of a numeric value to a variable is possible through the use of the infix operator `is`. Similarly, `write(value)` writes the specified value to the output file. These input/output commands violate the spirit of pure logic programming by permitting a derivation to "do" something as a side effect.

Finally, Prolog adds to the pure logic model by including data structures within the language. You will recall that the pure logic model included only objects that were atomic items, whose meanings were not a part of the language.

Prolog permits structures and lists. We discuss only the **list** feature here. A list in Prolog is very similar to a list in LISP, as detailed in Chapter 10. It is defined as an ordered sequence of objects and lists. A list is written using its elements, which are separated by commas and enclosed in parentheses. For example,

```
[]
[a,b,c]
[a,b,[c,d],e]
```

are all lists. The first example illustrates the empty list, whereas the third shows that list elements may be lists themselves. The head of a list is the first element in the list. The tail of the list is the list that remains after the first element is removed. Examples of the heads and tails of lists are shown here:

List	Head	Tail
[]	undefined	undefined
[a]	a	[]
[a,b]	a	[b]

```
[[x,y],a]              [x,y]              [a]
[[x,y],[a,b]]          [x,y]              [[a,b]]
```

In Prolog, the head and the tail of a list can be specified by writing the list as

```
[X | Y]
```

If this notation is in place for a variable binding, X and Y will be bound to the head and tail, respectively, of the list. For example, a relation that defines the head of a list can be written as

```
head([H | T], H).
```

Then the goal

```
?-head([a,b,c],X)
```

will return

```
X = a
```

Similarly, tail can be written

```
tail([H | T],T).
```

Both head and tail can be found in one rule by

```
list([H | T],H,T).
```

Note that this last fact can be used to find the head or tail of a list, as in

```
?-list([a,b,c],X,Y)
X = a
Y = [b,c]
```

or to splice a list together, as in

```
?-list(L,a,[b,c]).
L = [a,b,c]
```

13.3 Example Programs in Prolog

In order that you might get a taste for the spirit of programming in Prolog, two example programs are developed in detail in this section.

13.3.1 ▪ Quicksort

Quicksort is conveniently implemented as a recursive rule in Prolog. We will assume that the general form of the quicksort rule is

```
quick(UnsortedList,SortedList)
```

where both variables represent lists, one that will be the input and the second that will be the sorted output. A sample goal using quick might then be

```
?-quick([12,19,9,4,14,16],X)
```

from which Prolog would derive

`X = [4,9,12,14,16,19]`

The `quicksort` rule will be defined using two other rules, `append` and `partition`. The rule `append` is of the form

`append(List1,List2,AppendedList)`

where `List1` and `List2` are the two lists to be appended and `AppendedList` is the result. For example, given

`?-append([1,2,3],[4,5],X)`

Prolog will derive

`X = [1,2,3,4,5]`

`Partition` is defined by

`partition(Pivot,List,LessThanPivot,GreaterThanPivot)`

Here, `Pivot` is any object and `List` is any list of objects. The rule `partition` results in all objects in `List` that are less than the pivot value being placed in `LessThanPivot`, whereas all objects greater than or equal to the pivot are placed in the list `GreaterThanPivot`.

We specify append and pivot later. Given their availability, we can define quick as follows:

```
quick([],[]).
quick([Pivot | Remainder],SortedList) :-
        partition(Pivot,Remainder,BeforePivot,AfterPivot),
        quick(BeforePivot,SortedBefore),
        quick(AfterPivot,SortedAfter),
        append(SortedBefore,[Pivot|SortedAfter],SortedList).
```

The first rule for `quick` is the recursion stopper. It says that the sorted empty list is an empty list. The second rule indicates that `Pivot` will be bound to the first object in the input list, and `Remainder` will be bound to the rest of the list. `SortedList` will be bound within the subgoals.

There are four subgoals for this second rule. The first is that partition is derived for list `Remainder` with pivot element `Pivot`. The two sublists generated by the partitioning will be bound to `BeforePivot` and `AfterPivot`.

Next, the subgoal `quick` is recursively derived twice with `BeforePivot` as input and `SortedBefore` as output and with `AfterPivot` as input and `SortedAfter` as output. These two derivations result in `SortedBefore` and `SortedAfter` being bound to the corresponding two sorted sublists. These sublists are then joined together with the pivot element in between by the append subgoal, binding the resulting list to `SortedList`.

The predicate append is easily constructed. Its form is

```
append([],List2,List2).
append([Head|Tail],List2,[Head|NewList]) :-
    append(Tail,List2,NewList).
```

The first rule says that the empty list appended to any list is the list itself. The second rule is recursive and indicates how a list can be appended based on the definition of append on its tail.

Next we examine the rules to implement partition.

```
partition(Pivot,[],[]).
partition(Pivot,[Head|Tail],[Head|BeforePivot],AfterPivot) :-
    Head<Pivot,
    partition(Pivot,Tail,BeforePivot,AfterPivot),
    !.
partition(Pivot,[Head|Tail],BeforePivot,[Head|AfterPivot]) :-
    partition(Pivot,Tail,BeforePivot,AfterPivot).
```

The first rule indicates that the empty list is partitioned into two empty lists, no matter what the pivot value. This serves as the recursion stopper. The second rule says that if the head of the list being partitioned is less than the pivot and if the tail of the list is partitioned into BeforePivot and After-Pivot, then the original list is partitioned by the list formed when Head is attached to BeforePivot and the list is attached to AfterPivot. The cut is included in this definition to prevent attempting the third rule for partition when the second one is derived. The third rule is then reached only if Head is greater than or equal to Pivot and its meaning is obvious.

The combination of the definitions for quick, append, and partition form a complete version of quicksort.

13.3.2 ▪ Finding the Shortest Path

Problems that require searching are good candidates for solution in Prolog since the built-in search strategy of Prolog can be effectively put to use. In this section we will examine definitions that solve the problem of finding the shortest path between two nodes in a directed graph.

We assume that nodes are atomic objects in our solution and paths are lists of nodes. For example, a path from a to b passing through g and h, successively, would be represented by the list

```
[a,g,h,b]
```

Lengths of the edges between two nodes and the lengths of paths are represented by integers.

A graph is represented by a set of adjacent relations, where

```
adjacent(X,Y,L)
```

means there is a directed edge from node X to node Y of length L. For example, Figure 13.3 illustrates a directed graph and the set of adjacent relations required to represent it in Prolog. The problem that we wish to solve is this: Given a directed graph and two nodes, A and B, of that graph, find the shortest path from A to B.

We will begin with a simpler problem, that of finding all paths from A to B. The Prolog predicate used to do this is

```
trip(Start,Finish,Path,Length)
```

where Start and Finish are the two given terminating nodes, Path is a derived path, and Length is the total length of Path. The relation trip will derive all paths from Start to Finish that do not make repeat visits to any nodes.

Before we describe the rules for trip, we first need to define two relations that greatly facilitate trip's definition. The first is a general list predicate called not_in, which is of the form

```
not_in(Node,Path)
```

where Node is an atomic node object and Path is a list of nodes representing a path in the directed graph. This rule is to derive successfully if Node is not one of the members of Path and fail to derive if Node is a member of Path. It is defined by

```
not_in(Node,[]) :- !.
not_in(Node,[Head|Tail]) :- Node<>Head,
                            not_in(Node,Tail).
```

We are now prepared for the workhorse of this solution, a relation called path, which is described by

```
path(Start,SubPath,SPLength,FinalPath,FPLength)
```

where Start, SubPath, and SPLength are a node, path, and length that are provided to the derivation. FinalPath and FPLength are a path and length that are derived. FinalPath is a path starting at node Start and finishing with SubPath. The derived length of FinalPath is FPLength.

FIGURE **13.3**   **Prolog Representation of a Directed Graph**

```
adjacent(a,b,5).
adjacent(a,c,6).
adjacent(a,d,8).
adjacent(b,d,4).
adjacent(c,b,7).
adjacent(d,b,4).
```

The rules for path are

```
path(Start,[Start|Tail],L,[Start|Tail],L).
path(Start,[Head|Tail],-SPLength,Path,PLength) :-
        adjacent(NewHead,Head,EdgeLength),
        not_in(NewHead,Tail),
        NewLength is EdgeLength+SPLength,
        path(Start,[NewHead,Head|Tail],NewLength,Path,PLength).
```

This definition requires some further explanation. The first rule simply states that if the given subpath already begins at node Start, we are done, and that subpath is the final path and its length is the final length. This is the recursion stopper.

The second rule is more complex. It says that a subpath can be built upon if a new head can be added that is adjacent to the present head, the new head is not in the present subpath, and a path can be built from Start using the newly created subpath (made by adding the new head). The operator "is," which is used in the third subgoal, is a nonlogic operator that always succeeds and causes the variable NewLength to be immediately bound to the specified sum. The recursion specified in this rule will then cause all possible paths to be derived.

The rule that derives all possible paths from Start to Finish is now defined by

```
trip(Start,Finish,Path,Length) :-
    path(Start,[Finish],0,Path,Length).
```

In other words, there is a path Path of length Length from node Start to node Finish if the Path can be built from the subpath of length zero consisting only of node Finish and starting at node Start.

In order to clarify the actions of these rules, we examine a simple derivation in Figure 13.4. Note how the Prolog search for solutions results in all solutions being found. The last attempt to use the edge from d to b illustrates how the not_in predicate is used to prevent paths that cross themselves.

FIGURE 13.4   **Derivation of Path from Node a to Node d**

```
path(a,[d],0,P,L).
adj(a,d,8),not_in(a,[]),NewLength is 8+0,path(a,[a,d],8,P,L).
                                                /P:=[a,d],L:=8
adj(b,d,4),not_in(b,[]),NewLength is 4,path(a,[b,d],4,P,L).
adj(a,b,5),not_in(a,[d]),NewLength is 5+4,path(a,[a,b,d],9,P,L).
                                                /P:=[a,b,d],L:=9
adj(c,b,7),not_in(c,[d]),NewLength is 7+4,path(a,[c,b,d],11,P,L),
   adj(a,c,6),not_in(a,[b,d]),NewLength is 6+11,path(a,[a,c,b,d],17,P,L).
                                                /P:=[a,c,b,d],L:=17
adj(d,b,4),not_in(d,[d]),...                    FAILS
```

The next challenge, now that we can find all paths between two nodes, is to derive the shortest of these paths. This solution is derived in a way that illustrates the expressive power of Prolog. The solution can be simply stated as

```
mintrip(Start,Finish,MinPath,MinLength) :-
    trip(Start,Finish,MinPath,MinLength),
    smallest(Start,Finish,MinLength).
```

This result says that `MinPath` is the shortest path if that path results in a successful derivation of `trip` and if `smallest` can also be derived. The relation `smallest` is derived if there is no trip from `Start` to `Finish` shorter than `MinLength`. The easiest way to determine this is to again generate all trips from `Start` to `Finish` and fail the predicate `smallest` in any case where the generated trip length is greater than the value of `MinLength`. If no failure is generated, the predicate succeeds. This is written in Prolog as

```
smallest(Start,Finish,MinLength) :-
    trip(Start,Finish,Path,PLength),
    PLength<MinLength,
    !,
    fail.
smallest(Start,Finish,MinLength).
```

This definition uses the built-in Prolog predicate `fail`, which fails whenever it is encountered. In the first rule, when a path is found with length shorter than `MinLength`, immediately we want to fail the derivation. The predicate fail does this, and the cut preceding fail prevents any attempt to derive the alternative rule for smallest.

Notice that in the derivation of mintrip for two nodes, `Start` and `Finish`, if there are N different paths (as derived by trip) from `Start` to `Finish`, for each path, `smallest` will try to compare by generating paths and comparing lengths until a path is found that is shorter than the present path or until all paths have been compared.

We can see that the order in which paths are generated can make a big difference in the efficiency of the derivation. Consider the example of Figure 13.3. It happens, in this case, that the paths are generated in increasing order by path length. The comparisons for shortest can then be listed as follows:

Test path	Test against
[a,d]	[a,d],[a,b,d],[a,c,b,d]
[a,b,d]	[a,d],fails
[a,c,b,d]	[a,d],fails

In total, 8 trips were generated in this derivation. If the trips had been generated in decreasing order of length, then 3 trips would need to be compared to each test path, and the total trips generated would be 12.

For general N, these figures are $3N-1$ for increasing length generation and $N^2 + N$ for decreasing length, making the difference between $O(N)$ and $O(N^2)$ solutions. In practice, the solution presented cannot guarantee the $O(N)$ solution, but the fact that the paths are generated in the order of increasing number of nodes in the path makes the increasing order of length more plausible and leads to a reasonably efficient solution.

C H A P T E R *13* Terms

cut   list
relation

C H A P T E R *13* Discussion Questions

1. The logic language model separates the statement of the problem from the method used to solve it. What are the advantages and disadvantages of this approach?

2. Prolog and SQL take very different approaches to implementing the logic model. Compare the two approaches and discuss their relative advantages.

3. Discuss the usefulness of the principles of resolution and unification in everyday logic. Give examples of their application.

4. Discuss the cut feature of Prolog. What kinds of programs could not be written if the cut were missing? Is the cut a convenience or a necessity?

5. Why would the search order for facts and rules in the knowledge base have to be stipulated for Prolog?

6. Discuss uses for `asserta` and `assertz`. How could `retract` be used?

7. Discuss the advantages and disadvantages of using many facts and few rules versus few facts and many rules in a Prolog program.

C H A P T E R *13* Exercises

1. Write your assertion of `prime(X)` from Chapter 12 in Prolog.

2. Give the result of applying resolution to the following pairs of clauses.
    a. A(t) if B,C(t)   B if D,E
    b. A(t) if B(t),C(t)   C(X) if D(X),E
    c. A(t) if B(t),C(t)   C(X)

3. Let's add the following rules and facts to the knowledge base from the previous question:

    ```
    grandchild(C,G) :- parent(G,C1), parent(C1, C).
    greatgrandchild(C,G) :- parent(G,C1), grandchild(C,C1).

    father(jim, fred).
    mother(beth, fred).
    father(jim, ann).
    ```

```
mother(beth, ann).
father(fred, joyce).
mother(helen, joyce).
father(fred, albert).
mother(helen, albert).
```

If the goal is

```
greatgrandchild(X,Y).
```

how many answers do we get? What are they?

4. Use the rules of Exercises 2 and 3, and write a general `greatgrandchild` goal. That is, the goal `greatgrandchild(X,Y,1)` will find all great grand-children, whereas `greatgrandchild(X,Y,2)` will find all great-great grand-children, and so forth.

5. Construct a logic assertion prime(X) that will verify X is a prime number for unbound X.

6. Consider the following Prolog knowledge base:

```
parent(X,Y) :- father(X,Y).
parent(X,Y) :- mother(X,Y).
ancestor(X,Z) :- parent(X,Z).
ancestor(X,Z) :- parent(X,Y), ancestor(Y,Z).
sibling(X,Y) :- mother(M,X), mother(M,Y),
                father(F,X), father(F,Y), X \= Y.
father(albert, jeffrey).
mother(alice, jeffrey).
father(albert, george).
mother(alice, george).
father(george, cindy).
mother(mary, cindy).
```

The question posed to the Prolog system

```
?- ancestor(X,cindy),sibling(X,jeffrey).
```

produces an answer of

```
X = george
```

Show the derivation of this answer in detail by tracing the derivation of the solution using resolution, unification, and backtracking.

7. Show a derivation of

```
head([[a,b],x,y],H)
```

to produce `H = [a,b]`.

8. Show a derivation of

```
tail([[a,b],x,y],T)
```

to produce `T= [x,y]`.

9. Consider the append predicate given in Section 13.3.1. Based on this predicate, develop a member predicate that verifies that an item is in a list.

CHAPTER *13*   Laboratory Exercises

1. Implement the Quicksort algorithm given in Section 13.3.1 and verify that it does what it claims.

2. Implement a solution to the towers of Hanoi puzzle. Your solution should define the predicate `hanoi` by

   ```
   hanoi (N):- move (N,left,center,right)
   ```

   to move `N` discs from tower `left` to tower `center` using tower `right` to assist. Implement this recursively by moving `N-1` from `left` to `right`, writing a message for moving one from `left` to `center`, then moving `N-1` from `right` to `center`.

3. Using the list structure, implement a `stack` structure. Operation should have an invocation similar to

   ```
   pop([a,b,c], I)
   ```

   and `I` would contain a after the operation.

4. Repeat Exercise 3 using a queue instead of a stack, and `dequeue` instead of `pop`.

5. Following up on Discussion Question 3, write a program that "learns" — that is, interactively adds to the knowledge base when it has been determined that knowledge is insufficient. For example, write a Prolog program to learn how to guess animals. The program could be "preprogrammed" with some rules and facts and questions based on those rules and facts, such as:

   ```
   Does the animal fly?  or  Does the animal have four legs?
   ```

   Notice that this program is interactive. Upon running out of questions, the program should request new information: What is the animal name and what question distinguishes this animal from others?

6. Verify your answers to Exercises 7 and 8 by writing "head" and "tail" in Prolog and demonstrating their use.

7. Implement the family tree facts and rules scattered throughout this chapter in Prolog. Verify that our answers work correctly. In addition, implement a new rule

   ```
   ancestor(X, Y)
   ```

   that checks that `X` is some ancestor of `Y`.

An Overview of the Object-Oriented Model

14.1 ▪ Introduction to the Object-Oriented Model
14.2 ▪ An Example
14.3 ▪ Comparison with the Imperative Model

The object-oriented approach to problem solving provides a model that consists of objects sending messages to other objects. This simple concept, along with some accompanying tools, forms a powerful technique that has become very popular in the first half of the 1990s. Languages that enable this approach by directly providing facilities to support objects and message passing are called object-oriented programming languages.

The object-oriented concept originated with the language Simula (Dahl and Nygaard 1966), which was a language intended for simulations. Simula 67 extended the object concept to a general-purpose language. Alan Kay adopted this approach as the foundation for his language Smalltalk in the early 1970s. Smalltalk, more than any other language, defines the object-oriented model. We introduce Smalltalk in Chapter 15. In the early 1980s, C++ was developed at AT&T Bell Laboratories by adding object-oriented features to the language C. C++ has become a very popular language for object-oriented programming, and we describe it in Chapter 16.

14.1 Introduction to the Object-Oriented Model

The fundamental concept of the object-oriented model is that of encapsulated, interacting objects, each with its own internal state and set of behaviors. The fundamental focus of this model is on the objects themselves as actors rather than as passive data that are acted upon by procedures or functions. Objects are given their identity (i.e., internal state structure and behavior definitions) through their membership in a class. These classes are arranged in a hierarchy to permit the inheritance of properties from one class to another. The benefits, components, and properties of this model are described here.

14.1.1 ▪ Benefits of the Object-Oriented Model

Four fundamental benefits of the object-oriented model have led to its increase in popularity:

1. *Close correspondence to the problem domain* — Frequently, the objects in programs correspond directly to objects in the problem domain, and their activities correspond as well. This is particularly true in the solution of problems using simulation. This correspondence greatly simplifies the construction of a computer solution.

2. *Reusability of software* — The inheritance of properties by one class of objects from another class without explicitly respecifying them is an important benefit of the object-oriented model. This method proves to be a very effective way to reuse data structures and code in a selective way, meaning that only the pertinent parts of a class of objects can be inherited, whereas those that do not apply can be redefined or deleted.

3. *Abstraction and encapsulation* — The object-oriented model carries with it all the abstraction benefits of abstract data types by permitting the data and actions of an object to be encapsulated within that object and dividing its contents between those that are public and those that are private.

4. *Concurrency* — Because objects often act concurrently in the problem domain, it is natural for them to perform concurrently in the object-oriented model. When such concurrency capabilities are available, the object-oriented model presents a natural way to exploit them.

14.1.2 ▪ Components of the Object-Oriented Model

The **object-oriented** model has as its fundamental entity the *object*, which consists of a local state and a set of actions that it can perform, called *methods*. These methods are activated when the object receives an appropriate *message*, and their actions consist of modification of the object's state and the sending of messages to other objects. The structure of an object's local state and the methods that it can perform are specified by the *class* that defines the object. An object is said to be an instance of its class.

Objects An **object** in the object-oriented model corresponds to the concept of data object, as introduced in Chapter 3. The major difference is that an object is active, whereas a data object is passive. Data objects were considered to be acted upon by outside agents, whose actions resulted in changes of bindings, usually the value binding of the data object itself. Objects, on the other hand, are active agents. They receive messages, but upon receipt of a message, they perform some actions, which include changing the value binding of their own local state and sending messages to objects.

The name and location bindings of objects are the same as for data objects. In many languages, objects are referenced by pointers and hence have no direct name binding. The value binding is the binding of the object to its local state.

The binding that differs the most is the type binding. In the object-oriented model, the concept of type is replaced by class. Properties of classes are discussed next.

Classes   A **class** is a template for objects. It consists of descriptions of the actions an object can perform and the definition of the structure of an object's internal state. In this way it is similar to an abstract data type, which defines the type data structure and procedures that apply to it. All objects that are instances of a class have the same defined internal state structure and are able to perform the same described actions.

A class is also an object itself, which means that it has its own state and actions as well. One action that all class objects can perform is to create an object that is an instance of the class itself. For this reason, classes actually create or manufacture objects according to the template they define and are sometimes referred to as object factories.

A further property of classes is that they exist in a hierarchical structure to permit the phenomenon of inheritance to take place. Basically, if a class is a subclass of another class, it selectively inherits the structure of the internal state and the actions from that class. This is described later.

Messages   A **message** is a request sent from one object to another for the receiving object to produce some desired result. A message is similar to a procedure call in that it has a name and parameters. The difference is that a procedure call is sent by one procedure to another procedure. The data that are to be used by the receiving procedure are the parameters sent with the call and the internal data store of the receiver.

In the case of messages, the sender and receiver are both objects rather than procedures. The receiving object performs some action, called a method, as a result of the message being received. The data used by the receiving object consist of the receiving object's internal state and the parameters sent as a part of the message.

Methods   A **method** consists of the operations that an object performs when it receives a message. There is a one-to-one correspondence between messages and the methods that are executed when a given message is received by an object of a given class. Objects of different classes might perform different methods for the same message if that message were bound to a different method in the definition of the two classes.

Whereas a message corresponds to a procedure call, the method corresponds to the procedure itself. The distinction between the two is more important in the object-oriented model, because when a message is sent, the sending object is not necessarily aware of the class to which the receiver belongs and hence cannot anticipate which method will be activated. This is typically not the case in imperative languages, especially those that are strongly typed.

14.1.3 ▪ Properties of the Object-Oriented Model

Although various definitions of the object-oriented model have been proposed, there are four key concepts that are common to these definitions. We describe these four concepts in this section.

Encapsulation The process of **encapsulation** is accomplished by hiding of an object's internal state and methods from external access. The structure of the internal state and the description of methods are all a part of the class to which an object belongs. Encapsulation is an essential ingredient for abstraction. It permits unnecessary details of implementation to be encapsulated within an object and hidden from other objects that interact with it.

In addition, encapsulation is important because it separates implementation from use. This means that changes can be made to the implementation of an object without users knowing about these changes, because the implementation is encapsulated inside the object. This is similar to the way an automobile engine remains encapsulated under the hood. If the engine is replaced by a rebuilt engine, that change is hidden from the driver, as long as the interface with the engine (steering wheel, accelerator, brake, etc.) remains the same.

In addition, encapsulation protects the internal state of an object from unauthorized access or modification. Because that state is hidden from the external world, an object's internal state may only be accessed through the object's own methods.

Inheritance One of the most important properties of the object-oriented model, especially in its support of reusability, is **inheritance**. The property of inheritance applies to classes. Class A is said to inherit from class B if A is a subclass of B and B is, in turn, a superclass of A. What A inherits from B is B's internal state structure and message/method pairs. Class A can then define additions to the internal state structure as well as new message/method pairs that allow it to extend its definition beyond that of B. Furthermore, selected inherited state data or message/method pairs may be changed from B's definition or removed altogether in subclass A.

The advantage of inheritance is that it makes possible the reuse of many of the features of a superclass without respecifying them. The ability to modify or remove inherited features selectively makes inheritance much more powerful.

As a result of inheritance, an entire hierarchy of classes can be constructed, with inheritance propagated down many levels. Such inheritance occurs naturally in many application domains. For example, we can consider the class `Person` to contain a certain internal state structure and methods that can be performed as a response to messages. A subclass of `Person` would be the class `Student` that inherits all the components of class `Person` but adds some components of its own. A subclass of `Student` might be the class `Senior`, which would inherit all of the components of Student (including those that Student inherits from Person) and add further components of its own.

The key to utilizing the power of inheritance is the construction of an effective hierarchy of classes. Some languages permit each class to inherit from only one superclass, whereas other languages permit a class to inherit from many superclasses. The latter is called **multiple inheritance**. For example, the class Graduate-student might inherit from two classes, Student and College-graduate.

Polymorphism   The quality of being able to assume different forms is called **polymorphism**. In the case of the object-oriented model, this quality refers to the ability to send a message to an object whose class is not known. In this case, the sender cannot predict the response of the receiver, because different classes might specify different methods for the same message. Polymorphism is the reason that the object-oriented model must take so much care to differentiate between message and method.

We have seen polymorphism before in the form of operator overloading. Such overloading allows the operator to specify its action without knowing the types of the operands. For example, an overloaded + specifies a different action when applied to two integers than when applied to two real numbers. Another form of polymorphism we have seen before is that defined by the generic feature of Ada. This case permits a procedure or package to be specified independent of type, although separate instantiations must be created for each different type to which the procedure or package is applied.

The type of polymorphism commonly used by the object-oriented model is related to the concept of inheritance. When a message is sent to an object and the sender specifies the receiver to be an object of class A, the receiver may actually be any class that is a descendant of A in the class hierarchy. The receiver then responds to the message using the method of its own class rather than that of class A, although the two may actually be the same through inheritance.

This type of polymorphism is more restrictive than general polymorphism, where the sender would need to know nothing about the class of the receiver. In this case, the sender must at least know a class that is an ancestor of the class of the receiving object. In the case of the preceding example, a message sent to class Person could be received by an object of class Student or Senior.

Dynamic Binding   The **dynamic binding** referred to in connection with the object-oriented model is the binding of message to method when a message is sent. This binding is dynamic if it is carried out every time a message is sent.

In connection with polymorphism and inheritance, when an object receives a message, it will search its class to see if there is a method associated with the received message. If so, it performs the binding and activates the method. If not, the superclass of the object's class is queried, and so on, until either a method is found for the message or a class is reached that has no superclass. If the latter occurs, the message was inappropriate for the receiving object. The binding is called dynamic because it occurs at run time.

The advantage of dynamic binding is that it permits the environment to change dynamically.

14.2 An Example

Example: Object-Oriented Programming   In this section we define the classes of this example through the use of a hypothetical object-oriented language, which we abbreviate as HOOL. This language is similar to Smalltalk but has a simpler structure. In Chapters 15 and 16 the same example is developed in Smalltalk and C++, respectively.

Refer to Figure 14.1 for the HOOL definition of class Account. The lines are numbered in this figure for ease of reference in the following discussion.

FIGURE 14.1   **HOOL Definition for Class** Account

```
1    Class Account

2    Instance Variables:
3        balance, monthlyReport, name, acctID

4    Class Variables:
5        TotalBalance, NumberOfAccts

6    Class Methods:

7        initialize
8            TotalBalance ← assign(Amount ← new).
9            TotalBalance ← assign(0.00).
10           NumberOfAccts ← assign(Integer ← new).
11           NumberOfAccts ← assign(0).

12       reportTotals
13           TotalBalance ← print.
14           NumberOfAccts ← print.

15   Instance Methods:

16       deposit(itemID, anAmount, date)
17           TotalBalance ← addon(anAmount).
18           balance ← addon(anAmount).
19           monthlyReport ← addline('DEP',itemID, anAmount,date,balance).

20       monthend
21           monthlyReport ← print.

22       open(id,custName)
23           NumberOfAccts ← addon(1).
24           balance ← assign(Amount ← new).
```

                                                                        (continues)

```
25              balance ← assign(0.00).
26              monthlyReport ← assign(Report ← new).
27              name ← assign(custName).
28              acctID ← assign(id).
29              monthlyReport ← titleLine(id,custName).

30        withdraw(itemID,anAmount,date)
31           (anAmount ← greaterThan(balance)) ←
32              ifTrue([errorReport ← append('overdrawn account')]).
33           (anAmount ← greaterThan(balance)) ←
34              ifFalse([balance ← subtract(anAmount).
35                      TotalBalance ← subtract(anAmount).
36                      monthlyReport ← addline('WTH',itemID,
37                                          anAmount,date,balance). ]).
```

Figure 14.1 illustrates the constituent parts of a definition of a class. First, variables are listed that belong to the class state and hence will be found in each instance of the class. In our example, lines 2 and 3 indicate that four variables belong to every object that is an instance of the class Account. These four variables and their meanings are described as follows:

balance	the present balance in the account
monthlyReport	the present version of the monthly report for the account
name	the name of the owner of the account
acctID	the identification code for the account

These variables are bound to objects themselves, which exist as part of the state of each object of class Account that is created. The classes to which these four objects belong are not specified in this declaration. In fact, their classes are dynamically determined at run time by assignments made to them, a property that is similar to dynamic typing. The classes to which a variable belongs can be determined from the methods, however, and these must be classes that are predefined in HOOL or user-defined in a class definition, such as the one in Figure 14.1.

In this case, balance is of class Amount, which is a fixed decimal class with two places after the decimal point and used for holding dollar and cent amounts. The variable monthlyReport is of Report class, which holds an array of strings, each string considered to be a line of a report. The last two variables, name and acctID, are of class String and hold the name of the customer and the account identification code, respectively. We assume, for this discussion, that Amount, Report, and String are predefined classes in HOOL, each with its own state structure and message/method pairs.

In addition to the instance variables, a class may have class variables specified. Class variables are objects that belong to the entire class and can be referenced by methods of any instance of that class. The relationship between instance variables and class variables is illustrated by Figure 14.2. Here there are three instances of class Account, each having the four instance variables.

FIGURE 14.2   Illustration of Instance and Class Variables in Class `Account`

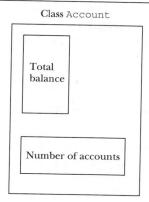

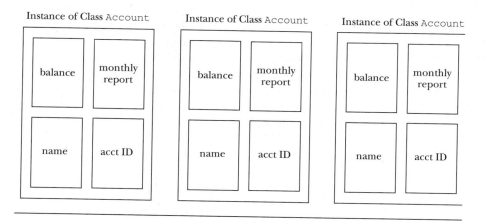

Notice that the class, its three instances, and all the variables are drawn as rectangles. This format indicates that all are objects.

In our example of Figure 14.1, we define two class variables: `TotalBalance` and `NumberOfAccts`. Here we follow the convention that class variable names begin with uppercase letters and instance variable names begin with lowercase letters. The same distinction is made for message names. `Total-Balance` is of class `Amount` and represents the sum of the balances over all instance accounts of this class. NumberOfAccts is of class Integer and contains the number of instances of class account that have been created.

Just as there are two types of variables, instance and class, so there are two types of methods defined. Class methods are activated by messages sent to the class object, whereas instance methods are activated by messages sent to instances of the class.

The syntax for the definition of a method is

```
method ::= <message-name> [(<parameter-id>{,<parameter-id>})]
   {<message>}
```

Here the message-name is the name of the message that activates the defined method. Each message can have parameters. The list of parameter identifiers indicates the number of objects that are to be received with the message and the names by which these objects are accessed in the body of the method. The body of the method consists of a sequence of messages sent to other objects. The format by which such message sending is specified in HOOL is

```
message ::= <receiving-object-id> ← <message-name>
              [(<parameter>{,<parameter>})].
```

This format specifies the receiving object's name to the left of the arrow and the message name and its parameters to the right of the arrow.

Consider lines 7–11 of Figure 14.1 as an example of a method definition. This method is a class method, so it is activated when the class object Account receives the message initialize. This method results in four messages being sent. The first, shown on line 8, sends the result of one message as the parameter for the second message. The first message, new, is sent to class object Amount. This action produces a result that is a new object of class Amount, which has not yet been given an amount value. This new object is then the parameter of message assign and results in class variable Total-Balance being bound to the newly created Amount object.

The second message (in line 9) results in the assignment of the Amount constant 0.00 to the newly instantiated Amount object, TotalBalance. Notice that lines 8 and 9 both send the message assign to object TotalBalance. The methods activated by these two messages are completely different, however, because TotalBalance belongs to a different class when the message in line 9 is sent. The first message is sent to an object of class Object, the initial class of all objects that are not otherwise classified. Class Object is very generic, recognizing a minimal number of messages. The first assign message results in TotalBalance becoming an instance of class Amount. The second message (in line 9) therefore activates the method associated with message assign in class Amount, because that is the class of the receiving object. This action illustrates the power of polymorphism. Lines 10 and 11 perform a similar function for NumberOfAccts.

A second class method is activated by the parameterless message report-Totals. It sends a print message to the two objects TotalBalance and NumberOfAccts, displaying the accumulated values of both of these objects, the first of class Amount and the second of class Integer. Note that again the two print messages result in different methods being activated, because they are sent to objects of different classes.

An object that is an instance of class Account responds to four different messages: deposit, monthend, open, and withdraw. We now examine the description of each of these instance methods in HOOL, as found in lines 15–37 of Figure 14.1.

The first is the method activated by the open message in lines 22–29. When received, this message is accompanied by two parameters, the first the ID number of the account and second the customer's name. Both these are objects of class String. The first message in line 23 sends the message addon to the class variable NumberOfAccts. This message adds its parameter's value (in this case 1) to the value of the receiving object (which is of class Integer). Lines 24 and 25 result in instance variable balance being instantiated as an object of class Amount and initialized to 0.00. Line 26 instantiates monthlyReport as a new object of class Report. Lines 27 and 28 result in instance variables name and acctID being assigned the values of the two parameter objects. Finally, line 29 sends message titleLine to monthlyReport, causing the title line containing the account ID and the customer's name to be the first line of the report for the receiving instance of class Account.

The methods activated by the message deposit and monthend are straightforward, and the reader should be able to interpret them with no difficulty. The method in lines 30–37 requires some further explanation, however, because this method requires the specification of a conditional test. Because all statements in HOOL are messages, we must perform conditional execution by message sending as well. The messages used for this are ifTrue and ifFalse. The receiving object for these messages is an object that is either TRUE or FALSE when evaluated. For example, in line 31 the message

anAmount ← greaterThan(balance)

results in TRUE if anAmount is greater than balance and FALSE otherwise. The message ifTrue has a single parameter that is a block of HOOL messages. As a result, the block is executed by the receiving object if that object has the value TRUE and is not executed if the receiving object has the value FALSE. In keeping with the spirit of object orientation, a block of messages must be considered an object that is an instance of some class. The message ifFalse is interpreted in the opposite manner, with the parameter block being executed if the receiver is FALSE. The square brackets are used to enclose a sequence of messages that are to be considered as a single block object.

With this interpretation of ifTrue and ifFalse, the reader can now understand the method for withdraw.

Next we extend our example to incorporate inheritance. We do this by creating two new classes, Checking and Savings, which are subclasses of the class Account. These are defined in HOOL in Figures 14.3 and 14.4. The

FIGURE 14.3   **HOOL Definition for Class** `Checking`

```
1    Class Checking
2        Superclass: Account

3    Class Variables:
4        MonthlyServiceCharge

5    Class Methods:
6        setServiceCharge(anAmount)
7            MonthlyServiceCharge ← assign(anAmount).

8    Instance Methods:
9        check(itemID,anAmount,date)
10           self ← withdraw(itemID,anAmount,date).

11       monthend(date)
12           self ← withdraw('SVC',MonthlyServiceCharge,date).
13           self ← monthend.
```

FIGURE 14.4   **HOOL Definition for Class** `Savings`

```
1    Class Savings
2        Superclass: Account

3    Class Variables:
4        InterestRate

5    Class Methods:
6        setInterestRate(aRate)
7            InterestRate ← assign(aRate).

8    Instance Methods:
9        monthend(date)
10           |interest|
11           interest ← assign(balance).
12           interest ← multiplyby(InterestRate).
13           interest ← divideby(12).
14           self ← deposit('INT',interest,date).
15           self ← monthend.
```

power of inheritance allows us to define these new classes succinctly, with many components inherited from their super class `Account`.

First we examine `Checking` in Figure 14.3. Notice that in line 2 this class is defined as a subclass of `Account`, which means that it inherits all the components of `Account`, instance and class variables and instance and class methods. In addition, one class variable, one class method, and two instance methods are added for this new class in order to include a service charge for the checking account. We assume, for simplicity, that this is a flat fee subtracted at the end of the month. The new class variable, `Monthly-ServiceCharge`, is set via the `setServiceCharge` message, whose accompanying method is defined in lines 6–7 of Figure 14.3.

Two new instance methods are defined. The first, `check`, defined in lines 9–10, is simply a synonym for the `withdraw` message. A new feature is introduced in line 10, where the object is specified as self, indicating that the instance object is to send the message `withdraw` to itself. Because it inherits `withdraw` from class `Account`, this message is a perfectly valid message for it to receive, resulting in the method given in class `Account` being executed.

The second instance method illustrates that an object is able to distinguish between messages with the same name but a different number of parameters. When an object of class `Checking` receives a `monthend` message with a single parameter, it sends itself a `withdraw` message to exact the service charge and then sends itself a parameterless `monthend` message. This message activates the method inherited from super class `Account`, which causes the `monthlyReport` to be printed. This case is an application of overloading to messages.

Figure 14.4 shows the HOOL definition of class `Savings`. The changes here implement the calculation of interest on the account.

This example illustrates all of the major features of object-oriented languages. The next two chapters show how these features are implemented in two popular object-oriented languages, Smalltalk and C++. This example is implemented in each of these languages.

14.3   Comparison with the Imperative Model

The concept of class in the object-oriented model is essentially identical to that of abstract data type. Both present an encapsulated definition of data structures and procedures, support information hiding, and are instantiated in objects. The major differences arise in the support that classes provide for polymorphism and inheritance. The following two sections compare the ways that HOOL differs from Ada in these two aspects.

14.3.1 ▪ Polymorphism

The closest concept to polymorphism in Ada is procedure/operator overloading. Here, the version of a procedure that is called is determined by the number and types of its parameters. Similarly, the method that is activated by the sending of a message is determined by the class of the object to which the message is sent.

The difference between these two concepts is the time of binding of the call to the procedure to be executed. In overloading within a strongly typed language like Ada, the types of all parameters are known at compile time; hence the call is statically bound to a procedure. In effect, one could consider the name of the procedure to be expanded by including the types of the parameters.

HOOL permits this binding to occur dynamically, because an object's class is not known until run time. Thus we can say that overloading is a form of "static polymorphism," where the action to be performed is bound statically to its call but is dependent on the number and types of parameters in addition to the name of the procedure or operator.

14.3.2 ▪ Inheritance

Although dynamic polymorphism is not essential for the object-oriented model, its presence in languages such as Smalltalk has resulted in it being included as a common enhancement. Inheritance is the one property that is generally used to distinguish languages as object oriented (Cardelli and Wegner 1985; Wegner 1987).

The only property of imperative languages that approaches inheritance is subtypes. Just as a subclass inherits all the properties of its super class, a subtype inherits all the properties of its parent type.

Subtypes, however, are a much more limited concept than inheritance, because they apply to only a limited set of possible base types, usually the scalar types. Imperative languages do not generalize this definition to abstract data types. This generalization is a major contribution of the object-oriented model.

C H A P T E R **14** **Terms**

object-oriented	encapsulation
object	inheritance
class	multiple inheritance
message	polymorphism
method	dynamic binding

C H A P T E R **14** **Discussion Questions**

1. To what degree is the concept of polymorphism implemented in Ada?
2. Consider useful ways to exploit polymorphism. Should operators such as + and – be included in this feature? Should selectors such as []?
3. Suggest a syntax for making polymorphism embrace these added language features.
4. What is the difference between inheritance and the use of include files, such as in the language C?
5. Identify some cases where multiple inheritance (the inheriting of the features of more than one object) could be useful.
6. Why is encapsulation an important property of object-oriented languages?
7. Based on our description and discussion of HOOL, evaluate the extent to which Ada is an object-oriented language.

8. How does the concept of class differ from that of type? How are they the same?

1. Add syntax definitions to the Ada language that would add the ability to specify inheritance. What difficulties arise in doing this?

2. Write the HOOL specification a class `interval`. This class will represent open intervals of real numbers and respond to the following messages:

```
setInterval(left, right)
leftEndPoint
rightEndPoint
overlap(anInterval)
```

3. Add a class to the set of HOOL classes developed in this chapter that provides a class for interest on checking accounts. This class will have all the capabilities of the class `Checking` but will add the interest at the end of the month as provided in class `Savings`.

4. Write a class for stacks in HOOL.

5. Write a class for queues in HOOL.

6. Consider the AVLtree data structure. An AVLtree is a balanced binary search tree. A binary search tree, in turn, is an ordered binary tree, which itself is simply a tree with a maximum of two children per node. Define this structure using polymorphism and inheritance using the HOOL syntax.

7. Extend the syntax of HOOL to allow multiple inheritance. How do the semantics change?

1. Implement an ADT for class `Amount` in an imperative language.

2. Implement an ADT for class `Account` in an imperative language.

Smalltalk: An Object-Oriented Language

15.1 ▪ Overview
15.2 ▪ Smalltalk Syntax
15.3 ▪ Class Hierarchy
15.4 ▪ Abstract Classes
15.5 ▪ An Example in Smalltalk

The object-oriented language Smalltalk is described in this chapter. It is studied as an implementation of the object-oriented model that is presented in Chapter 14. A detailed example written in Smalltalk is included.

15.1 Overview

Smalltalk was created by the Software Concepts Group at the Xerox Palo Alto Research Center. It consists of a powerful user interface and environment in addition to its language features. In this book, we concentrate on the language itself, but the environment has had a significant impact on the computer world as well, serving as a model for modern window-based systems.

The environment consists of windows, several of which can be on the screen at one time. Each window contains a different view of the present system. The user interacts with the Smalltalk environment through the use of pop-up menus that can be accessed through the use of a mouse. This environment greatly influenced the design of the Apple Macintosh, Microsoft

Windows, and X Windows user interfaces as well as those of many other modern systems.

Smalltalk uses five standard system windows. Other types of windows can be created as classes by the user. The five standard windows are the System Browser, the System Workspace, the File List, the Workspace, and the System Transcript windows. We briefly describe the function of each of these windows here.

The System Browser presents a list of all classes in the system in one subview. The user may select any one of these classes for further examination. When a class is selected, a list of messages that apply to that class appears in another subview of the window. When one of these messages is selected by the user, the method associated with the message is displayed in yet another subview. Through this window, the user may add or delete classes, add or delete messages, and modify methods. The System Workspace window contains Smalltalk definitions of various utilities. Through this window the user can examine and modify these definitions.

The File List window presents a subview consisting of a directory from secondary storage. Entries in the directory may be selected, in which case the selected file appears in a second subview. The text of the file can then be edited in that subview. The Workspace window can hold temporary text. It is used as a scratchpad area, and the System Transcript window contains all messages and output from the Smalltalk system.

The Smalltalk language implements all of the fundamental object-oriented concepts. In particular, every entity in Smalltalk is an object, and all operations are activated by sending messages to objects. The concept of class is fundamental. Every object is identified as having a defining class. In addition, inheritance is implemented through the definition of subclasses and super classes.

Smalltalk has a very simple syntax, consisting of only one basic type of statement: message sending. Collections of message-sending statements are used for the sole purpose of defining methods for classes. Classes are defined through the interactive environment by binding a name to the class, variable names to the class, messages to the class, and a method to each message. The syntax of Smalltalk is introduced later.

The power of Smalltalk comes from its built-in hierarchical collection of classes, called the **Smalltalk image**. These classes, although an integral part of the language, are treated like all other classes in that, being expressed in Smalltalk themselves, they may be deleted or modified by the user through the interactive Smalltalk environment. The user also has the ability to add newly created classes to the image. The structure of the Smalltalk image is described at a later point.

15.2   Smalltalk Syntax

Every statement in Smalltalk is a message-sending statement and appears within the definition of a method. The general form of a statement is

```
<statement> ::= <object> <message>
```

A period is used as a statement separator in Smalltalk. We next examine the form of each of the two component parts of a statement.

15.2.1 ▪ Objects

Objects can be expressed in four different forms: literals, reserved words, variables, and expressions.

Literals Smalltalk provides literals for representing instances of five different classes. Character literals are represented by a dollar sign, followed by any ASCII character. Examples are

```
$a    $?    $$    $*    $z
```

Numeric literals are written with digits, a minus sign, a decimal point, a lowercase letter e for expressing a power of ten, and a slash for representing fractions. The class of a numeric literal is determined by its format. For example, the following literals represent objects of class Integer:

```
1    -14    217
```

The following numeric literals represent objects of class Float:

```
6.28    -14.2    .7e12    33.5e-10
```

The following numeric literals represent objects of class Fraction:

```
1/7    -7/721    4/9
```

Literals representing objects of class String are strings of characters enclosed in single quotes — for example,

```
'This is a String literal'
'Special @+:$ characters are allowed'
'It''s also possible to include single quotes'
```

Literals of class Symbol are sequences of characters following a number sign (#). Each symbol must be unique — for example:

```
#aSymbol    #=    #S
```

An Array literal is a sequence of objects. The objects need not all be of the same class and they need not be literals. They are written by enclosing the sequence in parentheses, separating individual elements by spaces, and preceding the left parenthesis with a number sign (#). Examples of array literals are

```
#(1 $a v)        #('example' 2.4 7/9 $*)
```

Reserved Words In addition to literal representation of objects, there are five reserved words that represent specific objects in Smalltalk.

First, true and false represent the only objects of classes True and False, respectively. True and False are subclasses of class Boolean.

The reserved word `nil` represents the only instance object of the class `UndefinedObject`. Variables are bound to this object when they are created indicating an undefined state.

The reserved word `self`, when used in the definition of a method, is a pseudovariable that always refers to the receiving object of the message. The reserved word `super` also refers to the receiving object of the message, but with the object considered as an instance of the super class of its defining class.

Variables Within Smalltalk, there are six kinds of variables. These variables are all represented by identifiers consisting of a sequence of letters. No special characters are permitted in Smalltalk variable names. The convention used to express multiword names is to capitalize the first letter of every word after the first word. The first letter of an instance variable, temporary variable, or parameter is, by convention, always lowercase. The first letter of a class variable, class name, or global variable is always uppercase.

Instance variables are defined with a class definition and are private to each instance of that class. Each instance of a class, therefore, has the same set of instance variables, although the objects associated with these variables may differ from instance to instance. An instance object's instance variables are accessible only from the instance methods for that object.

Class variables are defined within a class and are accessible to every instance object of that class and its descendant classes as well as from the class methods of the class and all its descendant classes.

Temporary variables are defined only during the execution of a single method in which they are defined. When the method is completed, these variables cease to exist. These variables are declared at the beginning of a method definition by listing their names enclosed between a pair of vertical bars.

Global variables are accessible to all methods in the Smalltalk system. These names are listed in the system dictionary. Pool variables are shared among classes that specify them. They are listed in named pool directories.

Parameters represent objects passed into a method when it is selected by its corresponding message. They are private to the method and redefined upon every method activation. Variables are initially bound to the `nil` object, the only instance of class `UndefinedObject`. They are then bound to other objects by the assignment message. The class of a variable is the class of the object that was most recently assigned to it. Therefore, variables are dynamically bound to their classes.

The assignment of an object to a variable is specified in Smalltalk by using a left-arrow as the assignment message. An object is specified to the right of the assignment message, and that object is bound to the variable on the left as a result of the assignment message. The variable is bound to both the class and the value of the object found on the right side of the arrow.

For example,

a ← 6

binds the variable a to class `Integer` and object 6. Variable bindings are indirect in the sense that a pointer to the object is associated with the variable. For example,

```
a ← b
```

binds the variable a to the same class and object that is currently bound to variable b. It does not create a copy of the object.

Expressions   When a message is sent to an object in Smalltalk, the corresponding method returns an object as a result of its handling the message. In this way, the method behaves in a manner similar to a function. The returned object can then act as the recipient of a second message. The grouping of several messages into a single statement results in the construction of Smalltalk expressions.

For our discussion of expressions, we work with objects of class `Integer` and the messages +, ×, and − that are appropriate to that class. Note that operators are taken to be special forms of messages. Therefore, the expression

```
6 + 4
```

means that the message + is sent to 6, a literal object of `Integer` class with parameter 4. The return value of this message is the sum 10, another `Integer` object.

Therefore, the expression 6 + 4 represents an integer object returned from the handling of this message. Suppose we wish to multiply the result of the previous message by 2. We can do so with the following nested message:

```
6 + 4 * 2
```

This causes the message * to be sent to the object 6 + 4 with parameter 2. The resulting Integer object is 20.

Note that this is in opposition to the conventional precedence rules for arithmetic. The message-sending protocol of Smalltalk results in a strict left-to-right evaluation. Smalltalk does, however, permit the grouping of messages through parentheses. For example, the message

```
6 + (4 * 2)
```

returns the `Integer` object 14.

15.2.2   ▪   Messages

Smalltalk permits three types of messages, unary, binary, and keyword; they are distinguished by the number of parameters and the way the message is specified.

Unary Messages   A **unary message** is parameterless. Such a message is specified by identifiers with the first letter uppercase for a class message and lowercase for an instance message. Examples are

```
6 factorial
12 negated
```

Binary Messages A **binary message** is named by one or two special characters and always requires a single parameter, which follows the symbol that represents the message. Examples of binary messages are

```
6 + 5
'one' , 'two'
```

Keyword Messages A **keyword message** consists of one or more keyword/ formal parameter pairs. Both the keywords and the parameters are identifiers, and a keyword is separated from its corresponding formal parameter by a colon. The keywords for methods are chosen to make the reading of the message as explanatory of its function as possible. The message name is always given as the sequence of keywords, each followed by a colon. The number of parameters accepted by a message is always equal to the number of colons in its name. The mode of parameters is IN implemented by copy, although we must keep in mind that the parameters are bound to pointers to objects. Examples of keyword message calls are

```
6 gcd: 21
'test string' at:3 put:$x
```

15.2.3 ▪ Blocks

One type of Smalltalk object that has not yet been described corresponds to the block mentioned for HOOL. A Smalltalk block is a sequence of message specifications that is executable. A block literal is specified by placing the sequence of messages, separated by periods, inside of square brackets. Blocks are important tools for specifying conditional and iterative messages. But before we look at that use, let's illustrate the use of blocks for deferred execution.

Suppose we define the block

```
zeroOut ← [a ← 0. b ← 0. c ← 0]
```

This statement binds the variable `zeroOut` to the block of messages that bind `a`, `b`, and `c` to the `Integer` object `0`. This variable of class `Block` can then be executed at any time by sending the message `value` to `zeroOut` by

```
zeroOut value
```

The key concept here is that blocks of messages can themselves be considered to be objects. One important message that can be sent to such an object is `value`, just illustrated, which requests the block to execute itself.

This leads us to examine the Smalltalk approach to conditional execution. It consists of sending the message `ifTrue:` to a Boolean object (either `true` or `false`) and executing the single parameter of the message, a block object, if the receiver is true.

For example, the message

```
(x > y) ifTrue: [x ← y]
```

results in x being assigned the object bound to y if the value presently bound to x is greater than the value presently bound to y.

Similarly, the ifFalse: message executes the parameter block if the receiving object is false. Often the two messages ifTrue: and ifFalse: are sent consecutively to the same object. When consecutive messages are sent to the same object, the messages may appear after the receiving object separated by semicolons. For example, the following message sequence sets z to the maximum of x and y:

```
(x > y) ifTrue: [z ← x];
        ifFalse: [z ← y]
```

This sequence is equivalent to

```
(x > y) ifTrue: [z ← x].
(x > y) ifFalse:[z ← y]
```

Alternatively, Boolean objects can receive the single message ifTrue:ifFalse:, which contains two parameters of class Block. The preceding result can then be obtained by

```
(x > y) ifTrue: [z ← x]
        ifFalse: [z ← y]
```

Repeated execution of a block object is specified by the whileTrue: and whileFalse: messages. The receiving object of these messages is a block that returns a Boolean object when executed. The general form of the whileTrue: message is

```
<receiving-block> whileTrue: <parameter-block>
```

The resulting action is the repeated evaluation of the receiving-block, followed by the execution of the parameter-block, until the receiving-block no longer results in a true object. The following message sequences use the whileTrue: message to set logn to the largest integer less than or equal to $\log_2 n$.

```
logn ← 0.
temp ← n div 2.
[temp > 0] whileTrue: [temp ← temp div 2.
                       logn ← logn + 1]
```

Smalltalk also contains messages that implement variable-controlled iterations, but we do not discuss those here.

15.2.4 ▪ Definition of a Method

A method is defined as a sequence of messages separated by periods. Two special features of Smalltalk method definition should be observed.

First, a method may contain variables that are local to the execution of the method. These are declared on the first line of the message, with the variable names separated by spaces and the entire list enclosed in vertical bars. As mentioned previously, no class needs to be specified in this declaration, because classes of variables are determined dynamically as they are assigned objects.

The second feature is the ability to specify a return value for the method, which is done by preceding an object description by an up-arrow. The object following the up-arrow is then returned as the result of the message.

The method description in Figure 15.1 provides an example of the preceding features. The lines are numbered to facilitate reference in the following discussion and are not a part of the Smalltalk syntax.

In line 4, four local variables are declared. The location bindings for these variables hold for the duration of the method execution. Like all Smalltalk variables, they are bound to a class whenever they are assigned an object. Prior to that, they are bound to object nil of class UndefinedObject.

The variable n is an index into the string, recording the position of the current character of the string scan. The variable long is the length of the longest string of identical characters found. The variable lastchar remembers the last character scanned, whereas consec keeps a count of the number of consecutive identical characters at any point.

Line 16 indicates that the object bound to variable long is returned. Any object description preceded by an up-arrow indicates not only that the following object is returned, but also that the method is immediately terminated after the corresponding message returns its value.

FIGURE **15.1**   **Smalltalk Method Description**

```
1     longident
2       "This method computes the longest substring of
3       identical characters within the receiving string"
4       |n long lastchar consec|
5       n ← 1.
6       long ← 0.
7       lastchar ← self at: 1.
8       consec ← 0.
9       [n <= (self size)] whileTrue:
10        [(lastchar = (self at: n))
11            ifTrue:[consec ← consec + 1]
12            ifFalse:[lastchar ← self at: n.
13                    (consec > long)
14                        ifTrue: [long ← consec].
15                    consec ← 1].
16          n ← n + 1].
17       ↑long
```

15.2.5　▪　Definition of a Class

Class descriptions in Smalltalk consist of the following components:

1. *Class name* — The name of the class is, by convention, chosen to begin with an uppercase letter.

2. *Super class* — This is the name of the class from which the present class inherits variables, messages, and methods.

3. *Class variables* — Variables that belong to the class and are accessible to all instances of this class are called class variables.

4. *Instance variables* — Each instance object belonging to the defined class has a set of these instance variables, which are accessible only to the methods of the owning instance.

5. *Class methods* — Methods that are activated by messages to the class object are called class methods.

6. *Instance methods* — Methods that are activated by messages to instances of the class are called instance methods.

We illustrate this protocol description of a class by defining the class `Amount`, a class to represent an amount of money, consisting of dollars and cents. The definition of this class is found in Figure 15.2. Line 1 indicates that `Amount` is a **subclass** of class `Object` and hence inherits the protocol of `Object`, a super class of all Smalltalk classes.

Class `Amount` has no class variables and one instance variable, `total-Cents`, declared in line 2. This variable is bound to an object of class `Integer`, which is the total amount of cents associated with the amount of money.

`Amount` has one class method, `Dollars:Cents:`, which is used to instantiate an instance of this class. It is defined in lines 7–8. Line 7 is the message prototype, specifying `d` and `c` as formal parameters of the method. In line 8, `self` refers to the class object `Amount`, which is the only permissible recipient of this message. When `self` is sent the message `new`, this creates a new instance of class `Amount`. Class `Amount` inherits the class method `new` from its super class `Object`. This newly created object is then sent the message `dollars: d cents: c` to establish its initial value. This message is permissible to objects of class `Amount` and is defined in lines 38–39.

Nine instance methods are defined for class `Amount`, four callable by binary messages, three by unary, and two by keyword.

The binary message `*` permits the multiplication of an amount by any object of a numeric class. Note that the parameter `aValue` could be of class `Integer`, `Float`, `Fraction`, or any other class for which multiplication by an integer is defined. The variable `newTotalCents` is declared to be local to method `*` on line 12. This variable is bound to the result of multiplying the instance variable `totalCents` by the formal parameter `aValue` in line 13. Lines 14 and 15 create a new instance of class `Amount`, with its value represented by `newTotalCents`.

Similarly, the methods for binary messages `+` and `-` are defined in lines 17–21 and 23–27, respectively. The binary message `>` is used to compare two

FIGURE **15.2**   **Smalltalk Definition of Class** Amount

```
1    Object subclass: #Amount
2      instanceVariableNames: 'totalCents'
3      classVariableNames: ''
4
5    !Amount class methods !
6
7    Dollars: d Cents: c
8      self new dollars: d cents: c
9
10   !Amount instance methods !
11   * aValue
12     | newTotalCents |
13     newTotalCents ← totalCents * aValue.
14     ↑ Amount Dollars: (newTotalCents rem: 100)
15           Cents: (newTotalCents quo: 100)
16
17   + anAmount
18     |newTotalCents |
19     newTotalCents ← totalCents + anAmount totalCents.
20     ↑ Amount Dollars: (newTotalCents rem: 100)
21           Cents: (newTotalCents quo: 100).
22
23   - anAmount
24     |newTotalCents|
25     newTotalCents ← totalCents - anAmount totalCents.
26     ↑ Amount Dollars: (newTotalCents rem: 100)
27           Cents: (newTotalCents quo: 100).
28
29   > anAmount
30     ↑ totalCents > (anAmount totalCents)
31
32   cents
33     ↑ totalCents rem: 100
34
35   dollars
36     ↑ totalCents quo: 100
37
38   dollars: d cents: c
39     totalCents ← 100 * d + c
40
41   printOn: aPrintStream
42     self dollars printOn: aPrintStream.
43     $. printOn: aPrintStream.
44     (self cents < 10) ifTrue: [$0 printOn: aPrintStream].
45     self cents printOn: aPrintStream
46
47   totalCents
48     ↑ totalCents
```

amounts and returns the Boolean result of sending the > message to total-Cents, an instance of class Integer.

The methods for the three unary messages — cents, dollars, and total-Cents — return the cents part of the amount, the dollar part of the amount, and the total number of cents in the amount.

Two methods are activated by keyword messages. The first, dollars:cents:, is defined in lines 38–39. It accepts two parameters and modifies the total-Cents variable of the receiving object accordingly. The second, printOn:, accepts the name of a print stream as its single parameter and sends the appropriate characters for the amount to that print stream. Line 44 is required to support the printing of a leading zero character if the number of cents is less than 10.

15.2.6 ▪ Creation of Instance Objects

Each class in Smalltalk is itself considered to be an object that receives messages. This class object can receive any of the class messages specified for the class. The most important of the messages that the class object receives is the new message, which creates a new instance of the specified class.

For example, an instance of class Amount defined in Figure 15.2 can be created and bound to a variable a by the message

```
a ← Amount new
```

In this sense, the class object can be thought of as a factory for instance objects. On receipt of the new message, the class object manufactures an instance object of the defining class, returning it as the result of the message.

It is also possible to create additional methods that not only manufacture new instance objects, but also initialize those objects. The class method Dollars:Cents: defined in lines 7–8 of Figure 15.2 is an example of this.

15.3 Class Hierarchy

The image of a Smalltalk system is a hierarchy of classes consisting of a tree representing the subclass/super class structure used for inheritance. Many of the classes in Smalltalk are never intended to have instance variables. Rather, these **abstract classes** provide variables and methods that are to be inherited by a set of descendant classes. Each Smalltalk system comes with a large class hierarchy already built into the image. The user can then further enhance the image by adding new classes to this structure and modifying existing classes. These concepts are illustrated in the following sections.

15.4 Abstract Classes

We illustrate the concept of abstract class through the introduction of an example. Our example is the class Number, which is part of Smalltalk's built-in image.

Number serves as a super class for numeric classes such as Integer, Float, and Fraction. As such, its variables, messages, and methods are all inherited by these subclasses, so it defines those entities that are common to all of its subclasses. Because `Number` is an abstract class, there are never any instances of this particular class. It exists only to provide a template for its subclasses and their descendants.

In order to illustrate the different ways inherited methods are used, we examine five instance methods of class `Number` and the manner in which they are inherited by subclass `Float`.

First we consider the method for the binary message +. It is defined in abstract class `Number`, but its definition there indicates that the actual definition is deferred to subclasses. The message + needs to exist as a valid message in class `Number` because other methods of class `Number` use that message. However, because `Number` is an abstract class and has no instances, each instance that receives the message + is an instance of some subclass or further descendant of `Number`, such as `Float`, where + does have a complete definition.

Next, the unary message `abs`, which defines the absolute value operation, is defined for the abstract class `Number` and inherited by its subclasses as is, without any redefinition. For example, `abs` could be defined as

```
abs
    self < 0 ifTrue: [↑ self]
            ifFalse: [↑ self negated]
```

The messages < and `negated` are messages that, like +, are defined in `Number` but whose implementation is deferred to subclasses.

The message `numerator`, which is defined for class `Number`, is also inherited by class `Float`. This message is an example of a message that, although inherited, has no meaning for an instance of that subclass, because numerator does not make sense for a `Float` instance.

The message > is an example of a message that is inherited from `Number` by subclass `Float` in a way that is transparent in the definition of `Number`. By this we mean > is defined in the class `Magnitude`, which is the super class of `Number`. `Number` then inherits > from `Magnitude` and `Float` inherits it from `Number`.

Finally, `Float` contains instance messages that are unique to that class and not inherited at all. For example, the method associated with message `truncate` returns the truncated integer part of a floating-point number. This method is defined only in `Float`.

We summarize the five different ways message inheritance can occur in the following table.

Type of Inheritance	Example
Defined in super class but not implemented there	+
Defined in super class and inherited by subclass w/o redefinition	abs
Defined in super class and inherited by subclass but meaningless in subclass	numerator
Defined in super class of super class and inherited by subclass through its super class	>
Defined in subclass only	truncate

15.4.1 ▪ Important Smalltalk Abstract Classes

Each version of Smalltalk comes with a different set of abstract classes provided in its initial image. But there are certain abstract classes that have become more or less standard components of all Smalltalk implementations, serving as the building blocks for all other classes. We briefly summarize some of these classes in this section.

`Magnitude` abstract class provides the protocol for linearly ordered subclasses, including `Date`, `Time`, `Character`, and `Number`. The methods of class `Magnitude` that are inherited by all its subclasses include ordered comparisons and determining the larger and the smaller of two objects.

`Stream` is an abstract class for subclasses of positionable collections. These subclasses are used for accessing files or other input/output devices in a sequential manner. The messages of `Stream` allow accessing or updating the object at the current position and messages to change the current position in the stream. Subclasses of `Stream` include `ReadStream`, `WriteStream`, `ReadWriteStream`, `FileStream`, `PrintStream`, and `TerminalStream`.

`Collection` is an abstract class that represents either a structured or unstructured collection of objects. Many different types of collections with widely varying organizations make up the subclasses of `Collection`. Some of the more popular ones are `Array`, `String`, `Set`, and `Dictionary`. Different subclasses permit their elements to be accessed in different ways such as by position or by key.

Smalltalk also commonly contains abstract classes that support the use of window and graphic objects.

15.5 An Example in Smalltalk

Figure 15.3 lists the Smalltalk version of the class `Account`. This is a direct translation of the HOOL version of the same class, which was listed in Figure 14.1.

FIGURE 15.3   **Class Description of** `Account` **in Smalltalk**

```
Object subclass: #Account
  instanceVariableNames:
     'balance monthlyReport name acctID'
  classVariableNames:
     'TotalBalance NumberOfAccts '
!Account class methods!
initialize
  TotalBalance ← Amount new.
  TotalBalance dollars: 0 cents: 0.
  NumberOfAccts ← 0

reportTotBal
  |totReport|
  totReport ← WriteStream with: String.
  'Total Balance =' printOn: totReport.
  TotalBalance printOn: totReport.
```

```
    totReport cr.
    'Number of Accounts = ' printOn: totReport.
    NumberOfAccts printOn: totReport.
    ↑totReport contents
!Account methods!

balance
 ↑balance

deposit: itemID of: anAmount on: date
 TotalBalance ← TotalBalance + anAmount.
 balance ← balance + anAmount.
 monthlyReport nextPutAll: 'DEP';
              tab;
              nextPutAll: itemID;
              tab.
 anAmount printOn: monthlyReport.
 monthlyReport tab;
              nextPutAll: date;
              tab.
 balance printOn: monthlyReport.
 monthlyReport cr.

monthend
 |temp|
 temp ← monthlyReport contents.
 monthlyReport ← WriteStream with: String.
 ↑ temp

open: iD for: custName
 NumberOfAccts ← NumberOfAccts + 1.
 balance ← Amount new.
 balance dollars: 0 cents: 0.
 monthlyReport ← WriteStream with: String new.
 name ← custName.
 acctID ← iD.
 monthlyReport nextPutAll: acctID; cr

withdraw: itemID of: anAmount on: date
 (anAmount > balance)
  ifFalse: [balance ← balance - anAmount.
           TotalBalance ← TotalBalance - anAmount.
           monthlyReport nextPutAll: 'WTH'
                        tab;
                        nextPutAll: itemID;
                        tab.
           anAmount printOn: monthlyReport.
           monthlyReport tab;
                        nextPutAll: date;
                        tab.
           balance printOn: monthlyReport.
           monthlyReport cr.]
  ifTrue: [↑'Account overdrawn - withdrawal rejected']
```

This class has four instance variables, two class variables, two class methods, and four instance methods. We examine these in some detail and then we examine subclasses `Checking` and `Savings` of class `Account`.

15.5.1 ▪ Class `Account`

Class `Account` is an abstract class. Two class methods, `initialize` and `reportTotBal`, are defined in Figure 15.3. The class method `initialize` sets the class variable `TotalBalance` to an object of class `Amount` (as defined in Figure 14.4) and initializes that object to zero. This class variable represents the sum of the balances of all instance accounts. This class method also sets class variable `NumberOfAccts` to an object of class `Integer` whose value is zero. This result represents the total number of account instances that have been opened. The method associated with class message `ReportTotBal` constructs a report as an instance of class `WriteStream` and reports the total balance and the total number of accounts.

The instance method for `deposit:of:on:` is a method with three parameters. The first is an identification string for the deposit, the second is the amount of the deposit, and the third is the date of the deposit.

Message `withdraw:of:on:` sends as parameters the identification string, the amount of withdrawal, and the date of withdrawal. It also contains a test for the amount of withdrawal greater than the account balance to prevent overdrawing the account.

The method associated with `open:for:` creates a new instance of class `Account` and initializes its balance, monthly report, account ID, and customer name. The method associated with instance message `monthend` sends the report accumulated in `monthlyReport` to the printer and clears `monthlyReport` for the next month.

15.5.2 ▪ Class `Checking`

In Figure 15.4, class `Checking` is defined as a subclass of class `Account`. In addition to the protocol inherited from `Account`, `Checking` has one additional class variable, one class method, and two instance methods.

The class variable added is `MonthlyServiceCharge`, which is given its value in the new class method `SetServiceCharge`. The added instance method is `check:of:on` and is simply a renaming of the instance method `withdraw:of:on` from class `Account`. The instance method `monthend:` inserts the withdrawal of the service charge before sending the message `monthend` whose method is inherited from class `Account`. Note that Smalltalk distinguishes between the two messages `monthend` and `monthend:`.

15.5.3 ▪ Class `Savings`

Class `Savings` is defined in Figure 15.5. It adds the class variable `InterestRate` which is set by class method `SetInterestRate`. Instance method `monthend:` includes sending the message `calculateInterest` which for simplicity, calculates the interest on the monthly closing balance.

FIGURE **15.4**   **Class Description of** Checking **in Smalltalk**

```
Account subclass: #Checking
  instanceVariableNames: ''
classVariableNames: 'MonthlyServiceCharge'

!Checking class methods!
setServiceCharge: anAmount
  MonthlyServiceCharge ← anAmount.
  ↑MonthlyServiceCharge

!Checking instance methods!
check: itemID of: anAmount on: date
  self withdraw: itemID of: anAmount on: date monthend: date
  self withdraw: 'SVC' of: MonthlyServiceCharge on: date.
  ↑self monthend.
```

FIGURE **15.5**   **Class Description of** Savings **in Smalltalk**

```
Account subclass: #Savings
  instanceVariableNames: ''
  classVariableNames: 'InterestRate'

!Savings class methods!
  SetInterestRate: aFloat
  InterestRate ←aFloat

!Savings instance methods!

calculateInterest
  |totalCentsInt interest|
  totalCentsInt ← ((InterestRate / 1200) *
                    (balance totalCents)) truncated.
  interest ← Amount new.
  interest dollars: (totalCentsInt / 100)
        cents: (totalCentsInt rem: 100).
  ↑ interest

monthend: date
  |interestAmt|
  interestAmt ← self calculateInterest.
  self deposit: 'INT' of: interestAmt on: date.
  ↑self monthend.
```

C H A P T E R **15**   **Terms**

Smalltalk image   keyword messages
instance variables   super class
unary messages   subclass
binary messages   abstract class

C H A P T E R **15**   **Discussion Questions**

1. Smalltalk permits objects to be returned as a result of sending a message. How does this increase the power of these languages?

2. Contrast Smalltalk's manner of specifying multiple parameters (via keywords and colons) to that found in HOOL and imperative languages. Which do you prefer and why?

3. What is the difference between the relationship of a class to its superclass and the relationship of an object to its defining class?

4. Discuss the type of classes that could be derived from Smalltalk abstract classes. (For example, what classes other than `Array` could be derived from `Collection`, or what other types of arrays could be derived?)

5. How is an unconstrained array in Ada similar to an abstract class in Smalltalk? How is a generic package similar to an abstract class?

6. What are some advantages and disadvantages of having a modifiable built-in image in Smalltalk?

7. How should Smalltalk deal with multiple inheritance?

8. How is the concept of a block in Smalltalk different from the concept of block in an imperative language? How are they the same?

9. Classify the object construction and instantiation as a dynamic or static binding. What are the advantages of the approach you chose over the other approach?

C H A P T E R **15**   **Exercises**

1. The Smalltalk class `Fraction` has two instance variables, `denominator` and `numerator`, both of class `Integer`. Write the class method `numerator:` `denominator` which defines the value of a `Fraction` object.

2. Write the following instance methods for the class `Fraction` defined in Exercise 1:

   a. `* aNumber`
   b. `+ aNumber`
   c. `- aNumber`
   d. `/ aNumber`
   e. `< aNumber`
   f. `asFloat`
   g. `denominator`
   h. `numerator`
   i. `reciprocal`

3. Write the Smalltalk specification for the class `interval` from Chapter 14.

4. What will be the result of each of the final Smalltalk messages in the following?

a. a ←3. a + 4
b. a ←3. a + 4; -2
c. a ←3. a / 2 + 1
d. a ←3. a / (2 + 1)
e. a ←3. a + 6 / 2

5. If each of the following is preceded by

    a ← 5.
    b ← 2.

    what will be returned in each case?

    a. [a < b] ifTrue: [a + 1]
                    ifFalse: [b - 1]
    b. [b < a] whileTrue: [a ← a - 1. b * a]
    c. x ← 0.
       n ← a.
       [n > 1] whileTrue: [x ← x + n. n ← n - 1. x]

6. Write a Smalltalk method for each of the following on class `Integer`:

    a. sumOfFirstN
    b. factorial
    c. greatestCommonDivior:
    d. max:
    e. floorOfSquareRoot

7. Design the class hierarchy for the AVLtree specified in Chapter 14 exercises.

8. Design a `Precise` class, a class of floating-point numbers with unlimited precision.

9. Write the specifications for collections taken for granted in most languages: collections such as arrays, records, and sets.

C H A P T E R 15 **Laboratory Exercises**

1. Write a class definition for a stack in Smalltalk.
2. Write a class definition for a queue in Smalltalk.
3. In Smalltalk, implement the AVLtree class specified by your hierarchy in Exercise 7.
4. Likewise, implement the `Precise` class you designed in Exercise 8.
5. Write a class definition for real open intervals in Smalltalk. Objects of class `Interval` should accept the following messages:

    ```
    left        return the left end point
    right       return the right end point
    in: aFloat  return true if aFloat is in the interval
    in: anInterval
                return true is anInterval is contained
                in the receiving interval
    ```

C++:
An Object-Oriented
Language

16.1 Overview

The programming language C++ was invented by Bjarne Stroustrup (1986) in the early 1980s. It was designed primarily to extend the original C programming language to include "user-friendly" features such as strong type-checking and to embrace object-oriented concepts.

The concept of a C language extension is central to C++. The language was designed to be a superset of C, and, as a result, all C programs will compile using a C++ compiler. In fact, C++ was originally implemented by a translator that translates a C++ program into C and then uses a C compiler to compile the translated code. Although some compilers today compile straight C++, most are still implemented as translators.

We cannot cover all aspects of C++ in this chapter. Instead, we will focus on the extensions in C++ that implement object-oriented concepts.

16.2 Syntax

Because C++ is an extension of C, it starts with and then builds upon the syntax of C. We focus on the `class` construct in C++ and its use to implement the object-oriented model.

16.2.1 • Classes

In C++, classes are defined by the `class` construct. This construct allows the declaration of data elements and functions that are incorporated into objects of a class. Let us construct a small "string" class, much like that used in the example in Chapter 6. In that example, we used a declaration for a string (`char *`) and we defined three functions that could be used on strings, namely, `compare_string`, `read_string`, and `copy_string`. Therefore, a "string" class must incorporate the data that makes up a string and the functions — called **member functions** — that are defined to operate on strings. We can start with the following class description:

```
class String {
   char *data;

   int compare(String, String);
   String read();
   void copy(String, String);
};
```

Notice a few things about this class declaration. First, it is simply a declaration and not a complete implementation. C++ allows this type of separation. Second, note that the _string suffixes were eliminated, because they would have been redundant. Finally, note the C syntax that comes through this C++ specification (e.g., `char *` or the curly brackets).

Objects in C++ are simply variables that are declared to be of a specific class instance. Here the class is treated as a data type. To use our string example, we would declare a string object as

```
String str;
```

When an object is declared to be an instance of a class, the members of that class are accessible via structlike syntax. For example, we would reference the `data` member of a string as `str.data`.

However, referencing the data — the **implementation** — of a string violates the concept of encapsulation. To enforce this, C++ allows the distinction between private and public declarations. Private declarations are accessible only to member functions; public declarations are accessible to all parts of a program that can access the object. In our example, we should deny access to the data implementation but allow access to the operations. Therefore, we can respecify the class declaration:

```
class String {
private:
   char *data;

public:
   int compare(String, String);
   String read();
   void copy(String, String);
};
```

Allowing for hidden parts of a class specification makes initialization of a class difficult. For instance, how would one initialize the string to be empty when the data are inaccessible? Class initialization is so common that special features have been designed into C++ to allow it. These are called **class constructors**, and take the form of a function with the same name as the class. The converse operation — that of **class destruction** — is also supported in C++ if the programmer supplies a function with the same name as the class, prefixed with a ~ character. So, to complete the String declaration, we could use

```
class String {
private:
   char *data;

public:
   String();
   String(String);
   ~String();

   int compare(String, String);
   String read();
   void copy(String, String);
};
```

Notice that two String constructors have been given. The intent is that the first constructor gives an empty string and the second constructor initializes the String object to have the value of the string supplied as an argument. The special function ~String() is known as the class destructor and is executed whenever an object of class String is deallocated.

Consider the code in Figure 16.1 as a use of the String class. A string and pointer to a string are declared. First, str1 is read from the user; then str2 is initialized dynamically to be equal to str1. Finally, they are compared.

The example in Figure 16.1 is incomplete. We still need to provide the implementation of the member functions. This is done by the code in Figure 16.2. Often this code is kept separately in a different file to drive home the point of separate specifications. We need to note a few things about the C++ code in Figure 16.2 that we have not yet explained.

▪ First, comments in C++ start with the sequence // and end with the end of a line (C++ also recognizes the C comment syntax).

FIGURE 16.1   **An Example of the Use of the** String **Class**

```
main ()      {
  class String {
  private:
    char *data;

  public:
    String();
    String(String);
    ~String();
    int compare(String, String);
    String read();
    void copy(String, String);
  };

  String str1;
  String *str2;

  str1.read();
  str2 = new String(str1);
  if (str1.Compare(str1, *str2)) {
    printf("Equal\n")
  }
}
```

FIGURE 16.2   **The Implementation of C++** String **Class**

```
//*************************************************************
//
// string.cc -- a separately-compiled implementation of the String
//              c++ class.
//
//*************************************************************

// Some constant definitions

#define Max_Name_Length 128

#define EQUAL 1
#define GREATER_THAN 2
#define LESS_THAN 3

// Declaration of the String class itself

class String {
private:
  char *data;
```

(continues)

```
public:
    String();
    String(String);
    ~String();
    int compare(String, String);
    String read():
    void copy(String, String);
};

// String constructor for an "empty" string. We create the space
// and setup the data pointer.

String::String()
{
    data = new char [Max_Name_Length +1];
    data[0] = '\0';
}

// String constructor for a string copied from another string. We
// create the space, setup the data pointer, and call "copy" to copy
// the original string to the newly created one.

String::(String original)
{
    data = new char [Max_Name_Length + 1];
    data[0] = '\0';
    this ->copy(original);
}
// String destructor -- all we need to do is free up the data item.

String::~String ()
{
    delete [] data;
}

// "Compare" compares two strings and returns appropriate constant.
// Note that we setup two "char *" data items, then use the compare
// function from the C implementation.

int String::compare(String str1, String str2)
{
    char *s1, *s2;
    s1 = str1.data; s2 = str2.data;
    while (*s1 == *s2) {
        if (*s1 == '\0') return EQUAL;
        s1++; s2++;
    }
    if (*s1 < *s2) {
        return LESS_THAN;
```

```
        } else {
            return GREATER_THAN;
        }
}

// Read a string from the keyboard into the data element.

void String::read()
{
    gets (data);
}

// Copy a string into the current string (class). Here we must derive
// both string pointers (one from the current class, one from the
// function argument) and then we copy using the single while loop
// from the C version.

void copy (String str)
{
    char *s1, *s2;

    s1 = data;
    s2 = str.data;
    while (*s1++ = *s2++) ;
}
```

- Second, note that there is a different perspective with these routines than for the ones implemented in Chapter 6. The C routines in Chapter 6 worked from a source to a destination (consider, for example, copy_string). In C++, the destination object is implicit; it is the string object to which the message is being sent.

- Third, there are some cases where the class being defined must be referred to explicitly. Consider the class constructor in which a String class is passed. A copy routine is called to copy in the argument string. An explicit reference to the "current" class under definition can be made in C++ by reference to the variable this. This variable is defined to be a pointer to the current class; hence, the reference to the current class's copy routine must be made as this->copy(...).

- Finally, note how often the C code from the Chapter 6 example is useful here. In each case, the code is used after a bit of setup, which is needed to derive the required C constructs from the C++ characterization.

In C++, methods are the declaration of the functions; messages are the actual function calls. Therefore, the statement

```
str1.read();
```

from Figure 16.1 sends a message to the str1 object to activate the method associated with read.

16.3 Object-Oriented Properties

The implementation of object orientation in C++ has all the properties described in Section 14.2. We review them in this section.

Encapsulation is provided by two mechanisms in C++. First, by allowing the declaration of a class to have its own syntactic structure separate from the implementation of that class, the designers of C++ allow the state of a class to be maintained by the representation of data and member functions. Second, the separation of public and private sections allows the state to be maintained by and contained in the class structure.

Inheritance is a fundamental concept of C++ classes. One class, called the derived class, may inherit all of the specified members of another class, called the base class. For example, consider the definition of two classes, `employee` and `hourly_employee`.

```
class employee {
   public: employee ();
           ~employee ();
           void print ();
           void give_name (String);
   protected:String get_name ();
             String name ();
};

class hourly_employee : public employee
{ public:  hourly_employee ();
           ~hourly_employee ();
           void print ();
           void set_rate (float);
           float get_rate ();
   private: float rate;
};
```

In this example, `hourly_employee` is declared to be a subclass, or derived class, of `employee` by the appearance of `: public employee` in its class declaration header. This phrase indicates that `hourly_employee` inherits all the public and protected members of class `employee`. The visibility level `protected` is used for inheritance and means the protected members are accessible only to derived classes of the class in which they are defined. The protected items are, therefore, inherited by derived classes but are still not visible outside of the subclass structure. Public members, on the other hand, are accessible everywhere outside of the class, in addition to being inherited by derived classes.

In the preceding example, `hourly_employee` inherits three members of `employee, give_name, get_name,` and `name`. The class `hourly_employee` also defines `set_rate, get_rate,` and `rate` as members of the class that are not found in `employee`. The function `print` is in a third category, that of a redefined member. Therefore, `hourly_employee` does not inherit `print` from `employee`, although it is still accessible there, but rather defines a `print` function that will override the one it could have inherited.

Polymorphism is achieved in C++ by allowing the overloading of operators. Because function calls must be preceded by the object to which they belong, it is easy for the system to resolve the actual function that is being called. Therefore, if there were a String class, a Stack class, and a Queue class defined, all could have the same operation name, such as `print`, defined for them. In addition, operations with the same name may be defined with the same class, provided there is some way — either by number or type differences in the arguments — that the system could tell the functions apart and resolve the call uniquely.

C++ even allows symbolic operators to be redefined. The + operator for a string, for example, would be a nice way to express concatenation — that is,

```
s3 = s2 + "Hello World";
```

would result in the value of `s2` with `Hello World` appended being assigned to `s3`. Symbolic operators are defined as any function in C or C++, but the name of the function is the operator symbol prefixed by the word operator. That is, to define a + operator in the string class, we might express it as

```
String operator+(String, String);
```

A more sophisticated form of polymorphism is available through the declaration of virtual functions in C++, but this topic is beyond the scope of this discussion.

16.4 An Example in C++

Figures 16.3 through 16.5 list the C++ version of the class `Account` and two derived classes, `Checking` and `Savings`.

FIGURE *16.3* **C++ Declaration and Implementation of the** `Account` **Class**

```
// An Account Class -- general ops for maintaining an account

class Account {
protected:
   float balance;
   Report MonthlyReport;
   String AcctID, name;

public:
   Accounting (String);
   ~Account();

   float Balance();
   void Deposit(float, Date);
   void MonthEnd();
   void Withdraw(float, Date);
};
```

(continues)

```
// --------- The Implementation ----------------------------

Account::Account (String owner)
{
   balance = 0;
   name = owner;
   AcctID = nextID ();
}

Account::~Accounts() { balance = 0; }

float Account::Balance() { return balance; }

void Account::Deposit(float anAmount, Date date)
{
   balance = balance + anAmount;
   MonthlyReport.addline("DEP", AcctID, anAmount, date,
     balance);
}

void Account::MonthEnd()
{
   cout << MonthlyReport;
}

void Withdraw((float anAmount, Date date)
{
   if (anAmount <= balance) {
      balance = balance - anAmount;
      MonthlyReport.addline("WTH", AcctID, anAmount, date,
        balance);
   } else {
      errorReport.append("Overdrawn account");
   }
}
```

FIGURE 16.4   **C++ Declaration and Implementation of the** Checking **Class**

```
// A Checking Account
// A class based on the more generic "Account"

class Checking: public Account {
private:
   float MonthlyServiceCharge;

public:
   Checking (owner, float);
   ~Checking();
```

```
      void check(anAmount, Date);
      void MonthEnd(Date);
};

// --------- The Implementation ----------------------------

Checking::Checking(String owner, float msc)
{
   MonthlyServiceCharge = msc;
   name = owner;
   AcctID = nextID();
   balance = 0;
}

Checking::~Checking() { balance = 0; }

void Checking::check (float anAmount, Date date)
{
   Withdraw(anAmount, date);
}

void Checking::MonthEnd(Date date)
{
   Withdraw (MonthlyServiceCharge, date);
   this ->MonthEnd();
}
```

FIGURE 16.5   **C++ Declaration and Implementation of the** Savings **Class**

```
// A Savings Account
// A class based on the more generic "Account"

class Savings: public Account {
private:
   float InterestRate;

public:
   Savings(String, float);
   ~Savings();
   void MonthEnd(Date);
};

// --------- The Implementation ----------------------------

Savings::Savings(String owner, float ir)
{
   InterestRate = ir;
   name = owner;
```

(continues)

```
      AcctID = nextID();
      balance = 0;
}

Savings::~Savings() { balance = 0; }

void Savings::MonthEnd (Date date)
{
   float interest;

   interest= balance*InterestRate/12;
   Deposit(interest, date);
   this->MonthEnd();
}
```

The first thing to notice about these classes is that a "direct translation" from HOOL to C++ is not as straightforward as it was with the translation from HOOL to Smalltalk. The notion of super, or abstract, classes does not exist in C++. This notion is embedded in the idea of inheritance and of parent and child classes in a way, but it is not done exactly as in HOOL.

A second difference between HOOL and C++ is that C++ is derived much more from the imperative model than from the object-oriented model. This fact shows through in a variety of ways, including how the code is structured, how messages are sent, and how the system detects and uses classes that are already defined.

16.4.1 ▪ The Account Class

The class Account is a parent class to the Checking and Savings classes. In such a role, its definitions are inherited by the Checking and Savings classes, and some new ones are added. So we need some basic, general methods and variables in this parent class, leaving the child classes to define elements specific to those classes.

Note that the Account class has a constructor/destructor pair and then has four member functions. The private data stored with Account are composed of a balance, a monthly report of type Report (presumably predefined), and two variables of type String: the ID of the account and the name of the person who owns the account. Again, note that these are private and inaccessible to functions that are not members of this class.

The four member functions are defined in the class construct and then implemented. Note that two Report member functions are assumed. The first is addline and is used by Deposit and Withdraw. The second is harder to find. Note the only line in the implementation of MonthEnd is

```
cout << MonthlyReport;
```

In C++, the << operator is an output operator; it sends the object on its right to the output descriptor on its left. Cout is the predefined C++ descriptor for screen output. However, the << operator must be defined for whatever object is being printed. We assume it is defined for Report objects.

16.4.2 ▪ The Checking Class

Figure 16.4 defines the Checking class as a subclass of the Account class. It inherits members of the Account class — note that the "private" are declared to be "protected" there — and adds some elements of its own.

The only data element that is necessary is a new variable, MonthlyServiceCharge. This element should be set when the account is created, and so its assignment is included in the Checking class constructor.

Three member functions are added. These are the Checking class constructor, which adds the assignment of MonthlyServiceCharge to the functionality of the parent's constructor, the Checking class destructor, and a function to write checks.

A member function from the parent is refined. The MonthEnd function must include a deduction of the service charge. Yet, this functionality is to be *added* to the original, parent functionality. Note how this is done. Even though the name MonthEnd is overloaded, the parent function by that name is available by having no arguments, whereas the one from the Checking class has a single argument. Therefore, calling the parent MonthEnd after doing the withdrawal of the service charge does not cause a name conflict. (Note that the parent function would still be accessible even if the number of arguments were the same, but the syntax to access it would be confusing. This way is easier.)

16.4.3 ▪ The Savings Class

The Savings class is defined in Figure 16.5. Instead of a monthly service charge, we now need to calculate the interest every month. Therefore, in the spirit of the design of the Checking class, a new variable is added (InterestRate), a constructor/destructor pair is added, and the MonthEnd function is overloaded to provide a way to add the interest at the end of the month.

C H A P T E R ***16***   **Terms**

member functions	class constructor
implementation	class destruction

C H A P T E R ***16***   **Discussion Questions**

1. Compare C++ and HOOL. How are they similar? How are they different? Do this especially with the notion of a "class" and an "instance of a class." How can we differentiate class and instance variables in C++?

2. Compare C++ and Smalltalk. Look for differences and similarities. As with HOOL, look especially to abstract classes.

3. C++ encourages reuse of classes by allowing separate compilation of separate files and separate specification of declaration and implementation files. These are compiled into object files and linked into an executable sometime later. Compare this to Ada, which encourages reuse by entering modules into a library, or Smalltalk, which adds the definition to the current working space.

4. C++ relies heavily on C for its foundational structure. As stated in Section 16.1, most C++ compilers start out with a translator (called `cfront`) to turn C++ code into C. Evaluate this design decision. How could this be a big advantage? How could this be a big disadvantage?

5. How does C++ deal with multiple inheritance? Is it permissible?

6. C++ and Ada have similar features. For instance, both utilize overloading and both separate the definition and implementation of data objects. Yet, Ada is not considered object-oriented, but C++ is. What makes C++ object-oriented? What does Ada lack?

7. Classify the object construction and instantiation in C++ as a dynamic or static binding. What are the advantages of the approach you chose over the other approach? Compare this to the Smalltalk question you answered in the last chapter.

C H A P T E R *16* Exercises

1. Consider a C++ class called `Fraction` that implements a fraction as composed of a denominator and a numerator, both of type integer. Specify the declaration of the `Fraction` class. Include operators +, -, *, and / and relation <. Define operators numerator and denominator. Pay attention to how the fraction is initialized.

2. Define the `Fraction` class implementation of the operations in Exercise 1.

3. Define a nonmember function call `reciprocal` as follows:

```
float reciprocal(Fraction frac) { ... };
```

4. Based on the preceding definition of `Fraction`, how would one express each of the following?

   a. a fraction whose value is 3/7
   b. a fraction whose value is 3 3/8
   c. an if statement that tests if fraction f1 is less than f2

5. Write the C++ specification for the class `Precise` as you did in previous chapter exercises.

6. Add code to the examples in Sections 16.3 through 16.5 to implement the superclass and abstract class notions of HOOL and Smalltalk. Specifically, implement the `TotalBalance` and `NumberOfAccts` variables and the routine `reportTotals`. (*Hint:* You may need a data structure to hold various accounts.)

7. Design the class hierarchy for the AVLtree specified in Chapter 14 exercises in C++. Was the hierarchy different than for Smalltalk?

8. Design a `Precise` class, a class of floating-point numbers with unlimited precision, in C++.

9. Write the specifications for collections taken for granted in most languages: collections like arrays, records, and sets. Again, compare this to the answers you gave for Smalltalk.

C H A P T E R **16**   **Laboratory Exercises**

1. Write a program to test your specification and implementation of `Fraction`. Make sure you test `reciprocal` and all the operators.

2. Write a `Stack` class in C++ and implement it. Write a test program to test the operations.

3. Write a `Queue` class in C++ and implement it. Write a test program to test the operations.

4. In C++, implement the AVLtree class specified by your hierarchy in Exercise 7.

5. Likewise, implement the `Precise` class you designed in Exercise 8.

6. Redefine your class definitions of `Stack` and `Queue` that you implemented above as templates, such that they could be used with any data type. What changes did you make from the previous implementations?

An Overview of the Distributed Parallel Model

The distributed parallel model for programming is described in this chapter. The language considerations for defining and invoking parallel processes are presented and methods for communication between processes are studied. In addition, approaches to the synchronization of activities in parallel processes are discussed.

17.1 Introduction to the Distributed Parallel Model

Thus far we have viewed a program as a sequential process, working on exactly one task at a time, performing several tasks in sequence, one after another. In this section, we introduce the concept of **concurrency** — that is, the ability to do several processes at once — and discuss the manner in which concurrency can be represented in a programming language.

There are several actual processor configurations used to provide concurrent execution capabilities. **Multiprogramming** is the configuration used by a time-sharing system. Here, a single processor is shared by a number of processes, with the processes executing alternately under control of the operating system. **Multiprocessing** requires that separate processors be available so that multiple processes can each be executing on its own processor, exhibiting true simultaneous operation. All processors share a common memory, which can be used as a communication medium between the processes. **Distributed processing** also requires separate processors, but here each processor has its own memory. Distributed processors are connected via communication lines, such as an ethernet network.

For the purpose of our discussion of programming language features, the configuration used to implement concurrency is irrelevant. The language will provide an abstract method for viewing and implementing concurrency that can be implemented on any of the three configurations, although some language constructs fit more easily into one configuration than the others.

Concurrent units can be compared to procedural abstraction. Like procedures and functions, they are units of abstraction having their own, often sequential, definition. Like procedures and functions, their use in a program enhances the modularity and level of abstraction in a program by defining their own unit of binding and scope. Concurrent units are more general than procedures and functions, because they have their own thread of control that is independent of any "caller," or invoking mechanism. However, because of the closeness of the procedural and concurrent unit abstractions, concurrent units require all the same considerations as other procedural abstractions — namely, definition, invocation, and data sharing.

In any case, the major distinguishing feature is that once it is invoked, the invoking unit can proceed with its execution without waiting for the invoked unit to be completed, as illustrated in Figure 17.1. Therefore, in addition to the preceding considerations, two further considerations with concurrent units are the need for communication between concurrent units and the need to synchronize concurrent executions with respect to shared resources.

FIGURE **17.1**   **Concurrent Threads of Control**

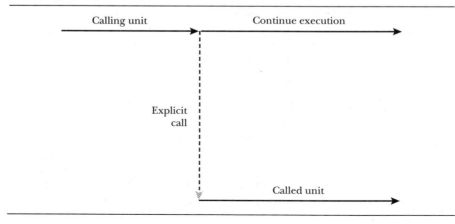

17.2 Concurrent Unit Definition

There are three primary models for the definition of concurrent units. The first follows the construct of the procedure definition with a definition by declaration. When the concurrent unit is declared, a binding is made between the name and the executable body. The unit can then be invoked concurrently by an appropriate reference to its name.

The second model for definition of concurrent units is that of a type. In this model, the definition creates a type rather than a process. Variables that are declared to be of that type are then bindings of names to executable units, and multiple executions of the same process type can be referenced by their distinct names.

The third model of concurrent unit definition is that of an in-line definition. Here, the definition of the concurrent unit takes the form of a new control structure in the language, using special syntax to designate a set of statements to execute concurrently.

For example, consider the program fragments in Figure 17.2. Parts (a) and (b) are written in Ada; part (c) is written in Concurrent Pascal (Brinch Hansen 1978). The major difference between parts (a) and (b) is when the process `array_sum` is started. In part (a), it is started when the procedure is called; no further control over when the process begins its execution is afforded to the procedure. In part (b), the task begins when the variable is declared, giving the procedure a small amount of control over when the task executes. In part (c), each pass of the loop is started in parallel with the other passes. These passes are started together when the enclosing procedure executes the `cobegin`. The enclosing procedure pauses for the conclusion of each pass at the `coend`.

These syntactic and semantic differences between parts (a) and (b) and part (c) result in a difference in the grain of concurrency. In Ada, concurrency is at the block level, allowing blocks of statements to execute concurrently with each other but sequentially within each block. In Concurrent Pascal, concurrency is at the statement level. Each statement between the `cobegin` and the `coend` statements executes in parallel. This means that the `sum :=` `sum + array[i]` statements in the `for` loop will run concurrently with each other. (Note that this fine grain of concurrency will more than likely cause the variable sum to be updated incorrectly. See Section 17.4 for the reason.)

17.3 Invocation of Concurrent Units

The invocation of concurrent units can either be implicit or explicit. Implicit invocation assumes that the concurrent process belongs to the program unit in which it is defined. Whenever a program unit begins execution, all concurrent units that belong to that unit (i.e., are defined in that unit) begin their execution simultaneously. When the master unit terminates, it will wait until all its concurrent units terminate before it returns to its invoking unit.

```
a.    procedure total () is
          sum: integer;
          task array_sum;
          task body array_sum is
             begin
                 sum := 0;
                 for i in (1..10) loop
                     sum := sum + arr(i);
                 end loop;
             end array_sum;
          begin
             -- task begins now!
             null;
          end total;

b.    procedure total () is
          sum: integer;
          task type array_sum;
          task body array_sum is
             begin
                 for i in (1..10) loop
                     sum := sum + arr(i);
                 end loop;
             end array_sum;
          begin
             sum := 0;
             declare
                 process: array_sum;
             end declare;
             -- task begins now!
          end total;

c.    procedure total;
          var sum, i: integer;
          begin
             sum := 0;
             cobegin
                 for i := 1 to 10 do
                     sum := sum + arr[i];
             coend;
          end;
```

This implicit invocation process is illustrated in Figure 17.3. Ada employs implicit invocation semantics.

Concurrent units that are invoked explicitly are invoked in one of two ways. For units declared explicitly as procedures or as types, their invocation

FIGURE 17.3   **Implicit Invocation of Concurrent Units**

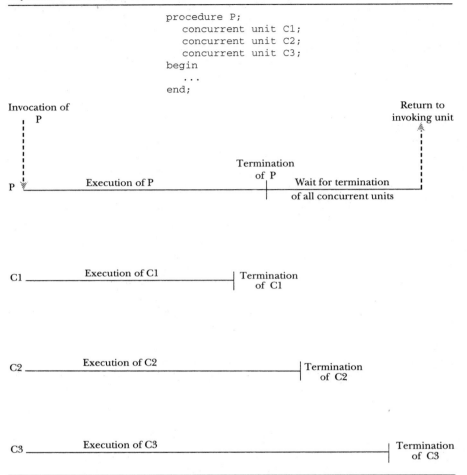

```
procedure P;
    concurrent unit C1;
    concurrent unit C2;
    concurrent unit C3;
begin
    ...
end;
```

is just like that for procedures — that is, as a statement abstraction through reference to the name to which the unit is bound by its definition. For units declared in-line, invocation is, by definition, explicit, accomplished through the special syntax of the statement declaration in the unit construction. Both these methods permit invocation of the concurrent unit at any point within the program unit in which it is defined.

Most methods of invoking a process have a **fork-join** type of behavior. The invoking master unit "forks" the invoked processes, splitting its own thread of control into multiple threads and becoming a process itself as it executes its own sequential code. When it completes its own parallel execution, it must wait for the "join" of its child processes — that is, the termination of these processes — before it can continue further sequential execution.

_____ *17.4*   <u>**Data Sharing**</u>

It is frequently necessary for concurrently executing units to share data with each other. Two models are commonly used to accomplish this. The first is the use of shared memory. This method is discussed in this section. The second model for data sharing, through information passing from one unit to another, is discussed in the next section.

When multiple concurrent units share memory, data exist that are global to all units in the sense that several units have access to that data. These data typically take the form of variables that all units can access or data structures held in memory for all units to use.

This type of sharing is illustrated in Figure 17.4 by Concurrent Pascal syntax. The example is made up of two concurrent units, P1 and P2, each of which uses the global variable N. It is important to note that the results of the program execution can vary, depending on the timings of the executions of the concurrent units. If the sequence is P1 followed by P2, then N results in the value 6. But, consider the sequence in Figure 17.5. Here P1 is executing N:=N+1 at exactly the same time that P2 is executing N:=N+2, and the result value is not the expected 6, but rather 4.

Figure 17.5 illustrates a potential problem that affects all concurrent units that share memory. Access conflict can occur when concurrent access of shared data is allowed. Thus, such access needs to be done with care, because it could lead to inaccurate results and affect the rest of the program's execution. The

FIGURE 17.4   **Concurrent Pascal Program Illustrating the Dangers of Data Sharing**

```
program Concurrent;
   var N : integer;

   concurrent unit P1;
   begin
      N := N + 1;
   end;

   concurrent unit P2;
   begin
      N := N + 2;
   end;

begin

   N := 3;
   cobegin
      P1;
      P2;
   coend;
   writeln(N);
end.
```

FIGURE **17.5**   **Execution of the Program in Figure 17.4**

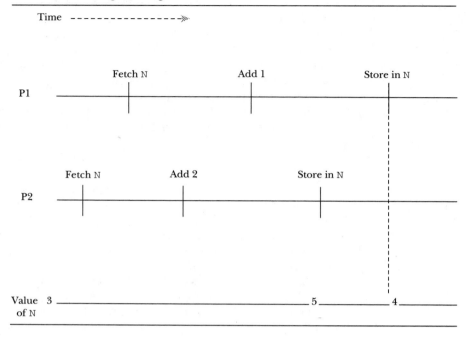

Time - - - - - - - - - - - - - - - -⫸

prevention of this kind of problem with shared variables is one of the major applications of synchronization, explained in Section 17.5.

Finally, examine the program in Figure 17.2(c). In Section 17.1, we explained that Concurrent Pascal's *grain of concurrency* is at the statement level, which means each pass of the for loop executes in parallel. Let's say that each pass performs the following sequence of statements to execute the loop's addition:

```
read sum
read arr[i]
add sum and arr[i]
write the result to sum
```

Now, if each pass were to perform each of the preceding steps at exactly the same time, the final result would write sum + arr[10] to sum, not what you might expect. Because of its grain of parallelism, Concurrent Pascal is particularly susceptible to this kind of data corruption.

17.5   Interprocess Communication

The second way that data is shared is through information passing from one unit to another, a method typically referred to as **interprocess communication** (IPC). We discuss IPC separately from shared memory, although a shared variable provides a very simple way for concurrent units to communicate. As with all ways of exchanging information, IPC requires a message sender and receiver. The different ways these two work together on exchanging the message result in two models for passing information between concurrent units: the mail model and the phone model. The difference between these two models lies in whether or not the receiving unit needs to attend to the message before the sending unit may proceed.

Under the mail model, information is sent by unit S to unit R and placed in a mailbox. Unit S can then proceed with its execution and unit R can come and retrieve the message at any later time. If more than one message is sent to the same mailbox, the messages are usually queued up within the mailbox so that unit R can successively retrieve messages until the mailbox is empty.

There are three ways that the mailbox might be identified, providing three different versions of the mail model. These three ways are distinguished by the way in which communication takes place and are illustrated in Figure 17.6. The many-to-one version is analogous to the way a typical post office mailbox operates, with messages arriving from any of a number of processes but destined for only one specific process. Therefore, the sender specifies the receiver of the message, but the receiver retrieves messages without needing to specify the sender.

The one-to-one version accepts messages from exactly one sender. Here the sender not only must specify the receiver, but when the receiver retrieves the message, it must specify the identity of the sender as well. A given mailbox then is identified with both the sending and the receiving processes. This situation is similar to a mailbox used to pass information from a boss to a secretary, where all messages come from the same sender and all go to the same receiver.

The many-to-many version accepts messages from many processes, and these messages may be retrieved by many processes. A sending process therefore places the message in the mailbox without specifying whom the receiver is to be. The next process to retrieve from that mailbox is then the receiving process. This is similar to a mailbox in an office with many bosses and many secretaries, where a boss puts a job to be done in a mailbox and the next available secretary retrieves the message from the box and does the job specified.

Under the mail model, the sender simply sends the message and does not wait for message receipt. The second model for passing information, the phone model, requires that the sending unit wait for the receiving unit to accept the message before proceeding. This is analogous to placing a phone call, where the caller must wait for the person called to respond before the message can be sent. The phone model is also known as the rendezvous model, where two people meet together at a prearranged location to pass information. By its nature, the phone, or rendezvous, model also synchronizes the two processes, because they must wait to make a simultaneous contact for the message to be sent.

There are two forms of the phone model, each with different views of waiting. In the first form, the sender waits for notification from the receiver only that the message had been received, and upon this notification, both units

FIGURE 17.6   **Three Types of Mailboxes for Concurrent Communication**

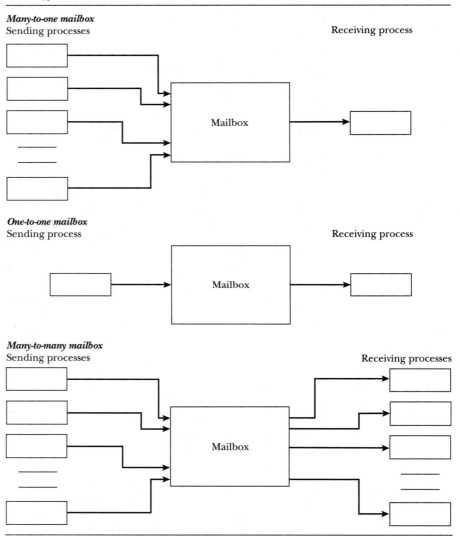

continue with their concurrent execution. In the second form, the sender waits for both message receipt and message processing. This second version of the phone model is similar to a procedure call; the caller calls the procedure, sending parameters, and must wait until this procedure returns, possibly with modified parameters. The analogy is so strong, in fact, that this second form of the phone model is typically referred to as a **remote procedure call** (RPC).

As with the mail model, the phone model might be one-to-many, one-to-one, or many-to-many.

17.6 Synchronization

Two processes that are executing concurrently frequently need to be synchronized. Often, this is necessary if several processes share the same resource, but only one can access the resource at a time. This is called **mutual exclusion**, an example of which is a set of processes accessing the same data. In order to protect the integrity of the data, only one process at a time should be permitted access to the data. We illustrated a problem with the lack of mutual exclusion in Figure 17.5.

In other situations, one process may need to wait until another process has completed some operation on a shared resource before the first process can proceed. This is called **mutual dependency**. An example of mutual dependency is one process collecting data while another operates on it. This case illustrates a pipeline, where the latter process should not be permitted to begin its operational activity until the collecting process has "filled the pipe" with sufficient data.

There are two common general approaches used by programming languages to specify the synchronization of processes. We will call these the *token* and the *gate* approaches.

The token approach makes use of a hypothetical token, which only one process may possess at a time. There are two operations, get-token and replace-token. If a process P executes a get-token command on token T and the token is not presently possessed by any other process, process P becomes the owner of T. If token T is already owned by some other process, then process P is suspended and must wait until the token is available again. Usually, when several processes are waiting for a token, they are placed in a queue, so the earliest arriving process gets possession of the token first. The process that possesses the token can execute a replace-token command, giving the token to the next process on the queue and permitting it to proceed. If there is no process on the queue, the token then becomes available.

The token approach can be used to implement mutual exclusion in a natural way. A token is associated with each shared resource. When a process wishes to use the resource, it asks for the resource's token with a get-token command. When a process has possession of the token, it has exclusive permission to use the resource. During the time a process has possession of the resource, any other process issuing a get-token command will be placed on a queue to await its turn to use the resource. After a process is finished with the resource, it makes the token available again through a replace-token command. Therefore, ownership of the token represents permission to access the shared resource.

The token approach can also be used to implement mutual dependency. Here the procedure performing the required activity on the shared resource will take the token and not replace it until that activity is completed to the point where the other process may proceed. The dependent process will request the token before proceeding to the part of its task that requires that the activity of the other process be completed.

The gate approach to synchronization works as follows. A hypothetical gate exists, which blocks the execution of a process. That process may proceed beyond the gate only if some other process comes along and opens the gate.

Gate synchronization is based on two primitive commands: wait and open. When a process executes a wait command, it will wait at the gate until the gate is opened, after which it may proceed with its execution. If other processes are presently waiting at the gate, this process joins them at the rear of a queue.

When a process executes an open command, it permits the process at the front of the queue to proceed and the rest of the queue to move up one position. After a single process passes through the gate, the gate recloses until another open is executed. If no process is waiting when the open command is reached, no action is taken. The gate simply swings open and then immediately recloses with no process passing through. In any case, the process executing the open command continues execution.

The gate synchronization allows for direct implementation of mutual dependency, with the dependent process executing a wait and the other process executing an open when the required activity is completed. The implementation of mutual exclusion requires the presence of a Boolean primitive that we call *waiting*, which is true if at least one process is waiting for the gate to open and false if none are waiting. A mutual exclusion can then be implemented by polling gate G and by including the following template in each participating process:

```
if busy(G) then wait(G);
mutually exclusive actions;
open(G);
```

As we mentioned in the last section, an additional form of synchronization is automatically implemented by the rendezvous version of the phone model of information passing, which requires the sending and receiving processes to synchronize before the message can be sent. We will examine this further in the next chapter, because it is the method used by Ada.

There are many languages with more concurrent features. We see two language examples in the next two chapters: Ada in Chapter 18 and Occam in Chapter 19.

C H A P T E R *17*   Terms

concurrency	interprocess communication
multiprogramming	remote procedure call
multiprocessing	mutual exclusion
distributed processing	mutual dependency
fork-join behavior	

CHAPTER **17**   Discussion Questions

1. What types of problems are best solved with a concurrent solution? What types of problems are best solved with a sequential solution?

2. Is there a type of problem to which the mail model applies more than the phone model?

3. At several places in concurrent processing, a queue is used. For example, messages that are passed under the mail model may be queued, and processes waiting to synchronize may be queued. Examine the possibility of making these priority queues, where the originating process assigns a priority to the activity that is queried. How might this be useful? How might this be implemented?

4. An additional problem can arise in the token approach to the mutual exclusion problem. If two processes request the token simultaneously and the token is a shared resource, there may be an associated mutual exclusion problem in accessing the token. Describe how this might happen and how it could be prevented.

5. Some languages — Ada is one of them — allow parallel features to be used regardless of the type of processor, even on uniprocessors. Discuss how this is possible. What is required of the implementation? Would this be easier if the operating system were multitasking?

6. In what situations are task types a useful concept? How would these situations be more difficult with a language without task types?

CHAPTER **17**   Exercises

1. Describe how you would simulate the gate approach to synchronization using only the token operations.

2. Describe how you would simulate the token approach to synchronization using only gate operations.

3. Divide-and-conquer algorithms can be nicely implemented concurrently. Describe how a concurrent quicksort might be written using any of the models introduced in this chapter.

4. One way to implement the token model is to have a variable called a semaphore mimic the action of the token. If the variable is 0, any process may take the token; it must make that variable value 1 to indicate the token is in use.

    a. Write a program in Concurrent Pascal demonstrating this concept.

    b. As mentioned in the discussion questions, the semaphore is itself a shared resource and is subject to the same mutual exclusion problems as other shared resources. Write a program in Concurrent Pascal to illustrate this.

    c. Can you write a section of code that guarantees mutual exclusion — both for a critical section *and* for semaphores used?

C H A P T E R **17**   **Laboratory Exercises**

For each of the following problems, use the language of your choice or simply design an algorithm.

1. Determine the IPC mechanism your language is using and write a program to demonstrate it.

2. Can you "simulate" other IPC mechanisms in your language? If you can demonstrate how to do this, write some demonstration programs.

3. A classic problem in concurrency is the *dining philosophers problem*, first suggested by E. W. Dijkstra in a paper published in 1971. The problem goes something like this:

> Five philosophers wish to philosophize together. As they philosophize, they also must eat to keep their strength up (thinking is a taxing activity). Thus, each goes through a cycle of eating and thinking, continually and asynchronously. Consider a table such as the one shown for the philosophers:

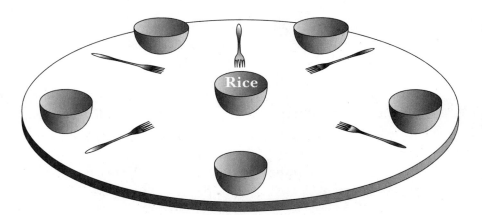

    Five bowls and five chopsticks (or, in another version, forks) are arranged alternately around a circular table. Each philosopher has his or her own place at the table. The center bowl of rice is continually replenished. To eat, each philosopher needs two forks. Only the two forks on either side of the bowl may be used. A fork may be used by only one philosopher at a time. The problem is to coordinate the use of the forks so that no philosopher dies of starvation.

    This problem neatly exemplifies many problems and solutions found in concurrent situations:

Deadlock can easily occur. If all philosophers pick up the left fork together, they will all wait for their neighbors to relinquish the other fork they require. They will all die waiting.

Starvation can occur. If two philosophers conspire against another, even if cooperation to avoid deadlock exists, philosophers can starve — not even get the chance to eat.

Mutual exclusion/synchronization is exemplified by the rule that no two philosophers may use a fork together. The one-at-a-time rule requires synchronization.

Implement a solution to the dining philosophers problem.

4. Another classic problem is the *producer-consumer problem.* For this problem, two processes, a·producer and a consumer, execute concurrently. The producer produces data one element at a time and places each element into a buffer of size *n.* The consumer retrieves elements one at a time from the buffer in the same order they were placed there by the producer.

    Implement a solution to this problem in your language and then add a twist: a "bucket-brigade" version. This version has a producer, a consumer, and an "intermediary" — a process that consumes from one queue and produces for another, as shown in the following diagram.

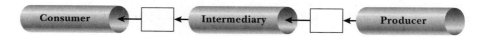

    Your "producer" may be very simple — such as producing a sequence of numbers. Your consumer should display the results that are retrieved from the queue. Your intermediary does not need to produce any output, although you will probably need some for debugging purposes.

5. Write a program that demonstrates the corruption of data through poor implementation of data-sharing protection. Then correct your program and demonstrate that your corrected version protects the data properly.

6. Does your language use the token or gate model for synchronization? Write a program to illustrate the *other* method.

Concurrent Units in Ada

In past chapters, we have used the language Ada as a vehicle for many examples. Ada was designed with concurrency as a foundational concept; thus, Ada provides concurrency model examples as well. Because of its design, Ada has more extensive concurrency capabilities than most other imperative languages. In this chapter, these facilities are described in the context of the models in the preceding chapter. We also examine extensions that Ada provides beyond the basic models.

_18.1_ Concurrent Unit Definition

In Ada, concurrent units are called **tasks**. Tasks are defined in the declarative part of a program unit in much the same manner as packages — that is, in two parts, the specification and the body. The specification gives the name of the task and specifies all points in the task body where interprocess communication can occur. These communication points, called *entries*, are declared along with their formal parameters. Entries are described later.

The task body is like any other program unit, consisting of a declarative part for locally defined objects and an executable part containing a sequence of statements. A task completes execution like any other unit and can have exception handlers appended.

In Ada, the definition of a task determines a task type of the specified name that can then be bound to variables in the containing program unit. When the word type is omitted from the task specification, a single task with the assigned name is created, and no variable declaration is required. Figure 18.1 gives an example of two sections of Ada code, yielding the same declarative results: two tasks, each with three entries. Thus, Ada permits both the procedure and the type model for task definition.

18.2 Invocation of Concurrent Units

The invocation of an Ada task is implicit. All task variables defined in the declarative part of a program unit (called the **master unit**) begin execution simultaneously with the master. The master unit may be a block, a procedure, or a function.

FIGURE 18.1 **Examples of Different Task Declarations**

a.
```
task type Bank_Task is
    entry deposit (acct: in accounts; amount: in real);
    entry withdrawl (acct: in accounts; amount: in real);
    entry balance (acct: in accounts; amount: out real);
end Bank_Task;

task body Bank_Task is
    -- task definition is skipped
end Bank_Task;

First_National, National_Bank_of_Detroit: Bank_Task;
```

b.
```
task First_National is
    entry deposit (acct: in accounts; amount: in real);
    entry withdrawl (acct: in accounts; amount: in real);
    entry balance (acct: in accounts; amount: out real);
end Bank_Task;

task body First_National is
    -- task definition is skipped
end Bank_Task;

task National_Bank_of_Detroit is
    entry deposit (acct: in accounts; amount: in real);
    entry withdrawl (acct: in accounts; amount: in real);
    entry balance (acct: in accounts; amount: out real);
end Bank_Task;

task body National_Bank_of_Detroit is
    -- task definition is skipped
end Bank_Task;
```

Ada tasks can be invoked explicitly but only by relying on the explicit semantics of other language features and not those of task invocation. Consider the code in Figure 18.1(a). The following declaration declares a pointer to a task instance:

```
Bank_of_Fargo: access Bank_Task;
```

Note that the pointer has not yet been instantiated, so no task instance yet exists. It now takes a statement such as

```
Bank_of_Fargo := new Bank_Task;
```

to instantiate the task and start its execution. Note that, although we appear to have explicitly controlled the invocation of a task, we have actually relied on the explicit semantics of pointer data creation to start the task.

Ada uses **fork-join semantics** for process invocation. The master will not complete its termination until all its concurrent tasks have terminated. Therefore, if the master unit completes all its statements but some of its member tasks are still active, it will wait until all these tasks terminate before it proceeds with normal termination and returns to its invoking unit.

18.3   Data Sharing

Data can be shared among tasks in Ada through the use both of shared memory and of interprocess communication. Shared memory is employed through the use of global variables. Because tasks share the same environment as their master program unit, they have access to all data that are in the environment of the master. Accessing shared data needs to be done with care, however, because the order in which different tasks will access the data is undetermined unless some form of synchronization is used. Ada provides a weak mechanism for protecting shared variables. This protection takes the form of a pragma. **Pragmas** in Ada are compiler directives that may vary from one implementation to the next. The pragma "SHARED_VARIABLE_UPDATE" can be used to specify which variables need protection from corruption by concurrent tasks.

18.4   Interprocess Communication

The preferred form of data sharing is through the IPC mechanism, or **entries**. Ada uses the semantics of the remote procedure call to implement IPC; entry behavior is similar to many-to-one communication under the phone model. Entries have parameters that are passed in the same way that procedure parameters are passed, with the three modes of IN, OUT, and IN OUT. An entry is called by specifying the destination task, the entry name, and the actual parameters, much like calling a procedure. The destination task requests an entry by an accept statement, which receives the parameters that can then be used in the block of statements associated with the accept statement. As with procedures, the communication can be in either or both directions, depending on the mode of the parameters.

The synchronization associated with entries is the phone model approach described in Section 17.4. The calling task places the call to a specific task. If that task is presently waiting at an **accept statement** for the called entry, the two tasks **rendezvous**, the called task executes the statements attached to the accept statement, and then both tasks proceed with their executions. If the called task is not presently waiting at a matching accept statement, the calling task is placed on a queue to wait for a rendezvous.

Consider the example of the two tasks shown in Figure 18.2. The tasks are called ONE and TWO, with ONE calling the entry MEET, which is declared in task TWO. The action of task ONE is to calculate X using procedure CALCULATE, synchronize with TWO at MEET, sending X and getting back Y, and then use X and Y in procedure USE_IT. ONE will wait at its call to MEET until TWO reaches its accept statement. Task TWO will get a value of Z from procedure OBTAIN and then accept a call to MEET. If ONE has not yet called MEET, TWO will suspend until the call is placed. When the synchronization occurs, ONE is suspended and MEET takes in the value for formal parameter A. After calculating values for formal parameter B and local variable Z, the processing of MEET terminates. At this time, the value of formal parameter B is sent to actual parameter Y in ONE, ONE resumes execution at its call to USE_IT, and TWO resumes execution with its call to DISPLAY.

FIGURE **18.2** **An Example of Ada Tasks**

```
task ONE;

task body ONE is
    X,Y : integer;
begin
    CALCULATE(X);
    TWO.MEET(X,Y);
    USE_IT(X,Y);
end ONE;

task TWO is
    entry MEET(A : in integer; B : out integer);
end TWO;

task body TWO is
    Z : integer;
begin
    OBTAIN(Z);
    accept MEET(A : in integer; B : out integer) do
        B := FN1(A,Z);
        Z := FN2(A,Z);
    end MEET;
    DISPLAY(Z);
end TWO;
```

Figure 18.3 illustrates the interaction of a task with its master unit. This program will result in the integer values from 1 to 10 being printed, but not necessarily in order. The integers 1 to 5 will appear in increasing order, as will the integers 6 to 10, but the two lists will be merged in the output in an indeterminate manner. For example, one run of the program in Figure 18.3 produced the output

```
1 6 7 2 3 8 9 4 5 10
```

18.5 Synchronization

The same mechanism that implements interprocess communication in Ada also implements synchronization. Because the accept statement can work with a code block or without a code block, it can implement both forms of the phone model in Section 17.4, and it implements the gate mode from Section 17.5. Figure 18.4 contains an Ada program that illustrates the synchronization facilities of Ada entries.

FIGURE 18.3   **An Example Ada Interaction of Task with Master Unit**

```
with TEXT_IO; use TEXT_IO;
procedure TEST_TASKS is

    package INT_IO is new INTEGER_IO (integer);
    use INT_IO;

    task TEST;

    task body TEST is
       COUNT : integer;
       begin
          for COUNT in 1..5 loop
             put(COUNT);
             new_line;
          end loop;
       end test;

    begin

       for MAIN_COUNT in 6..10 loop
          put(MAIN_COUNT);
          new_line;
       end loop;

end TEST_TASKS;
```

FIGURE 18.4 **An Example Ada Program Synchronizing Facilities of Entries**

```
with TEXT_IO; use TEXT_IO;
procedure TASKS3 is

--Two tasks, each with one entry

    task T1 is
        entry t1_entry;
    end T1;

    task T2 is
        entry t2_entry;
    end T2;

    task body T1 is
        begin
            put_line("In T1: before first accept.");
            accept t1_entry do
                put_line("In T1: in first accept.");
            end t1_entry;
            accept t1_entry do
                put_line("In T1: in second accept.");
            end t1_entry;
            put_line("In T1: terminating.");
        end T1;

    task body T2 is
        begin
            put_line("In T2: before first accept.");
            accept t2_entry do
                put_line("In T2: accepting the entry.");
            end t2_entry;
            T1.t2_entry;
            put_line("In T2: terminating.");
        end T2;

begin
-- Main program. At this point, the main program
-- and its two tasks begin execution concurrently.

    put_line("In main: before calling T2.");
    T2.t2_entry;
    put_line("In main: after calling T2.");

    put_line("In main: before calling T1.");
    T1.t1_entry;
    put_line("In main: after calling T1.");

    --Terminate, waiting for tasks to terminate.
    put_line("In main: terminating.");
end TASKS3;
```

(continues)

Output from preceding Ada Program:

```
In T2: before first accept.
In T1: before first accept.
In main: before calling T2.
In T2: accepting the entry.
In T1: in first accept.
In main: after calling T2.
In main: after calling T1.
In T1: in second accept.
In T1: terminating.
In T2: terminating.
In main: after calling T1.
In main: terminating.
```

In fact, Ada extends the gate model to include the monitoring of multiple gates in its implementation of mutual exclusion. This powerful feature in Ada is implemented through the use of **selective waits** to accept one from a number of pending synchronizations. This feature is rather complex, and we do not attempt to describe all of its capabilities here. We instead examine the basic structure of the selective wait and its use of guarded commands.

First we examine the unguarded selective wait. In this case, a task is waiting for any of several accept statements to be called. This is similar to a receptionist waiting for any of several phones to ring. When one does ring, the receptionist responds to that phone. If two or more ring simultaneously, the receptionist chooses one at random to answer. Similarly, the select statement permits a task to wait on all of several different accepts to be called. When one is called, its associated handler is executed, and the task continues executing beyond the select. If more than one is called simultaneously, one of the called accepts is chosen in an indeterminate manner. The form of the select is

```
select
    accept MEET_1 do
        HANDLE_1;
    end MEET_1;
or
    accept MEET_2 do
        HANDLE_2;
    end MEET_2;
or
    accept MEET_3 do
        HANDLE_3;
    end MEET_3;
end select;
```

This construct will wait until at least one of the accept alternatives is called. If none of the alternatives is called, it will wait forever. Ada provides a way to avoid this situation by expressing one of the alternatives as a DELAY. Consider the following example:

```
select
   accept MEET_1 do
      HANDLE_1;
   end MEET_1;
or
   delay 1.0;
   HANDLE_2;
end select;
```

This construct will wait up to one second for MEET_1 to be called. If it has not been called by that time, HANDLE_2 will be executed, and the task will proceed beyond the select. A special case of DELAY is ELSE which has the same effect as DELAY 0.0. This is chosen by the select construct if none of the accepts have a call pending at the time the select begins execution.

Ada also permits **guards** to be placed on alternative conditions in a selective wait. To understand the role of guards, let us return to our example of the receptionist handling multiple phones. Some of the phones may have conditions placed on them, specifying when they are to be connected and when they are to be disconnected. For example, Phone 1 may need to be connected only on Mondays, phone 2 is connected only on the first day of the month, and phone 3 is connected only when the Dow Jones average is greater than 3400. When the receptionist comes to work, he or she first determines which phones to connect by evaluating each of the guard conditions. The receptionist then operates as above, handling the first phone that rings, choosing a phone at random if two or more ring simultaneously. Of course, the disconnected phones can be ignored, because they will never ring. If it ever happens that all the phones are disconnected, we consider that an exceptional condition, because the receptionist can then go home.

The Ada representation of the preceding situation is expressed by the following guarded select statement:

```
select
   when day_of_week = MONDAY =>
      accept PHONE_1 do
         HANDLE_1;
      end PHONE_1;
or
   when day_of_month = 1 =>
      accept PHONE_2 do
         HANDLE_2;
      end PHONE_2;
or
   when DOW_JONES > 3400 =>
      accept PHONE_3 do
         HANDLE_3;
      end PHONE_3;
end select;
```

The guard conditions are evaluated just once, when the select statement begins. These evaluations determine the open alternatives. The first alternative called that has an open guard is then handled, with the choice being made at random if more than one is called simultaneously. If all guards are false and an `else` alternative has not been specified, a `PROGRAM_ERROR` exception is raised.

Entry calls may be timed in Ada as well. This construct also utilizes the keyword `select`. For example,

```
select
    TASK_1.MEET_1;
or
    delay 5.0;
    NO_ANSWER_ACTION;
end select;
```

will wait 5 seconds for `TASK_1` to execute an accept for entry `MEET_1`. If this does not occur, procedure `NO_ANSWER_ACTION` will be invoked, and the task will proceed to the statements following the select. This is analogous to placing a phone call and hanging up if nobody answers in 5 seconds.

A delay of 0 seconds can be expressed by

```
select
    TASK_1.MEET_1;
else
    NO_ANSWER_ACTION;
end select;
```

This will invoke `NO_ANSWER_ACTION` if `TASK_1` is not waiting at an accept for `MEET_1` at the time the entry call is made.

A summary of the syntax of Ada concurrency is given next:

```
Concurrency
Language: Ada

    task specification ::=  task [type] <identifier> [is
                                {<entry-declaration>}
                            end [<identifier>] ];


    task-body ::=    task body <identifier> is
                         [<declarative-part>]
                     begin
                         <sequence-of-statements>
                     [exception
                         <exception-handlers>]
                     end [<identifier>];


    entry-declaration ::= entry <identifier> [formal-part];


    entry-call ::= <identifier> [<actual-part>];
```

```
delay-statement ::= delay <expression>;
                        [<sequence-of-statements>]

accept-statement ::= accept <identifier> [<formal-part>] [do
                        <sequence-of-statments>
                     end [<identifier] ];

else-alternative ::= else <sequence-of-statements>

select-statement ::=    select
                            <select-alternative>
                            {or <select-alternative>}
                            [<else-alternative>]
                        end select;

select-alternative ::= [when <condition> =≥]
                            <accept-statement> |
                            <delay-statement>

select-entry-call ::=   select
                            <entry-call>
                            [<sequence-of-statements>]
                            <else-alternative> |
                            <delay-statement>
                        end select;
```

18.6 Ada Examples

Example: ATM Management   In this section we develop the simple concurrent Ada program shown in Figure 18.5 to simulate the actions of an automated teller–type application. Our system supports six accounts, which are accessible to all users. The task data_manager accepts two entry calls, lock and unlock. The entry lock is a request from a user for exclusive access to an account and has an in parameter, the name of the account, and an out parameter, a Boolean done that indicates whether the account was accessible and therefore able to be locked by this entry. If the account is already locked, done is returned as false.

FIGURE **18.5**   **ATM Manager in Ada**

```
-- ATM management in Ada
with TEXT_IO; use TEXT_IO;

procedure ATM is
    package INT_IO is new INTEGER_IO(integer);
    use INT_IO;
    package FLT_IO is new FLOAT_IO(float);
```

(continues)

```
-- Accounts are composed of a name and an amount of money.
type account_name is (Acct1, Acct2, Acct3, Acct4, Acct5, Acct6);
amount : array (account_name) of float;

--Declare the manager of all data.
task data_manager is
   entry lock(account: in account_name);
   entry unlock(account: in account_name);
end data_manager;

--Declare a task type for the user so we can declare many users.
task type user is
   entry identify (id: in integer);
end user;

users: array (1..5) of user;

--This task handles the locking and unlocking of accounts.
task body data_manager is
   type lock_states is (locked, unlocked);
   lock_status: array (account_name) of lock_states;
begin
   for a in account_name loop
      lock_status (a) := unlocked;
   end loop;
   loop
      select
         accept lock(account: in account_name; done: out boolean) do
            if lock_status(account) = unlocked then
               lock_status(account) := locked;
               done := true;
            else
               done := false;
            end if;
         end lock;
      or
         accept unlock(account: in account_name) do
            lock_status(account) := unlocked;
         end unlock;
      else
         delay 5.0;
      end select;
   end loop;
end data_manager;

--This simple user process handles one type of transaction:
--    the transfer of $100 from Acct1 to Acct2.
task body user is
```

```
        ok: boolean;
        id_number: integer;

    begin
        --Get the user number from the main program.
        accept identify(id: in integer) do
            id_number := id;
        end identify;

        --Lock Acct1
        loop
            data_manager.lock(Acct1,ok);
            if ok then exit; end if;
        end loop;
        put("User #); put(id_number); put_line("has grabbed Acct1.");

        --Lock Acct2
        loop
            data_manager.lock(Acct2,ok);
            if ok then exit; end if;
        end loop;
        put("User #"); put(id_number); put_line("has grabbed Acct2.");

        --Make the transfer.
        amount(Acct1) := amount(Acct1) - 100.0;
        amount(Acct2) := amount(Acct2) + 100.0;
        put("User $"); put(id_number); put_line("has made transfer");

        --Release the locks.
        data manager.unlock (Acct1);
        put("User #"); put(id_number); put_line("has unlocked Acct1");
        data_manager.unlock(Acct2);
        put(User #");put(id_number); put_line("has unlocked Acct2");

    end user;

begin -- Main program
    -- Initialize
    amount (Acct1) := 1000.0;
    amount (Acct2) := 1000.0;
    put_line ("Initialized accounts, starting users.");
    --Start users by identifying them.
    for i in 1..5 loop
        users(i).identify(i);
    end loop;
end ATM;

Initialized accounts, starting users.
User #    1 has grabbed Acct1.
User #    1 has grabbed Acct2.
```

(continues)

```
User #    1 has made a transfer
User #    1 has unlocked Acct1
User #    2 has grabbed Acct1.
User #    1 has unlocked Acct2
User #    2 has grabbed Acct2.
User #    2 has made a transfer
User #    2 has unlocked Acct1
User #    3 has grabbed Acct1.
User #    2 has unlocked Acct2
User #    3 has grabbed Acct2.
User #    3 has made a transfer
User #    3 has unlocked Acct1
User #    4 has grabbed Acct1.
User #    3 has unlocked Acct2
User #    4 has grabbed Acct2.
User #    4 has made a transfer
User #    4 has unlocked Acct1
User #    5 has grabbed Acct1.
User #    4 has unlocked Acct2
User #    5 has grabbed Acct2.
User #    5 has made a transfer
User #    5 has unlocked Acct1
User #    5 has unlocked Acct2
```

The task data_manager first initializes all locks to be unlocked. It then proceeds to a nonterminating loop, where it awaits calls to either lock or unlock.

Each user has an associated task of type user. These tasks are structured in an array of tasks named users. Each user task first accepts identify, which establishes its id_number and then attempts to lock Acct1 and Acct2 through entry calls to data_manager. When these accounts have been successfully locked by the user, the user task t transfers $100 from Acct1 to Acct2. After the transfer, the two accounts are unlocked using the unlock entry call.

Example: Sieve of Eratosthenes   One approach to generating prime numbers is known as the **sieve of Eratosthenes**. The basic idea is that the positive integers are, in increasing order, sent through a sequence of filters that remove some integers and pass the others on to the next filter in the sequence. Whenever an integer n is tested, there already exists a filter for each prime that is smaller than n. Each filter passes on only those integers that are not divisible by that filter's associated prime number. When an integer has passed through all the filters, it is known to be prime, because it is not divisible by any prime smaller than itself. Such an integer will then have a filter established in its honor so that all larger integers can pass through it.

This method is an excellent candidate for concurrent processing, because all the filters can operate concurrently. An Ada program for the sieve of Eratosthenes is given in Figure 18.6. Each filter is defined as a task. Because the number of tasks needed is not known at compile time, we introduce dynamic tasks through the creation of type `filter_task`, which is a pointer to a task of type `filter`. Each `filter` task then creates a new `filter` task to which it will pass integers that are not divisible by its prime. Every `filter` task assumes the first integer passed to it has already passed all previous filters and is, hence, the prime associated with the present filter.

FIGURE **18.6**　　**Sieve of Eratosthenes in Ada**

```ada
with TEXT_IO; use TEXT_IO;

procedure SIEVE is
    package INT_IO is new INTEGER_IO(integer); use INT_IO;

    -- First, define the filter type.
    task type filter is
        entry number_stream(number : in integer);
    end filter;

    type_filter_task is access filter; --point to a filter task
    first_filter : filter_task;
    numbers : integer;

    function new_filter return filter_task is
    begin
        return new filter;
    end new_filter;

    task body filter is
        next_filter : filter_task;
        prime, num : integer;
    begin
        accept number_stream (number : in integer) do
            prime := number;
        end number_stream;
        if prime > -1 then       --NOTE: "-1" is an end-of-numbers flag.
            put (prime); new_line;
            next_filter := new_filter;    --Spawn a new filter.
            loop
                accept number_stream (number : in integer) do
                    num := number;
                end number_stream;
                if num = -1 then
                    next_filter.number_stream(num);
                    exit;
                end if;
                if num mod prime /= 0 then
                    next_filter.number_stream(num); -- Pass the number on.
                end if;
            end loop;
```

(continues)

```
        end if;
    end filter;

begin -- Main program. Generate the initial list of integers.

    put("Enter end of integer range: ");
    get(numbers);
    first_filter := new filter;

    put_line("All primes in the range are: ");
    for i in 2..numbers loop
        first_filter.number_stream(i);
    end loop;
    first_filter.number_stream(-1); -- Flag the end-of-numbers.
end;
```

C H A P T E R **18**   **Terms**

task	accept statement
master unit	rendezvous
fork-join semantics	selective wait
pragma	guards
entries	sieve of Eratosthenes

C H A P T E R **18**   **Discussion Questions**

1. Why did the designers of Ada elect to describe a task in two parts, like a package, instead of one part, like a procedure?

2. Can you devise a situation where implicit invocation can cause problems? When is explicit invocation desired?

3. Why did Ada's designers allow several different alternative accept statements in a select statement but only one entry call in a select statement? Can you devise a situation where multiple entry calls would cause problems?

4. Why did Ada's designers "allow" implicit invocation to take place at all? Because they designed tasks to be implicitly invoked, they could have denied the possibility of implicit invocation altogether. Why did they not design Ada this way?

C H A P T E R **18**   **Exercises**

1. Consider how a quicksort might be implemented concurrently. Write the task specification for such an implementation.

2. Write the necessary task bodies for the implementation of a concurrent quicksort.

3. Consider the example in Figure 18.4. Construct two other sequences that are possible, given the constraints of the Ada semantics.

4. Given the following Ada program, TASKING_MANIA, which of the given output sequences is legal?

```
with TEXT_IO; use TEXT_IO;
procedure TASKING_MANIA is
    task t1;
    task t2 is
        entry entry1;
    end t2;
    task t3 is
        entry entry1;
    end t3;
task body t1 is
    begin
        select
            t2.entry1;
        else
            put_line("T1: dying");
            terminate;
        end select;
        put_line("T1: entry call accepted");
    end t1;

task body t2 is
    begin
        accept entry1;
        put_line("T2: accepted entry1");
        t3.entry1;
        accept entry1;
        put_line("T2: accepted entry1 again");
    end t2;

task body t3 is
    begin
        t2.entry1;
        accept entry1;
        put_line("T3: accepted entry1");
    end t3;

begin
    null; -- main program needs at least a null statement
end TASKING_MANIA;
```

a. T2: accepted entry1   **b.** T2: accepted entry1
    T1: dying   T1: entry call accepted
    T3: accepted entry1
    T2: accepted entry1 again

c. T2: accepted entry1   **d.** T1: dying
    T3: accepted entry1   T2: accepted entry1
    T1: entry call accepted   T3: accepted entry1
    T2: accepted entry1 again   T2: accepted entry1 again

   e. T1: entry call accepted
          T2: accepted entry1
          T3: accepted entry1
          T2: accepted entry1 again

5. Modify the Sieve of Eratosthenes example given in the text so that all printing is done by a *print-server* — that is, a task that loops through a select statement waiting to service centralized printing requests. You will need numeric and string printing routines in the server.

6. Ada abides by remote procedure call semantics with respect to interprocess communication. You are to determine whether the other forms can be "simulated" in Ada — that is, whether Ada IPC semantics can look like no-wait send or wait-for-notification send. In both cases, if simulation is possible, write a program that demonstrates the required semantics; if simulation is impossible, write a paragraph (in English) that justifies your decision.

7. Write a program that demonstrates how semaphores do not protect "critical sections" completely.

C H A P T E R *18*   **Laboratory Exercises**

1. We stated that the IPC mechanism in Ada is the remote procedure call. Write a program to demonstrate the semantics.

2. Can you "simulate" other IPC mechanisms in Ada? If you can demonstrate how to do this, write some demonstration programs.

3. Implement a solution to the dining philosophers problem in Ada.

4. Implement a solution to both producer-consumer problems given in the last chapter.

5. Write a program that demonstrates the corruption of data through poor implementation of data-sharing protection. Then correct your program and demonstrate that your corrected version protects the data properly.

6. Implement and run the Sieve of Eratosthenes from the listing in Section 18.6. Perform the following experiments:

   a. Try to discover the largest prime number it will generate. Why is this number significantly less than the largest integer number Ada will represent? What else is affecting it?

   b. Implement a solution where the end of the number stream does not need to be indicated by a -1 value. Implement this so that a process could be signalled to stop at any time.

   c. Solve the problem stated in (a) above. How would you change the Sieve solution in Section 18.6 such that higher prime numbers could be generated?

Concurrent Units in Occam

The programming language Occam is based on parallel concepts, modeled after CSP [Hoare (1978)], and designed for a set of computers called Transputers, manufactured by the INMOS Corp. It is simple in its structure and syntax and is not designed for complex mixtures of programming requirements. It does, however, exemplify parallel structures very well, and it is very instructive to examine as a parallel language. We do so in this chapter.

19.1 Concurrent Unit Definition

In Occam, concurrent units are called processes. Processes are defined in-line, using an alteration of the declaration of sequential code. Occam mandates that sequences of statements be declared as either sequential, using the SEQ keyword, or parallel, using the PAR keyword. For example, a sequence of code might look like

```
SEQ
  input1 ? x
  input2 ? y
  z := x + y
  output ! z
```

This is declared to be a sequential series of four statements, sequential because the SEQ keyword forces one statement to be executed at a time. However, simply changing the SEQ keyword, as in

```
PAR
  input1 ? x
  input1 ? y
  z := x + y
  output ! z
```

indicates that each of the four statements are executed in parallel. By this syntactic structure, Occam does not bear the "sequential bias" of an imperative, essentially sequential language with concurrency a built-in feature. Rather, Occam has concurrency at its foundation.

Figure 19.1 contains some interesting examples of SEQ and PAR keyword interchanges. Because all declarations are in-line, process types are not possible.

19.2 Invocation of Concurrent Units

The invocation of an Occam process is explicit, because a process begins execution as it is declared through an in-line declaration.

Occam processes adhere to fork-join semantics. The block of parallel code does not terminate until all its statements have completed parallel execution. This is especially important in Occam, because sequential and parallel blocks are interchangeable. Fork-join semantics allow parallel blocks to start and finish in the same manner as sequential blocks.

19.3 Data Sharing

As with Ada, data in Occam is shared through the use of shared memory and interprocess communication. Shared memory is organized in layers of scope surrounding blocks of code. Declarations apply to the immediately following block. As an example, consider the following code:

```
INT w:
SEQ
  INT x,y :
  SEQ
    w := 10
    x := 0
    y := 0
    out ! x
    out ! y

  INT z:
  PAR
    z := 10
    z := z + w
```

FIGURE **19.1** **Examples of Different Task Declarations in Occam**

a.

```
PAR                                          PAR
    chan ? x                                     chan ! z
    y := y + 2        is equivalent to           chan ? x
    chan ! z                                     y := y + 2
```

b.

```
SEQ                                          SEQ
    SEQ                                          chan ? x
        chan ? x                                 x := x + y
        x := x + y    is equivalent to           z := z * 2
    SEQ                                          chan ! z
        z := z * 2
        chan ! z
```

c.

```
PAR                                          PAR
    process_init ()                              process_init ()
    PAR                                          start (10)
        start (10)    is equivalent to           finish (15)
        finish (15)                              x := x + 1
    SEQ                                          again ()
        PAR
            x := x + 1
            again ()
```

d.

```
PAR                                          SEQ
    SEQ                                          PAR
        call_it (10)                                 call_it (10)
        call_it_again (20)                           call_it (20)
    SEQ               is this                     PAR
                          equivalent to?             call_it_again (20)
        call_it (20)                                 call_it_again (30)
        call_it_again (30)
```

This code is a sequential block of two blocks, one sequential and one parallel. The variable w is declared in the outer block and is accessible to the two inner blocks. In the inner sequential block, the variables x and y are accessible, along with w from the outer block; in the inner parallel block, the variable z is accessible along with w. In Occam, there is no built-in protection mechanism for shared variables.

19.4 Interprocess Communication

Channels are the IPC mechanism in Occam. Channels need to be declared before they are used. Input on a channel is performed using a ? notation, as follows:

```
chan1 ? v
```

This expression reads the value of the variable v from the channel chan1. The ! notation is used to write a value to a channel:

```
chan1 ! v
```

This expression writes the value of variable v to channel chan1.

Channels are declared as variables, and Occam scope rules apply. Channel names are bound statically and are part of the name space their declaration implies. Communication across channels is synchronized; a channel read is blocked until a write to the same channel takes place, and vice versa.

Figure 19.2 shows the example from Figure 18.2 rewritten in Occam. Note that there are no process names, but by using a procedure definition mecha-

FIGURE **19.2**   **Example from Figure 18.2 Rewritten in Occam**

```
CHAN OF INT MEET:
PROC One ()
  INT X, Y:
  SEQ
    CALCULATE (X)
    MEET ! X
    MEET ? Y
    USEIT(X,Y)
:
PROC TWO ()
  INT Z, A:
  SEQ
    OBTAIN (Z)
    MEET ? A
    MEET ! FN1 (A,Z)
    Z := FN2 (A,Z)
    DISPLAY (Z)
:
PAR
  ONE ()
  TWO ()
```

nism in Occam, we can give the same type of abstraction. The channels are given the same names as the entries from Figure 18.2. The process in procedure ONE sends X and then waits to get Y from procedure TWO. After receiving Y, it calls USEIT to do further work with X and Y. TWO obtains Z and then waits on channel MEET to receive A. Once A has been received, TWO sends back the results of a function computed on A and Z. It then adjusts and displays the value of Z.

Note that the example in Figure 19.2 is subtly different from the example in Figure 18.2. Because there are no remote procedure call semantics in Occam, the value of Z is adjusted with the call to FN1 *after* the rendezvous is over. In Figure 18.2, the value of Z is adjusted *during* the rendezvous. This is a small difference, but it is significant.

Figure 19.3 illustrates the interaction of two tasks. The program in 19.3(a) will result in the same output as the Ada program from Figure 18.3. It is much shorter and more to the point. The program in 19.3(b) illustrates the combination of repetitive and parallel constructs. This program results in 10 processes, all created at once, each printing a different value of COUNT.

Figure 19.4 illustrates Occam with the Occam version of the Ada program in Figure 18.4.

FIGURE **19.3**   **Two Examples of Task Interaction in Occam**

```
a.    PAR
      INT COUNT:
      SEQ COUNT = 1 for 5
        output ! COUNT
      INT COUNT:
      SEQ COUNT = 6 for 5
        output ! COUNT


b.    INT COUNT:
      PAR COUNT = 1 for 10
        output ! COUNT
```

FIGURE **19.4**   **Example from Figure 18.4 Rewritten in Occam**

```
CHAN OF INT channel1, channel2:
PROC T1 ()
  SEQ
    Screen ! "In T1: before first input"
    channel1 ? any
    Screen ! "In T1: after first input"
    channel1 ? any
    Screen ! "In T1: after second input"
    Screen ! "In T1: terminating"
  :
```

(continues)

```
PROC T2 ()
  SEQ
    Screen ! "In T2: before first input"
    channel2 ? any
    Screen ! "In T2: after first input"
    channel1 ! 100
    Screen ! "In T2: terminating"
:
PAR
  T1 ()
  T2 ()
  SEQ
    Screen ! "In main: before sending on channel2"
    channel2 ! 100

    Screen ! "In main: before sending on channel"
    Channel1 ! 100

    Screen ! "In main: terminating"
```

19.5 Synchronization

Because there is no remote procedure call semantics in Occam, synchronization is simple and occurs only through channel communication. Therefore, Occam semantics can implement only the first form of the phone model from Section 17.4. The semantics do, however, implement the gate model from Section 17.5.

Like Ada, Occam extends the gate model by allowing multiple channels to be examined for input or output potential. In Occam terminology, these are **alternative processes**. There are two forms of alternatives in Occam; the first is the unguarded alternative:

```
ALT
  chan1 ? x
    ...code block
  chan2 ? x
    ...code block
  chan3 ? x
    ...code block
```

The channels are examined, top down, and the first channel with input is taken and its code block is executed.

Occam also permits guards to be placed in conjunction with the checking on each channel. This process works the same way it does for Ada. Consider the example of the guarded receptionist from Section 18.5. Here, our receptionist is handling multiple phones. Some of the phones may have conditions placed on them specifying when they are to be connected and when they are to be disconnected. For example, phone 1 may need to be connected on only Mondays, phone 2 is connected only on the first day of the month, and phone 3 is connected only when the Dow Jones average is greater than 3400. When the receptionist comes to work, he or she first determines which phones to connect by evaluating each of the guard conditions. This situation can be expressed by the following guarded alternative:

```
ALT
  (day_of_week = MONDAY) & phone1 ? msg
    ...code block
  (day_of_month = 1) & phone2 ? msg
    ...code block
  (DOW_JONES > 3400) & phone3 ? msg
    ...code block
```

Guards are evaluated once per statement execution. The first alternative with both the guard evaluating to TRUE and input on the channel is taken and its code block is executed. Unlike Ada, if no guards are TRUE, no error occurs — but the process this executes in is halted.

This chapter does not attempt to give the complete syntax of any Occam construct. Therefore, we do not summarize the concurrency syntax here as we did for Chapter 18. Those interested in Occam are referred to Pountain and May (1987) and Occam (1988).

_19.6_ Occam Examples

Example: ATM Management   In this section we develop an Occam program to simulate the actions of an automated teller application. This program is shown in Figure 19.5 and mirrors the application written up in Figure 18.5. The program is composed of two procedures (Data_Manager and User) and a main program. The main program initializes two accounts, defined by the array amount, and calls the Data_Manager and five User procedures in parallel. Note the sequencing of the initialization steps and the parallel section; notice also that, once the parallel code is reached, execution is designed to be as parallel as possible.

The Data_Manager first declares two constants through VAL statements — locked and unlocked — and declares an array of six locks. It then initializes all locks to be unlocked. It launches into a loop (the while TRUE statement) that perpetually executes an alternative process. This alternative checks two channels, lock and unlock, for input. The input on these is the account number to lock or to unlock. If we are to lock, either the status is set and the value 1 is returned (actually *sent back* through the lock ! 1 statement) if the account is unlocked or the value 0 is returned if the account is already locked. If there is input on the unlock channel, then the status is set to unlocked. If there is no input on any channel, then the delay procedure is called, and the program sleeps for a few seconds.

FIGURE 19.5   **ATM Manager in Occam**

```
CHAN OF INT lock:
CHAN OF INT unlock:

PROC Data_Manager()
  VAL unlocked IS 0:
  VAL locked IS 1:
  [6]INT lock_status:
  INT acct:
  SEQ
    SEQ acct := 1 for 6
      lock_status[acct] := unlocked
    while TRUE
      ALT
        lock ? acct
          IF
            lock_status[acct] = unlocked
              SEQ
                lock_status[acct] := locked
                lock ! 1
            TRUE
              lock ! 0
        unlock ? acct
          lock_status[acct] := unlocked
        TRUE
          delay()
  :
PROC User (INT id)
  INT done:
  SEQ
    lock ! 1
    lock ? done
    while done <> 1
      SEQ
        lock ! 1
        lock ? done
    lock ! 2
    lock ? done
    while done <> 1
      SEQ
        lock ! 2
        lock ? done
    amount[1] := amount [1] - 100
    amount[2] := amount [2] + 100
    unlock ! 1
    unlock ! 2
  :
```

```
SEQ
  amount [1] := 1000
  amount [2] := 1000
  PAR
    Data_Manager()
    PAR id := 1 for 5
      User(id)
```

Each `User` procedure locks account 1, locks account 2, transfers $100, and then unlocks both accounts. Note that "locking" actually means sending a lock request to the `Data_Manager`. Note also the polling loop around each lock.

Example: Sieve of Eratosthenes   The Occam version of the Sieve of Eratosthenes is quite short, but it is a bit tricky to specify. The dynamic nature of the sieve algorithm eludes the semantics of Occam somewhat — Occam is a very static language. Although invocation of processes is dynamic, the creation of data objects is static, tied by declaration to compile-time bindings. Thus, the channels must be allocated by array ahead of time and parceled out to each new process by incrementing a counter.

Aside from this restriction, the program in Figure 19.6 is very similar in construction to the one in Figure 18.6. Each filter assumes the first number in its stream is the prime, and the value of $a - 1$ is the signal to stop the algorithm. The procedure `Filter` is called recursively — *and in parallel* with the while loop that processes the stream of numbers; that action gives the code its dynamic nature.

FIGURE 19.6   **Sieve of Eratosthenes in Occam**

```
CHAN OF INT starter:
[25] CHAN OF INT primechans:
INT i, count:
PROC Filter (VAL CHAN OF INT stream)
  INT prime, num:
  SEQ
    stream ? prime
    IF
      prime > -1
        SEQ
          output(prime)
          count := count + 1
          PAR
            Filter(primechans[count])
            SEQ
              stream ? num
              while num <> -1
                IF
                  num = -1
```

(continues)

```
                    SEQ
                      further ! num
                      STOP
                  TRUE
                    IF
                      num REM prime <> 0
                        further ! num
                      TRUE
                        SKIP
          TRUE
            STOP
      :
      SEQ
        count := 1
        PAR
          Filter(starter)
          SEQ i :=2 for 100
            starter ! i
```

Terms

channels   alternative processes

Discussion Questions

1. What are the advantages of using in-line declaration — as in Occam — versus the way Ada declares tasks? What disadvantages are there?

2. Can Occam programs be broken up into modules easily? Why or why not?

3. As a language, Occam is much "terser" than Ada. Compare an `accept` statement in Ada with the ? construct in Occam. Is this terseness an advantage or a disadvantage? Which do you think would cause you to make more mistakes in programming?

4. Occam receives data through the ? construct, whereas Ada uses the parameter mechanism built into the `accept` statement. Discuss functionality that can be done with Ada that cannot be done in Occam.

5. Likewise, Occam sends data through the ! construct, whereas Ada uses the parameter mechanism built into the remote procedure call. Discuss functionality that can be done with Ada but not in Occam.

Exercises

Refer to the exercises from Chapter 18. These are intentionally similar.

1. Write the implementation of a concurrent quicksort in Occam.

2.   Consider the example in Figure 19.4. Construct two other sequences that are possible, given the constraints of the Occam semantics.

3.   Examine Figure 19.1.

   a. For each of the fragments (a) through (c), explain why they are equivalent.

   b. For the fragment (d), explain why they are not equivalent? Can you give an equivalent fragment?

4.   Given the following Occam program, which of the given output sequences is legal?

```
PROC T1 ()
  SEQ
    ALT
      entry1 ? ANY
        SKIP
      TRUE
        Screen ! "T1: Dying"
        abort
      Screen ! "T1: entry accepted"
:
PROC T2 ()
  SEQ
    entry1 ? ANY
    Screen ! "T2: accepted entry1"
    entry1 ! 2
    entry1 ! ANY
    Screen ! "T2: accepted entry1 again"
:
PROC T3 ()
  SEQ
    entry1 ! 3
    entry1 ? ANY
    Screen ! "T3: accepted entry1"
:
PAR
  T1
  T2
  T3
```

   a. T2: accepted entry1   **b.** T2: accepted entry1
           T1: dying   T1: entry call accepted
           T3: accepted entry1
           T2: accepted entry1 again

   c. T2: accepted entry1   **d.** T1: dying
           T3: accepted entry1   T2: accepted entry1
           T1: entry call accepted   T3: accepted entry1
           T2: accepted entry1 again   T2: accepted entry1 again

   e. `T1: entry call accepted`
       `T2: accepted entry1`
       `T3: accepted entry1`
       `T2: accepted entry1 again`

5. Modify the Sieve of Eratosthenes example given in the text so that all print-ing is done by a *print-server* — that is, a task that loops through a select state-ment waiting to service centralized printing requests. You will need numeric and string printing routines in the server.

6. Occam abides by synchronization semantics with respect to interprocess communication. You are to determine whether the other forms can be "sim-ulated" in Occam — in other words, whether the IPC semantics can look like no-wait send or wait-for-notification send. In both cases, if simulation is pos-sible, write a program that demonstrates the required semantics; if simula-tion is impossible, write a paragraph (in English) that justifies your decision.

7. Implement semaphores in Occam. They can be implemented as variables — but also in the form of channel IPC communication. Write a program that demonstrates how semaphores do not protect "critical sections" completely.

C H A P T E R 19 **Laboratory Exercises**

Refer to the Lab Exercises from Chapter 18. These are intentionally similar.

1. We stated that the IPC mechanism in Occam is channel communication. Write a program to demonstrate the semantics.

2. Can you "simulate" other IPC mechanisms in Occam? If you can demon-strate how to do this, write some demonstration programs.

3. Implement a solution to the dining philosophers problem in Occam.

4. Implement a solution to both producer-consumer problems given in Chap-ter 17.

5. Write a program that demonstrates the corruption of data through poor im-plementation of data-sharing protection. Then correct your program and demonstrate that your corrected version protects the data properly.

6. Implement and run the Sieve of Eratosthenes from the listing in Section 19.6. Perform the following experiments:

   a. Try to discover the largest prime number it will generate. Why is this number significantly less than the largest integer number Occam will rep-resent? What else is affecting it? Compare this to the Ada solution.

   b. Implement a solution where the end of the number stream does not need to be indicated by a –1 value. Implement this so that a process could be signalled to stop at any time.

   c. Solve the problem stated in (a) above. How would you change the Sieve solution in Section 19.6 such that higher prime numbers could be generated?

Bibliography

Abelson, H., G. J. Sussman, and J. Sussman. 1985. *Structure and Interpretation of Computer Programs.* Cambridge, Mass.: M.I.T. Press.

American National Standards Institute. 1983. *Reference Manual for the Ada Programming Language.* ANSI/MIL-STD-1815A. Washington, D.C.: U.S. Department of Defense.

Backus, John W. 1978. "Can Programming Be Liberated from the von Neumann Style?" *Comm. ACM* 21, no. 8: 613–641.

Boehm, Corrado, and Giuseppi Jacopini. 1966. "Flow Diagrams, Turing Machines, and Languages with Only Two Formation Rules." *Comm. ACM* 9, no. 5: 366–371.

Brinch Hansen, P. 1978. "Distributed Processes: A Concurrent Programming Concept." *Comm. ACM* 21, no. 11: 934–941.

Burstall, R., D. MacQueen, and D. Sanella. 1980. "HOPE: An Experimental Applicative Language." *The 1980 LISP Conference*, Stanford University, Santa Clara Univ., pp. 136–143.

Cardelli, Luca, and Peter Wegner. 1985. "On Understanding Types, Data Abstraction, and Polymorphism." *Computing Surveys* 17, no. 4: 471–522.

Church, Alonzo. 1941. *The Calculi of Lambda-Conversion. Annals of Mathematic Studies*, no. 6. Princeton, N.J.: Princeton University Press.

Clocksin, William F., and Christopher S. Mellish. 1987. *Programming in Prolog.* 3rd ed. New York: Springer-Verlag.

Dahl, Ole-Johan, and K. Nygaard. 1966. "SIMULA — An ALGOL Based Simulation Language." *Comm. ACM* 9, no. 9: 671–678.

Dijkstra, Edsger W. 1968. "Goto Statement Considered Harmful." *Comm. ACM* 11, no. 3: 147–148.

———. 1971. "Hierarchical Ordering of Sequential Processes." *Acta Informatica* 1, no. 2: 115–138.

———. 1975. "Guarded Commands, Nondeterminancy, and Formal Derivation of Programs." *Comm. ACM* 18, no. 8: 453–457.

Genesereth, Michael R., and Matthew L. Ginsberg. 1985. "Logic Programming." *Comm. ACM* 28, no. 9: 933–941.

Gordon, M. J., R. Milner, and C. P. Wadsworth. 1979. *Edinburgh LCF.* Berlin: Springer-Verlag.

Hoare, C. A. R. 1969. "An Axiomatic Basis for Computer Programming." *Comm. ACM* 12, no. 10: 576–583.

———. 1972. "Notes on Data Structuring." In *Structured Programming,* edited by O.-J. Dahl, E. W. Dijkstra, and C. A. R. Hoare, pp. 83–174. New York: Academic Press.

———. 1978. "Communicating Sequential Processes." *Comm. ACM* 21, no. 8: 666–677.

Hogger, Christopher J. 1984. *Introduction to Logic Programming.* Orlando, Fla.: Academic Press.

Hudak, Paul. 1989. "Conception, Evolution, and Application of Functional Programming Languages." *Computing Surveys* 21, no. 3: 359–411.

Iverson, Kenneth E. 1962. *A Programming Language*. New York: John Wiley.

Jensen, Kathleen, and Niklaus Wirth. 1985. *Pascal Users Manual and Report*. 3rd ed. Berlin: Springer-Verlag.

Kernighan, Brian W., and Dennis M. Ritchie. 1988. *The C Programming Language*. 2nd ed. Englewood Cliffs, N.J.: Prentice Hall.

Kosaraju, Rao. 1974. "Analysis of Structured Programs." *J. of Computers and System Science* 9, no. 3: 232–255.

Kowalski, Robert A. 1979. "Algorithm = Logic + Control." *Comm. ACM* 22, no. 7: 424–436.

Liskov, Barbara H., and John V. Guttag. 1986. *Abstraction and Specification in Program Development*. Cambridge, Mass.: M.I.T. Press.

Marlin, C. D. 1980. *Coroutines: Lecture Notes in Computer Science 95*. New York: Springer-Verlag.

Milner, Robin, Mads Tofte, and Robert Harper. 1990. *The Definition of Standard ML*. Cambridge, Mass.: M.I.T. Press.

Naur, Peter, ed. 1963. "Revised Report on the Algorithmic Language Algol 60." *Comm. ACM* 6, no. 1: 1–17.

Occam. 1988 Inmos, Ltd., *Occam 2 Reference Manual*. Englewood Cliffs, N.J.: Prentice Hall.

Pountain, D. and D. May. 1987. *A Tutorial Introduction to Occam Programming*. Oxford, England: BSP Professional Books.

Rubin, Frank. 1987. "GOTO Considered Harmful." *Comm. ACM* 30, no. 3: 195–196.

Sammet, Jean E. 1969. *Programming Languages: History and Fundamentals*. Englewood Cliffs, N.J.: Prentice Hall.

Scott, D. S., and C. Strachey. 1971. "Towards a Mathematical Semantics for Computer Languages." *Symposium on Computers and Automata*. Brooklyn, N. Y.: Polytechnic Press, 19–46.

Stroustrup, Bjarne. 1986. *The C++ Programming Language*. Reading, Mass: Addison-Wesley.

Sussman, G. J., and G. L. Steele, Jr. 1975. "Scheme: An Interpreter for Extended Lambda Calculus." *M.I.T. Artificial Intelligence Memo 349*.

van Wijngaarden, Aard, B.J. Mailloux, J. E. L. Peck, and C. H. A. Koster. 1969. "Report on the Algorithmic Language ALGOL 58." *Numerische Mathematik* 14, no. 2: 79–218.

Wegner, Peter. 1972. "The Vienna Definition Language." ACM *Computing Surveys* 4, no. 1: 5–63.

———. 1987. "Dimensions of Object-Based Language Design." *ACM SIGPLAN Notices* 22, no. 12: 168–182.

Wexelblat, Richard L. 1981. *History of Programming Languages*. New York: Academic Press.

Wikstrom, A. 1987. *Functional Programming Using Standard ML*. Englewood Cliffs, N.J.: Prentice Hall.

Wirth, Niklaus. 1985. *Programming in Modula-2*. 3rd ed. New York: Springer-Verlag.

Index